Empire of Law
in Colonial Mexico

Empire of Law and Indian Justice in Colonial Mexico

Brian P. Owensby

STANFORD UNIVERSITY PRESS

STANFORD, CALIFORNIA

Assistance for the publication of this book was provided by
The University of Virginia.

Stanford University Press
Stanford, California

Printed in the United States of America on acid-free, archival-quality paper

Library of Congress Cataloging-in-Publication Data
Owensby, Brian Philip
Empire of law and Indian justice in colonial Mexico / Brian P. Owensby.
p. cm.
Includes bibliographical references and index.
ISBN 978-0-8047-5863-5 (cloth : alk. paper)
ISBN 978-0-8047-7662-2 (pbk : alk. paper)
1. Indians of Mexico—Legal status, laws, etc. 2. Indians of Mexico—
Government relations. 3. Indians of Mexico—History.
4. Justice, Administration of—Mexico—History. 5. Mexico—
History—Spanish colony, 1540–1810. I. Title.
F1219.3.L4O93 2008
972'.02—dc22
2007028909
Typeset by Thompson Type in 10/12 Sabon

For Bronwyn

Contents

Acknowledgments

This book bears an enormous debt of gratitude. Through the many research trips to Mexico and Spain and while writing, I have enjoyed the generous support of several University of Virginia Summer Research Grants, a Sesquicentennial Fellowship, and a semester's leave provided by the University of Virginia Alumni Board of Trustees. The National Endowment for the Humanities provided a Summer Research Fellowship at a crucial time in my endeavors.

I owe endless thanks to the many people from Charlottesville to Mexico City, Madrid, and Seville who helped me find and consult the books and manuscripts that made the research for this book so exciting. I would especially like to thank Sra. Dulce María Liahut Baldomar, director of the Central Historical Archive at the Archivo General de la Nación and Rocío Romero Hernández at the Archivo General de la Nación (AGN) in Mexico City. I am very grateful to the AGN's Sr. Berinstein, whose encyclopedic knowledge of the archive helped me decide where to look for certain things and steered me away from blind alleys. The generous professionals in Sala 4 kept me in reading material and reminded me when it was time to take a break. The kind people at the AGI in Seville were marvels of efficiency and willingness to help. I also am in debt to the fine staff at Interlibrary Loan and LEO at the University of Virginia's Alderman Library. This project would not have come to fruition without their unstinting help and goodwill.

Many colleagues and friends have left their mark on this book. My colleagues Chuck McCurdy, Allan Megill, Elizabeth Meyer, Eric Midelfort, Ruth Hill, Lenard Berlanstein, and Alison Weber offered comments and encouragements at early points. Professor Paul Halliday provided a sounding board for broad questions of framing and conceptualization at crucial moments in my thinking. Professor Tico Braun and Professor Fernando Operé listened to my ideas while we pedaled away on Sundays, probing and encouraging. Tico's genius with titles saved me from myself more than once. Chris Gist was very patient with my insistent pleas for help in preparing the maps. At the AGN, Professor Ben Vinson provided comradeship and timely advice more than once. Martin Nesvig generously kept a watchful eye over document requests in my absence. Professor Fritz Schwaller and Professor Susan Kellogg shared valuable time in agreeing to read those parts of the argument dealing with Nahuatl. I am also indebted to members of the Washington Area Symposium on the History of Latin America, and in particular Professor John Tutino, Professor Mary Kay Vaughn, Professor Barbara Weinstein, and Professor Daryle Williams who heard and debated several facets of the broader work and provided valuable feedback and support. I benefited enormously as well from the opportunity to present parts of my work to Professor Nathan Wachtel's seminar on colonial Latin America at the École des Hautes Études en Sciences Sociales in Paris in March 2006. An anonymous reader provided important criticism in the final stages of writing. Margaret Pinette was patient and precise throughout the editorial process.

I am profoundly grateful to doña Estela Villalba Caloca, who twice provided me a home in Mexico City, and to Cecilia Brown, who made it possible. I would also like to thank my family-away-from-home in Mexico City, Alfredo Muñoz Téllez, Lucy Brown de Muñoz, as well as Alfredo and Sebastián, who didn't treat me like an old guy. Sundays at their house reminded me of why I missed my own home and refreshed me for the archive.

My mom, brothers, and sister always asked how it was going and actually listened when I told them. My dad engaged and probed. My wife and daughter put up with more than anyone and were always as eager to see me upon returning from a trip or emerging from my garrett as I was to see them. Thanks are not enough.

Brian Owensby
Charlottesville, December 2007

"As well as long, the history of the Empire is complex: it is not a simple tale in which one thing happens after another and causes explain effects and effects are in proportion to causes. Nothing of the kind. The history of the Empire is strewn with surprises, contradictions, abysses, deaths, and resurrections."

—Angélica Gorodischer, *Kalpa imperial*

CHAPTER ONE

Opening

In seventeenth-century New Spain, amid the continuing chaos of conquest, orderly people whose lives and lands had been invaded a century earlier made their own a system of laws imposed by an empire that sought both to exploit and protect its most vulnerable subjects. They did so by bringing their troubles before judges at the local level and tribunals in Mexico City. Indian claimants, individuals and collectives alike, came to see the law as a means to justice and a position from which to speak. Many defended land and liberty, sought redress for abuses by Spanish and Indian officials, insisted on the enforcement of royal provisions regarding labor conditions, contested village elections and local power, and strained to punish the guilty. Some employed the law as a means to personal advantage, taking land, putting people to work, or ousting rivals from office. Regardless of motivation, tens of thousands of Indians across a long century came to understand what the law could do and how it might disappoint. They recounted their woes, but did so from the conviction that they had more to tell than their suffering. In the telling, they acquired and refined a vocabulary of grievance and redress and developed ideas of protection, liberty, possession, guilt, autonomy, voice, common good, rebellion, and reconciliation. They also learned to make the most of their status as tributaries. While addressing themselves to local conditions, they forged an ever-tenuous relationship to a distant king. Through their active engagement with law they glimpsed justice. And by pursuing justice, they created an enduring politics of colonial lives.

Law was present in the relationship between Indians and Spaniards from the very start. During the years of military conquest, a Spanish notary would, on the eve of a battle, face the city or settlement under threat and read out a document known as the *requerimiento,* or requirement. Initially drawn up by royal lawyer Juan López Palacios Rubios, the document demanded that the Indians acknowledge the Holy Catholic

Church as "Ruler and Superior of the whole world." In the name of the pope and the Spanish monarchs, the document called upon the Indians to allow the gospel to be preached. If they refused, war would be waged against them, "as to vassals who do not obey," and they would be subjected "to the yoke and obedience" of the church and the monarchy and enslaved. If they did not oppose the preaching of God's word, they would be spared and priests would minister to them. After the document was read, the assembled troops served as witnesses and the notary produced a *testimonio,* or legal acknowledgment that proper procedure had been followed. As soon as the ink was dry, Spanish troops, and their allies, were legally free to attack.[1]

It is easy to dismiss the requerimiento as little more than an absurdity of conquest. It might be read across a great distance, or muttered as Spaniards approached a sleeping village. A notary or captain might proclaim it to trees or empty huts.[2] In fact, the document was less concerned with actually warning the Indians than with satisfying the demands of Christian conscience. Theologically, unbelievers could not be conquered without giving them an opportunity to come to Christ of their own free will, God's great gift to man. To have fought them without issuing a warning would have been to deny free will an opportunity to work. And while Palacios Rubios himself and others "laughed often" when regaled with tales of how the requerimiento had been executed, and friar Bartolomé de las Casas could not decide whether to laugh or to weep, the requerimiento contained within it the crucial recognition that indigenous people, under the specific circumstances of willing conversion, were entitled to royal protection.[3] While this legal status seemed more often honored in the breach during the first decades of encounter between Spaniards and Indians in Mexico, the ambit of its relevance grew through the sixteenth century as conquerors and conquered learned to live in each others' presence.

During the decades following the fall of the Aztec capital Tenochtitlan in 1521, newly converted Indians, now vassals of the Spanish king, began to seek justice. By the 1530s, Indian leaders had begun to appear before the audiencia, Mexico City's high court, to protect land and to dispute political arrangements between themselves and Spaniards, and among themselves. Four decades later, Indians had become quite self-consciously litigious. Writing to King Philip II in the early 1570s, a group of Indian leaders expressed amazement at their own penchant for legal dispute. "In the time of our gentility we did not often have lawsuits," they noted. "[N]ow that we are Christians we have many lawsuits, with other natives as well as with the Spanish people of your Majesty."[4] Spaniards, especially in Mexico City's officialdom, also began to comment on how the Indians were given to lawsuits. By 1600, law and its processes figured centrally in the lives of indigenous individuals and communities.

It has been said that the Spanish empire took shape "under the inspiration of law."[5] Perhaps no other conquest and colonization, certainly none in modern European history, made such a point of its laws and judicial institutions as did Spain in America during and after the sixteenth century. This is the impression one takes from the vast record of legal activity housed at the General Archive of the Nation in Mexico City and the General Archive of the Indies in Seville. Thousands of volumes in crabbed notarial hands testify to the centrality of law in the conqueror's imagination and to the Indians' close engagement with Spanish law during the colonial period. Curiously, what we know of that engagement remains limited. One of the great oddities of history writing about colonial Mexico—and colonial Latin America more generally—is the mismatch between the volume of legal documentation involving Indians and the attention historians have paid to the processes they represent. Scholars have always drawn on the deep and almost inexhaustible vein of legal source material to reveal aspects of life under Spanish rule. Much less frequently have they sought to understand legal processes themselves and the role they played in mediating the relationship among people very differently situated in Spain's empire in the New World.

To a certain extent, the thin study of Indians' involvement with Spanish law bespeaks a broader inattention to matters of law in viceregal Latin America. Through much of the twentieth century, the study of colonial law focused almost exclusively on jurisprudence and its philosophical foundations. Scholars writing in Spanish set out to order and understand the vast corpus of law and learned commentary known as *derecho indiano*—the law of the Indies. Royal decrees, compilations of legislation, jurists' treatises, the deliberations of king and council, the proclamations and orders of viceroys came to be parsed and analyzed with great insight.[6] And not a little celebration, for on paper royal legislation protecting the New World's Indians seemed enlightened compared to the "imposed law" of nineteenth- and twentieth-century European colonialism.[7]

This approach called forth a reaction from scholars who insisted that the texts of imperial law misrepresented reality. These historians came to see Spain's law in the Americas as an impressive formalism largely disregarded in practice. Against derecho indiano's tendency to generalize from the written record while scanting law in practice, these scholars saw a nearly systematic failure to enforce royal decrees protecting the Indians. Far from being "one of the wisest, most human, and best coordinated" legal systems ever applied in a colonial situation, Spanish law seemed to mock justice.[8] Debate over law and its role in colonial Latin America eventually converged on the question of whether a *Black Legend* of Spanish cruelty toward the Indians or a *White Legend* of Spanish benevolence best described Spain's New World empire.[9] Although both sides recognized that such distinctions produced little light, the sharpness of the contrast underlay much debate that followed. While some argued for a more nuanced approach in seeking to understand the interplay of the "economic and ecclesiastico-humanitarian motives of empire," it became common to dismiss the law as largely "irrelevant" to, "alien, therefore without moral force" in, or "separated, divorced" from the everyday lives of Indians.[10]

Efforts to breach the impasse came when historians began to focus on America's concrete reality alongside derecho indiano's text-driven approach. In Peru, Steve Stern used court records to show that indigenous litigants and petitioners had adopted legal tactics to defend land and challenge abusive labor practices.[11] In Mexico, Woodrow Borah's research demonstrated that from the 1590s forward the institutions of law proved a powerful draw to Indian claimants.[12] In other words, up close, law could be seen for anything but an irrelevancy in Indians' lives.

While in certain regards Stern and Borah held similar concerns, they parted ways on the broad question of how to understand law's role in the lives of indigenous people. Borah argued that law needed to be studied because it was "basic to the experience of mankind whenever and wherever two peoples have come into contact for more than very short periods."[13] He wanted to understand how Mexico's Indians had adjusted to the imposition and acceptance of Spanish law over time. Stern, by contrast, argued that the problem with law in colonial Peru was not its inefficacy, as had earlier been thought, but the Indians' very success before Spanish judges. By reducing the sphere of outright arbitrariness, and by providing complainants a measure of justice, law undermined a "wider, more unified, and independent movement" on behalf of indigenous people. In effect, by giving indigenous litigants a reason to hope for justice, law "rooted exploitation into the enduring fabric" of Indians' lives.[14]

From this point forward, law played a limited role in historical accounts of colonial Latin America's Indians. Instead of the quieter and more ordered processes of law that interested Borah, or the hegemonic processes identified by Stern, revolts and direct resistance carried the day among historians.[15] Law might figure as background to resistance, or as the trigger to rebellion, but few scholars sought to understand law on its own terms, or asked why Indian claimants persisted in challenging Spaniards and each other in court. Once law had become a "mask for colonial power," there was little reason to study the inner workings of legal process, or to take seriously the proposition that indigenous people might care deeply about legality.[16]

A few scholars refused to surrender law's centrality in Indian lives. Historian William Taylor noted that "law does not have to be the 'ordered irrelevancy' it has become in Latin American social history, if our questions are not limited to whether or not rules and decrees reflected social realities, whether or not they were enforced, whether or not law was a tool of oppression."[17] From those who have followed in this vein, we have learned that law shaped family life and property relations among the Aztecs of central Mexico, that northern New Spain had a dynamic "legal culture" after 1700 that gave Indians a role in shaping regional administration, and that penal law in Quito represented a "common enterprise" allowing the humble as well as the powerful a measure of influence over legal outcomes.[18] More recently, an edited volume has called for a "new social and cultural history of law" in Latin America, though of the dozen or so essays only one dealt with viceregal law, and that only at the tail end of the eighteenth century.[19]

A chief reason for slighting law in Latin America has been the tendency to see it through the prism of *the rule of law*.[20] At its most basic, the rule of law insists that impartial, rational, impersonal, universal rules govern legal process, rather than the personal whims of individuals. Administration and adjudication are separated from one another, and politics and law are not supposed to mix. The general supposition is that "modern" legal systems have more or less achieved this condition. The rule of law, as with so many other signs of "modernity," thus became the benchmark by which Latin America's legal-historical experience was judged deficient On this view, Latin America has lacked rule of law in the past and suffers from "the (un)rule of law" in the present.[21] The unspoken implication is that these two facts are related to one another historically. Such a formulation suggests indifference to the history of law in Latin America.[22]

My point is not that the rule of law, broadly conceived, is irrelevant to thinking about law in Latin America. The problem is that as an idea it is a "transplanted philosophy" that bears an ambiguous relationship to Latin America's pasts and histories.[23] While the rule of law has deep roots in Western political thought, it flowered as a defining idea of modern societies under the aegis of nineteenth-century Anglo-American legal history, which understood law's historical trajectory as the unfolding of the "rule of law" over time.[24] Latin American historians' relationship to this narrative has always been equivocal, at best, because the histories of Latin America have differed so profoundly from the histories of England and the United States. Yet without the rule of law as a benchmark, Latin American historians have shied away from law as an object of inquiry. For if it is an axiom that law in Latin America did not give rise to the rule of law, would-be legal historians would have to commit themselves to studying its failure to do so, a project most scholars have not found compelling enough to pursue.

Developments in legal scholarship and legal history began to challenge uncritical acceptance of the rule-of-law idea during the last quarter of the twentieth century. Theorists and historians in the United States argued that law had never been a value-free, politically-neutral body of rules.[25] Historically, it had been a source of power distributed unevenly through society. At any given moment, what counted as "law" did not result from the autonomous and rational evolution of formal doctrine, but from contests between the powerful and the less powerful over the meanings and practices of law and legislation in the heat of legal and political conflict. Freed from teleological notions of law's development over time, and setting aside the idea that law can be understood either as an expression of disembodied, formal rules, or as the exercise of naked power, historians could now take account of what was happening on the ground in legal proceedings. Litigants and witnesses were not merely acted upon by law and its agents, they "participated" in the process by which legal decisions were made. Formal rules did not dictate outcomes so much as written law and actual practice existed in tension with each other, and common people navigated multiple, overlapping legal structures, choosing the ones that best advanced their interests within the constraints of their circumstances.[26]

Such an approach implies a set of conceptual tools more in keeping with the multiform history of law in Latin America, for it recognizes both that law is an expression of power and that people pursue their interests through it. Recognition of the centrality of power in the workings of law, however, does little to tell us how law actually worked. According to legal scholar Steven Winter, to say that the law is finally an expression of power elides the question of what power is and how law comes to be expressed through it. " '[P]ower' can not work as a foundational account of justice, morality, law, or anything else because at each level and every step of the way, the capacity to exercise power is itself contingent on some complex set of social conventions and understandings."[27] This means that power will remain shrouded so long as we persist in seeing human agency in terms of the opposition between freedom and determination. We must, says Winter, see human acts in terms of "contingency and constraint," which in the final analysis are one and the same because "our very ability to 'have' a world" depends on the preexisting social practices and conditions—the constraints—that set the frame of individual and collective lives.[28] On this view, human beings do not act from freedom so much as they act in relation to constraints that are simultaneously the condition of their being able to act at all.[29] What people can think, what they can envision and aspire to, are products of the circumstances in which any individual or group finds itself.[30] Unmoored from circumstances, no one would know what to want or how to go about getting it, nor would they know when they had achieved anything. Thus, in seeking to understand how and why people have acted, we must inquire into their circumstances as deeply as possible and seek to grasp how they have acted from and through them.[31]

Human actions unavoidably produce conflict. One way of conceptualizing law is to see it as a means by which peace is preserved against the constant threat of discord. From this vantage, law substitutes words for clubs in the hope that parties to a dispute will live to fight, or not, another day. As such, law, though inherently about contest, is also intrinsically about how "those who live together . . . express themselves through it and with respect to it." It is, in short, a highly contentious conversation over how a community lives, the norms it obeys, the things its members value. Legal precepts, principles, and rituals not only embody the rules by which conflict in any given reality is adjudicated, they are also "signs by which each of us communicates with others."[32] As a result, however local a dispute may seem, legal process is always part of a wider societal conversation about what is right or wrong, acceptable or unacceptable, just or unjust in a given "normative universe."[33]

My chief aim in this book is to listen in on just such a conversation, one that took place among Indians and Spaniards in viceregal New Spain. I have focused on the seventeenth century because it represents the period when people who first met in the violence and dislocation of Spain's sixteenth-century invasion of Mexico converged on the enduring legal ground rules for living together in a shared social order. This century, roughly spanning the early 1590s and 1700—from the establishment of the General Court of the Indians to the dynastic change from Hapsburgs to Bourbons—is often elided in historical accounts of early modern Mexico.[34] Wedged between a sixteenth century looking back to conquest and an eighteenth century looking forward to independence, it has no obvious center of historiographical gravity. It has been characterized variously, as a period of consolidation, as a diminuendo transition to a mature colonial society. More recently it has been described as an era of "singular complexity" during which multiple and fragile compromises were reached over how Indians and Spaniards would live together.[35] I have chosen to see these portrayals as constrasting perspectives on a broader process. From the Indians' point of view, the seventeenth century was in many ways a quieter one than the sixteenth. Military conquest had largely abated, except at the margins of empire, and the indigenous population began to recover from its long decline after 1521. At the same time, the decades after 1590 were ones of profound economic, social, and political change that strained frail social arrangements, set individuals and communities in competition with each other, subverted established political ideas, and enhanced local against distant royal power.[36] Law and its processes figured centrally in how Indians and Spaniards confronted these circumstances.

I begin from the premise that law in seventeenth-century Mexico, as elsewhere, is best seen in terms of the complex, open-ended interplay between recognized legal principles and the words and actions of all who took part in legal proceedings—complainants, witnesses, advocates, interpreters, notaries, and judges. Together these participants created "legal meaning," not by some rational process of divining legal rules, but through the struggle to interpret how those rules would apply in concrete situations. In that struggle they allowed themselves to be governed by procedures designed to ensure an orderly treatment of issues. In Spanish law, this interaction came to be recorded as individual episodes of legal process known as "cases."

This book is first and foremost about cases involving indigenous men and women who brought petitions and filed lawsuits—transcripts of the agonistic conversation regarding human relations in seventeenth-century Mexico. I have focused on cases raising fundamental issues in the lives of these colonial subjects—the yearning for royal protection, struggles over the possession of land, disputes regarding labor relations and liberty, efforts to order tribute relations, the concern for village autonomy and governance, and the desire to see the guilty punished for their crimes. By reading case records against each other and in light of more formal sources of law and jurisprudence, I argue that Indian claimants connected with and helped to forge a powerful vocabulary of legal meaning. From the cases I also seek to recover something of the texture, quality, and depth of experience of those who came before the law with their grievances and pleas, and how their participation shaped legal outcomes.[37]

That participation was irreducibly mediated. Indian petitioners and litigants typically retained advocates known as *procuradores* to prepare documents and conduct cases. These procuradores, in turn, acted from what they knew of the legal principles and procedures underlying litigation. In communicating with their procuradores, and in all official court proceedings, Indian clients generally relied on interpreters to translate from indigenous languages to Spanish, and back. With rare exception, case records contain only Spanish translations of indigenous words.[38] Thus, a voice emerging from any given case is in no way the "true" or "original" voice of this or that person apart from the litigation. It is simply the voice of that person—complainant, respondent, witness, or, for that matter, judge—as a participant in the proceeding. This seems confining only if we insist on the idea of severing individuals from their circumstances.[39] Once we surrender this notion we can hear from the cases themselves—the voices of people who knew that in the consequential conversation of law they were constrained to say and do certain things rather than others if they wished to prevail.

Law is a "resource in signification." It enables human beings to "submit, rejoice, struggle, pervert, mock, disgrace, humiliate, or dignify," and I would add relate, separate, hope, and despair. Yet, the written traces of law—the texts of legislation, the treatises that expound legal principles, the cases that record the process of litigation—are barely adequate to convey this vast "expressive range" and its tangled meanings.[40] Although the law is made of words, the flat, page-bound scrawl that survives any given legal encounter in colonial Mexico can only hint at the experience of those whose lives became enmeshed in the workings of law in action.

From a historian's vantage, this represents an unavoidable paradox of legal documentation. At first glance, the archives of Indian litigation seem incredibly rich and dense. Individual lawsuits can run to hundreds of pages in a tight notarial hand, and thousands of two-page petitions can seem an embarrassment of riches. Upon close inspection, these documents present enormous perplexities. Despite all the writing, much remains shadowy about the encounters these records depict: How did a party decide to file a petition? Why did a lawsuit continue over months or years at great expense or why was it dropped after a certain point? Why did a particular case turn out as it did and how did parties understand the outcome? One must read a case knowing that a great part of what defined a legal encounter lay beyond the record—the often-times grueling trip to Mexico City, conversations with the procurador, efforts to line up witnesses, behind-the-scenes negotiations with an opposing side, the aggrieved party's decision that he had had enough. Attending to context and to the details of process can help fill in some of these gaps. But this leads to a second problem. The very granularity implied in such an approach seems at times to stymie generalization.

To face these challenges, I have relied on a dynamic structure to reveal broad conceptions and still express the inherent contingency and fluidity of individual encounters. To this end, the chapters are organized around certain fundamental ideas—protection, possession, liberty, guilt, voice in village governance, vassalage—expressed across hundreds of short petitions and full-blown lawsuits.[41] Because these ideas were not stated abstractly, for legal meaning "must first germinate in action and then take root in our forms of life," the intimate circumstances and procedural details of individual cases are critical to understanding them.[42] Each chapter, thus, represents a three-way fugue among "the facts" of a case given by witnesses or litigants, recognized sources of law and legal principle (such as royal decrees, legal treatises, and compilations of law), and the processes, procedures, and practices that mediated parties' actions.

Chapter 2 grounds this effort by fleshing out the process by which Spaniards and Indians came into relation during the sixteenth century. A final section introduces basic elements of Spanish law in the New World as they had taken shape by roughly 1600. Chapter 3 considers the flowering of the *amparo* petition over the seventeenth century, during which time Indian petitioners from across New Spain traveled to Mexico City in search of royal protection. My central concerns in this chapter are to discern something of petitioners' experiences and to draw from the amparos themselves the vibrant language of royal protection that formed the baseline of Indian expectations of law. Chapters 4 and 5 examine this vocabulary of protection in the context of struggles over land and labor, revealing the instability of "possession" and uncovering indigenous ideas about "liberty" in the colonial context. Chapter 6 peers deeply into a number of criminal cases to show how participatory these proceedings could be in local situations and how struggles over the meaning of criminal wrongdoing could help secure social peace, or disrupt it. Chapter 7 examines heated contests over village governance. I show that these were far from just local affairs, for issues of autonomy, collective liberty, and relations to Spanish power were at stake in any case that got as far as Mexico City. Chapter 8 proposes a rereading of the rebellion of Tehuantepec in 1660–61. I argue that the unfolding of events may be understood in terms of an abiding concern for and relationship to the king's law as an always-equivocal instrument for confronting official misconduct and negotiating with viceregal authorities.

Litigation's role in the lives of Mexico's indigenous subjects cannot be reduced to a hard-edged instrumentalism. Too often, it has been supposed that Indians lacked any genuine thoughts beyond the impulse to survive or get on with life, that their relationship to Spanish rule could be summarized as one of resistance, rejection, reaction, fear, or indifference. This book argues for another view. If "colonial situations breed confusion," they also nurture a commensurate desire for order.[43] Law was a medium through which Indians expressed that desire within the broad range of their experience. In the heat of legal contest, indigenous people in Mexico came to ideas of their own about where they stood in the colonial world of Spain's ocean-spanning empire.[44] In doing so, they articulated hard-scrabble lives to the erudite texts penned by Spanish jurists and commentators. Over the seventeenth century, this interaction gave rise to colonial law's cosmopolitan context as the grievances of Indian villagers who paid tribute to a distant king met the aspirational ideals of Spanish imperial legality.

Nor is this simply a matter of watching Indian claimants litigate. Taylor has noted that one of the great advantages of the historical study of "the operation of law in relationships of inequality" is that it allows us to "examine politics without . . . leaving out most of the population as 'unpolitical.' "[45] Law and its processes, in other words, can be thought of as politics by another name, a means to "reclaiming the political" for the colonial period.[46] Law in early modern New Spain was not only about how the colonizers controlled the colonized. It was also about how the crown sought to exert control over its Spanish vassals who so often flouted royal decrees, especially those regarding treatment of the Indians, and how Indian subjects went about trying to have those laws enforced.

Nineteenth-century English legal historian F. Maitland noted in 1898 that "[i]f we speak, we must speak with words; if we think, we must think with thoughts. We are moderns and our words and thoughts can not but be modern. Perhaps . . . it is too late for us to be early English. Every thought will be too sharp, every word will imply too many constraints."[47] It is also too late to be early Mexican. The same modern sharpness of words will cut into our ability to connect with indigenous litigants and petitioners, with the witnesses who testified for them or against them, with the procuradores who helped and opposed them, with the judges who ruled on their cases, and even with the decrees and treatises of law in relation to which they were acting. Our ingrained sense of what law is, a modern sense, will constantly interfere with our ability to understand Spanish law in early modern Mexico on its own terms. Historian Victor Tau Anzoateguí understood the problem from the perspective of Latin American colonial law. In its openness, its flexibility, and its willingness to relax principles and precepts in any given case, the law of the Indies (derecho indiano) can seem fatally flawed. Yet such a conclusion, says Tau, can only come from a modern, "rationalist" conception of law, a conception rooted in the notion that a proper legal system must be closed, complete, and self-sufficient. This idea is "inapplicable" to viceregal law precisely because it blinks legal reality.[48]

My own experience as an attorney confirms Maitland's and Tau's admonitions. When I first started to read cases for this book, I kept searching for cognates to what I knew from U.S. law and procedure. I recognized that procedure might be different, but at every turn I wanted to find equivalents in colonial law. Sometimes I would find them. Other times not. The question then was how to make sense of the gaps. At times the issue tied me in knots. I would spend days consulting legal treatises, manuals of procedure on some arcane point. I kept track of how often such gaps occurred in cases. Sometimes I would find a rule, sometimes I would discern a practice rather than a principle. Other times not. The other times continued to frustrate me, I see now, because I was looking for a closed, complete, and self-sufficient system.[49] Gradually, I came to realize that I was dealing with no such thing. There were, quite simply, lacunae that could not be filled, contradictions that could not be reconciled, decisions for which I could find no rationale beyond a casuist's sense regarding justice in a particular situation.[50] All participants in New Spain's legal system, from Indian claimants, to procuradores, witnesses, notaries, interpreters, and judges, would have understood this intuitively. What we might see as examples of gross injustice, or arbitrariness—the absence of a requirement that judges write opinions, for instance—were simply part of the legal world as they experienced it. This is not to say they were blind to arbitrariness, as many cases attest. It is to recognize that they could see the law and hope for justice only from the perspective of their circumstances—as is true always and everywhere.

CHAPTER TWO

Ordering the Circumstances of Encounter

Law does not happen in a vacuum. It is always and everywhere a matter of deep context, of the way the world is arranged, of relations among the things of human existence. In this lay the New World's challenge for Spanish law: amid the novel circumstances of encounter between Spaniards and indigenous peoples everything remained to be arranged—the relations between men, between men and things, between rulers and ruled, between ideals and practice. No principle of law could dictate the form and shape of these relations. Those thrust suddenly into each other's presence had no choice but to rebuild the world from the ground up, to discover from within the struggle to survive and achieve how they would order their shared existence.

LABOR, LAND, MARKETS

From the beginning, new men in this old world assumed they could take whatever their will fixed on. Closing his epic account of the conquest of Mexico, fray Diego Durán noted that after the fall of Tenochtitlan in 1521, "the Spaniards went from conquest to conquest, subjecting the land. They went here and there, from town to town, conquering and pacifying. After each town was taken, a Spaniard would ask [Hernán] Cortés to grant it to him and he then received it as an *encomienda*. So it was that *juste vel injuste* [justly or unjustly] men, women, and children were taken, branded on their faces, and sold as slaves for the mines or as servants." Those not sold were given over to the service of Spaniards. Nor were Spaniards alone in gaining power over people and land during the conquest. Durán tells of a young Nahua woman of Hueyapan who, astride a Spanish horse, led her townsmen against the warriors of Tetela, vanquishing them. "When he realized the bravery of the woman, Cortés granted her the control of the two towns of Tetela and Hueyapan in the name of his Majesty."[1] Land and people—during the hundred years following conquest, these were the axes of struggle and aspiration in Mexico, for Indians and non-Indians alike.

Until 1550, people were the prize of conquest. *Conquistadores* and *encomenderos* accumulated Indians, put them to work, and sold them; friars sought them out, preached to them, and baptized them: each according to his jurisdiction over body or soul. Yet if during these years the logic of booty governed relations between Spaniards and Indians, economic concerns quickly came to the fore. Indians were needed to mine silver, till land, and serve in Spanish shops and homes. For many Spaniards slavery seemed the obvious answer, a recognized practice dating to the middle ages. No less crucially, the Indians themselves seemed familiar with the concept. In the pre-Hispanic world, the *tlacotin* were people who did not own themselves. Witnessing the purchase and sale of tlacotin in the *tianguis* or Indian markets during the 1520s, Spaniards assumed they were seeing the slavery they knew, neither realizing nor caring that *tlacotli* status was less confining and less permanent than that of Spanish *esclavos* (slaves).[2] In 1527, Spaniard Francisco Díaz obtained a license to allow him to "rescue" tlacotin from an Indian market so they could be branded and sold in Mexico City. A few lonely voices spoke against such practices. Franciscan friars wrote to the king in 1529, asking that he stop the branding of Indians and deliver them from servitude, "so that they might become true Christians."[3] The crown heard these laments, but understood that the settlers must provide for themselves, lest the colony perish.

These were the origins of the Spanish use of indigenous labor in Mexico—the enslavement of Indian bodies as an extension of conquest, paralleled by a critique grounded in a concern for Indian souls.[4] During succeeding decades the crown found itself pushed to address this tension. Over strident opposition from the New World, Charles I, king of Spain—Charles V, Holy Roman Emperor—passed a series of measures in the 1530s and 1540s asserting Indian liberty and regulating the use of indigenous labor. Royal decrees and instructions to the viceroys condemned the poor treatment of Indians, by Spaniards and Indian nobles alike, but always within the context of assuring tribute, which at this time was still paid in kind, and with an eye to keeping peace among and between Spanish encomenderos and Indian *principales* (nobles).[5] This political and legislative process culminated in promulgation of the New Laws of 1542 which, among other things, declared the Indians free by nature and not subject to enslavement under any circumstances.

The fate of the New Laws is well known. Peruvian viceroy Blasco Núñez Vela lost his life to angry encomenderos in 1544 after attempting to enforce them. Apprised of Nuñez's demise, Mexican viceroy Antonio Mendoza opted in favor of noncompliance. While this represented the first stirrings of a sense that local power could thwart royal will in the New World, the New Laws were not dead letters. Over ensuing decades, many of their provisions, especially those regarding Indian enslavement, gained traction in law and everyday practice. Indian slavery persisted in isolated pockets into the 1550s, and work conditions in *obrajes* (textile manufactories) and mines and on some haciendas may have approached de facto slavery. But from roughly mid-sixteenth century, no person in New Spain could legally own an Indian. Nor, according to a 1549 law, could Indians be compelled to perform personal service for Spaniards, though this prohibition was routinely ignored until the 1630s.[6]

By 1550 it was becoming clear to all but the encomenderos themselves that the encomienda simply could not adequately supply New Spain's needs in the long run. Some began to argue that a new system for allocating Indian workers had to be found. The origins of this gathering labor crisis can be traced to the epidemic of 1546–48.[7] Smallpox and typhus had been abroad in the land since the 1520s. Between 1521 and the early 1540s, as many as ten million of Mexico's twenty-five million people died. In the three years from 1546 to 1548, typhoid fever reduced the indigenous population to around six million.[8] Encomiendas, whose productivity had been patchy since the 1530s, were decimated, though encomenderos saw no alternative that could preserve their status and ensure their continued control of the dwindling native population.

Disease was not the whole story behind the crisis of labor. From the 1540s onward, encomenderos commonly complained that Indians simply would not stay put in their villages. Unable to pay their tribute, villagers often fled—to other pueblos where they were not on the tribute rolls, or to the *monte* or wilderness beyond the reach of Spanish power. Only moderation of tribute demands could keep them from leaving, an early hint of the role flight would play in the relationship between rulers and ruled.[9]

In response to the crisis, the crown created the *repartimiento* system, under which workers from Indian villages rotated through a labor draft.[10] A certain proportion of villagers—generally somewhere between 1 and 2 percent, depending on the season—were required to appear in a local market on a certain day so that they might be sent off to nearby encomiendas, haciendas, mines, and obrajes, depending on the composition of the local economy. This was not slavery, at least not according to the crown's reasoning, for such labor was justified as serving "public utility" rather than private gain. To this extent, repartimiento labor represented a departure from pre-Conquest labor arrangements, precisely because it purported to advance the public good by delegation to private

parties. Before conquest, men and women had served together at the behest of a local official acting on behalf of the community at large. Their
labor might involve repairing roads or buildings, or farming corporately
owned fields, but did not imply work on behalf of a private individual.[11]

Administration of the new system fell to royal officials, usually Spanish *corregidores* or *alcaldes mayores*. By controlling the labor bottleneck, these local justices enjoyed great power. Not all Indians were subject to the draft. Indian workers called *mayeques,* who in pre-Hispanic
tradition fell somewhere between the enslaved tlacotin and the free commoners called *macehuales,* remained under the power of local Indian
nobles until the end of the sixteenth century.

In densely populated central areas, the repartimiento worked reasonably well. Indians' work conditions improved somewhat, despite the
more than occasional corruption of corregidores and alcaldes mayores.
Toward the fringes of empire, however, where populations were sparser
and viceregal authority more tenuous, the system, through the 1590s,
was characterized chiefly by the abuses it fostered.

Through the mid-sixteenth century, when people were more numerous,
Spaniards had concerned themselves little with land as such. For a for-
tunate few, the encomienda permitted a measure of control over indigenous populations. During the early decades after 1521, these encomenderos, lords of whole Indian villages, made little effort to own land.
Their attitude reflected the legal and political environment of conquest.
In 1532, Francisco de Vitoria had argued that Indian land belonged to
the Indians. Regardless of their status as unbelievers, he insisted, they
could not be dispossessed by war or other coercive means.[12] Although
this position seemed to undercut its authority in the New World, the
crown ultimately accepted Vitoria's doctrine because it followed that if
the Indians' land could not be taken from them, the indigenous people
themselves could not be permanently possessed by the encomenderos.
By 1550 this proposition was accepted law.

But as Indians continued to die in catastrophic numbers, large tracts
of land emptied out. With no one to claim or work them, they were
available for the taking by Spaniards. Those who had not been granted
an encomienda were especially attentive to such opportunities, though
astute encomenderos also perceived the growing importance of property.
Spaniards could not legally dispossess Indians, but with so much vacant acreage, many took land whose rightful possessors had either died
or scattered. Fitfully and unevenly, the benign neglect of land among
Spaniards began to give way to an intensifying interest in its acquisition
from the 1550s forward.

At the same time, it was becoming clear that the Indians alone could not feed a growing Spanish population. Cities were hard pressed. In 1544, bishop of Oaxaca Juan de Zárate sent a letter to prince Philip (later King Philip II), complaining that there was no wheat in the city of Antequera. A decade later, viceroy Luis de Velasco wrote to Charles V that Mexico City's "necessity [was] as great as that suffered by a city besieged," since its 200,000 mouths could only be fed by the sweat of Indian labor, whose number was dropping.[13]

Vacant lands and a growing food crisis galvanized poorer and unemployed Spaniards, and some encomenderos, to seek land. In this they were encouraged by Spanish officialdom. An *oidor* (judge) of the *audiencia* (Mexico City's superior worth) in Mexico City noted in 1561 that all viceroys since Mendoza had allowed Spaniards to "sow wheat on lands that were found not to be tilled by the Indians."[14] The quick success of these early agricultural ventures, and Indians' preference for corn over wheat led many Spanish residents in the Mexico City-Puebla region to take up agriculture.[15] Farms sprang up, filling the interstices left by native death.[16] With agriculture on a firmer footing, related spheres of economic activity began to expand. North of Mexico City, the number of Spanish cattle and sheep ranches rose steeply after 1560, just as grants of sheep-grazing lands to Indians were plummeting.

Although this was the beginning of Mexico City's status as the economic hub of New Spain, other regions underwent similar transformations. Indian death and flight from the hinterlands of Oaxaca also left lands vacant, stimulating Spanish wheat production after 1550. There, too, royal grants for Spanish cattle estancias rose after mid-century.[17] More generally, increases in crop production and stock raising gave a fillip to commerce, which in turn led to improved road systems. Regional and intercity trade picked up.

Most of these enterprises, whether wheat farms or cattle and sheep ranches, still relied chiefly on repartimiento workers, though a few had begun to experiment with wages. Through the 1560s, Indian commoners came to resent the repartimiento, as well as the many other labor obligations heaped on a rapidly shrinking population. By the 1570s, repartimiento quotas had in many places risen from 1 to 2 percent to over 2 percent, and in certain cases after the 1580s, quotas reached 4 to 5 percent for ordinary work, and 8 to 10 percent for seasonal labor.[18]

As these numbers suggest, the repartimiento was beginning to buckle under the dual pressures of a diminishing labor force and growing Spanish demands. Disease continued to collect a heavy toll in lives, peaking every so often in ravaging pandemics that saw the indigenous population drop to three million by 1570 and to less than two million by

1585.[19] At the same time, native people scattered across the landscape, fleeing disease and increasingly burdensome tribute and labor exactions. Birth rates dropped. Labor, thus, remained in short supply, just as Spanish agriculture was taking off. African slaves were one response to the problem, though the twenty-five thousand who had arrived by 1570 represented a miniscule proportion of Indian lives lost during these years. Like the encomienda before it, the repartimiento as a means of allocating labor was collapsing by the 1580s.

The years between 1570 and 1590 were ones of upheaval in land tenure as well. Throughout the sixteenth century, Spaniards had bought Indian land or acquired it through *mercedes* (royal land grants). Outright usurpation was forbidden by the New Laws—a ban not infrequently circumvented in practice—so Spaniards would often first buy land from Indian owners and later perfect their claim by requesting a *merced*. They were aided in this by the fact that during most of the sixteenth century indigenous villages and individuals eagerly sold land to Spaniards, demanding only proper payment. Land, after all, was one of their principal resources in hard times.[20] Spaniards also found opportunity in indigenous depopulation. Those who cultivated Indian land abandoned in the face of disease and abuse could often apply for a royal grant of possession. The church, too, contributed to the alienation of native lands, receiving property in bequest from pious Indians and then making it available to Spanish hacendados.

The precise pattern of land transfer varied dramatically by region. In Morelos, ambitious Spaniards skimmed off the best Indian land with the hope of establishing sugar cane haciendas. By contrast, Oaxaca's indigenous peoples lost relatively little land up to 1600, despite disease and migration. In Nueva Viscaya, far to the north, miners established vast estates in lands thinly peopled and virtually without law.[21] In central regions, the expansion of cattle and sheep ranches pressed hard on properties held by native villages. By viceregal order, unoccupied land was regarded as common pasture. As Indian lands emptied out, and even where they had not, Spanish ranchers became bolder in allowing their droves to range widely.[22] Indians complained bitterly that cattle and sheep overran fields, trampling and eating crops. Villagers were often forced to flee the destruction, creating more vacant land.[23]

The expansion of pastoralism in central New Spain also led to squatting. Indeed, taking land without legal title appears to have been the most common way Spaniards obtained property up to 1600, even as Indians more often gained land by legitimate royal grant.[24] Illegal seizures became so prevalent among Spaniards in certain areas because it was so difficult for those lacking access to the levers of political and

economic power to obtain mercedes. In Puebla, city officials favored clients, retainers, and family members. In Celaya, miners parlayed their irrigation rights into possession and later ownership. Elsewhere, investors
and big landowners from Mexico City, with ready capital, swallowed
up property. From Guadalajara, one audiencia oidor complained to the
king in 1585 that large estancia owners had cornered land, with the
result that "other inhabitants . . . cannot find a single site left, owing to
the quantity of land occupied, or rather, usurped, in a manner contrary
to all reason."[25]

In short, by the close of the sixteenth century, native commoners
or *macehuales,* faced an acute problem. They could not compete with
Spaniards and Indian caciques and principales in obtaining royal land
grants. Spaniards were entitled by law to own land, and Indian nobles
and village leaders could claim ancestral rights to particular plots of land
for their own use. Macehuales could not make such claims, since Spanish
law held that individual native commoners had no property rights over
preconquest corporate lands.[26] Corporate claims had a greater chance
of success. A village might argue, through a cacique, that land tilled in
earlier times had merely been left fallow in the face of mass death, a
claim which Spanish law recognized. But there were no guarantees:
caciques could not always be trusted to act on behalf of the villages they
purported to represent, and Spaniards opposing such claims could easily muster witnesses to say that a particular plot of land had never been
cultivated. As a last recourse, villages might file suit at the audiencia in
Mexico City, but they struggled uphill against Spaniards, who knew and
understood the law and its ways.

Even so, litigation became more common as pressure on land use
increased. Up to the 1550s, most land disputes had been between Indian
towns arguing over boundaries. From the 1570s forward, land contests
increasingly pitted Indians against Spaniards, especially in the core
around Mexico City and Puebla. In the middle decades of the sixteenth
century, Spaniards had become more aggressive in taking land, just as
Indians showed themselves willing to sell or rent it to Spaniards, often
with little legal formality.[27] Although regions differed, it is fair to say
that by the 1580s decades of poor registration procedures had made a
shambles of land tenure, inviting dishonesty on all sides.

By 1590, the crises of land and labor had converged. Repartimiento could
not provide enough labor to feed New Spain's cities and was interfering
with tribute collection. At the same time, land disputes had become a
source of political instability, as conquerors and conquered squared off in
court and in the fields. In many regards, labor was the more intractable

of the two problems: there simply were not enough Indians to do all the work that a growing Spanish population demanded. By contrast, land claims could be sorted out by clarifying registration procedures.

This was the gist of the *composición de tierras* enacted by royal decree in 1591. The doctrine had deep roots in Spanish legal culture. Growing out of Germanic vengeance laws, brought to Iberia by the Visigoths, the principle underlying composición was to repair, *componer,* a juridical breach—originally, a violent dispute between families—that threatened social order.[28] Of course, conditions in the New World were very different, but this ancient doctrine seemed to offer a way of bringing order to an increasingly anarchic situation. According to the 1591 decree, all disputed lands reverted to the crown, which reserved to itself the power to distribute to the Indians lands necessary for their sustenance.[29] In practice, the law was limited largely to Spanish claimants, who appeared in court to make good their de facto ownership, paying a fee to the crown in exchange for a grant recognizing legal title. After 1600, and with special intensity between 1631 and 1645, the composición legalized decades worth of seizures and usurpations of indigenous lands by Spaniards.[30] More crucially, composiciones became the chief means by which Spanish owners acquired land between 1600 and 1700.

Indians were not completely excluded from this process of settling land claims. They continued to receive royal grants, though rarely through composición because they generally could not outbid affluent Spaniards. This did not stop them from applying for and obtaining land grants. According to one study, Indians in the Valle del Mezquital received ninety-four mercedes between 1589 and 1599, to Spaniards' fifty, even as Spaniards continued to squat on land far more often than Indians (ninety-three to thirty-eight). Much the same happened elsewhere.[31] Alongside mercedes, the crown made available to Indians the *amparo,* or protective judicial order, for land possessed by indigenous villages or even individual Indians. Caciques especially, though not exclusively, benefited from the amparo which, like the composición, was rooted in the idea that the king owed a special responsibility to protect his most vulnerable vassals. Indians flooded into Mexico City between 1590 and 1592, filing amparo petitions to protect their lands.[32]

One of the principal effects of the amparo was to enable Indian caciques to sell land with relative ease. Over the final decades of the sixteenth century many potential buyers of Indian lands, especially Spaniards, had come to distrust the caciques' representations regarding ownership amid the expanding chaos of property claims. A buyer who could see a seller's amparo for a particular plot knew that he was far less likely to be challenged by a third party claiming to be the rightful owner, and if he did he would go to court with a rebuttable presumption in his favor.

Impoverished or overworked caciques often sold uncultivated and un-
populated plots: "I have no use of the land at all, because it lays waste and
I have a lot of other land to work," was a typical explanation for putting
property on the market.[33] In the Valley of Puebla, such sales often involved swamplands along major rivers, places where crop cultivation was
difficult, at best. In this way many Spaniards acquired land that had once
belonged to Indians and, as speculation became more common, began to
sell them off and buy better plots with which to expand their estates.

Composición and amparo coincided with another important reform
straddling the end of the sixteenth and the beginning of the seventeeth
centuries—the *congregaciones*. Civil congregaciones involved "congre-
gating" or "reducing" Indians who because of epidemics and flight had
scattered across the landscape. Dispersion complicated tribute collection
and evangelization. The idea behind the congregaciones was to gather
Indians so they could hear the gospel and pay tribute. It was a process
driven by a profound sense within Spanish political and ecclesiastical
officialdom that it was not right for people to live strewn to the four
winds. Tribute, the need for labor, and evangelization were at stake, certainly. But at a deeper level, Spanish political sensibilities demanded that
people live alongside one another, for *convivencia*—living together—
was the only basis for a just and human society.[34]

A first wave of congregaciones washed over native communities between 1550 and the mid-1560s. The policy was put into practice throughout New Spain, over the active opposition of some Indians, who feared
they would lose lands left behind.[35] When the dust had settled, tens of
thousands of Indians had been moved from their original homes, though
few were forced beyond the boundaries of the pre-Hispanic territorial divisions into which they had been born.[36] Many simply refused to move.

The second round of congregaciones took place between 1598 and
1606. Not more than 15 percent of the total Indian population of New
Spain was forced to abandon their homes.[37] In peripheral areas few were
affected. Elsewhere, as in Morelos, where sugar was emerging as a cash
crop, villages were hard hit as hacendados grabbed displaced workers. As
before, the new regulations specifically sought to protect Indian lands,
by forbidding any vacated plots from being taken or alienated. And while
the majority of congregaciones appears to have taken place without incident, some villagers opposed removal, as they had earlier, complaining
that despite legal provisions, they would end up losing land. In fact, thousands of hectares do appear to have escheated to the crown, property
which often found its way into Spanish hands through later mercedes and
composiciones.[38]

Still, it would be a mistake to see the congregaciones as simply a
land grab. By stabilizing indigenous communities, the congregaciones

oftentimes created a new baseline for Indian property claims. Village lands were recorded and written down, which often made it harder for opportunists to proceed by outright usurpation. The law explicitly forbade Spaniards from taking abandoned plots. Under the congregaciones, Indian villages in the Valley of Puebla retained farming lands, as well as rights to pasturage and water. A similar story appears to hold for Oaxaca.[39] In such places, much property freed up by congregaciones did pass to Spaniards, either by purchase, merced, or composición, though mostly in places where population was thin or along ancient political territorial borders at the edges of more densely peopled areas.[40]

Crucially, the crown seems to have heard Indians' concerns regarding ancestral lands. Barely had the congregaciones been carried out when in 1607 viceroy Luis de Velasco II began to grant special permission for people to return to their villages of origin. Some congregaciones disintegrated quickly as people hurried home. Some took deeper root, becoming permanent abodes for those who lived there. Others disbanded initially but later reformed.[41] In all cases, people and their communities were responding locally to the same pressures they had faced since conquest—tribute, labor, and evangelization.

Just as order was being put to New Spain's land tenure system, its chief mode of allocating labor, the repartimiento, was beginning to fail.[42] Most hacendados and farmers continued to use the draft when it was available, but some began to seek other ways of meeting their labor needs. By the late sixteenth century, hacendados were beginning to attract workers by paying them. In the Valleys of Mexico, Puebla, and Oaxaca *gañanes*—permanent, hired workers—had been employed since the 1580s. In mining zones, forms of wage labor had been in place from early on. Among landowners, wages remained an exception to reliance on the repartimiento, but their spread did reveal an incipient fracture among employers—between those financially flush enough to pay workers and those who were not.

Turn-of-the-century land reforms came just when the food crisis in New Spain was giving new momentum to agriculture. The process was constrained by the shortage of workers. As hacendados and farmers began to chafe against the labor draft, murmurings against the corregidores could be heard. Some began to argue against the repartimiento altogether. Hacendados who took this position saw little future in coerced labor. Nor were the Indians silent. In areas where the repartimiento pressed most heavily, villagers began to speak up. Commoners from Tlaxcala, for instance, complained in 1591 that the repartimiento controlled by the caciques and principales of their province was abusive—each week they had to provide six hundred workers.[43]

In 1601, the crown responded by abolishing the agricultural repartimiento. At least in principle, Indians could now work for whomever they chose and had to be paid a wage. Though the decree did not completely eliminate the labor draft, it did cut away much of the ground on which it stood. But the law was hampered by the circumstances of its birth: it did not so much resolve the labor problem as favor financially independent farmers over a larger and poorer group lacking the resources to compete in a wage market. A backlash ensued. Faced with food shortages, viceroys could not afford to let arable land lie fallow for lack of workers. And so, in 1609, the crown curtailed the 1601 decree's broad sweep. The expressed intention of ending the repartimiento remained, but an exception was made for wheat farms which, as the principal source of food for Spanish cities, were declared a matter of "public utility," allowing other farmers who did not grow wheat to cloak illegal labor practices.[44]

The repartimiento issue simmered for the next three decades. Toward 1620, the Indian population bottomed out at almost a million souls. Villagers, overburdened by tribute and labor obligations, began to flee in search of less onerous situations. Increasingly, employment on haciendas represented a welcome haven. Wages were relatively high, and many employers were so desperate that they readily agreed to pay workers' tribute shares in order to keep them on the farm. Under the circumstances, Indian villages became bolder in opposing the repartimiento. It was not uncommon for village leaders to reject calls for workers.[45] Although this represented a deepening resistance to the coercive aspects of repartimiento, it is almost surely true as well that so many workers had opted for wage labor that villages simply had no one to spare.

As with the encomienda decades earlier, the repartimiento's moment had passed. It limped through the 1610s and by the 1620s was moribund. In 1632–33 the crown again issued decrees abolishing it once and for all, less a bold legal initiative than recognition of an accomplished fact. Since the turn of the seventeenth century, repartimiento had become the major obstacle to wage labor, which many hacendados and Indian communities alike had come to see as the only viable option for allocating workers. From different perspectives, both were more confident than fifty years earlier that they could make their way through markets—just as it was becoming clear that there were few other alternatives.

REPUBLICS, COMMUNITIES, INDIVIDUALS

Before the Spaniards' arrival, central Mexico had been a densely populated, urbanized, sedentary civilization. City states, or *altepetl*, had dotted the landscape, allied with or opposed to the dominant Mexica. Many languages were spoken across this region, with Nahuatl a lingua franca from north to south. Ritualistic wars remained entangled with religious practice, political governance, and daily life.[46] Beyond the Aztec sphere of influence lived other peoples—the Chichimecas to the north, less sedentary, more resistant, and more bellicose, and the Maya to the far south, less concentrated, more fugitive, and more autonomous.[47]

As Spanish officials assumed power in New Spain, indigenous people faced a pressing social and political question. From the beginning Spaniards had referred to the people of the New World as "Indians," the rubric born of Columbus' mistaken impression that he had reached the Indies. Natives themselves, however, do not seem to have thought of themselves as such. During the early decades after conquest the word *indio* rarely appeared as a loanword in Nahuatl texts. "Indians" preferred to speak of themselves as the residents of this or that altepetl, town, or pueblo, insisting on their "microethnicities" over and above all other labels.[48] In calling them *indios,* Spaniards were not merely recognizing and naming an existing difference between themselves and these New World others, so much as they were creating new categories: they were "inventing" the Indians and thus themselves in relation to the Indians.[49]

At first, the label lacked emotional or social content for indigenous people. It was a forced name bespeaking the conquerors' power over the vanquished. Through it, natives became a subject population of tributaries and workers. Yet the word *indio* was always an ambivalent expression of control, for it figured simultaneously as a basis for royal protection. An early royal decree dispatched by Queen Isabel to the governor of Hispaniola embodied this ambivalence, noting that the "indios" were not subject to enslavement, though they could be made to work, so long as they were properly paid, "as the free people they are."[50] All subsequent legislation regarding the Indians' status under Spanish rule expressed this irresolvable tension.

The need both to exploit and to protect the Indians led, over the course of the sixteenth century, to a policy of segregation between the "Republic of Spaniards" and the "Republic of Indians." No one piece of legislation enshrined this outcome. It evolved as the crown responded to complaints by Indians and Franciscan friars regarding Spanish excesses. Decrees announced in 1550 forbade Spanish "vagabonds" from living in Indian villages and required encomenderos to obtain licenses before sending their servants and retainers into them. Two decades later, encomenderos and their families were barred from Indian villages, except for short visits. In 1578 the principle of residential separation received its fullest statement to that time, when blacks, mestizos, and mulattoes, as well as Spaniards, were forbidden to live among the Indians.[51] Friars, who had pushed this policy, hailed separation: "For the same reason that there cannot exist a good manner of republic and friendship between wolves and sheep, there cannot exist a good manner of republic, confederation and league between Indians and Spaniards."[52] Of course, friars had every reason to exaggerate Spanish abuses, for they craved uncontested control over the natives, the better to save their souls. Even so, their position seems more or less to have been accepted by the Council of the Indies and the king himself as a touchstone of relations with New Spain's indigenous people.

From the crown's perspective, separation made sense not only because of the need to subject and protect the Indians, but also because it followed from a fundamental tenet of Spanish imperial politics—Indians were entitled to govern themselves under Spanish rule. Initially, this meant that principales and caciques retained power over native communities. Over time, the scope of their authority shrank in the face of depopulation, congregaciones, and the imposition of new layers of Spanish bureaucratic control. By the 1560s caciques retained jurisdiction over pre-Hispanic political regions, but answered to Spanish officials above them. In effect, indigenous political power was confined to the local level.

Under the policy of separation, and beneath the lowering cloud of calamity that darkened the sixteenth century, many aspects of indigenous lives remained unchanged. Nobles and caciques continued to dominate everyday life at the village level. Indigenous people still spoke their own languages—which added a baffle of insulation between Indian communities and Spanish interlopers. As in the past, they grew crops, went to market, traded with each other, even paid tribute much as they always had. And yet, they were as keenly aware of their new lords as Spaniards were of them. The problem both sides faced was how these two republics were to communicate.[53]

Though at first most ordinary Indians had little to do with Spaniards—caciques did most of the talking—the trend of the sixteenth century was toward more pervasive contact between Indians and Spaniards. Interpreters emerged as the most common means of communication and remained so throughout the seventeeth century. At the same time, Spaniards were divided over how to confront the issue of language. Some, including King Charles V, thought Indians should learn Spanish. Franciscan missionaries disagreed: "Your majesty should command all the Indians learn the Mexican language [Nahuatl], for in every village there are many Indians who know this language and learn it easily."[54] Their motivation is obvious: having learnt Nahuatl, the friars were reluctant to give up their privileged access to indigenous society. In 1570, after much debate and waffling, Philip II commanded that "all Indians shall learn one language, and that shall be the Mexican tongue [Nahuatl], since it can easily be established as the universal language of the Indians."[55]

Many scorned the new policy. Away from central areas, friars began to realize that Nahuatl was no easier to teach than Spanish. In 1599, these sorts of complaints led Philip III to reverse his father's policy and order missionaries to go back to learning local languages. Far from establishing Castilian as the language of empire by 1600, crown policy had continually strengthened indigenous tongues as the tool of conversion. This ensured that native languages would remain the principal means of communication between the two republics, with Nahuatl an indigenous lingua franca among Indians whose first languages were Tarasco, Otomí, Mixteca, and many others. Even so, many Indians did learn Spanish, enough that Spaniards began to refer to them as *ladinos,* a word that over the seventeenth century took on a sense of impudence, craftiness, and cunning.[56]

Despite popular support for the idea of separation, and official zeal on its behalf, the two republics could not keep people rigorously apart. During the first decades after conquest, before separation had been fully articulated as policy, Indians had kept largely to themselves, especially in the countryside, where Spaniards relied on caciques to collect tribute and organize labor. Toward mid-century this had begun to change. As markets picked up, more traders peddling cloth and pulque traveled the roads linking communities. The repartimiento brought large numbers of Indians together with Spanish employers and hacendados, laying the groundwork for wage labor later on. Waning of the encomienda after 1560 created new economic possibilities and drew Indians into market and credit relationships with Spaniards and others. Congregaciones in 1550–65 relocated thousands of Indians into larger villages and cities where Spaniards lived and where Spanish and Indian children might play together in the streets. In commercial and mining zones, prostitution took root alongside concubinage and more fleeting affairs of the heart and loins.[57] Not surprisingly, by 1600 more Indians spoke Spanish than ever—though no policy of crown or church could claim credit for that.

By the early seventeenth century the border between New Spain's two republics, while legally solid, was in practice almost infinitely porous. There was simply too much coming and going in the pueblos; too much upheaval in Indian lives; too much Spanish need of native labor; and too much intercourse—social, cultural, and sexual—for such a line to hold. The idea behind separation, advocated most vigorously by Franciscan friars and supported by two kings, had been to shelter the Indians from Spanish excesses. New Spain's reality was another—a forced coexistence that multiplied and tightened the sinews of connection almost inexorably.

According to Alonso de Zurita, a judge of the Mexico audiencia during the 1550s, social and political life in the Aztec core, which he considered to be the most "principal and general of New Spain," had been well- and properly ordered before conquest. Strong rulers, firm hierarchies, rigorous justice, and clear and durable arrangements for the living of everyday life—these were the emblems of "good governance."[58] Political authority had radiated outward from the central palace, where the *tlatoani* or lord presided over the altepetl, to the *calpolli,* wards bearing common tributary obligations and holding common land rights.[59] The tlatoani, in turn, had answered only to the Mexica emperor, who collected tribute but did not otherwise interfere in local affairs. Commoners' loyalties and identities appear to have revolved around the calpolli and the altepetl, perhaps in that order of importance. This, wrote Zurita to the king in the mid-sixteenth century, is what had been "unmade and knocked down" since the coming of the Spaniards.[60]

The unmaking of indigenous order was not simply a razing of all social and political structures. It proceeded along uncertain vectors resulting from complex, crosscutting forces. One of the first effects of conquest and its aftermath was to splinter the far-flung Aztec world, more a "mosaic of towns" than an integrated empire, into its constituent elements.[61] Before 1521, altepetls had more or less constantly sought greater independence and wider autonomy within the limits of Mexica tributary control. Even within the altepetls, there had been ceaseless pressure from the calpollis to gain land rights and to diminish central control over local affairs.[62] For many within the Aztec world, the early years of conquest by Spaniards represented an opportunity to pursue autonomy more vigorously than had been possible under the Mexica. Yet when they succeeded, it was against the backdrop of growing Spanish control over indigenous life. In an important sense, efforts by Indian leaders to assert autonomy against pre-Hispanic rivals provided an unwitting aid to Spanish efforts to exert control.

At the same time, the Spanish practice of relying on existing social and political boundaries pulled obliquely against the forces of fragmentation. Up to the 1550s, altepetl and calpolli boundaries remained largely unchanged from pre-Hispanic times. Encomienda and parish limits often ran along altepetl borders, just as Indian villages and their lands tended to track calpolli holdings. In effect, preconquest divisions were reproduced, and the bases of collective and individual identity remained in place. In some respects these divisions were strengthened. Congregaciones after

1550, by insisting on centralized settlements, reinforced the altepetl. When the *cabecera-sujeto* system was created in the 1550s and 1560s— under which each province was ruled by a main town, or *cabecera,* to which smaller towns, or *sujetos,* were politically subject—it mapped almost directly onto the altepetl.[63]

As the sixteenth century wore on, other forces began to impinge on the altepetl as a viable source of political power and social identity. Massive depopulation exacerbated fragmentation as whole villages vanished and people found themselves jettisoned into a rapidly changing landscape. Altepetls began to dissolve into calpollis and other small territories rooted in the occupation of land. From the 1560s forward, new tribute and labor obligations, including the repartimiento, began to drive a wedge between altepetl/cabeceras and calpolli/sujetos. Simultaneous introduction of the corregimiento also undermined the altepetl as a stable source of identity, for corregidores frequently grouped several altepetl together into a single jurisdiction, subordinating cabecera towns to central authority.

As obligations mounted and populations dwindled, Indian communities began to do as they always had—to seek autonomy from outside control. Land, always central to calpolli lives and livelihood became, under colonial circumstances, the distilled essence of local identity. Communities would stop at nothing to protect their lands. A town in litigation over land might take possession of the parcel in question on the eve of a judicially ordered survey, even build an entire settlement overnight in order to strengthen its claim.[64] Where links to the altepetl weakened over time, a sense of belonging buoyed calpollis amid the sixteenth century's tempest. So strong was this sense of local connectedness that calpollis often stayed together even when displaced by the congregaciones, forming new barrios unto themselves if put in the same town as another group. Whole communities might decamp for new places, as did a group of four hundred Tlaxcalan families who in 1591 migrated north to the Zacatecas region to help pacify the Chichimecas.[65] The altepetl's hold on the indigenous imagination might be slipping; the calpolli's remained vital to the very idea of community—though it was hardly untouched by the maelstrom swirling around it.

Perhaps nothing weighed so heavily on a sense of corporate belonging among Indians as economic changes encouraging and forcing people to respond to circumstances as individuals.

It is an old story by now that Spanish emigrants to the New World were in search of opportunity. Social mobility in sixteenth- and seventeenth-century Spain was a real if limited possibility, though all but unachievable for the vast majority of Spaniards.[66] For such people, the New World represented a chance for a better life. They might not gain great wealth or ascend the peaks of status, but they had a greater chance of securing their futures there than in Spain. Over the course of the sixteenth century tens of thousands of Spaniards sailed to Mexico to pursue their dreams.[67]

There is more to this story than just flows of people and a straightforward ambition for betterment. During the late sixteenth century and through the first half of the seventeenth century, Spain underwent a cultural shift in which Spaniards began to imagine that they could—and had no choice but to—act for themselves in the world. As Calderón de la Barca put it through a character in one of his early seventeenth-century plays, "king and kingdom unto myself, I live alone with myself."[68] This sense of aloneness appears to have been rooted in an intensified competition for prestige, material reward, and petty power. Of course, everyday life continued to be defined by estates and hierarchies. But growing numbers of Spaniards began to nurture the idea that they could exert control over their lives, knowing that aspirations could as easily founder.

This made for an anxious contest. According to contemporary writers, personal life was lived on a war footing. Early in the seventeenth century, Suárez de Figueroa lamented that "our life is but a continuous and perpetual war, without any sort of truce or peace." Not much later, Saavedra Fajardo claimed that among Spaniards "people arm themselves against each other, and everyone lives in perpetual distrust and suspicion." At mid-seventeenth century, Jerónimo de Barrionuevo worried about the broader consequences of a so thoroughly individualistic approach to life: "each pursues his own business and not the common and good of all, as a result of which everything goes wrong." In the process, "some enrich themselves making others poor."[69] These were the wages of a generalized sense among ordinary people that they had no choice but to determine their own destinies in the world.

This attitude was no less pronounced among Spaniards in the New World, a place where common folk could more readily play out their dreams than in the Old World. As Bernal Díaz, one of Cortés's soldiers noted in his chronicle of the conquest, Spaniards came to Mexico in good measure "because there was wealth."[70] In this place even a petty trader with no capital could make his way, perhaps prosper modestly, and when trying to persuade his nephew to join him from Spain could write of "the ease you will have here."[71]

At the same time, as in Spain, an atmosphere of struggle pervaded everyday life, inspiring deep personal and moral misgivings. Around 1600, an anonymous poet wrote an unflattering sonnet to Mexico City:

"greedy" merchants, "presumptuous" gentlemen, women who sold themselves for money, "many friends, but few true ones," blacks who did not
obey their masters, masters who did not rule their households, "a thousand pretenders" hanging on the viceroy, "auctions, markets, cacophony, confusion"—"in sum this is what happens in this city."[72]

Another anonymous poet from the early seventeenth century made
essentially the same point, at somewhat greater length and with greater
pathos, in his "Romance to Mexico."[73] One afternoon, while reflecting
on his sorry state, the protagonist finds his mind swept up in the whirl of
Mexico City, where "gallant gentlemen and gracious women," lawyers
and theologians rub shoulders with successful merchants. In the gilded
swirl of "silver, cattle, wheat and gems," he realizes that, like the weights
of a clock, some people "rise while others fall." All of a sudden he enters a
house where four alluring women sit. One of them, a beautiful young girl
not more than fourteen. She asks him who he serves, whether he has any
estate, and what his name is. Answering that he serves no one and that
his cape would cover what estate he has, he says his name is Jerónimo. At
that point he loses all hope, knowing he cannot furnish the jewels, rich
emeralds, and snow-white nacre he assumes she yearns for and deserves.
In the heat of the moment, he understands that it is not true that Venus
rules on this earth and that love can achieve anything; rather, "[self] interest accomplishes all." This phrase becomes a refrain, punctuating the
lament Jerónimo pours out to the girl. In this Mexico, he tells her, "men
live without faith/without God, without law, without soul/and the one
who knows more/promotes himself, adulates and cajoles." Such people
"fool" others, even their own kin, so that there is no place in the world,
countryside or plaza, where "[self] interest" does not hold sway. After a
while, this "beautiful ingrate" tires of his jeremiad, telling him that his
words are "banal." Now his "enemy," she asks to play cards, but he has
nothing to stake. He stands and tells the ladies that if they wait he will fetch
money. He leaves, "engulfed in their flames," damning his fortunes and his
disgrace, intent on pursuing his "high enterprise" because, "I must say, if you
will pardon me, [self] interest can accomplish anything."

If Spaniards in the Old World and the New World experienced the
thrill and anxiety of pursuing individual aspirations in much the same
way, there was a crucial difference between them: in Mexico a subjugated
population was clay to the Spanish desire to shape a personal fate. This
was the origin of the accusation that New World Spaniards were corrupted
by "great greed" and "malice."[74] "To a man seeking power," noted Juan
de Mariana in 1599, "every poor man is a very great opportunity."[75] Nowhere was this more painfully obvious than in sixteenth- and seventeenth-
century New Spain. Not only could the Indians be put to work, but their

very presence reinforced the ascendancy of Spaniards from modest backgrounds who otherwise lacked status. Those who could, and not only
Spaniards, had every incentive to take ruthless advantage of the Indians.
In doing so, they helped remake the Indian world, not so much to render
it in their own image, as the friars had wanted, but to splay it open for appropriation.[76]

Combined with official policies—tribute, congregaciones, repartimiento—this diffuse but powerful energy among Spaniards subjected the
natives to enormous pressures. In the earliest decades after conquest,
Indian nobles clung to power and prestige in colonial life. They had land,
office, lineage, and authority inherited from the pre-Hispanic past—
which allowed them, at times, to match Spaniards themselves in abusing
indigenous commoners. By contrast, through most of the sixteenth century the macehuales faced a world that was little more than an arena in
which they were acted upon.

Only toward 1600 did it become possible for any significant number
of Indians to imagine they might make individual accommodations in a
world that had long been governed according to corporate identities. As
the repartimiento began to fail and hacendados bid against each other
for wage labor, *gañanía*—permanent employee status—permitted growing numbers of individuals to conceive of destinies apart from village life.
They did so under tight constraints, negotiating terms with employers,
arriving at informal, often lasting arrangements. Wages, even debt peonage, opened up opportunities for indigenous laborers. Skilled trades-
men could earn three or four times the going rate for agricultural labor.
Workers who sought release from repartimiento obligations might pay
their employers to hire substitutes. By taking on debt they made it harder
to leave a particular job, but also more difficult for an employer to send
them packing. Such possibilities expanded as wage rates increased after
1580.[77] Changes in land tenure also affected opportunities for chart-
ing an individual course. Through most of the period, land remained
predominantly corporate, at least for commoners. After 1580, with the
emergence of a real estate market in central Mexico, more people were
able to buy and own land privately, even if only very small parcels.[78] In
Oaxaca the situation was less altered by century's end, though there too
the record reveals land sales and privately owned plots.[79]

Gañanía did not imply complete separation from village life. Wage
workers might set up households within the boundaries of an hacienda
and still keep in close touch with home villages, returning for religious
festivities and family events and contributing to communal labor to this
village's corporate lands.[80] On the other hand, labor shortages and the
spread of wages between 1580 and 1620 led many Indians to break with

village life. Some went north, where they joined mestizos, mulattoes, and blacks in the go-go world of silver mining or hired themselves out to local haciendas. Others joined mule trains and took up the itinerant life. More commonly, Indian families chose to reside on hacienda property, attaching themselves more or less permanently to emerging estate communities organized around economic production rather than around ethnic identities rooted in a specific place linked to the pre-Conquest past.

As resident gañanes, they might defend the hacienda in times of crisis, as happened in 1638 when a bailiff who came to arrest the *mayordomo* of a Spanish hacienda met stiff resistance from the Indians, blacks, and mulattoes who lived there. In return, many hacienda owners, acutely aware of the need to keep workers as the repartimiento faded, assumed certain duties toward their employees, making sure they did not starve, assisting them in times of illness, extending credit, and taking part in marriages, baptisms, and funerals.[81] Of course, a moral economy was far from universal, and many gañanes sweated for hacendados who wasted little energy or money cultivating personal reciprocities with their employees. But especially when labor was short up to 1630, such employers often had little choice other than to make concessions to workers in order to retain them.

People who struck off on their own remained a distinct minority. Those who severed ties with villages formed part of a somewhat more hispanized segment of the native population, one that gravitated to cities, large estates, and mining zones. Between them and those who remained bound to the village a gulf was opening. To one side were those who lived by community obligations, people whose lives were ordered according to tribute schedules, religious festivities, and the repartimiento, where it was still honored. To the other was the growing number of Indians who found a "personal solution" in gañanía, independent skilled labor, or private ownership.[82] Though in language, dress, habits, expectations, and aspirations those who remained rooted in the villages and those who moved on were diverging, they were not on their way to becoming two recognizably different groups of Indians—for those who took the path away from the *pueblo de indios* ended up in the world of mestizos rather than in a world of alternative "indianness."

KING, GOVERNANCE, LAW

The king, declared *Las Siete Partidas*—Spain's medieval legal code which still stood in the sixteenth and seventeenth centuries as a pillar of Spanish legality—is a vicar of God, "appointed over the people to maintain them in justice and in truth in temporal matters." Justice, in turn, "is one of the things by which the world is better maintained and regulated . . . like a spring from which all rights flow . . . a firmly established virtue . . . which gives and apportions his rights to every individual." Thus is the king called the "heart and soul of the people," for justice is the "life and support of the people." In his treatise on kingship, Aquinas echoed *Las Partidas,* speaking of the king as the "shepherd" who made it possible for men "to live in the society of many" and "assist his fellows" in forming a "perfect community." "Political happiness," maintained St. Thomas, followed when each person occupied a particular place in the social order and there was no "repugnance" among society's members.[83] To this end, according to sixteenth-century political writers, the just king "makes himself available to all in every duty of life; no one in his helplessness, no one in his loneliness is kept away . . . [h]is ears are open to the complaints of all."[84]

This was not idle theory. As Philip II noted in his instructions to the viceroy of Naples in 1558, "the people was not made for the sake of the prince, but the prince was instituted at the instance of the people."[85] The king's job, according to Philip, was to "work for the people" and dispense justice, so that there should be "good government." A republic could not long survive if its constituent elements were at war, any more than could a body whose hands and feet attacked one another. As head of the realm, the king was responsible for coordinating relations among men so as to secure "peace, which is the principal social good"—justice by another name.[86] As one historian has characterized the matter: "[T]he principal task of government was considered to be that of adjudicating between competing interests, rather than that of deliberately planning and constructing a new society . . . Administration in the sense of the formulation of policy was incidental to jurisdiction."[87] Royal jurisdiction operated less by a mechanical application of law than by appealing to the spirit animating the law, to ensure that each member of the body politic received all due rights and privileges—"to each that to which he is entitled," in the words of the *Las Partidas.*[88]

This was no mean feat in Spain's far-flung empire. In Europe alone, the empire stretched across several Iberian kingdoms—Castile, Aragon, Catalonia, Valencia, Navarre—and included the kingdoms of Sardinia, Naples, and Sicily. In the New World, the difficulties of projecting royal authority were hugely magnified. There, as elsewhere in the Spanish empire, the king represented the ultimate source of political power. But in New Spain and Peru, efforts to rule "constituted a challenge . . . without precedent in European history."[89] So "difficult [was] the governance and direction of those realms which are so distant," so diverse and complex the conditions of rule, and so pervasive the laxity of ordinary Spaniards and others in heeding the king's word, that the Spanish crown in the sixteenth and seventeenth centuries wielded a tenuous, at times erratic, authority in New Spain.[90]

By 1600, the Indians had, across an immense distance, been incorporated into the empire's body politic as legitimate, if subordinate, members. This fact defined a central political problem of the New World: how to extend the king's justice to a large population of indigenous people? The answer given by the crown after 1550 was to allow viceroys to appoint corregidores and alcaldes mayores, royal officers with regional jurisdiction over Indian populations. But as successive kings and viceroys came to understand, these men were often "less than reliable instruments of royal authority."[91] Poorly paid and facing enormous opportunities to take advantage of the Indians, these officers frequently pursued private interests at the expense of public concerns and in flagrant violation of royal will. In other words, the king had no guarantee against those who "strive more sluggishly for the common good."[92]

The problem was of a piece with broader political and cultural trends: more and more Spaniards in the late sixteenth and early seventeenth centuries were acting as though individual interest were separate and distinct from any broader social obligation. If it remained true in principle that "the common good is the end of each individual member of a community," in everyday life individuals were learning to "live for oneself" and call it liberty.[93] Political writers of the early seventeenth century worried that the pillars of social order were swaying precariously with the tremors of rapid change. For them, and for those involved in governance, "conservation" was the political problem of the day. Under these circumstances, king and counselors alike sought to balance liberty and the common good, which did not mean conserving each individual thing unto itself, so much as conserving the relations of each thing to all others. Individual things—people, estates, offices—might change, but so long as the web of relations among things was not torn, society could remain stable. "It is better to conserve than to conquer," wrote Baltazar Gracián in the 1630s, offering a chastened vision of the impulse that had dominated the sixteenth century and brought the New World into a Spanish orbit.[94]

It was through a fog of change and challenge and across the huge cultural and geographic span that separated the New World from the Old World that Mexico's indigenous people squinted to behold their king. Through most of the sixteenth century little is known of what they saw. Those closer to larger towns and cities might see royal portraits and representations in the context of religious and political processions or, as when Charles V died, in funerals. In certain places, Indians might attend plays in which the king was represented by a live actor on stage or in Corpus Christi processions in Tlaxcala in 1539. The children of Indian elites might see the king represented in chapbooks and primers of Spanish history. From these and other traces, such as coins bearing the royal image, many Indians doubtless recognized the symbols of kingly power: crown, scepter, and royal raiments. Through much of the sixteenth century, this image may well have been filtered through remembered images of pre-Hispanic rulers. For instance, the backs of a deck of playing cards dating from the mid-sixteenth century, depicted Cuauhtemoc in profile, sitting on a throne, bearing a distinctly indigenous crown, with a spear in one hand while the other gestured in a commanding way. Toward the margins of empire, most indigenous people probably had at best only the sketchiest image of the king.[95]

In many regards, this was not so different from the way ordinary Spaniards experienced the king by the seventeenth century. A central tenet of royal authority during and after the reign of Philip II was that the king should be invisible to the great masses of his subjects. He was to rule justly on their behalf, but it was felt that he would be more revered if he remained largely unseen by common eyes. The same basic principle held that the Sacred Host should be displayed only during the Holy Sacrament, in order to ensure veneration at the appropriate moment. King and God, then, were tightly joined in the representation of power. Indeed, in 1586 Philip II ordered that he be addressed simply as *señor* (lord), the same word used to refer to God. Eschewing bishops' and viceroys' long list of titles, Philip was emphasizing, as did kings to follow, his singularity as monarch. This is why viceroys, who were only the king's living image, relied so heavily on the display and performance of royal power: where the king's invisibility exalted his authority, the viceroy's authority had to be made visible.[96]

This would have seemed familiar to many indigenous people in the sixteenth century. Among the Aztecs, the tlatoani, or emperor, was largely an unseen ruler. Ordinary people were supposed to bow their heads in his presence. Under Spanish rule, indigenous petitioners acknowledged their status as vassals of the Spanish king even as they adhered to pre-Conquest norms of behavior in the face of power. According to a chronicler of the period, at the "mere mention" of God, church, or king, they would prostrate themselves and refuse to say a word.[97]

Seeing, thus, was not the chief basis for connecting with the Spanish monarch. More often, and increasingly over the sixteenth century and into the seventeenth century, indigenous petitioners conjured an image of the king in legal documents. Plaintiffs from Huejotzingo in 1560 opened their petition, written entirely in Nahuatl, with the words: "Our lord sovereign, you the king don Felipe our lord, we bow low in great reverence to your high dignity, we prostrate and humble ourselves before you, very high and feared king through omnipotent God, giver of life."[98] And they continued, figuratively trying to make the king visible, even while straining for him to see them:

> [W]e who dwell here in New Spain, all together we look to you, our eyes and hearts go out toward you; we have complete confidence in you in the eyes of our Lord God, for he put us into your hands to guard us, and he assigned us to you for us to be your servants and your helpers . . . [V]ery high majesty, remember us, have compassion for us, for very great is the poverty and affliction visited on us who dwell here in New Spain.

Though this pre-Conquest ornamentation faded somewhat as time went on, this basic notion of a ruler who took the form of a powerful superior, connected to God, who could extend his hand to dispense justice to his lowliest vassals suggests a baseline for Indian conceptions of the Spanish king. In 1681, over a century after the Huejotzingo petition, a Oaxaca Indian filed an otherwise unremarkable document echoing the florid Huejotzingo letter. Domingo de Ramos, in a document written originally in Mixtec, opened his statement complying with a judicial order by referring to himself as "a poor commoner of our lord God and a commoner of our lord King." In a subsequent petition filed to oppose the accusation against him, he once again mentioned "our lord King and the royal arms" and asked "for justice."[99]

Though law and legal process represented a vital link to the crown, perhaps the most powerful emblem of the king's presence among the Indians of New Spain was tribute. Though collected largely by native caciques at the behest of Spanish corregidores, tribute was understood to be *royal* tribute, distinguishable in principle from the *derramas* (extra levies) laid on the Indians by friars, alcaldes mayores, corregidores, Indian *gobernadores* (elected village governors), and others who so often acted for private gain. The importance of tribute ran in both directions between Indian vassals and the king. On one hand, tributary obligations perfused Indian lives. Most villages paid tribute two or three times a year, which had a direct impact on the local use of land and labor. Village projects—to build churches, drain swamps, improve land, repair roads, or dam streams—were often subordinated to tribute obligations, for unmet quotas could mean problems with caciques and local Spaniards. On the other hand, Spanish kings from Philip II forward appear to have exercised great care in trying to manage the tributary relationship, as evidenced by the continual flow of royal decrees regarding tribute. After all, alongside religion, nothing touched Indian lives more directly or more pervasively. Of course, royal solicitude was not unqualified, for the crown had to balance a need for revenue and the pursuit of other interests against its concern for indigenous vassals. Nor was royal regulation always effective in preventing abuse at the local level, where the king's power was weakest.

Still, the king remained an important, if remote presence in the lives of Mexico's Indians. They felt royal authority as one might feel the subterranean rumblings of distant power. Their experience of that power was fundamentally local, at a time when the ordering of local rule was very much in flux.

Through the early decades after conquest, indigenous political structures had been remarkably robust. So long as the altepetl retained its vigor, indigenous caciques retained power within native communities. In the face of mid-century congregaciones, the creation of corregimientos (under the jurisdiction of a Spanish corregidor), and the introduction of the repartimiento, caciques found their power slipping. For the crown this was a matter of policy. Before 1560, caciques soaked up a substantial portion of royal tributes. Their influence at the local level needed to be weakened if the crown was to capture more revenues at a time when Indian populations were plummeting. To this end, the king issued decrees instituting yearly elections in an effort to prevent any cacique from gaining lasting control over village life. Although nobles occupied these offices at first, over time commoners also came to be involved in local politics.

At the same time, the crown sought to standardize tribute collection. In the 1560s, Philip II ordered the creation of a consistent, uniform head tax, abolishing the practice of collecting tribute from lands worked in common. Control over receipts from such lands had given caciques enormous discretion regarding tribute payments. As part of this reform, royal orders also required that tribute be paid either in money or maize. This measure made it more difficult for caciques and others to underreport what they were collecting. When tribute had been payable in food, textiles, firewood, fodder, or turkeys it had been almost impossible to keep accurate accounts. Under the new provisions, tribute was still assessed by town, but now according to head counts, with each tributary paying the same amount. In 1578 a further regulation established clear schedules for tribute payment to prevent encomenderos, clergy, and Indian leaders from levying excessive tributes or fudging receipts. Though these measures were nowhere uniformly applied, Indian communities appear to have welcomed the changes. Schedules and capitation meant that local officials could keep track of how much tribute was due, enabling them to contradict those who might claim they owed more, as late sixteenth-century documents attest.[100]

There was no shortage of opposition to these measures. Encomenderos found themselves slowly undercut by royal regulation. Up through the 1550s, they had relied on an unfettered ability to use the Indians as they saw fit. The thicket of laws passed after 1542 constrained them, especially as Indians began to appear before legal tribunals. Encomenderos struggled against these measures, but ultimately were "tamed."[101] Nor did Indian caciques go quietly. They often fought crown policies as best they could, understanding that their sway over the macehuales was at stake. Even after losing direct control they continued to influence villages through faction politics, though no longer commanding unquestioned support from villagers, especially when they competed with each other for influence.

Conflicts within towns and villages were endemic. Caciques complained that they were "being dispossessed and deprived of the absolute authority and income that they formerly had."[102] New officials, now elected annually, strained to establish their authority in the context of a novel political arrangement for community governance. Spanish corregidores strove to work out the implications of their jurisdiction over Indian lives. The minutes of a meeting of the Tlaxcala *cabildo* (governing council) in 1556 hint at the complexities these crosscutting interests could produce.

Since conquest, Tlaxcala had enjoyed a special relationship to the Spanish crown because of its alliance with Cortés against the Mexica in 1521. Tlaxcalan rulers expected fair treatment from Spain. In the meeting minutes, written entirely in Nahuatl, with an interpreter translating for the Spanish corregidor, who was present throughout, the cabildo debated the question of whether to obey a viceregal decree ordering the removal of Tlaxcala's duly elected governor, who had been accused of stealing land and fields. Statements by individual cabildo members make clear that Tlaxcala had only recently pacified deep conflicts over land and governance among its four cities. A Spanish judge by the name of Santillán had come to "set things right," establishing a rotating governorship and settling property claims. Opinions on how to respond to the viceroy's order removing the gobernador spanned a wide range. Some worried that the viceroy had turned against them: "Since we are vassals of the emperor and our ruler the viceroy governs us, if it is really he himself who wants this, it is not good." Others feared that allowing removal of the gobernador would open the door to renewed conflict. As one alcalde anxiously asked: "The ordinances of Santillán are being destroyed; are there to be disputes again?" Others still supported the viceroy, noting that, as the king's vassals "we will obey, since he is the representative of our ruler the emperor." More than anything, cabildo members wanted to know "who went to tell the lord viceroy?" None supported the accused official, but all seemed genuinely worried that someone, perhaps one of their own, had gone behind the cabildo's back, prompting one member to warn against their being "ruined by secret [words]."[103] These minutes are powerful testimony that Spanish rule over Mexico's Indians did not rest mainly on strict obedience. Everything from royal and viceregal orders to requests by a local corregidor could be subject to discussion and negotiation.[104]

The prevalence of debate within Indian communities, was a direct reflection of the fundamental problem of Spanish rule in Mexico. Corregidores had jurisdiction over vast rural areas comprising dozens of towns and thousands of tributaries. Communications were slow and unreliable and had to be conducted in translation, which did not so much impede understanding as offer Indians a refuge from coercive clarity and strict interpretation. As one of the Tlaxcala cabildo members admitted in advocating the removal of the gobernador, "Often we are accused of misinterpreting what is said." In short, the reality of Spanish colonial power was holographic. At each level—local, regional, viceregal, and royal—the issue was the same: power could be exercised only by admitting that the Indians would contest and negotiate it at every step.[105]

Asserting a connection to the king was one way New Spain's Indians sought to figure their stance amid colonial complexities. In 1570, for instance, the caciques and nobles of "Mexico, Tezcuco, Tlacupan and of other provinces and villages of New Spain," wrote a letter to Philip II accusing Spaniards, encomenderos as well as clergy, of levying excess tribute, invading lands, and all but enslaving Indians. Referring to the king as a shepherd and a father, and "kissing the royal feet," they pleaded for "protection and defense" and begged greater enforcement of decrees against mistreatment.[106]

Such expressions of unity were made over deep divisions among and within Indian communities, for "indian society was rarely unanimous in its conception of self-interest."[107] As the minutes of the Tlaxcala cabildo hint, towns could be at odds with one another, or at least uncertain about the proper course of action in any given situation. Even within towns, barrios might reflect factional conflicts. These, in turn, converged with a beggar-thy-neighbor attitude among barrios, villages, and towns. Such conflicts became particularly intense in contests over cabecera status, because cabeceras could demand labor and tribute from subject towns. Alternatively, two cabeceras might join a jurisdictional battle over which of them ruled a particular town and thus controlled its labor supply.[108]

In other words, leaders and principales of indigenous towns shared with local Spanish officials the same basic motivation—to profit from the macehuales. Hence the dilemma of colonial governance: Spanish kings had ample authority to protect Indian commoners even while ensuring tribute, but their ability to do so was limited by competing interests and by vast distance. As a consequence, "power was widely dispersed, not concentrated in king's and notables' hands" and, whether from the direct opposition of encomenderos, the self-serving corruption of corregidores, the recalcitrance of Indian nobles, or the pursuit of survival by commoners, the crown faced unending challenges to achieving its goals.[109]

And yet, local relations and conditions more often than not produced workable outcomes. While reports of bad corregidores and greedy caciques are easy to find, all the evidence indicates that in most situations people got on and fulfilled their basic obligations to the crown. Corregidores had a strong incentive to listen to Indian leaders, and take them seriously, for timely tribute collection and labor supply depended on their collaboration. Indian leaders, first caciques and later elected officials, also had a stake in cooperating with the corregidores, for without tribute and repartimiento requirements enforced from above, they would have had a more difficult time putting the commoners to work. Macehuales, especially toward the turn of the seventeenth century, found greater if still limited opportunities to say "no" to excessive demands by encomenderos, corregidores, and principales—in effect to negotiate the terms of their subjection.

In other words, though Spaniards and Indians often found themselves at odds, they were never simply opposed. And while resentments could run deep, social, economic, political, legal, and even personal relationships often precluded a sharp sense of separation. Indians might sue Spaniards, but they might also join Spaniards to sue other Indians or on other occasions seek allies among Spaniards against other Spaniards. The intensity and frequency of such interactions also differed according to time and place. For the most part, entanglements among Spaniards and Indians seem to have exerted a stronger gravity on social life than did any impulse to mutual isolation.[110]

Law was crucial to this convivencia—this living in each others' constant presence. By spelling out rights and obligations and offering a process for their adjudication, it gave a firmness to arrangements that might otherwise have been little more than passing agreements of convenience. It represented, as well, an emanation from an "invisible" king, his will expressed in an imperfect world with regard to which his knowledge was incomplete. As such, law was a channel of communication joining king and commoner. It was also a language and process by which people could speak to each other across the chasm of conflict.

Yet law was not a thing unto itself, a sphere of *judicial* or *juridical* activity separate from *politics*. Jurisdiction, understood as the right to judge, underlay all politics, the thick slab on which authority and power were built. Though the ground beneath this slab, which dated to the Middle Ages, had begun to shift, there was throughout this period no real distinction between the judicial and the political.[111] The king sat at the pinnacle of Spanish law and enjoyed the most wide-ranging jurisdiction, but he did not legislate alone. Many, likely most laws affecting the New World were drafted by the Council of the Indies, though successive kings did take cognizance of particular issues. Over the sixteenth and seventeenth centuries, laws governing the treatment of the Indians were one of these issues. The problem, of course, was that the king had to rely on distant officials of uncertain zeal and probity to administer those laws.

Indian litigants and petitioners were not deterred. First nobles and later commoners came to understand the power of seeking legal redress. Early on they discovered the role law could play in disputes over land, as when in 1531 the Indian gobernador of Xaltocan joined a Spanish encomendero against the Indian leaders of Tenochtitlan and Tlatelolco, and six years later won a judicial order awarding possession of property.[112] Throughout the sixteenth century, lawsuits of this sort served as a school where Indians mastered the intricacies of legal process and the possibilities and pitfalls of litigation.

The idea of legal process and dispute was hardly new in Mexico. Bernardino de Sahagún noted that before conquest Aztec rulers had been concerned "with the pacification of the people and the settling of litigations and disputes among them, and for this reason they elected wise and prudent judges." At the base of the system had been a general jurisdiction rooted in the calpolli, or ward. There, a local leader served as a judge for claims and petty crimes arising in his area. Above him sat a panel of twelve judges who heard cases in the first instance but also considered appeals. Every twelfth day, the ruler would meet with these judges to hear the most difficult cases. Witnesses were brought and the judges, "who were very skilled at arguing," would examine and cross-examine them to determine the truth of a matter.[113] If postconquest reports are to be believed, judges were honest, making no distinction among people, "important or common, rich or poor." One judge who showed favoritism toward an important Indian against a common man, noted Zurita, was strangled. In the new trial, the verdict favored the common man.[114] Nor was this just a system of customary law informally and inconsistently applied. Though pre-Hispanic legal systems varied, law among the

Aztecs followed established procedures.[115] Juan de Pomar-Zurita noted that cases were not to last more than eighty days, and all sentences were passed "according to the laws that their kings had."[116]

A legalistic sensibility had marked language itself. The Nahuatl word *nahuatilli,* depending only on the presence or absence of a prefix, could be used to denote both law in a general sense (the Latin *ius*) and law in the sense of specific legal rule (the Latin *lex*). Etymologically, *nahuatilli* meant "to speak in a loud voice," suggesting that the law was understood to be a set of commands to be obeyed. These commands were feared for their rigor. In criminal contexts, law was often compared to a wild beast into whose claws one "who stirred up justice" might fall or to a trap that would leave the guilty "quivering before authority." In general, Nahuatl resorted to vivid metaphors and everyday language to connote the meaning and mechanics of law and process. Tribunals were "places of listening" (compare the Spanish word *oidor,* one who hears, for audiencia judges) and to judge something was to "know" it. To render judgment and pass sentence was to cut the head off a case (compare the Spanish *cabeza de proceso,* the head of a trial, to denote the opening statement of a case). Words for punishment ranged across verbs meaning "to advise" or "to correct," to metaphors involving sticks and stones, and cold water. Actual punishment was known for its severity, ranging from admonishment and public shaming, to exile, drowning, hanging, and quartering.[117]

We should not suppose, thus, that the structures and procedures of Spanish legality represented a great novelty for many of Mexico's Indians.[118] As in preconquest Aztec law, the first resort in colonial law was almost invariably local. The Indian gobernador of a village or town was the holder of a *vara de justicia,* or staff of justice, that served as an emblem of judicial authority. He disposed mostly of small matters. He was free to apply customary law so long as it did not contradict natural or divine law. Above the gobernadores sat the Spanish corregidores or alcaldes mayores (terms all but synonymous by the late sixteenth century). They handled disputes over land, debts, theft, assault, and women within communities. As in the calpolli before conquest, these officials combined administrative and judicial functions. Although they had authority to order corporal punishment, they generally preferred fines and banishment.[119] And though in principle alcaldes mayores were to be "pure, honest, exemplary" and "not to be so rich that they oppress the poor of their jurisdiction, nor have dealings or derive profits" from them, corruption among them was legendary.[120] This may have been particularly so in the remote precincts of empire. In 1604, Licenciado Gaspar de la Fuente, on a tour of inspection in New Galicia, wrote an indignant letter to the king detailing the abuses of local corregidores: "In this realm judicial offices are held for the private good of a few individuals, not for your vassals' general welfare, as is your intention."[121]

Above the alcaldes mayores, good and bad, sat the audiencia, which could hear from the king's subjects on all manner of cases, such as land, inheritance, mistreatment of Indians, abuses of power, and disputes over local governance. Its competence included cases in the first instance as well as appeals. At this level, there was often a full complement of legal personnel: eight *oidores,* or superior judges, four regular judges who heard criminal and civil matters, two prosecutors, one civil, one criminal, a chief bailiff, a chief chancellor, and a variety of ancillary personnel, as well as notaries, interpreters, and *procuradores* (soliciters) on behalf of Indian petitioners.[122] The presence of so many professionals meant that the process was taken seriously, from verifying evidence and deposing witnesses, to summoning parties, imposing fines for delay, and providing notarized copies of judgments so that appeals might be pursued.

Indians had access to this evolving system from the earliest times. As the king's vassals, they could not be denied the right to seek royal justice. Starting in the 1530s, indigenous claimants appeared before corregidores or took matters to the audiencia in Mexico City. Through most of the following half century, lawsuits remained uncertain avenues of relief. By the last quarter of the sixteenth century, many in Spanish officialdom had begun to express concern that ordinary Indians lacked ready and effective legal recourse. Macehuales were among the most disadvantaged. Pedro de Gante noted in a 1552 letter to the king that caciques had become "avid litigators" off the "sweat of the Indian commoners, whose belongings are sold in order to litigate." Even among Indian leaders there was great discontent. Around 1570, an unnamed Indian noble complained to Alonso de Zurita that "the Indians had given themselves over to lawsuits because you [Spaniards] had forced them to," by which he seems to have meant that Spanish actions had left indigenous people no option other than to defend themselves in court, which had not been their way before conquest. Nor was their schooling in law an easy one. The Indians who bring lawsuits, Zurita reported his interlocutor as saying, "never reach what they want, because you are the law and the judges and the parties, and you cut into us wherever you want, and whenever and however you like."[123]

These few words crystallized what, by the end of the sixteenth century, had become a crisis of law as applied to the Indians. Viceroy Luis de Velasco II wrote to the king in 1590 advocating the creation of a special court for Indian matters. The crown's response was to establish a new tribunal—the *Juzgado General de Indios* (General Indian Court).

The Juzgado sat in Mexico City, headed by the viceroy and run by a legal assistant, usually a trained lawyer, whose job it was to adjudicate lawsuits brought by Indian claimants. The Juzgado enjoyed original jurisdiction when Indians sued other Indians or when Spaniards sued Indians. Cases in which Indian plaintiffs sued Spaniards were handled through ordinary channels at the audiencia.[124]

Indigenous claimants quickly came to prefer the Juzgado to other tribunals. Although by law they could bring a petition against a Spaniard only before the audiencia, Indian clients learned that if they filed petitions for administrative—as opposed to judicial—relief with the viceroy, they could claim the Juzgado's jurisdiction even in cases against Spaniards. The reason they could do so hinged on the distinction between administrative and judicial remedies.

Spanish government was divided among four branches: administration, justice, treasury, and military. Justice was handled by the audiencia and its subsidiary officers. Anything pertaining to royal finances, however, such as tribute, fell within the viceroy's purview as supervisor of the treasury. In the early 1590s, viceroy Velasco had advocated creation of the Juzgado so that the Indians might have a quick and effective remedy against abuses by Spanish officials. Philip II had agreed in principle, though he did not accept Velasco's recommendation that the viceroy have jurisdiction over cases in which Indians were plaintiffs against Spaniards. Instead, he granted the viceroy full powers to investigate alleged wrongdoing by royal officers and order them to enforce royal law. The effect of this was to empower Indian claimants to complain not only of corregidores' illicit actions but also their refusal to enforce the law against other Spaniards. This amounted to a political compromise that assured ordinary Spaniards they would not be dragged directly into court by Indians, but allowed Indians to seek refuge in the viceroy's administrative powers. Indians responded with great enthusiasm, applying for administrative relief, especially decrees of royal protection— amparos—in large numbers from the 1590s forward.[125]

The general extension of Spanish law and its reception in the Indian world, culminating with establishment of the Juzgado, represented a considerable normative and institutional accomplishment. Broadly speaking, it was made possible by the dominant sixteenth-century view regarding the "steady perfectibility of the social order," even in a place so different and challenging as the New World. Throughout the century of conquest, Thomist writers such as Vitoria, Suárez, Soto, and Mariana had succeeded in defining politics—synonymous with governance—in terms of pursuit of the common good. They stressed the search for complementarities and affinities among seemingly disparate phenomena. By looking for commonalities in the world, rather than assuming difference, they held out the possibility of creating order and balance through the combination of elements that might otherwise have been dismissed as incommensurable. On this view, a principled flexibility allowed deep philosophical commitments—to the inherent stability of the social order, the natural reasonableness of man, and the possibility of moral rulership—to stand and even thrive in the face of competing interests and profound differences.[126] This flexibility was a response to the novel and distinctive challenges of ruling the New World, a dynamic fulcrum on which were precariously balanced three different understandings of *law:* law as the legal order ensuring "good government" (*derecho*); law as legislation, a written code promulgated by legitimate authority (*ley*); and law as an unwritten norm regarding the problem of order and human relations (*costumbre*).

Toward 1600, this balance began to teeter in the face of growing political and philosophical concerns. Sixteenth-century confidence that the common good could be achieved and social order perfected gave way to a gathering pessimism regarding the fortunes of human communities. Chastened by the seeming permanence of the Reformation, by the deepening sense that humankind was "self-serving rather than self-realizing," by the widening rift between politics and morality, by the raucous greed of Spanish settlers, and by the fact that indigenous people in the New World had not become the model Christians and vassals many had hoped, seventeenth-century Spanish writers retreated somewhat from the grand abstractions of the sixteenth-century Thomists to an abiding concern for securing society against the forces of dissolution.[127] Writers such as Pedro de Ribadeneyra, Sebastián de Covarrubias, Saavedra Fajardo, and many others focused on particular problems, advising rulers to attend, above all, to concrete circumstances rather than broad principles.[128]

This preoccupation with particularity and circumstance found expression in law through a renewed emphasis on casuistry in legal decision making. The casuistic imperative had a long pedigree, descending from Roman and medieval notions of legal judgment. Celsius had defined the law as "the art of the good and the equitable," less a science and methodology than a principled response to the unavoidable multiplicity and plenitude of human life. Spanish jurists of the sixteenth and seventeenth centuries held this same line, emphasizing cases over fixed laws. Plato himself, noted fray Luis de León in 1583, had been of the view that written laws were not the best form of government, for they were too static to accommodate changing circumstances. "Particular cases," observed León, "were many, and they vary, by circumstance and time." Good government depended on the spirit of *ley viva,* the living law given by the ruler who attends closely to the particularity of each thing in his charge. For God and Nature, wrote another theologian, had created "particular and singular things," rather than genera and species.[129]

According to Covarrubias's 1611 dictionary of Castilian, the *case* was not only the thing that had happened, but "the occasion and proposition upon which the determinations of law and decree are made; and in lawsuits the first thing that is agreed upon is the case or the facts, which are the same thing." Francisco Bermúdez de Pedraza reiterated the point in his 1612 primer for law students. In a chapter entitled "Why jurists proceed more by facts than by general rules," he explained that because all law consists of facts and "any small variation of fact changes the law," there could be no "universal rule for everyone." Indeed, "rules in law" were "dangerous," for "what else does human fragility do than produce varied facts and a diversity of circumstances, which are what form instances and exceptions? Because as law wants nothing more than clarity, and from generality more often than not is born uncertainty, it seemed more useful to apply a law to each cause."[130]

Perhaps nowhere in the Spanish empire were multiplicity and particularity more mind-bogglingly evident than in the New World. In the words of late sixteenth-century poet Bernardo Balbuena, Mexico was a place "of varied shapes, faces and countenances/of varied men, of varied thoughts . . ./ . . . men and women/of diverse color and occupations/of varied estates and varied viewpoints;/different in languages and nations/in purposes, goals and desires,/and at times in laws and opinions." The crown had been aware of the New World's astonishing variety from the very beginning. Bowing to situation, Charles V in 1526 had ordered an early governor of Tierra Firme to act according to conscience, since "that land is so new and very different from Spain." Not until 1614 did the crown finally order that only legislation written expressly for the New World carry the weight of law there.[131] In the interim, law was an open-ended experiment in adapting Castilian norms to a novel world. Even after 1614, written law remained suspect before the New World's distinctiveness. Writing from Peru, mid-seventeenth century jurist Solórzano y Pereira recognized that a single rule could not "take the measure of all cases . . . because these alter and vary, according to the difference and variation of their quality and circumstances."[132]

Casuistry, in other words, was not an unswerving principle. By its very nature it was prone to change and sensitive to situation. This is precisely why it proved such a supple response to the challenge of creating legality in a new land. Over the seventeenth century, as the corpus of royal edicts, decrees, and ordinances grew, and as jurists such as León Pinelo and Solórzano y Pereira compiled, systematized, and commented on them, written law began to take on greater importance. But never by displacing a concern for the case as such, an approach which remained influential in New Spain's legal culture down to the eighteenth century.[133] System, in the sense of written law in and for itself, remained an important secondary concern. Although judges had an obligation to the letter of the law, at the end of the day, they were supposed to find a just outcome in each individual case. This was not to be an exercise in arbitrariness—though such an approach was open to abuse. It was, instead, to be a principled and disciplined search for the particular truth of each case on its own terms by appeal to and close comparison of relevant authorities and in light of experience.[134]

The elaboration of law was not exclusively a process dictated from on high. Royal edicts and viceregal willingness to enforce them were indispensable. But without indigenous participation it is unlikely laws regarding treatment of the Indians could have retained much force or legitimacy among conquered peoples. Legality became reality because, over the sixteenth and seventeenth centuries, Indian petitioners, first caciques and nobles and later commoners, took law and legal process seriously. They learned of the law from criers, from documents posted in public places, from the pulpit (Charles V ordered that the New Laws be announced in Mexico's churches), and from each other. They watched as their procuradores drafted and filed petitions. They listened to the words interpreters used in tacking back and forth between languages. They came to understand that a lawyer's opinion could carry great weight in a proceeding. They learned to write wills, to contest and defend property, to complain of abuses, to seek liberty, to defend community autonomy, to insist on and face punishment, and to back away from too conclusory an outcome when community peace demanded compromise.[135] Above all, they learned to press their grievances against each other and Spaniards as well.

Even before the advent of the Juzgado, caciques and nobles from Mexico City's environs had expressed amazement at their own litigiousness. In letters to the king in 1570 and 1574, they marveled at their own penchant for lawsuits since the Spaniards' arrival. They asked that their cases be dealt with speedily and that something be done to control costs, "given that we are poor and ignorant." Unlike Zurita's anonymous informant, who seemed to despair of the law—"because you [Spaniards] are the law and the judges and the parties"—these leaders, appealing to the mercy and prudence of a distant king, harbored a hope that the law might be made an instrument of their survival and agency in a world in which they had not chosen to live.[136] The axis between these two positions might be thought of as the constitutive tension that defined the Indians' relationship to law, and hence Spanish rule, throughout the viceregal period.

≈

During the long century after the fall of Tenochtitlan one might have expected a hush of defeat to have fallen over the Indian world. It did not. That world was eclipsed by the encounter with new Spanish rulers, but it was not extinguished. Despite demographic calamity Indian communities and individuals survived. Amid demands for labor and tribute, faced with competition over land and assaults on community, drawn into a new spiritual world, they struggled against oblivion by adapting. They were not of a single voice and rarely expressed anything so compact as a unified agenda. Much of the time they could not even be sure what was in their best interest, so changeable were the circumstances of their lives.

One thing remained constant. Over this century, all of the crown's efforts and experiments of rule came down to law. Every major change was heralded by royal decrees, and viceroys and other royal officers, with greater or lesser zeal, sought to enforce them as they confronted the difficulties of interpreting royal will against recalcitrant realities. Indians were not idle in this process, bringing lawsuits, against each other and against Spaniards, always seeking more effective means of conveying their concerns and securing their interests, as individuals and as communities. In the company of procuradores, notaries, lawyers, interpreters, judges, and many others, they began to cultivate their own understandings of law and justice, understandings rooted in their condition as people at once succored and beset.

By the late sixteenth century, through the mutual actions of Spaniards and Indians, conquerors and vanquished, law circulated widely in the colonial body politic. Enough so that by 1588 Jesuit José de Acosta could insist that "the multitude of Indians and Spaniards form one and the same political community, and not two entities distinct from one another. They all have the same king, are subject to the same laws, are judged by a sole judiciary. There are not different laws for some and for others, but the same for all."[137] There was much wishful thinking in this assertion and not a little self-congratulation. Above all, this view glossed over the complexities of what was, in fact, a novel situation—in which a Spanish legal system that had emerged under a given set of historical circumstances became a means to the negotiation of colonial difference.

CHAPTER THREE

Help Us and Protect Us

In early 1640, a small delegation of Indians from the village of San Miguel de Mesquitic trudged wearily into Mexico City. The *gobernador* and one or two other officers of the republic had set out from their village shortly after the turn of the new year to seek help against a Spaniard who was trying to take their land.[1] They had traveled eighty arduous leagues on foot from the northern silver-mining province of San Luis Potosí—a two-week trip—to appear before the Juzgado General de Indios.[2] Having secured lodging, they had made for the audiencia hoping to find someone who could draft and file a petition on their behalf. They may have had a fair idea of what they were doing, for leaders of their community had made a similar trip twenty years earlier.[3] They knew, for instance, to avoid the mountebanks who hovered at the edge of the city hoping to ensnare unsuspecting Indians new to the legal game. They may even have had a specific person in mind to represent them. José de Çeli, a procurador at the Juzgado, had helped two Indians from a village near San Miguel in 1638. Anyone familiar with the bustling corridors of the audiencia would have mentioned his name and pointed the gobernador and his officers toward Çeli's table, where he sat drafting petitions and advising clients.[4]

In a sense, their arrival in Mexico City may have been something of a homecoming for these village leaders. As noted in the petition, they spoke for a group of Indians who decades earlier had left "their homes, their lands, their kin, and many other comforts" in Tlaxcala, twenty-five leagues or so from Mexico City, to move to the far northern frontier of New Spain to help "reduce" the "rebellious" Chichimecas—a people widely thought of as barbarous—by attracting them to "our holy Catholic faith."[5] And they had succeeded, or so they insisted, claiming to represent the "*común* [the collective] and all the native inhabitants, Tlaxcaltecos and Chichimecas" of the village. The thrust of their petition was that Spaniard Pedro Días del Campo and certain other people were trying to usurp lands the king himself had granted them to compensate their sacrifice and service.[6]

Specifically, declared the petition, Del Campo and his confederates, "with a powerful hand and favored by the local justices," had "dared to enter" lands held by the Indians of San Miguel pursuant to a royal provision dating back to the late sixteenth century. Viceregal orders confirming their claim had been of little avail in the recent dispute. Trespassers, "carried away by their greed" and with "neither proper title nor reason," had sent their cattle and sheep to graze on the Indians' land, "laying waste to and destroying" the pastures. Adding insult to injury, Del Campo's servants had stolen onto the land to cut down trees and had taken all the wood which the residents of San Miguel generally harvested and sold to the mines in San Luis. To make matters worse, stated the petition, some Jesuits have wrongfully claimed a piece of land and begun to litigate, a process the villagers could ill afford. Finally, concluded petitioners in a Jobian tone, certain other Indians, following the trespassers' example, had begun to come on the land and take wood. In the face of all this, village leaders had tried to resolve matters legally by asking that the land be properly surveyed and marked, but no local justice had been willing to do so. On the contrary, the *alcalde mayor* and *teniente*—the Spanish justice and his lieutenant—had done everything in their power to "tie [petitioners'] hands," delay San Miguel's lawsuits, and stymie enforcement of the viceroys' earlier orders, thereby preventing the Indians "from pursuing their justice."

By way of remedy, the gobernador and his officers asked that the royal provision and subsequent viceregal orders recognizing the legitimacy of their claim be enforced and that the trespassers be evicted and commanded not to allow their stock animals to wander loose. They requested that the land be surveyed and its boundaries marked. Local justices, especially the alcalde mayor, should be ordered not to interfere.

The Juzgado sent the petition to the audiencia's crown attorney and to its own legal adviser, both of whom pronounced in favor of the Indians, acknowledging the great service they had done for the king in helping subdue the Chichimecas. The tribunal then issued a writ of amparo—protection—confirming the village of San Miguel in the "quiet and pacific possession" of the claimed land. In closing, the tribunal agreed that the local alcalde mayor should stay out of things, ordering instead that the matter be handled by *receptor* Juan de Meras—an itinerant judge answerable directly to the audiencia—who was in the area of San Luis Potosí conducting the alcalde mayor's *residencia,* or posttenure audit. Failure on the receptor's part to settle the matter within a "brief time" would result in penalties against him. Finally, petitioners were to be sent a written confirmation—a *testimonio*—that the order had been executed as issued.

This small drama was only one among thousands of similar petitions filed by Indians from across Mexico during the seventeenth century. Whether from as near as Mexico City's outlying districts or as far as the remote southern province of Tehuantepec, Indians brought their grievances and their hopes for royal protection—amparo—to the viceroy in Mexico City.

By 1640, when San Miguel's leaders took their complaint to the capital, the bare legal requirements for filing an amparo petition with the Juzgado were well established: petitioners had to be Indians (because the Juzgado was a special jurisdiction limited to Indians), the written petition had to allege some sort of individual or collective harm, and it had to request the king's protection in the form of an enforceable order. As a nonadversarial proceeding—the party complained about rarely appeared to tell its side of the story—the writ was not legally complex. Even so, most petitioners retained legal counsel to help them draft and file their petitions. Procuradores such as Çeli, not full-fledged lawyers but with considerable legal experience, knew best how to present a petition for maximum impact on judges' minds.[7]

Usually the tribunal ruled on the validity of a claim very quickly and issued an order within days. Typically, an amparo was directed to a named justice, often an alcalde mayor or corregidor in a particular jurisdiction, though at times the order would instruct any justice to whom it was presented to execute it, effectively giving the bearers of the order a choice of judge. Notification was entrusted to "any person who knows how to read and write," usually a notary, but in a pinch any other person who could read and understand the order. With an amparo in hand, petitioners were free to use it when and as they pleased. Frequently they went straight to a notary in their home jurisdiction and asked that it be officially served on the justice named. Less often, especially when seeking to prevent a harm rather than redress one, petitioners would hold the order in abeyance to use at an opportune moment in an ongoing lawsuit or as a way of launching a legal offensive.

A critical aspect of the amparo was its limited legal effect: as an administrative, rather than judicial order, it aimed to protect a petitioner without speaking to the merits of any ongoing or future litigation. Thus, if ownership of land was truly in dispute, the protection afforded by the amparo would hold only until the matter had been settled or decided at law. By presenting an amparo, the holder legally ensured that a judge would hear both parties to a dispute before any binding legal action could be taken. And so amparos issued to Indian petitioners very often closed by indicating that any opposing party wanting to question the order should do so in the Juzgado itself, in effect protecting Indian petitioners against having to appear before judges friendly to their adversaries.

For the period between the early 1590s and roughly 1700, I have found more than 2,500 amparos issued by the Juzgado pursuant to all manner of petitions.[8] Of these, I culled a sample of more than 450 for close scrutiny.[9] As a source, the amparos are fairly straightforward. What comes down to us are not the raw material of the proceedings—original petitions and court working documents—but notarial copies of the petitions and orders issued by the tribunal. Only successful petitions found their way to the written record.[10] With rare exception, these cases summarize the petition, provide a statement of legal opinion by the Juzgado's legal adviser, and close with the viceroy's order. The entire document generally appeared in the hand of a single scribe. The summary of the petition was not verbatim and in most cases referred to petitioners in the third person—*he, she,* or *they*—reflecting the mediated quality of petitioners' accounts, although first person petitions are not uncommon. The variety of language and fact situations across the amparos indicates that notaries were true not only to the gist of the petitions, but to the nuances of narrative and to petitioners' and procuradores' use of language, legal and otherwise.

Although the San Miguel case is wordier than most, it was quite simple at the core: cattle and sheep belonging to certain people were intruding upon the petitioners' land, destroying crops, and these same people were stealing wood that the Indians of San Miguel depended upon to sustain themselves. The words used to frame this harm are striking. People had not merely trespassed, but with a "powerful hand" and "favored by local justices" they had "dared to enter" the land. Led by their "excessive greed," they were "laying waste" to the countryside, preventing the "miserable Indians" from enjoying the fruits of their own land and labor. And when the people of San Miguel had tried to survey the parcel in question they had found "their hands tied, so that they could not pursue their justice."

This language was not cribbed from some legal form book indicating how amparo petitions should be written. It was instead a richly metaphorical idiom that brought the moral underpinnings of amparo into sharp relief against New Spain's realities. More to the point, this idiom, which developed over the course of the seventeenth century as indigenous petitioners raised an ever-widening array of issues with procuradores like Çeli, represented a chief means by which Indians came to understand and imagine their relationship to the law and to a distant king.

We cannot eavesdrop on the exchange between procurador and client. Çeli probably began by asking the gobernador and his men to explain the matter and posed questions as he went, already shaping a legal narrative. The record does not indicate one way or another whether this conversation proceeded in Spanish or back and forth between Nahuatl and Spanish. As Tlaxcaltecos, the San Miguel delegation almost certainly spoke Nahuatl. No less plausibly, the conversation could have been conducted in a kind of hodgepodge of the two languages, for Çeli worked so often with Indian petitioners that he may have understood some Nahuatl. The Indians may also have spoken quite a bit of Spanish. While ordinary villagers might have only native tongues, those who dealt with officialdom often had considerable command of Spanish. Essentially, the amparos are condensations of these conversations, followed by the tribunal's legal action in the form of orders.

These documents present significant methodological challenges. Because they are fundamentally mediated, perhaps more insistently so than many other legal records, it is difficult to isolate petitioners' voices from the interpreter's dubbing, the procurador's framing of a narrative for legal effect, and the notary's summarizing of the petition. While there are rewards for careful listening, moments when petitioners can be heard through other voices, there are limits to what can be made out.

Once this is understood, what appears as a constraint becomes an opportunity. The many instances in which the distinctiveness of individual voices is muffled are a reminder that these documents are the transcripts of a collective conversation—among petitioners, procuradores, interpreters, corregidores, judges, the viceroy, and constructively, the king—regarding the meaning of royal and legal protection in colonial circumstances: petitioners told their woes, but in doing so drew on their knowledge or sense of what the procurador needed to hear, interpreters relayed what they heard using phrases experience told them would communicate relevant information to procuradores, who listened to these tales and shaped them to best effect by requesting further detail from petitioners. Participants themselves may not always have known precisely where one voice left off and another picked up. They did know that as far as the tribunal was concerned, petitions spoke for petitioners and orders spoke for the king's law.

THEY ARE UNDER MY PROTECTION

In broad terms, the tale of how the *residentes* (native residents) of San Miguel ended up in Mexico City in 1640 is the story of how medieval Spanish legal principles, New World circumstance, and juridical innovation converged to produce the possibility of redress for people who might otherwise have had no hope of remedy.

According to the *Las Siete Partidas*—Alfonso X the Wise's thirteenth-century compilation of medieval Spanish law—the king possessed the power to draw up a letter to protect his subjects from "wrong . . . violence . . . or injustice." In principle, this protection knew no distinction of rank or status. *Las Partidas* enjoined the monarch to "love, honor, and protect his people"—"the union of all men together, those of superior, middle, and inferior rank."[11] His duties in this regard ran along three tracks: to protect the people against his own power; to protect them against each other; and to protect them against foreigners and other external threats. The first of these prohibited the king, and those acting on his behalf, from treating his people "in an improper manner, as he would not desire that others treat him." In this way he would forge a "union" between himself and his subjects "which cannot be broken." To protect the people against each other, and especially to prevent violence and injury among them, *Las Partidas* declared that the king must "maintain law and justice, and not permit those of superior rank, who may be arrogant, to seize, rob, or take by force the property of their inferiors, or injure them." To accomplish this, so that his subjects might live "in security, and each one enjoy what he possesses," he had to "restrain the proud and strengthen the humble." Finally, the king should shield his subjects in every way he could from external attack, be "their wall and their refuge" against foreign enemies.[12]

The established precept that the king bore toward his subjects a duty of protection crossed the ocean with Spanish faith, arms, and rule in the sixteenth century and encountered a new and unprecedented challenge—whether the New World's indigenous people were to enjoy the same protections and royal solicitude as Spaniards themselves. The legal, philosophical, and practical quandaries posed by this challenge were acute. Conquistadores and encomenderos treated indigenous inhabitants as a prize or a resource. Many theologians, jurists, and practical men concluded that the Indians were little better than beasts. And yet, the crown continually, if not always consistently, pushed the idea that the Indians were entitled to royal protection. Early decrees declared that the Carib Indians of Cuba were "free and subject to no servitude." The 1512 Laws of Burgos extended this idea, calling for good treatment of all the New World's Indians. While this legislation was laced with exceptions and largely unenforceable in the immediate chaos of conquest, it enshrined a significant if inchoate axiom of protection for Indians. The encyclical *Sublimis Deus* of 1537 declared the Indians "truly men," and the New Laws of 1542 held unambiguously that the Indians were entitled to the king's protection.[13]

By mid-sixteenth century, the central dilemma of rule in the New World had been clearly delineated. On the one hand, Spain's only justification for its occupation of these lands rested on an obligation to convert the natives to Christianity.[14] Since Christian doctrine did not recognize different classes of believers—because all men were equal in the eyes of God—the Indians were on a theological par with Spaniards.[15] Their humanity, defined by their capacity to accept Christian faith, entitled them to protection under the law, commensurate with their place in the greater scheme of society. On the other hand, indigenous workers were the indispensable resource of the New World. These two interests tugged and pulled against each other throughout the sixteenth century, creating a dynamic tension at the core of colonial life. Ideologically, this tension found a kind of equipoise in the idea of the Indians' tutelary status. Legally, Indians were likened to minors, that is, fully human people who could not be left to rule themselves. They could be made to work— to ensure they were not idle and for the common good—but they could not be abused. And so, they required defense against those who would take advantage of them.

Effective protection was long in coming. Through most of the sixteenth century the Indians' legal status remained unresolved. By law their land could not be taken. And after the 1550s, they could not be enslaved. But they were still subject to the encomienda, which masked so much excess, and to personal service, which so often could not be distinguished from slavery. The first step in the process by which the "humble" were strengthened against "arrogant" superiors, in the words of *Las Siete Partidas,* involved legal acknowledgment of the Indians' vulnerability in relation to the powerful. An idea stretching back to Constantine and rooted in scripture, the doctrine of *miserabilis* held that certain people, whose helplessness inspired compassion, enjoyed special protection as "personas miserables"—wretched persons. During the late Middle Ages and after, writers had spoken of widows, orphans, pupils, minors, servants, captives, imbeciles, the aged, paupers, peasants, and even the weak generally as miserables.[16] At its core, the doctrine expressed a concern for those who wandered the wilderness of the world without a protector, people such as orphans, who lacked fathers, and widows, who lacked husbands—all those, as *Las Partidas* noted, who may "suffer wrong or violence from others more powerful than they."[17] This was in keeping with scripture: Exodus enjoined rulers not to "deny justice to your poor people in their lawsuits" and Deuteronomy bade rulers "not deprive the alien or the fatherless of justice."[18]

Although recognized in sixteenth-century jurisprudence, the doctrine of miserables had applied only to *individuals* who stood naked before the powerful. The notion that a whole people—an entire ethnic group,

in modern parlance—should fall under the rubric of *miserables* represented a juridical innovation of the first order. After 1521, the ambit of
the term *miserables* gradually widened to embrace Indians in recognition of their vulnerability at the hands of licentious Spaniards. Starting
in the 1560s and increasingly thereafter, Mexico's native people came to
be explicitly referred to as *miserables* in official communiques between
Madrid and Mexico City. Up to 1580, the word was more often used
rhetorically than as a term of legal art. Toward the end of the sixteenth
century, *miserables* began to take on a more distinct legal meaning.
Royal decrees began to hold that Indians were entitled to certain privileges at law—speedy trials, free legal counsel, diminished responsibility
for truth telling, choice of judges under certain circumstances, lesser
punishments—that did not reach Spaniards generally.[19] In 1593, the king
ordered that the Indians "be more protected as people who are more
miserable and of less defense."[20] A treatise written in Peru in 1602 noted
that "the poor and personas miserables, in litigation with a powerful
person" were entitled to special recognition in courts of law, because "it
is natural for the powerful to oppress the poor."[21]

Despite this language of paternal concern, decrees favoring the Indians
often went unenforced. Without a routinized legal form expressing the
principle of protection short of lengthy and costly litigation, royal edicts
remained little more than admirable statements of intention. In other
words, indigenous people lacked the "simple, inexpensive, quick and effective legal remedies" they needed to make good on the promise of
the crown's protective legislation.[22] The problem was deeply systemic.
Indeed, by the late 1580s the incorporation of native people into Spanish
law and polity seemed on the verge of failure, and the royal bureaucracy—both in the viceroyalty and the metropole—began desperately to
seek an answer to the problem.

This is the point at which the writ of amparo took center stage.
Between 1590 and 1592, viceroy Velasco II recognized the Indians'
status as *miserables* in institutional terms by establishing the Juzgado
General de Indios—the General Indian Court. With strong royal backing, the new tribunal threw open the audiencia's doors to indigenous
claimants.[23] While "before it had not been easy" for the Indians to be
heard in court, viceroy Velasco wrote to his successor in 1595, now they
did so "with great ease and brevity."[24]

One of the most important effects of this new access was to make
the writ of amparo widely available to Indian petitioners. Response to
the tribunal hints that New Spains' Indians may have been no less desperate than royal bureaucrats to clarify their legal status. During the
tribunal's first two years, the audiencia issued three hundred petitions

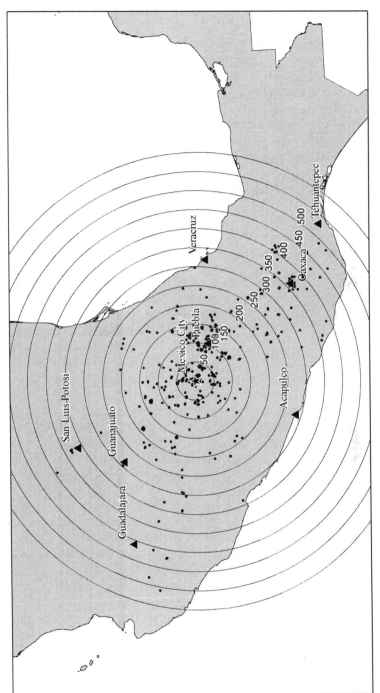

FIGURE 1. Amparos (n = 428) in terms of distance from Mexico City (each concentric circle represents 50 km).

for amparo, suggesting a tremendous demand for a quick and effective remedy.[25] Much had changed since the middle of the sixteenth century. The administrative and judicial infrastructure on which the amparo depended for its efficacy had taken shape between the 1550s and the 1580s. Jurisdictional boundaries had hardened somewhat, and local justices were not so thinly scattered across Mexico's vastness. At the same time, the turmoil raised by the first wave of *congregaciones* had finally begun to subside and Indian communities once again enjoyed a measure of stability.[26]

Spanish kings knew that their orders regarding good treatment of the Indians often went unenforced, when they were not flouted outright. Yet it would be a mistake to assume that these laws, and the principle of protection underlying them, were dead letters.[27] No legal arrangement perfectly inscribes itself upon the messy realities of the actual world— perhaps most especially in the New World, where the fount of royal justice fell below a distant horizon. It was a place where the king's wishes, while more than rumor, were less than undoubted commands, a place where the convergence of an exploitative imperative and a protective impulse condensed into a fog of ambivalence that often hid the abuse of vulnerable colonial subjects.

By 1600, the Indians of Mexico understood this. Law for them was not reducible to the issue of how closely litigation fit the word of law. Decades of experience told them that the law was by its very nature fickle.[28] Whether in disputes with Spaniards or with other Indians, petitioners knew that "justices (sometimes) favor[ed] the powerful."[29] The amparo, they understood, afforded the vulnerable a counterweight to local power. And yet, the amparo was also available to the powerful. Native officials and others often went to court seeking amparos whose effect was to dispossess or subjugate other Indians. This irony was not lost on petitioners. As with all legal forms, the royal amparo became an instrument by which rich and poor, powerful and vulnerable alike sought to exercise some control over their world. It was the opportunity to do so that brought indigenous petitioners by the thousands to Mexico City over the seventeenth century, as Fig. 1 clearly shows.

STAYING POWERFUL HANDS

Early amparos were simple affairs, rarely running to more than half a page. Up to 1630, a majority were land cases involving a trespass of persons or livestock. The language used to describe injury, even at this initial stage, was quite uniform. In case after case, petitions complained that malefactors had "entered" or planned to "enter" upon the land in order to cause them "wrong and damage" (*mal y daño*). Intent was crucial to these small narratives of harm. The trespass alleged was never inadvertent. Rather, wrongdoers were accused of seeking to "impede the use of a land grant" or "disturb and take the land," and of doing so "forcibly and without right," "unjustly," "without other cause," or out of "hatred and enmity" (*odio y enemistad*). Petitioners, by contrast, were invariably depicted as having held the land by long-established right, by inheritance, or "quietly and pacifically"—as people who were minding their own business until a villain came to prey on them.[30] These petitions were nothing if not legal morality tales.

The moral in all of these stories subtly expressed the underlying legal idea of amparo—that the vulnerable required protection from the strong. In many cases, the narrative effect was heightened by key phrases charging or hinting at an abuse of authority. Pablo de Gaona, an Indian from Acarem, about thirty leagues northeast of Mexico City, accused an Indian noble of trying to take land "on his own authority." Andrés Oçolotl claimed that an Indian woman, with "the favor" of an Indian justice of the peace in the village of Calamaya, was trying to take the deed and title to his land. Joana Verónica of Guautitlan alleged that an Indian painter called Simón, "favored by Spaniards and by the interpreter of the village court," was trying to dispossess her of land she had bought fifteen years earlier.[31]

These cases raise a critical question: who was committing the acts that led petitioners to travel such distances to have their complaints heard? Indians frequently accused other Indians. Indeed, during the first years of the Juzgado a petition was more likely to identify another Indian than a Spaniard as wrongdoer. Less commonly, a petition might accuse Spaniards and Indians of acting together. Occasionally, Indians would complain of the treatment they suffered at the hands of mestizos, mulattoes, and blacks. More often, petitions made no reference to an evildoer or blamed "some people" (*algunas personas*), "certain people" (*ciertas personas*), or sometimes "insidious persons" (*personas insidiosas*).[32] Whether petitioners were wary of naming Spaniards for fear Spanish judges might turn against them is impossible to know; later petitions do more often complain of Spaniards than Indians. But from these earliest cases it is clear that with regard to certain issues, especially land, Indians felt they required as much protection from other Indians as from Spaniards.

In late 1619, the gobernador and officers of republic of the city of Guanajuato complained that the Spanish chief bailiff (*alguacil mayor*) of the local court was engaged in private commercial dealings with the residents of his jurisdiction. According to the petition, he forced them to buy calves at inflated prices and when they failed to meet their installment payments locked them up "on his own authority," without a proper judicial order. Because he was the brother-in-law of the village notary, who "threatens" them, they "dare[d] not complain" to the local justice, for only the notary could issue the documents they would need to pursue a remedy. They asked the viceroy for protection, noting that private dealings of this sort were contrary to law. Viceroy Fernández de Córdova agreed, ordering the local justice of Guanajuato to put a stop to the bailiff's impositions.[33]

Compared to the earlier cases, there was a new tone here. The concern for *mal y daño* and abuse of authority had not dropped away. But now coercion and intimidation were expressed more directly and more clearly. What had been hinted at before, the way powerful figures in a given community could overawe and bully ordinary people, had become explicit. In part this was because the forcible sale of goods and arbitrary imprisonment could not be as easily disguised as trespassing. Cattle wandering over the land could be chalked up to inattentive shepherds. An attempted land grab could almost always be camouflaged as a legal effort to regain property lost. The bailiff's actions in the Guanajuato case were unmistakably coercive: he forced petitioners to accept the calves and arrested them when they failed to pay up.

Over the following two decades, amparo petitions followed this line and gradually enriched their narratives of harm with a more dramatic idiom of duress. More than land was at stake in these cases, though land continued to be a bone of sharp contention. The people of the village of Cotepec, for instance, complained in 1620 that the black servants of the administrator of mines at Tocomilco, near Oaxaca, entered their village and homes, "stealing what they have" and "forcing their wives." Compounding the injury, a servant of don Alonso de Gusmán, minister of mines in the region, had one night entered a home in the village and, with the staff of justice in hand, told the family that he was going to take a son and daughter off to the mines. Hearing this, the two young people fled to the hills. Noting how important it is "to attend to the protection of the natives of your jurisdiction," the viceroy ordered the local corregidor to investigate and proceed against any blameworthy individuals and otherwise protect the Indians from further bother.[34] A string of later petitions continued in the same vein, referring to the myriad ways Indians could be "compelled" or "obliged" to do things they otherwise would not have done and which by law they were under no obligation to do, such as perform personal service, pay excessive tithes or surtaxes during religious celebrations, or being taken "by force" to work in the mines.[35]

At the core of these and similar cases was a growing sense that Indians' wills could not be arbitrarily overridden. An amparo from 1632 crystallizes the point. The gobernador and officers of the village of Malinaltenango, twenty leagues southwest of Mexico City, asserted that land on which they grazed their own cattle was being invaded by Miguel García and other Spaniards who, "with force and violence enter on said lands against the will of the Indians." The petition, drafted and filed by procurador Joseph de Çeli (also referred to as José de Çeli), made a specific point of referring to the "great importance of conserving the Indians in this place," since they tend to the road and bridge that are the only access to the mines at Zacualpa, where his majesty's silver comes from. Dozens of other cases refer to the Indians' "will" in this explicit way.[36] Just as many, without doing so, bring into focus how Indian petitioners sought to use the amparo as a shield against coercion in its various guises.[37]

By the late 1630s, petitions had begun to braid together notions of compulsion, violation of will, and a growing concern over corrupt and well-connected local officials. In 1640 the gobernador and officers of Acambaro, Michoacan, traveled the thirty leagues to Mexico City to lodge a complaint against don Melchor Lorenzo, who they claimed was interfering with town elections and upsetting long-established customs of local governance. Although he had arrived in the area only four years earlier, said the petition, don Melchor was "favored" by the Spanish alcalde mayor of Celaya, as well as by the local priest, because he was a "rich Indian." Concerned that they would not get a fair hearing locally, the officials of Acambaro had decided they had no choice other than to seek help at the Juzgado. With Bernardo López de Haro drafting and filing their petition with the tribunal, they alleged that don Melchor had sought to have himself named gobernador of the village so that he might put the Indians to work on his hacienda, as he had done three years earlier when the alcalde mayor had "violently appointed" him to the governorship of Acambaro, "against the Indians' will."[38]

As such cases attest, a crucial development in the amparos between the 1620s and the 1640s was that native petitioners became far more willing to challenge and name Spaniards directly in their pleadings. Vague references to *certain people* persisted, but as often as not petitions during these years clearly identified wrongdoers by name or, in the case of officials, by the position they held. And where in the 1590s more amparos were filed by Indians against other Indians, by the 1630s petitions against Spaniards significantly outnumbered those against Indians.

This trend continued into the following decades. Of the one thousand or so amparos issued by the Juzgado in the 1640s and 1650s, nearly half were against Spaniards, whereas about a third were against Indians.[39]

The 1640s might thus be thought of as a coming of age for the amparo. Nearly fifty years had passed since the first explosion of petitions in the 1590s, and Indians from all over Mexico had become familiar with the writ as a legal resource of first resort in their disputes with others. The amparo of these decades bears the stamp of mature legal expression. Coercion, variously depicted as physical force or overweening influence, had always been an important theme in the petitions. During the 1640s and 1650s, what had been a somewhat scattered and diffuse sense of duress and intimidation condensed into one of the more succinct and eloquent legal metaphors of this period—the *mano poderosa,* or powerful hand.

Numerous petitions bespeak the plasticity and reach of this expression. Virtually anyone who enjoyed wealth, office, or influence (even the reflected influence of a servant) could be characterized as acting with *a powerful hand.* There was the rich Indian woman, doña María who, according to the residents of Santiago Tecali, was trying to take their land, "with a powerful hand." There was Spanish encomendero Sebastián Beltrán, who the Indians of Ysmiquilpa accused of taking advantage of his position as a minor local official to impose illegal tributary burdens, "with a powerful hand." Spanish mill owner Nicolás Barreto, charged the Indians of Santo Domingo Ticoman, had come on their land and dug a stream to divert their water to his mill. And there was the unnamed Indian gobernador who, out of "hatred and bad faith," lent his brief authority to a clique of church cantors with a personal grudge against Juan Diego, who traveled several weeks from distant Amilpa to bring his complaint and plea for protection before the viceroy.[40] In these, and in hundreds of other petitions during these years, the idea of a *powerful hand* distilled the amparo's protective essence into a potent metaphor. Although it said nothing directly of the Indians' vulnerability as miserables, its imagery bespoke their need for protection. One could almost see doña María's hand snatching land belonging to powerless others, or feel Sebastián Beltrán's fingers squeezing excess tribute from the villagers of his jurisdiction, or watch Nicolás Barreto's hand scraping a stream bed across Indian land, or witness the unnamed gobernador brandishing his fist on behalf of his cantankerous cantors.

It is difficult to know when and how the words *powerful hand* acquired currency. More than likely, the *hand* as a metaphor for power found its first use somewhere in the vast corpus of Spanish legal and political discourse, where body imagery was common.[41] For instance, a royal ordinance from 1541 explained that Spaniards were not to have "any hand or entry into the Indians, or any power, or command over them."[42] Here, as in the petitions, the *hand* was a malignant force, a metaphor of unjust coercion against vulnerable people. But it was not always so. A century later, Saavedra Fajardo in his widely read *The Idea of the Christian Prince* wrote that the king's "powerful hand" could, in chaotic times, remind his subjects of the need for order.[43] The contrast between the two usages is striking. In one, the hand seems an almost disembodied agent of disruption and overreaching. In the other it retains a sense of strength, but as a sign of order and connected legitimacy. There was perhaps no more evocative metaphor of the political problem of colonial life from the perspective of Indian petitioners seeking the king's protection than this polysemic image of the hand.

Stray references to powerful hands in amparos before the mid-1640s indicate that its use was not altogether a new idea in pleadings. A petition filed on behalf of the gobernador of Tepoxoxuma in 1631 complained that a local Indian official refused to obey him because of the "powerful hand he has from the priest."[44] In 1633, a petition asserted that the Spanish alcalde mayor, with the "powerful hand" he had from being the "intimate friend" of the rich Indian gobernador of the village, was trying to take his clients' land.[45] In these and other instances of the powerful hand through the early 1640s, the emphasis was squarely on the sense that one who had the hand, either of office or favor, was capable of great harm toward ordinary Indians.

As of the late 1640s, the expression began to be used more readily. By the late 1650s, *powerful hand* had become a conspicuous and striking phrase of art in the petitions. Although coincidence of timing is not causality, it bears noting that of the three hundred or so petitions between 1630 and 1680 invoking the powerful hand, about 90 percent date from after 1647, the year Juan Solórzano y Pereira published his monument to Spanish law in the Indies, the *Política indiana*. In an important section on the New World encomienda, listed in the index under "poderosos" (powerful people), Solórzano states that "the powerful whenever they decline to evil and allow themselves to be carried away by unbridled greed, not only improve their own situation with the power they gain, but more importantly this power gives them *a greater hand with which to inflict wrong and damage* [mal y daño] *upon the poor and humble even more powerfully.*"[46]

We can only speculate as to whether those who prepared petitions for Indian clients in the 1640s and 1650s actually read this passage. It is certainly a possibility. After all, Solórzano's *Política* was the first systematic treatise on New World law to appear in Spanish, a kind of vulgate of two earlier works in Latin on the laws of the Indies, precisely the sort of thing an on-the-ball procurador might browse through. And because it was in Spanish and boasted a good index, procuradores like Çeli, who mostly were not fluent latinists, could easily have consulted the book, which was available in at least one of Mexico City's bookshops as of the 1650s.[47] Solórzano y Pereira's sentence not only recalls sporadic use of the hand image in amparo petitions during the 1630s and 1640s, but employs the phrase *mal y daño,* one of the legal expressions most commonly used in early amparos. If nothing more, this metaphorical characterization of the relationship between the powerful and the powerless in the New World so closely paralleled the one implied by the words *powerful hands* as to suggest that the idea had simply become part of the legal zeitgeist.[48]

That Spanish procuradores were responsible for introducing the term *powerful hands* into the amparos does not imply that the phrase was empty of meaning for their clients. Given the time, money, and hope Indian petitioners invested in filing these claims, it is hard to imagine they simply recited their woes to a procurador and left the matter at that. The whole point of what they were doing was to connect with the structures of Spanish power and authority as represented in law. Why else travel so far and at such great expense? And so, precisely that which led procuradores to employ the powerful hand image in their pleadings— its immediacy, its expressive economy, its descriptive power—also afforded Indian complainants a grounded understanding of the principle of amparo as it had been expressed over several decades. A 1656 petition framed in the first person plural and without a procurador's name accused a group of Spaniards of "want[ing] to take our church with a powerful hand."[49] While these Indians from San Juan Sitaguaro, Michoacan probably had the help of a notary in drafting the petition, repeated use of "we" and "our" suggests that the wording was basically their own, the result of a long, collective learning process regarding the possibilities of protection in their straitened circumstances.

USEFUL TO THE REPUBLIC

In contemporary political theory, the amparo represented a pact between the king and his most defenseless subjects, each in reciprocal obligation to the other with respect to the common good. The king's side of the bargain was clear. By protecting his subjects the king acted for the common good, of which just law was the chief ordering principle. Aquinas had been firm on this point.[50] The neo-Thomists updated the idea. Francisco Suárez, for instance, concluded that "law was the ordering of reason toward the common good, promulgated by the one charged with care of the community."[51] Toward the end of the sixteenth century, Jesuit Pedro de Ribadeneyra wasted no words in describing the king's obligation: "The king is tied to the public good and to the defense of his people."[52]

For their part, subjects owed obedience to the law insofar as it was ordained to the common good. According to Jesuit Domingo de Soto, each citizen of a human community was, like the king, beholden to the common good.[53] For Soto, as for others who looked to Aristotle in making sense of politics, human society resulted not from a contractual decision to congregate, but from human beings' natural inclination, given by God and expressed through reason, to live in common with others.[54] Francisco de Vitoria had argued the point in his 1528 *Relectio* on civil power, "to mankind Nature gave 'only reason and virtue,' leaving him otherwise frail, weak, helpless, and vulnerable, destitute of all defense and lacking in all things." As a result, he concluded, "it is in fact essential to man that he should never live alone."[55]

The king's duty of protection was rooted in the inherent frailty of the human creature, whose only real hope was an ordered political community. Life in common, however, did not by itself suffice to secure such a community. Individual members were under an obligation to maintain society and seek its perfection, each according to his station. Solórzano y Pereira enshrined this principle in New World legal discourse. It is "ridiculous," he wrote, to think that men first "lived like beasts in solitary life, in the wilds, mountains, and jungles, because this would be repugnant to his definition." Rather, insisted Solórzano, man's natural place is a republic, a "body composed of many men and many members who help each other and lighten each others' burdens." Quoting St. Thomas, he concluded that all men were obliged to give this help: "The city will be perfect and well governed when the citizens help each other at times and each promptly and conscienciously does what he should according to his station."[56] And because just laws create the conditions for the realization of this goal—which is nothing less than the common good—all men must obey the law. The political pact implied here was straightfoward: subjects submit to the king's power on condition that such power be used exclusively to promote the common good.

All of this lay just behind the ink of a royal decree inserted into an order of amparo protecting land claimed by residents of Tepetlixpa, a village two to three days' hike from Mexico City. The petitioners arrived at the audiencia in August 1629, bearing a legal order dated August 17, 1611, enforcing in their favor a 1604 royal decree originally addressed to the Indians of San Juan Botocho, a village dozens of leagues off in the distant northern province of Celaya. Two decades earlier, the residents of San Juan had been swept up in the congregaciones of 1595–1604 and forced to abandon homes and communities. They had sought the 1604 decree to protect land they were leaving behind. How the Indians of Tepetlixpa had come by the text of the original 1604 decree is unclear. But it is certain that they had been safeguarding the enforcement order referring to it since 1611.

Opening with the words "His Majesty the King," the 1604 decree stated that the "principal aim" of the "reductions" was to ensure that the Indians "participate spiritually and temporally in a Christian polity with the least discomfort to them as possible." Only in this way, could the Indians "who are scattered in the broken mountain solitudes and without settlements, be reduced to settlements where they can be well ministered to and live politically in moderation." Those forced to move, continued the decree, might at a later time go back to their villages of origin and reclaim their land, so long as their churches and houses could be put into good repair. If upon their return "some persons" have entered and taken the land, the local justice would evict the trespassers and install the "miserable Indians," so that under no circumstances such lands remain in the power of Spaniards.[57] In 1611, petitioners from Tepetlixpa had sought and obtained an enforcement of this decree applied to their own situation. In 1629 they were asking nothing more of the tribunal than that it affirm the 1611 order. The court agreed and issued the amparo.

The language of the 1604 decree on which the Tepetlixpa petitioners relied in 1611 and again in 1629 amounted to a small lesson in Spanish political theory. The description of people "scattered in the broken mountain solitudes and without settlements" is a powerful evocation of the view that human beings were meant to live in community rather than as isolated individuals. This was why Tepetlixpa's residents could be made to abandon their villages in the face of dwindling populations and limited resources for conversion: their humanity demanded they not be left to the mountain solitudes, even if they had wished it—though we should not assume they did.

Of course, the lofty aspiration of securing human communities did not stand apart from pragmatic concerns, such as tribute collection, or from the impositions of evangelization, the only justification for Spanish rule in the New World. But the king was not oblivious to the heavy burden "reduction" cast upon the Indians. Royal decrees from the sixteenth century had established that while the Indians could be compelled to move, so that they "not live divided and separated in the hills and mountains," their relocation was to be conducted with "utmost forebearance and moderation . . . with gentleness and mildness, without causing inconvenience."[58] Echoing these earlier words, the 1604 decree insisted that removal be done "with the least discomfort [to them as] possible." Nor had reduction been merely a pretext for usurpation. The decree carefully set out the conditions under which displaced Indians might return to their villages and created a mechanism by which to restore them to their land, even if doing so meant dispossessing Spaniards. Public good, in this case the creation of Christian polities, might trump the Indians' desire to stay put, but it did not do so irrevocably.

We can only guess at the extent of the Indians' "discomfort" in this process. In 1604, when the original royal decree was issued, the province of Celaya had been a crossroads of profound demographic change. Starting in the 1560s, immigration had brought new residents to the area—Tarascos, Otomies, and Mexica from further south—even as others, the unreduced Chichimecas, had fled northward. Epidemic disease around 1580 cut the number of tributaries to about 3,500, nearly half of what it had been just a decade earlier. By 1600, the number had dropped to about 2,000, and Spaniards, mestizos, mulattoes, and blacks eager for land had begun to move in. A wave of local reductions swept over the region in the mid-1590s, carrying San Juan Botocho with it. The story was similar in Chalco, Tepetlixpa's province. In the last three decades of the sixteenth century the number of tributaries dropped by more than half to under 10,000, already catastrophically down from fifty years earlier. In this context, twenty scattered estates in one corner of the province were reduced to eight pueblos, among them Tepetlixpa.[59]

This document does not reveal how the reductions of San Juan and Tepetlixpa proceeded. Perhaps the villagers resisted and faced violence. Perhaps they fled to the hills, hoping to outwait the Spaniards. Or perhaps they left their homes resigned to their plight or glad for any escape from what had become untenable situations. Whatever the case, it might be best to think of their "discomfort" not so much in terms of the momentary shock of removal, but in terms of the broader circumstance of calamity which had been their lot through the sixteenth century.

Unbowed by their plight, the residents of San Juan and Tepetlixpa took their grievances to Mexico City. San Juan went to secure a copy of the 1604 royal decree in the hope of using it to return home at some later date. This may have been especially important in Celaya at the time, given the large number of land-hungry non-Indians drawn to the area throughout the sixteenth century. For their part, the villagers of Tepetlixpa somehow or other came across the 1604 decree, grasped its legal significance, and in 1611 used it as a lever to obtain their own legal insurance, specifically citing the Celaya Indians' use of it. In doing so, the Tepetlixpa petitioners revealed their understanding that forced reloca-tion, however harsh it may have seemed at the time, had not constituted an absolute dispossession.

As a legal proposition, reduction for the purpose of establishing a Christian polity did not imply loss of dominion—"the right to have, possess, enjoy, use and dispose of some thing as it may best seem to the owner of the thing"—over the Indians' lands.[60] Vitoria had summarized the crux of the matter in 1539: the Indians could not be "robbed of their property, either as private citizens or as princes, on the grounds that they were not true masters."[61] Too often in the sixteenth century, Vitoria's words meant little in the face of Spanish land grabs. Such abuses had led to the promulgation in 1591 of a law that jurist Antonio León Pinelo in-terpreted as holding that land could neither be given nor sold in a man-ner that would harm the Indians.[62] Decades later Solórzano y Pereira spelled out what had long since crystallized as the firm rule: Indians did not lose rights over their land simply because of a reduction.[63] The remedy fashioned in the 1604 decree, recognized in the 1611 enforce-ment order, and affirmed in the 1629 amparo—that Indians were enti-tled to return to their home villages and eject any Spaniards who might be there—expressed this notion in a concrete context and taught the petitioners what they might expect from the law.

Although royal decrees clearly favored the Indians, deeper currents of meaning ran beneath the letter of the law. From a legal and political standpoint, the Tepetlixpa Indians' move to another village, whether forced or not, had been for the common good—evangelization and secur-ing a properly ordered Christian polity. Jurists, from sixteenth-century authorities up through Solórzano y Pereira in the mid-seventeenth cen-tury, held unanimously that the common or public good could not be subordinated to mere private ends.[64] Domingo de Soto put the issue in a broader New World frame in his *De la Justicia:* "If the overseas king-doms had not been conquered for any reason other than that their riches be used to serve Spain, if they had been submitted to laws directed ex-clusively to our benefit, as if they were our slaves, the decorum of justice would have been broken."[65] Failure to restore petitioners to their land would have amounted to allowing actors seeking only private gain to take advantage of a public act directed to the common good. Such an inversion would have violated fundamental precepts of Spanish law and political order. The residents of Tepetlixpa, who doubtless had never read Soto, appear nevertheless to have intuited this in filing their peti-tion. The essence of their argument, made with the king's own words from the 1604 decree, was that they had lived up to their part of the pact implicit in the reductions: they had left their lands so that they might be incorporated into a Christian polity. Now they wished only that the king recognize their contribution to the common good by protecting them from those whose greed would lead to private gain at their expense.

From the tribunal's perspective there was a solid legal foundation for this claim: petitioners deserved amparo because they were *useful* to the common weal. A royal decree from 1601 made the point without equivocation: "Because the Indians are useful [*útiles*] to all and for all, all must watch out for them, and for their conservation, since everything would cease without them."[66] Without Indians the fields from which New Spain was fed would not be tended, nor silver flow to royal coffers, nor the scut of day-to-day life be done. Tribute would not be paid. Masses would not be heard. In other words, the 1601 decree's superficially utilitarian tone rested on a much deeper sense of *usefulness* as an acknowledgment that the whole colonial edifice was shouldered by the Indian masses, without whom it would collapse. The Tepetlixpa petitioners were in essence reminding the viceroy, and indirectly the king, of this fact, and claiming from it the right to recover their land.

But a danger lurked in the principle of usefulness, for not a few Spaniards invoked the common good to justify abuse of the Indians. Solórzano y Pereira recognized the danger: "common good and usefulness" should not "weigh more heavily" on the Indians than on anyone else, as countless laws indicated.[67] By law and by principle, Indians were useful in the same way all citizens of a properly ordered Christian polity were—by contributions, according to their station, on behalf of the greater social whole.

Numerous petitions for amparo suggest that by the early seventeenth century the advantages and perils of claiming usefulness—*utilidad*— were widely understood among indigenous amparo petitioners. In 1591, over a decade before the decree of 1604 had crystallized matters, Thomás Aquino of Tlaxcala signed up to help subdue a group of fierce, unconverted Indians far to the north. Having taken the precaution of leaving his house and land to his son, he sought an order of amparo so that no one would be able to take the land in his absence. His petition to the Juzgado began by noting that he was on his way to "serve your Majesty at the settlements in the Chichimecas." And though the petitioner almost certainly did not draft the request himself—the record indicates that the petition was filed "on behalf of Thomás Aquino," probably by the Juzgado's procurador for Indians—the statement of moral reciprocity between himself and the king was clear: he was giving up house and land to march to inhospitable territory to "reduce" "brave and spirited warriors" in the king's name.[68]

While the idea of a moral relationship to the king never faded, later amparos indicate that it came to be expressed in more explicitly legal and instrumental terms. Tribute, precisely because it bespoke a political as well as an economic relationship, was one of the most universally recognized and easily asserted legal reciprocities between Indians and the king. Rather than complain only of coercion in its various guises, Indian petitioners in tribute cases specifically alleged that their ability *to sustain themselves and pay tribute* was being interfered with by Spaniards or other Indians.

During the 1590s, when most petitions straightforwardly asserted some kind of threat to land, or complained of violence or influence, only the occasional amparo referred in this way to tribute. In the 1630s and 1640s, the expression began to appear far more often, and by the 1650s it had become a commonplace in the petitions. In 1649, Juan Diego in Amilpa complained that the Indian gobernador of the town, "with a powerful hand and out of hatred and bad faith" had mistreated him "in word and deed" even though Juan was a "quiet and peaceful person of good life and customs who had always tried to work for his own sustenance and to pay his tribute." In 1681, several petitioners from the village of Asumpción Milpa, in the jurisdiction of Xochimilco, just outside of Mexico City, filed an amparo petition insisting that certain people in a neighboring village were mistreating them and stealing wood with which they "sustained themselves and their children and grandchildren and pay Royal tribute and do all the other things to meet their needs." Their procurador argued that this caused harm "not only to my clients but to the common good," for which reason they ought to be protected. Similarly, a 1695 petition filed by officers of San Bartolomé de Capuluac in Metepec, without the services of a procurador, pressed their complaint against Spaniards who sought to yoke their village to debt peonage by insisting that if the viceroy did not provide a remedy, "great harm will follow to the common good."[69]

These last two cases were unusual in so explicitly invoking the *common good* and connecting it to petitioners' suffering. Most petitions along these lines sought to highlight the moral compact implicit in the relationship between survival and obligation. It was a point at once obvious and powerful. Through their experience of harsh weather, overwork, mistreatment, and persistent want, petitioners knew in their own flesh that if they could not feed and clothe themselves they could not meet tribute obligations. They knew as well that tribute was not optional. Their lives, so close to the margin between life and death, were thus tightly linked to the fortunes of the governing structures whose burdens made their existence so precarious. By playing on the inescapability of their tributary obligations, amparo petitioners sought to turn not just the letter of the law but its underlying rationale in their favor. Royal power to collect tribute had deep historical roots and from the sixteenth century forward had been connected to the idea of the common good. According to Solórzano y Pereira, numerous authorities had held that tribute constituted the very "nerves of the republic," which ensured the "health and conservation of everyone." As a consequence, "tributes should be paid with pleasure by all, since they redound to common utility and assure the stability and firmness of the republic."[70] Of course, *all* did not pay tribute—Spaniards and mestizos were exempt—and *pleasure* doubtless is not how the Indians would have described their tributary duties. Nevertheless, by the mid-seventeenth century Indian petitioners seemed to have learned from legal experience that paying tribute at all aligned them with the idea of the common good, furnishing them a powerful means of claiming the king's protection.

Willingness to acknowledge tribute carried the charge it did in part because so many Spaniards acted out of purely selfish motives, heedless of the common good, or at least that is how it seemed to treatise writers of the day. In 1599, Juan de Mariana's *De Rege et Regis Institutione* had laid the problem bare in a chapter on the poor: "The rich are corrupted by power," he wrote with uneffaced censure. "To a man seeking power every poor man is a very great opportunity."[71] Mariana was hardly the first and certainly not the last to express such concerns. Solórzano y Pereira was typically blunt. He condemned New World Spaniards who refused to dirty their hands and instead "enriched themselves solely by the sweat and work" of the Indians.[72] In another section of the *Política* he pressed the point further, noting that while well-off Spaniards, bore a "greater obligation to look to the defense and conservation of the Indians," their riches often made them "more given to vice, haughtier, and less affected and attentive to the love and service of our kings and their commands." As a result, concluded Solórzano darkly, they think they no longer "need to aspire to or expect anything from royal hands," perhaps most especially in the New World, "so far from the royal presence."[73]

This was no idle worry on Solórzano's part. The middle third of the seventeenth century was a period of high anxiety over economic and political change. From the 1630s forward, encomenderos had been joined by corregidores and alcaldes mayores in taking advantage of New Spain's Indians. In 1646, the year before the *Política indiana* was published, the Puebla city council wrote to King Philip IV complaining of the "rapacity and avarice" of the corregidores.[74] Amparo petitions in this same vein are legion. Particularly after the labor draft for haciendas was outlawed in 1633, corregidores were given a freer rein to pursue their own private affairs, usually at the expense of those they were charged with protecting.[75] Where this happened, Indians were often left defenseless, emboldening ordinary Spaniards and Indian officials to squeeze whatever benefit they might from the situation.

Indian commoners pushed to the limits of forebearance had a final option: they might threaten to flee their villages. By intimating their willingness to walk out on their obligation to be *useful* they could dramatize the gravity of their circumstances. Solórzano recognized that no Indian could be faulted for fleeing mistreatment, because the mere fact of collecting tribute did not give Spaniards dominion over the persons and property of the Indians.[76] Even so, flight was not a threat to be made lightly, since it hinted at rebellion against the established order. But carefully done it could signal to ruling authorities, not least the viceroy, that a local situation was dangerously out of kilter.

This was the central message of a petition filed by the residents of San Francisco Ystquimastitlan in 1655.[77] The core of the claim was a memorandum written in Nahuatl by the petitioners and translated into Spanish for the Juzgado's benefit. A long document, it opened by noting "our sorrow and grief" and went on to lay out ten specific complaints against the man who, according to the document, illegally claimed to be their gobernador. The detailed description of the gobernador's abuses—excessive tithes, taking other men's wives, flogging people who opposed him, stealing their calves—rested solidly on two broad pillars: the gobernador had usurped his position from the legitimately elected gobernador, contrary to royal law, and he and the local priest had so "unsettled the village" that the inhabitants would leave if something was not done. Petitioners appear to have understood the risks of the game they were playing, and they hastened to add that "prostrated we ask for your help" to confirm their gobernador. In short, the threat of flight represented a further means by which Indians could indicate their willingness to abide by the colonial compact if only they would be protected from those who saw in other men only a very great opportunity.

COMMON GOOD, ROYAL AUTHORITY

As a matter of first principles, the crux of the problem native petitioners faced in such cases was a blurring of the bright line between public and private. The idea of the common good demanded this sharp distinction, for otherwise men would not be able to tell when they were acting privately and when publicly. As a montage, the amparos represent a determined effort by petitioners to keep the idea of the public from being trampled by private greed. Some amparos from these years, none before 1630, refer explicitly to *private ends (particulares fines)* or *private ends and interests (particulares fines e intereses)*.[78] In these cases, the complaint was always the same: someone, whether a Spanish corregidor, local priest, private citizen, or Indian gobernador or official, was acting to advance private ends rather than the common or public good.

Many other cases made the same basic point without invoking these particular phrases of legal art. In a petition from 1655, the gobernador and officials of Guamantla, just outside Puebla, complained that the executor of a Spaniard's estate sought to take possession of a house attached to a church they had constructed with their own hands. With the help of procurador Agustín Franco, they argued that the executor had no right to take the house from them. "It is not possible that the said house should be held by a private person, who would have no right to it since [the house and church] were a work in common." Moreover, concluded the petition, the house and church in question "belong to his Majesty," so that it is the Indians of Guamantla who have "possession in community, since they worked without salary or stipend."

A whole theory of public and private, the very spring of the larger idea of the common good, rests within these few phrases. Whatever else petitioners may have understood by the terms *private (particular)* and *common good* or whether they thought to use them at all in any abstract way, one can almost hear them telling procurador Franco that the executor had no right to do what he pretended. *After all, we built these buildings, with our own hands, with alms and donations from neighbors and we built the house as part of the church so that our ministers might have a place to live. One person cannot own it because all of us worked on it and we did it without pay or reward. How can this man take for himself what we worked on so hard for the benefit of everyone in the pueblo?* In short, the church could not be taken for purely private advantage, because it had been built by the community as a whole for the common good.

Persuasive as such an argument may seem, it was an equitable rather than a legal one—rooted in notions of "equality, rectitude, goodness, pious spirit, and a good intention to do justice" rather than in strict adherence to the letter of the law.[79] Franco understood this and knew that his clients' position would be stronger if they could assert an explicitly legal claim. And so the petition argued that the house "belongs to his Majesty." Far from an ornament of flattery, this phrase invoked a principle deeply chiseled in New World law—that all churches in the Indies belonged to the king. In the New World, because of the *Patronato*—the special authority over New World affairs ceded to the Spanish monarchy by the papacy—Spanish kings held exclusive power to erect churches.[80] Technically, all colonial churches were built at the expense of the king's tributes.

We cannot know whether the community of Guamantla sought permission to build the church before starting its work (by law it was supposed to seek a license). Whether it did so or not, the petition sought to transmute their effort into a service on behalf of the king, amalgamating equitable and legal arguments into a single substance, conflating the Indians' religious and tributary obligations, and making the Indians into the king's loyal servants. By invoking the king's grandeur and by citing a legal principle harking back to royal decrees issued in the sixteenth century, petitioners were reminding the viceroy that far more was at stake here than just possession of one little building out in the middle of nowhere.[81] And even if petitioners themselves did not formulate quite so crystalline a legal understanding, their concern resonated with the broader question of whether private greed would be allowed to trump not only the common good but the king's authority.

There was no greater danger in this latter regard than the power of *personas validas* (favored people) to manipulate the law to personal advantage, or ignore it altogether. Concern for *favor*—as when a powerful person favored one party over another in a legal dispute—goes back to the earliest amparos. From roughly the 1650s, however, relationships that might previously have been characterized in terms of favor came to be described in the amparos as *valimiento*. Such cases often overlapped with those employing the powerful hand metaphor. What distinguishes them is the frequency with which the accused *valido* is characterized as projecting authority because of an enduring relationship with some official, usually a corregidor, alcalde mayor, or Indian gobernador. Thus, the residents of the pueblo of Chila felt they could not complain to the local Indian justice about abuses they were suffering at the hands of the local Indian cacique, because the justice to whom they would have gone was himself an "indio valido" of the very same cacique. Other petitions referred often to personas validas or to *personas validas de personas poderosas* (validos of powerful people).[82] The implication in all of these is that valimiento involved something shading from mere circumstantial favoritism to an association more intimate and more sharply redolent of official impropriety.

Such cases echoed a more generalized anxiety over valimiento within the Spanish empire. Dozens of writers held forth on the issue of office holders chosen on the basis of their "friendship" with the king. Some supported the practice as necessary and beneficial. Others rejected it as a blight on the body politic. The absence of the term *valido* in the amparos before 1650 strongly suggests that it appeared in connection with this broader anxiety and specifically in the context of a growing concern over the abuses of corregidores and alcaldes mayores in the New World. The Puebla city council had complained to the king of the corregidores' "avarice and rapacity" in 1646. By all accounts, the problem had only worsened through the 1650s. In 1663, the bishop of Oaxaca Alonso de Cuevas y Dávalos wrote to the king's council of the Indies that the viceroys had "an excessive number of retainers and dependents" who are often appointed to corregimientos.[83]

One of the earliest and most strident declarations against validos appeared in 1615 in fray Juan de Santa María's *Tratado de república y policía cristiana.* Santa María's chief concern was for the king's sovereignty, which he felt was too easily undermined by the validos who thronged the throne.[84] Of course, when Indian petitions accused people of being validos, they were not talking about anything so grand as royal prerogative. Theirs were local concerns, of how what one amparo referred to as "corruptela" (petty corruption)—a word often used in royal edicts to describe corregidores' abuses—made it difficult for petitioners to pursue their justice.[85]

The broader implication was clear. In the context of citing their role as tributaries who by their very essence contributed to the common good, petitioners were hitching their fate to the king's authority. Local officials who acted out of private motive and allowed their power to be used by others, turned their backs on the king's most exposed subjects and made a hash of laws he had decreed to protect them.

Amparo petitions rarely put the matter so bluntly. Instead, by the 1650s they resorted to a formula—*in contravention of* or *contrary to that which is prohibited by royal decree*—that simultaneously had legal effect and served as a metaphor for describing ongoing affronts to the king's law. Petitions most often cited a small number of laws: decrees banning *castas* and Spaniards from Indian villages; decrees outlawing personal service by Indians; bans against the labor draft; laws indicating how much and in what kind tribute was to be paid; ordinances regarding how village elections were to be conducted; and decrees forbidding priests from forcing their congregants to give them food or pay tithes other than in wheat, cattle, and silk.[86] Some petitions not only referred to specific royal decrees and viceregal orders, but claimed to have kept copies of them in their files.[87] In all of these, the point made was decidedly local—a particular law was being violated at a particular time and place. Their cumulative effect, however, was broader—to indicate both to Indian petitioners and to those concerned for royal power, not least the king himself, that justice was a matter of constant struggle against those who saw the world largely as an arena for private action.

Solórzano y Pereira, discussing the limits on Indians' personal service, summarized the matter pithily: against the "yielding and humble condition of the Indians" must be set the "great greed" of the Spaniards who would use them, which was why the "many laws and ordinances made for their relief and defense" have not "sufficed to remedy their oppression and injury."[88]

The elected officers of San Andrés Atzala in the jurisdiction of Xalatzingo, near Puebla, would almost surely have agreed with Solórzano, but would doubtless have included greedy Indians among those who vexed them with oppression and injury.[89] According to their 1659 petition, don Pedro Cortez, an Indian from San Andrés, had conspired with Captain don Amaro Velázquez, the Spanish alcalde mayor, to have himself appointed gobernador of the town. Their chicanery had failed after petitioners obtained a viceregal order installing don Melchor de los Reyes as the legitimately elected gobernador. Fearing Velásquez would simply snub them, petitioners had presented the viceroy's order to the corregidor of a neighboring jurisdiction, asking him to enforce it. The corregidor had accompanied the petitioners to appear before Velázquez, who lost his temper when confronted with the accusation. Despite the corregidor's presence, Velázquez had given the staff of office to Cortez and proclaimed him gobernador. He then threatened to have Reyes and others flogged if they opposed him and arrested the notary responsible for memorializing the proceedings. At that point, the whole community had gone into the street proclaiming Reyes as their gobernador "in order to escape from the tyranny and slavery in which don Pedro Cortez had them." In addition to his other abuses, the petition charged Cortez with selling some village Indians to Spaniards and mulattoes and with threatening to hang six Indians as rebels. Cortez had also imprisoned Diego Ramírez for traveling to Mexico City to fetch the official document approving Reyes's election. The viceroy ordered Velázquez to stop issuing orders and further commanded him to release any Indians he might have in jail, threatening him with loss of office if he failed to comply. He also banished Cortez from the jurisdiction for as long as petitioners held office.

Although Cortez's and Velázquez's actions spoke for themselves, the petition's reference to "tyranny and slavery" was not an idle one. While not a term with legal effect in these circumstances, it powerfully evoked the Indians' situation in terms the viceroy and his legal advisers could easily make sense of, as procurador Salamanca surely understood. Cortez, with Velázquez's support, had unlawfully seized a political office subject to election within an Indian community and terrorized the village's people. By arresting the notary and locking up Ramírez, they had effectively sought to cut the connection between the Indians of San Andrés and royal law in Mexico City. Among treatise writers there were no surer signs of tyranny than when a ruler came by his position illegally, "exercise[d] an oppressive power" over the people, "aggrandized his own house to the ruin of his subjects," and forsook his obligation to dispense justice.[90] Of course, they were concerned with the acts of a Prince, not with the abuses of a petty despot in the Mexican countryside. But by referring to *tyranny*, the petition invited the viceroy to see the Indians' situation as a microcosm of the broader political universe within which his most vulnerable vassals had learned to use the language of amparo against those who evinced little concern for the common good or the king's authority.

FOUND IN TRANSLATION

Most of indigenous petitioners' learning happened in translation. And while those who had more frequent contact with Spaniards could often get by in Spanish, translation could not be avoided. The Juzgado, and Indian petitioners as well, insisted on the presence of interpreters in all legal proceedings. This mediation is all but impossible to get at directly in the amparos, since mostly we have only translated texts. Still, it is worth noting that by the mid-seventeenth century, Nahuatl, the most widely spoken native language in central Mexico, bore the clear marks of long engagement with Castilian. Words adopted from Spanish into Nahuatl were common, and many of them reflected Indians' engagement with Spanish law and legal process. Taken together, they amounted to a barebones lexicon of procedural terms relevant to filing legal petitions: *escritura* (document with legal effect); *royal tribunal, notification, original* (of a document); *proof, witness, traslado* (authorized copy of a legal document); *testimonio* (notarized copy of a legal document); and *king, viceroy, justice, order, judge, lawsuit, petition, procurador, corregidor, appeal.*[91]

The challenges of translation may help account for the repetition of certain key phrases in the amparos. For instance, one of the advantages of the term *powerful hand* as a way of invoking the amparo idea is that its metaphorical qualities and elemental corporality spanned the distance between indigenous languages and Spanish and between lay and legal vocabularies. Almost any human can instantly relate to the image of a great hand taking land, throttling reluctant workers, knocking down buildings, tying someone up, or holding someone back from traveling to Mexico City. At one level, the word *hand* stands in for the people who performed these acts. At another, deeper level *powerful hand* seems to suggest something less tangible, something like power itself. Either way, the term *powerful hand* was an economical, intuitive, and vivid way of describing and categorizing actions that were contrary to law and of casting those who performed them in a morally indefensible role.

Although many Indians, particularly those closer to Mexico City, spoke some Spanish and could have made sense of *mano poderosa* without need of translation, most who heard it would have done so in translation.[92] Native petitioners spoke many different languages, but Nahuatl remained the lingua franca among indigenous groups. For this reason alone it is worth pausing to make some superficial observations regarding how *mano poderosa* might have been understood among Nahuatl speakers. Words for *hand* and *powerful* were easily found, and the agglutinative properties of Nahuatl allowed their combination without great problem. As in Spanish, *powerful* itself does not appear to have been a negative term in Nahuatl, though in the context of the amparos the phrase *powerful hand* was clearly meant to convey the improper use of power. There is, thus, every reason to think Nahuatl speakers would have understood what was implied by a literal translation of *mano poderosa* in legal proceedings. Nahuatl was and is a richly metaphorical language, and Nahua judicial procedure had tended to use "common everyday words" rather than specialized terms of art.[93]

The Metaphors of Andrés Olmos open a slit window of insight onto this issue. A Franciscan friar, Olmos was among the first clergy in the New World. In 1547, he wrote a Nahuatl grammar entitled *The Art for Learning the Mexican Language*. "The Metaphors," forming one part of the book were, in essence, poems written in Nahuatl dealing with religious and ethical themes. Some were headed by a Spanish gloss. Others were not. Overall, they appeared to have been intended to reflect the quality of elite discourse among pre-Columbian Aztecs.[94]

Although they cannot be taken to represent the speech of commoners a century and more after conquest, these poems do suggest that Nahuatl speakers could have understood a translated version of *manos poderosas* (*powerful hands*) quite readily. Metaphor XII, with the Spanish heading "servant or vassal of someone," defines a servant as one who *acts as hands* for another, indicating that those who spoke Nahuatl were willing to understand *hand* metonymically. Metaphor LI, describes the thief not by saying he steals (where the Spanish gloss reads *Thief who everything clouds and steals*), but through a series of characterizations regarding his hands that concludes with a commentary on his character: *He is malicious of hand, he is clever of hand/he is conceited of hand, he is quick-handed./Recklessly he grabs things./He is not a true person./He pants, he is foolish, he is shallow-hearted.*" While the idea of power is absent here, this Metaphor conveys the thief's character through negative constructions regarding his hands, much as the amparos' *powerful hands* were a way to characterize the abuse of which petitioners complained. Metaphor XIV, on sentences of death, does come close to a sense of power through *hand* imagery: *"After the act, the ruler casts him down, hurls him away./Finally the ruler rips him asunder."* Although the Nahuatl word for *hand* (the word is *maitl*, shortened to *ma* when in combination) appears explicitly in only one of these (*hurls*), the other verbs *cast* and *rip* imply the actions of hands. What this suggests is that in Nahuatl, a hand could be thought of as powerful through its capacity for destructive violence, a frequent meaning of the phrase *powerful hand* in the amparos.[95] And as in Spanish, the Nahuatl word for *power* and its related usages signified the ability or faculty for doing a thing.[96]

The word *amparo* can be approached in much the same way. Metaphor II refers to the relationship between parents and children as the foundation of all authority and segues to a broader sense of offering cover or shade: *A mother, a father is as/a foundation, and a covering/like the silk cotton tree, the cypress tree./They afford shadow, shade, shading/as a cool bower, as a spindle.* The first line dovetails nicely with the paternal nature of the Indians' tutelary relationship to the king, enshrined in viceregal law. In this regard, it is worth noting as well that Covarrubias's 1611 dictionary of Castilian gave as an example of *amparo* one who opens his arms to catch a child who is about to fall. Allusions in the second and third lines to *covering, shadow, shade,* and *shading* communicate a clear sense of protection and shelter. Here there were very close parallels to Spanish. The Spanish gloss heading Metaphor II read "Father, mother, lord, captain, gobernador who are like a protecting tree."[97] The Royal Academy's 1726 Spanish dictionary offered the following entry for *hacer sombra* (to make shade): "to favor and protect [*amparar*] someone, so that with their protection they can be seen to or respected." Molina's Spanish-Nahuatl dictionary gave for *amparo* and related words Nahuatl equivalents deriving from the root *toctia*, which with different prefixes could mean to fortify or hide behind something. Molina also equated several Nahuatl words for taking shelter from the sun or sheltering behind some thing with the Spanish word *amparo*.[98]

The *common good* too was susceptible to meaningful translation into Nahuatl. Entries in Molina's bilingual dictionary suggest that a literal translation of *bien común* into Nahuatl might have drawn on words for *good* (*qualli yectli*) and *thing or asset belonging to everyone or held in common* (*nepan axcatl*). Beyond a literal approach, the metaphorical qualities of Nahuatl offered rich possibilities for conveying the idea behind *common good* more obliquely, as Olmos's Metaphors hint.

Metaphor III depicted the holder of authority as one who *bears the burden, cradling it* or *bearing it in his arms,* the holder of authority as one who *embodies the town,* and consequently *he protects, he governs.* This Metaphor connects closely with Metaphor XLIII, which describes the good ruler as one who *serves the town as water, serves the town as a hill* and *serves as public word.* In Nahuatl, *altepetl* was the word for *town,* literally the combination of the words for *water* and *hill.* To say that the ruler *serves as water* and *serves as hill,* then, was to say that the ruler by his very essence *embodies the town.* The Spanish gloss for this Metaphor read as follows: *Rules well the lord that populates, honors and adorns his town.* This is in stark contrast to Metaphor XXII's characterization of bad government. In those lines, the bad ruler *causes dust to puff up, to billow above, to rise up, he demolishes it, disperses it,/he cracks it, he splits it,/he throws it in the river, he hurls it from on high./He endangers them, he muddies them, he vanquishes them, he scatters them./He alone casts down his father, throws down his mother./He alone becomes foolish.* Similarly, Metaphor XLIV, for which the Spanish gloss was *Destroys the lord or gobernador the town,* condemned the person who *throws mud, stirs anger, destroys, erodes, strews dirt,* for by his actions he *exhausts the town.*[99] Although no direct correspondence is possible here, the similarity in tone to the amparos's condemnations of those who acted out of private motive are tantalizing.

Of course, none of this stands as direct evidence of how Nahuatl speakers saw and expressed their world in the mid-seventeenth century. Nor does it say anything of those who spoke the dozens of other languages.[100] But it does offer some sense that speakers of native languages could readily understand what was meant by *powerful hands,* connect with the idea of *amparo,* and distinguish between a ruler who ruled for the common good, thus *embodying the town,* and one who acted out of private motive and by his actions *exhausted the town.* Certainly the many corregidores, alcaldes mayores, Indian gobernadores, and validos of whom petitioners complained would have figured alongside the latter.

Translation is never perfect. But it is often good enough. What this analysis and more pointedly thousands of successful amparo petitions suggest is that Indian petitioners and Spanish procuradores, notaries, and judges were, in the main, able to make themselves understood through the muffle of linguistic difference.

REACHING JUSTICE?

Even so, it was a struggle, for the Indians' efforts to be heard were fraught with the paradox of their circumstances. As tributaries of the king, they were subject to laws whose purpose was to ensure the often-inefficient exploitation of those who Solórzano y Pereira referred to as "the feet of the republic."[101] At the same time, as tributaries of the king they were entitled to protection from those who would oppress them. It was in the vast gray zone between these competing interests that so many Spaniards, Indians, and mestizos sought their opportunities, and ordinary Indians without any particular power fought to be protected.

In this context, local justices' capacity to short the circuit between law as announced in Madrid or Mexico City and its enforcement in the countryside was considerable. Time and again, petitioners came before the Juzgado requesting new orders to confirm or enforce older ones that were no longer being honored. More often than not, inconsistent enforcement was woven into the very fabric of law as it played out in everyday life. In 1684, a group of residents from the village of Tlacotepeque appeared before the Juzgado complaining that a viceregal order issued in 1677, exempting them from service in the nearby mines of Sultepeque, was no longer being upheld. A new alcalde mayor had taken office in 1682, and petitioners asked that he honor the order, as the previous officeholder had. He refused, arguing that the exemption had been granted because the Indians needed time to work on their church, and because that work had been completed they should return to the mine. He promised to consult with the viceroy on whether the order should continue in force. In the meanwhile, he was sending them back to work. Through their procurador, petitioners claimed that the alcalde's sole duty was "blindly to obey, comply with, and execute" the order as presented to him. In essence, stated the petition, the order held that the Indians could not be made to work in the mine without a proper hearing and legal ruling. By returning them to the mine, the alcalde had suspended the effect of an earlier viceregal order and had denied petitioners their day in court. The viceroy agreed and, on pain of 500 pesos fine, commanded the alcalde to abide by the old arrangement until further notice.[102]

There is no way to know with certainty what prompted this alcalde mayor to renege on the earlier order and in doing so risk offense to his viceroy. Being in charge of a mining district, he had substantial responsibility to make the mine produce and considerable opportunity to enrich himself while doing so, a duty and opportunity in constant tension with his (probably less heartfelt) obligation to uphold royal law and protect the Indians from abuse. Noticing that work on the church had ceased, he may have seen a chance to beef up the mine's labor force. He doubtless read the order presented to him by the Indians of Tlacotepeque and understood its import. In refusing to enforce it, he may have wanted to see just how far he could push local residents. The answer appears to have been "not very." The church was still in need of repair, insisted petitioners. Work had been slow in recent times, they said, because ninety townspeople had died in the last seven years, straining the villagers' ability to pay tribute, work on the church, and ensure their own survival.

Their legal trump card was that the original order had stated without equivocation that they could be sent back to the mine only after work on the church was complete. The new alcalde probably understood just how difficult it would be to prevail on that issue. As they hinted, petitioners could argue that repairs on the church were not done yet and would be able to offer a compelling reason for delay—the number of deaths in recent years. The alcalde may well have suspected the Indians were lying, or at least shading the truth on this point; and he may even have been right. But he would likely have had a tough time testing the proposition, since burial and baptismal records were in control of the priest whose church the natives were working on. The previous alcalde mayor may have understood this balance of power and chosen not to disturb it. The new one may have done so as a kind of experiment to see what leeway he might have with local people. There is no evidence of further litigation on this matter, suggesting that the new alcalde learned his lesson and decided to leave well enough alone.

Still, a local official wanting to withhold the law's effects from those it aimed to protect had numerous options. A renitent justice might stoop to jurisdictional shenanigans. The residents of Cuitlacan had gone before their corregidor to complain of a Spaniard who was cutting and taking their fruit trees and trespassing on their land.[103] The corregidor had refused to hear them, stated the 1643 petition, alleging that as a minister of the Cruzada (an honorary military organization) he lacked jurisdiction over their lawsuits. This was balderdash pure and simple, since membership in the Cruzada bore no relation to his job as corregidor, as the Indians probably knew. Before the Juzgado, petitioners concluded that because of the corregidor's inaction, they "have not been able to reach justice." The viceroy granted the petitioners' order. Not amused by his underling's antics, the viceroy warned that if the Indians appeared before the Juzgado again on this matter, he would send someone to enforce the order and charge that person's costs and salary to the corregidor himself.

In other cases, the pinch point might be a local notary, as petitioners from Metepeque complained in 1686. They claimed to have a viceregal order assuring their possession of a marshland and cattle shed. The notary, they charged, refused to serve a viceregal order on the corregidor (probably with his connivance), which meant that the order had not been executed. Petitioners asked the viceroy to compel the notary to serve the order on the justice in question within a brief period. In a sharp tone, the viceroy, whose authority was now in play, commanded the notary to present the order to the nearest royal justice within two days of seeing it and return a sworn statement indicating enforcement, on pain of 20 pesos fine for noncompliance.[104]

These cases bring front and center the question of how and to what extent amparos were backed by measures to ensure execution. On paper, the issue seemed to be taken quite seriously, which stood to reason. Legal forms with the power to compel people to do or stop doing something must be put into force if they are to endure. And the amparo was not just any order. Every writ of amparo began with the viceroy's name, often listing his full titles, making it clear that he spoke from the power of his office and as the representative of the king, whose decrees were often cited in the petitions and orders themselves. His authority, and indirectly the king's, was always on the line when Indians came before the Juzgado. When successful petitioners presented an order of amparo to a local justice, they were invoking that authority and relying on its power to awe or at least intimidate. To this end, Spanish law gave teeth to the tribunal's orders. Fines were common and easily scaled to fit the situation, ranging from the 20 pesos threatened against the notary from Metepeque, to the 500 pesos with which the Juzgado menaced the alcalde mayor from Tlacotepeque. Indian officials might also be fined or in more serious cases warned that noncompliance could result in banishment to a textile manufactory for a year, a punishment from which Spaniards were reserved. A particularly refractory corregidor might be put on notice that he had better execute the order in question, or face a fine of 1,000 pesos and denial of office.[105]

Beyond the merely minatory, the viceroy could take more active steps to ensure enforcement of his orders. Of these, the *receptores*—judges answerable directly to the viceroy, who could be sent to execute an order regardless of local jurisdiction—were the most important. Receptores might be itinerant judges conducting the residencia of an outgoing corregidor in a given area. Such a person would be given a viceregal commission to investigate and dispose of a matter nearby. Alternatively, an order might designate as receptor any justice to whom it was presented. In essence, this allowed successful petitioners to draft a justice to enforce an unexecuted order. They had to be careful in doing so, lest the judge in question feel too greatly imposed on by lowly Indians.

The Juzgado appears to have reserved the threat of sending a receptor for the most egregious cases of judicial nonenforcement. In 1641, a petition filed by the residents of several villages in Xiquilpa asked the tribunal to send a receptor to enforce an earlier amparo protecting them from an invasion of cattle upon their land and to free a woman from involuntary service. The corregidor had flatly refused to abide by the order, not least because he was holding the woman in question. Petitioners noted that they had been before the Juzgado many times with these same complaints, "without reaching justice." They asked the viceroy to dispatch a receptor to investigate the situation and enforce the previous order, so that they "need not return to this court at great expense." The tribunal agreed, dispatching a receptor to look into the matter and execute all relevant orders, on pain of a 200 peso fine for failing to do so.[106]

A receptor could also be an effective means of facing down jurisdictional mischief by local justices. The foot-weary residents of Guaniqueo told of the runaround several local officials had sent them on in 1669. Pursuant to a lawsuit in which they were embroiled, petitioners had obtained an order addressed to their corregidor, who sat in Patzcuaro, the provincial capital of Valladolid. They asked him for a testimonio confirming execution of the order. Replying that he lacked jurisdiction over the matter (a blatant falsehood), the corregidor told them to see the public notary in the city of Valladolid, ten leagues from Patzcuaro and about seven leagues away from their village. Presented with the order, the notary there also refused to execute it, telling petitioners that they needed to see a second notary for the testimonio. This fellow charged them 21 pesos and set them to crisscrossing the countryside for three weeks, detaining them in Valladolid several days, sending them on to Salvatierra, and finally back to Patzquaro again. Then he promised to deliver it to their village, where they had returned for religious festivities. And still they had no testimonio. The only reason for this, charged petitioners, was that these three officers of the king's justice were in cahoots to sabotage their lawsuit. The tribunal agreed that enough was enough and sent a receptor, in Celaya at the time, to put an end to the Indians' woes and order any notary he could find to issue the testimonio petitioners sought.[107]

On occasion, a receptor was the last resort when all semblance of legality had broken down in a jurisdiction. Indian petitioners from San Miguel Almoloya in Metepeque were at wits end when they came before the Juzgado in 1680. Three years earlier, they had obtained an order permitting them to rebuild their old village of Santa María Nativitas Almoloya, which their ancestors had occupied before a reducción early in the seventeenth century. Two years later a receptor had been sent to execute the edict. Despite clear documentary support for the Indians' claim—including grants from the king and testaments showing inheritance—the receptor faced tenacious opposition from the Conde de Santiago, a local landowner and nobleman. The receptor had nevertheless completed the legal process of putting petitioners in possession of the land and granting them a license to rebuild. No sooner had they erected a crude structure where the village's old church had stood than the Conde's servants appeared one night, spears and guns in hand, and burned the building to the ground, stole an image of the Virgen de Guadalupe, knocked down the bell that had been hung, and chased the villagers off the land. Petitioners were before the Juzgado asking once more that a receptor be sent so that they might "reach justice." After consulting with his legal adviser, the viceroy agreed and commissioned a second receptor to enforce the previous orders and return petitioners to their peaceful possession of the land.[108]

What is most striking about this account is the total absence of a corregidor or alcalde mayor in the petitioners' narrative. This was not a case of an overweening local official. It was, rather, a situation seemingly without local law. In 1679 a receptor had put the residents of San Miguel in possession of their land, but he had been unable to protect them as the Conde's men despoiled the fragile community with impunity. The petition makes no mention of seeking out a local solution, for there appears to have been none. Instead, the residents of Almoloya hustled the ten leagues or so to seek help from the Juzgado.

In a microcosm, this case suggests how significant a resource the amparo could be for New Spain's Indians during the seventeenth century: access to the center was crucial to their ability to defend local claims and concerns. It hints as well at the importance of local justices. There was never a guarantee that corregidores would side with Indian petitioners against the likes of the Conde de Santiago—the opposite was often the case. Even so, and despite their well-deserved reputation for corruption and self-dealing, the corregidores' very presence served as something of a check-rein on those who might otherwise terrorize and threaten the vulnerable. Unreliable though they might be, local justices were answerable to the viceroy—hierarchically and legally—largely because so many Indian petitioners took the trouble to hold them to account. Corregidores and alcaldes mayores might evade Mexico City's orders, but they could not ignore them completely. The Conde, by contrast, mustered his thugs, sent them to Santa María Nativitas and took what he wanted by force, a reminder, perhaps, of what might have been if Mexico under Spanish rule had been truly lawless.

Despite the drama of receptores who strode in to resolve situations of sharp local tension, the viceroy's principal means of ensuring enforcement of his amparo orders was petitioners themselves. Thousands of petitions make clear that the Indians had to be ever vigilant of their rights. This was the premise of a procedural formula that tied off so many of the amparos, especially from the 1630s forward: that petitioners receive a *testimonio,* a copy of the proceedings so that they might protect their rights in law.[109] Ordinary Indian petitioners, thus, not the tribunal or the regidores, were the first line of enforcement for the king's laws and the viceroy's orders. From their experience, they came to understand that the amparo's promise of protection required an immense investment of money, time, energy, and hope, even as they knew that success was never assured: corregidores might manipulate jurisdiction, laws and orders might be narrowly interpreted, and notaries might give them the runaround. On occasion, receptores themselves might be the sticking point in enforcement of the king's laws, as when the residents of the villages of Villa Alta de San Yldefonso went to Mexico City to complain that a number of these justices were extorting money from the villages by auditing their community account books.[110]

For all that, writs of amparo seem often to have had the desired effect: land was recovered, rigged local elections overturned, oppressive tribute payments rolled back, corrupt gobernadores turned out, and churches protected. Indian claimants held the Juzgado and its amparos in high regard. An Indian couple from San Martín Tlanpan, Cholula, filed an amparo petition requesting that an overbearing Spanish farmer be forced to litigate before the Juzgado, "since naturally they would choose it for their defense."[111] And there was other evidence of the amparo's vigor: the locally powerful at times did everything they could to prevent petitioners from obtaining an order in the first place. This is what petitioners meant when they complained they were being stopped by threats or by force from "pursuing their justice." On this point the tribunal minced no words: "no one is to impede their coming to this court to ask for their justice," concluded a 1657 amparo issued to petitioners from Quexotzingo who alleged that unnamed parties had barred them from traveling to Mexico City.[112] The tribunal's adamance was a sign of how deeply questions of viceregal power and royal authority were tied up with the law's mandate that the Indians be protected. Petitioners' insistence on making pilgrimage to that cynosure of power and authority represented a staunch refusal to adandon themselves to the despair of the unprotected.

≋

Through thousands of petitions and countless conversations with their procuradores and each other, Indian petitioners of seventeenth-century Mexico mastered an idiom of amparo that helped them seek the sanctuary of protective laws and drew them within the yearning intimacy of a distant king's embrace. From the depth of their dignity before the unceasing insult of conquest, they understood that the refuge they sought was imperfect and that the king's arms, while long, were weak. This does not appear to have dampened their enthusiasm for, or at least their engagement with, the idea of amparo.

By the latter half of the seventeenth century, Indian petitioners had a powerful vocabulary of harm and wrongdoing for framing amparo petitions and for understanding their situation in legal and political terms. As miserables, they knew their vulnerability burdened the royal conscience. *Mal y daño* and its cognates described their suffering in immediately recognizable ways. Where powerful hands grasped and struck and took, the amparo expressed petitioners' hope for and belief in the possibility that, to quote Saavedra Fajardo, "the powerful hand of the king" might reach out and shelter them.[113] Through the idea of the common good they could imagine themselves as something other than merely fodder for the greedy. By their willing—and unavoidable—usefulness as tributaries they contrasted favorably with the validos who so often seemed to act contrary to royal decrees. Of course, Spanish procuradores, not Indian petitioners, introduced these phrases into the amparos. But petitioners learned. And though we cannot know with certainty, it seems altogether likely that Indian clients would have used what they had learned in talking to their procuradores about amparos.

Some sense of this possibility comes from petitions framed in the first person and lacking a procurador's name. This is not proof that petitioners filed on their own without help. In most cases at least an interpreter and someone to write down their story would have been present, though Indians frequently served as interpreters and villages often had their own notaries. But the immediacy of "we" in these petitions does seem one step closer to the petitioners' own voices. In a case from 1655, the petitioners began: "[W]e say that even though we were sent a Royal Provision which with all due solemnity we here exhibit so that justice will protect us," two servants of don Lorenço de Monrroy, "in contravention and violation [of the king's law]," came to our village, tied up Francisco Matheo and forcibly took him to Monrroy's hacienda to work. Similarly, a 1656 petition complained that Spaniards were trying to take "our lands" from which "we sustain ourselves and pay our royal tribute and hold our festivities as is our obligation," and "with a powerful hand they seek to take our church." Indians from Cuernavaca opened their 1687 petition by noting that "we are poor tributaries" unable to pay our tribute because a local Spanish rancher "has taken our land" and we have not taken any of his "because we are poor and unprotected Indians." "Help us and protect us," they pled, "as our protector that your Excellency is of the whole kingdom and of the poor more than others since our Lord brought you for this." In 1714, the gobernador of Anenequilco, Cuatla wrote a report to the viceroy, noting that Francisco de Godoy with "powerful hand has taken control of land granted by your Majesty." As "your Majesty's loyal vassals and wishing to remain vassals," we ask that our land be returned.[114]

These cases hint at how thoroughly Indian petitioners internalized the idiom and idea of amparo during the seventeenth century. This did not require that they understand these terms exactly as their procuradores did. Ordinary Indians did not write or read learned treatises or spend their lives crafting petitions. They were no more jurists than they were theologians: just as their religious understanding formed at the meeting point between Spanish theology and everyday religious experience, their understanding of law crystallized at the convergence of Spanish legal theory and their experience under Spanish rule, of which law was a central part. They were not trying to make law; they were trying to protect themselves—to secure property, prevent an increase in tribute, or escape an abusive employer. By seeking protection, Indian petitioners came to know the king's law as a practical and moral resource.

Their actions had profound implications for the colonial social order. By gaining a measure of protection and solicitude, they held their rulers accountable to the law's best intentions. In doing so, they invested the broad idea that the weak required protection from the strong, the "humble" from the "arrogant" and "powerful," with day-to-day significance, breathing life into a notion that might otherwise have been a curiosity of legal doctrine or merely a measure of Spanish hypocrisy. At the same time, by assimilating themselves to *personas miserables* through the amparos, they played to the ambivalence of a term haunted by an abiding sense of Indian inferiority. Solórzano y Pereira, for instance, while insisting that the Indians be protected, characterized them as possessing a "short capacity" for managing their own goods or enjoying the liberty of their own persons. Alonso de la Peña Montenegro, former bishop of Quito, agreed in his *Itinerario para parrocos* in 1663, a manual for parish priests, that the Indians needed protecting, yet in doing so he burdened them with all manner of character deficiencies to justify their privilege at law—they were superstitious, drunk, dishonest, cowardly, timid, and inarticulate.[115]

Nor should we imagine that the amparo was unequivocally an aid to the innocent. As many of these cases suggest, amparos were often used in disputes within Indian villages and at times were employed as the instruments of internal mischief and factionalism. Indeed, throughout the seventeenth century, Indians were not dramatically less likely to file petitions against other Indians, even members of their own communities, than against Spaniards, or castas. Dissensions from within, no less than forces from without, could trigger the desire for the law's protection.

CHAPTER FOUR

Precarious Possessions

⟫

On thousands of occasions over the seventeenth century, an alcalde mayor, corregidor, or other royal officer took a person by the hand and led him along the boundaries of a piece of land. Along the way, the person would stop to point out features of the terrain—hills, gullies, trees, or streams, or markers such as crosses—and indicate where boundary lines fell. With witnesses gathered, sometimes whole villages numbering hundreds of people, the person would pull up weeds from the ground and cast them to the winds, throw stones in all directions, and tell people to leave the premises, a kind of symbolic eviction demonstrating the intent to hold the property against all others. The officer would then ask the assembly if anyone objected to the person who had performed these acts being given the land. If no voice rose, the person was officially *put in possession* of the land in *His Majesty's name*. The notary who watched the proceeding then asked the witnesses to sign and added his own signature. At that point, the person could claim to be "in possession"—*en posesión*—of the land. If someone protested, as not uncommonly happened, the possession document might go unsigned until underlying legal disputes were resolved, which might take days, months, or years.[1]

Indians in villages across New Spain were intimately familiar with this legal ritual, known as an *acto de posesión*—act or ceremony of possession. They participated as owners receiving possession of land, as witnesses, and as observers. Sometimes they applauded the outcome—as when they, a friend, or a village leader took possession of land. Other times they attended grimly to a procedure that signaled the loss of property to someone else—another Indian, a Spaniard, or a casta. Sometimes the land had been disputed between different indigenous villages. Other times the act of posesión marked the end of a contentious chapter between a village and a local hacendado.

As practiced in seventeenth-century New Spain, the act of posesión was a simple affair—a walking inspection of borders, pulling weeds, throwing stones, and an opportunity for objections to be voiced. And yet, the placidity of this ritual cloaked what may have been the thorniest political issue in New Spain: who actually held land. While not all who claimed land performed an act of posesión—in private transactions, one party might simply occupy land, without fanfare or legal process or, crucially, the presence of a notary—the ceremony represented the public touchstone of property relations in colonial Mexico. Its artful corporality and its procedural simplicity, rooted in older traditions, represented the broader notion of posesión, a pivotal idea on which turned Indian litigants' understanding and experience of landholding and, given the centrality of land to their lives, to Spanish rule more generally.

As with all legal ideas, *posesión* was a term that took on meaning in the arena of judicial contest, a place where the concrete circumstances of everyday life met the abstractions of law. My goal here is to bring that moment of encounter and confrontation into tight focus in order to understand something of how process and procedure informed the relationship indigenous petitioners and litigants bore to land.

LAND BETWEEN LEGALITY AND REALITY

Elements of the ceremony of posesión had ancient roots. *Las Siete Partidas* had declared that "possession" consisted in "the act of placing the feet" on a piece of land, as a sign of a person's "will to obtain it" and "enter it and hold it."[2] *Possession* was to be distinguished from *property,* or what Roman law referred to as *dominium.* "Property" had to do with the "*señorío,*" the ownership or legal right a man has over a thing; "possession" with "tenancy" or holding of a thing, the bodily occupation of it against others. And because it was more difficult to prove ownership of property than the "mere holding" of it, parties were more likely to succeed in court by claiming possession than by asserting ownership. In essence, posesión amounted to a rebuttable presumption of ownership. Or as *Las Partidas* put it, if persons claim property, but cannot prove ownership, "those in possession can always hold it."[3]

The role this distinction played in the New World can be traced back to the earliest debates about the Indians' status in the face of Spanish conquest. Vitoria argued vigorously that the Indians retained ownership over their land and property. All dominium, he claimed, derived from God, the creator of all things, so that "no one may have such dominion unless he is given it by God." Since the New World's native inhabitants—and he appears to have been thinking of New Spain's Aztecs rather than the island peoples of the Caribbean—had been "in undisputed possession of their property, both publicly and privately" before conquest, they could not be "dispossessed without due cause." The Spanish king, concluded Vitoria, had only *dominium jurisdictionis* over these lands—jurisdiction rather than the outright ownership of *dominium rerum*—which meant that he lacked true property rights in them.[4] And if the king had no right of property in the New World, it followed that ordinary Spaniards could make no greater claim to ownership than their king. In effect, the Indians' possession of their land was unassailable at law. If from a modern perspective this seems tortured reasoning, it is important to acknowledge that Vitoria's argument became the legal and theoretical baseline for royal decrees seeking to protect Indian lands from Spanish usurpers.[5]

As legal doctrine, the idea of indigenous possession was in sharp tension with one of the crown's chief concerns in the early years after conquest—to reward those who had subdued the new kingdom. The crown's answer to the problem drew on another medieval institution, the encomienda which, in the New World, amounted to a license to control Indian labor power in a particular geographic area.[6] By denying property, or even possession of land to the conquerors, the crown sought to prevent the emergence of a landed aristocracy similar to the one that was beginning to challenge royal authority in Spain. Encomenderos might control the labor of people living in a given place, but they did not enjoy ownership rights of the land. Yet the encomienda proved only a temporary obstacle to those seeking land. Even as the crown began to legislate against the encomienda—most famously by denying inheritability in the New Laws of 1542—encomenderos found ways to perpetuate their influence over indigenous people and to gain control over property itself. They were not alone. Late-arriving Spaniards who had missed out on the encomienda also began to seek property as a means to security, or even comfort, putting increasing pressure on the possession of land from the mid-sixteenth century forward.

From a legal perspective, the paradox of the situation was that the crown itself had not claimed outright ownership of lands actively worked by Indians.[7] Technically, these remained in the hands of Indians. And yet, by century's end the king had asserted property rights over uncultivated Indian land, known as *tierras baldías* or vacant lands—despite Vitoria's conclusion that the crown lacked property rights in the New World.[8]

The broad context of this decision represented the crown's effort to ensure agricultural production, both to sustain the kingdom of New Spain and to provision the mines producing silver for the royal treasury. In theory, the king was not free to dispose of such lands at whim, for as one mid-sixteenth-century commentator noted, "the authority of the king rests on this principle, . . . that the king must preserve the common good against private interests."[9] As royal decrees across the sixteenth and seventeenth centuries make clear, the common good was understood in terms of political and economic urgencies expressed in the relationship of indigenous people to land.[10] The crown recognized that the Indians had every right to possess, live on, and use their lands and indeed mandated that Indians and their descendants "remain on the land."[11] Yet, massive death and migration among Indians through the early seventeenth century created ample opportunities for attentive Spaniards to gain control of property.[12]

As villages fell to disease in the mid-sixteenth century and as survivors fled, lands opened up, leading to endless legal wrangling over what was to count as tierras baldías. Spanish law had long held that the first person to occupy vacant land was entitled to possess it.[13] In central Mexico, Spaniards cited this principle in claiming lands located at the borders of neighboring altepetl. Before the conquest, these lands, which often ran along rivers, had served as buffers between different, sometimes competing political territories.[14] Indians generally treated such lands as commons, subject only to the collection of wood and water. During the early decades following the fall of Tenochtitlan, Indian caciques gave little thought to these lands, since they had played a limited role in native property relations. Spaniards occupied and held them, often with little opposition from Indian leaders. Indeed, when caciques took any notice at all of such lands, they often were more than willing to sell them.[15]

By law Spaniards could not simply usurp Indian land. In practice, the absence of systematic record keeping and uncertainty regarding the legitimate bases of possession enabled many Spaniards to gain control of great swaths of realty during the first half century after conquest. They did so by sale, above board or below, depending on the situation, by leveraging encomienda privileges and positions of political power, and by applying to the king for royal land grants.[16] Throughout this period, the crown demanded that its indigenous vassals feed the kingdom and pay tribute by working the very land that had become the object of relentless competition from the 1560s forward, especially in central Mexico.[17] Land, in short, was part and parcel of the crown's political and economic relationship to its new vassals, a relationship defined in terms of a palpable tension between the king's Indian and Spanish subjects.

The question of land in New Spain was so extraordinarily fraught for another reason: having held that the Indians were legally entitled to possess their lands, the crown faced the problem of articulating indigenous notions of property and possession to Spanish ones. Before 1521, the Nahua had recognized several different categories of property: lands held corporately by temples or community houses; lands held by the ruler; lands held personally by nobles; and district lands, often held in usufruct by individual commoner households. In Oaxaca, Mixteca land tenure appears to have been highly fragmented across the landscape and individual ownership limited. Households were not supposed to hold more land than they could cultivate. In these and other cases, indigenous ideas of property often lacked direct parallels in Spanish law and the interaction among different forms of property seemed to defy strictly individual notions of possession. A further difference between Spanish and indigenous ideas of land had to do with boundaries. Size of holdings had never been central to Indian conceptions of property, and most had never been measured or marked. Spaniards, by contrast, insisted that property lines be clearly spelled out and marked on the land itself.[18]

Despite these differences, there was a vital point of contact between indigenous and Spanish notions of land as they played out in the New World. Indian conceptions of possession tended to be tightly connected to the idea of productive use. Among the Nahua, for instance, commoners might hold land in usufruct, even be allowed to pass it on to children, but if the land ever stopped being cultivated, it escheated to the community, to be given to someone who would put it to work. The same appears to have been the case among the Mixteca in Oaxaca.[19] During the postconquest period, this sensibility regarding land resonated with the crown's deep concern to ensure productivity. The crown asserted possession of tierras baldías in part because they were uncultivated. It wanted to promote continuous planting and harvesting. Efforts to protect Indian lands, thus, were as much about ensuring that indigenous farmers be able to farm—and pay tribute—as it was about legal, political, and humanitarian concerns. In other words, it appears that in the New World the crown, like preconquest indigenous societies, understood possession, at least in part, as the exercise of a "social function."[20]

The irony here is that just as New World circumstances were reinforcing a legal understanding of property as being inseparable from its social role—in a sense, establishing an always slippery common ground with preconquest indigenous notions of property—individual Spaniards in Mexico appear to have been moving toward a more individualized, Roman conception of ownership.[21] Under Roman law, an owner bore no obligation to use land productively: he could choose to plant and harvest or let it lie fallow—a decision his alone to make. As the encomienda weakened late in the sixteenth century and as Indian lands opened up, individual Spaniards increasingly saw possession of land as a "visible sign of prestige" and "one of the few safe forms of investment," regardless of productivity.[22]

As with virtually every other aspect of colonial life, law straddled the contradictions of these two positions. Petitions for royal land grants—mercedes—often cited the "utility" of putting a particular parcel of land into production and the granting document, signed by the viceroy in the king's name, might acknowledge this utility and require grantees to "work and cultivate" the property in question. Mercedes might also limit ownership by forbidding sale for several years until the land had been made productive, warning grantees that failure to abide by the conditions could result in loss of property and any improvements on it. This more insistent phrasing that land be put to productive use, however, did not run consistently through the mercedes. Some grants, often for grazing land (an activity more difficult to verify than crops in the ground), might barely hint at what an owner intended to do with the property. In these mercedes, the focus seemed to be on spelling out the owners' rights and quieting title.[23]

Despite these variations, one limitation on the use of land appears to have remained relatively constant across the mercedes: no grant could be approved if doing so would "prejudice" the Indians.[24] This stipulation became a source of bitter contention between Spaniards eager for property and Indians intent on protecting individual and collective holdings. And though, in the words of viceroy Gastón Peralta in 1567, mercedes were often granted without "as careful a determination that third parties would not be harmed as there should have been," the formula itself signaled the crown's continued willingness to recognize Indian possession and cultivation as critical aspects of land tenure through the sixteenth and seventeenth centuries.[25]

Nor did the legal challenge of land boil down to a simple struggle between Indian communities and Spaniards. As native hierarchies loosened under the pressure of warfare, disease, and novel forms of local governance, commoners began to perceive opportunities for gaining possession of land. Before conquest, commoners had been barred from owning land individually. They might hold it across generations, but they could not sell or alienate it. Spanish law, by recognizing all Indians as vassals of the king, opened the door to individual and collective landowning by commoners. Indigenous nobles sought to defend position and privilege by concentrating land in their own hands. The contest was fierce. Over the sixteenth century, and into the seventeenth, litigants developed strategies for retaining or gaining access to land, according to their circumstances, with the result that Indians more often litigated property matters against other Indians than against Spaniards.[26] Even so, the relationship was not invariably antagonistic. In 1601, for example, the cacique of San Juan Batista Quauhtinchan, sold land he had inherited from his father and grandfather to the Indian commoner Simeón de Castro, who paid 12 pesos.[27]

Amid this competition, possession of property was rarely stable. It tended, rather, to be "a pattern of multiple, overlapping, and residual rights."[28] Legitimate transactions, such as mercedes, sales, donations, rental agreements, and testaments, blended, at times imperceptibly, with usurpations, squatting, fraud, unfair dealings, and outright violence as methods for acquiring property.[29] Indian individuals and communities commonly sold and rented land to Spaniards, often under direct pressure, though more frequently in response to conditions of time and place: if land was a good investment for Spaniards, it was a ready resource for communities and individuals in times of distress.[30] And while indigenous holders may have been more likely than Spaniards to do things by legal means, Indians routinely squatted on lands belonging to others. They even usurped property outright, as suggested by Bernardino Vázquez's admission in his will that land he had held and used for years actually belonged to someone else.[31] Regional differences in land tenure could be pronounced. In central Mexico, Spaniards exerted enormous pressures on property, especially near larger towns and cities, dispossessing indigenous communities and individuals of huge stretches of terrain by the early seventeenth century. In Oaxaca, by contrast, far more land remained in Indian hands through the sixteenth century and beyond.[32]

If by 1600 there had been a substantial transfer of land from Indian to Spanish hands and if Indian communities and individuals often contested property, this outcome was neither a failure of law nor a straightforward consequence of law as an instrumentality of domination. It was, rather, a consequence of the law's limitations before the novelty of the New World's complex realities, a situation in which the crown sought both to secure Indian lands and to satisfy the clamor of Spanish vassals for property.

The crown had no choice but to suppose that Spanish law might successfully mediate this quandary: it had no other instrument with which to order land tenure. That law had a record of rigor and effectiveness. It had long stood squarely against those who took land illegally. In Castile, where land was scarce and dear, property lines were carefully drawn, memorialized in legal documents, and marked on the land itself. *Las Siete Partidas* specifically discussed the need to punish those who mismeasured land, established false boundaries, changed landmarks without a judicial order, or resorted to fraud in the sale of land.[33] Usurpation and other illegalities were routinely undone and culprits punished.[34] In short, the law of property relations in Spain, the norm to which the king and his advisers looked, was fairly orderly.

In the New World, by contrast, the gap between reality and legality yawned wide, perhaps wider in matters of property than any other area of law.[35] In Mexico, unlike Spain, land was abundant. As Indian communities withered or fragmented, Spaniards found a field of opportunity, for indigenous property norms had not stressed precise measurements or careful drawing of boundaries. And while royal decrees tried to shelter Indians and their lands, the status of these new vassals remained unsettled through most of the sixteenth century, so that struggles over land intensified as a distant law strained against local conditions.

As the sixteenth century drew to a close, land tenure had become a shambles. The complex articulation of corporate lands, individual ownership, and generational usufruct that had characterized preconquest property had shattered under the blows of countless occupations, usurpations, and sales. Spaniards had taken much, especially from individual native landholders. Indian caciques competed with each other over parcels large and small. Individuals and communities jockeyed for position. And native commoners had gotten in on the game as well.[36] There simply was no order to property relations.

By the early 1590s, the crisis had reached such proportions that King Philip II resolved to act. Referring explicitly to the "disorder" in land, he decried the fact that so much property was "possessed without just and true titles."[37] To remedy this situation, he asserted the crown's absolute control over all vacant lands in the New World. In 1591, three decrees ordered that the Indians be confirmed in all the lands they worked and given any further land necessary to their sustenance. All other property, said the king, would belong "free and unencumbered" to the crown. Philip then commanded Spanish landholders to exhibit their titles before the audiencia. Lands lacking proper title were to revert to the crown as vacant. Owners whose titles were found to be defective faced the option of paying a *composición*—a fee—to clear their title, or of losing their land to the crown. In fact, few Spanish landholders lost property in this process. Many of the haciendas and farms in question were quite productive. By asserting its right to take improperly titled lands, the crown could serve the common good by "returning" lands to their owners, who would keep them in production, contingent on payment of a fee.

Composiciones figured crucially in the land tenure regime through the first half of the seventeenth century. Up to the early 1640s, most were granted to individual Spanish landholders. Between 1643 and 1646, however, viceroy Conde de Salvatierra declared a collective composición pursuant to which groups of landowners across central Mexico negotiated blanket settlements for a single, agreed-upon fee.[38] Despite the apparent safeguards of this convoluted process, composiciones frequently ended up by legalizing prior usurpations of Indian lands, especially during the collective settlements of the 1640s. Spaniards would come to the composición process armed with documents purporting to prove ownership, with evidence of long-standing possession and culti-vation, all of which might be true. After all, Indians often sold property to Spaniards for reasons of their own and even connived with Spaniards to circumvent laws limiting the sale of native lands. But a composición could just as easily cover up earlier takings at the expense of indigenous villages. And once granted, a composición was virtually impossible to undo.[39] It should be noted that there was a deep fiscal rationale under-lying the composiciones: royal coffers were strapped for cash. As one composición decree noted in its preamble, the treasury was "in debt and consumed by great expenses."[40] In other words, as ever in colonial legis-lation, the crown sought to balance competing goods: to order the chaos of land, garner money for the treasury, and protect the Indians.

PROTECTING POSECIÓN

Indian landholders were as acutely aware of the crisis in land tenure by 1590 as the king was. Between 1590 and 1592, hundreds of native petitioners went to Mexico City seeking royal amparos to protect their holdings. Although Indians had always been legally entitled to file such petitions, jurisdictional confusions had limited their ability to do so. When viceroy Velasco II began to hear amparo petitions directly, native petitioners from across New Spain flocked to the audiencia with brief but poignant tales of usurpers and confidence men and went back home with viceregal orders granting royal protection and stating that they not be dispossessed without a legal hearing. As of 1592, they could bring their grievances to the newly formed Juzgado General de Indios.

The flurry of amparo petitions during the early 1590s represented a vigorous response by indigenous landholders, individuals as well as com-munities, to the uncertainties of possession. The language of the peti-tions, and orders pursuant to them, condensed several relatively straight-forward propositions that set a legal baseline for subsequent land dis-putes involving indigenous petitioners and litigants. One of the most basic concepts in these early petitions was that of continuity through time. Repeatedly, petitions by native communities alleged that land had been possessed and cultivated for a period of years—from ten, to twelve, to eighteen, to fifty—or, more vaguely, "for much time until now," from "time immemorial," or since "our gentility." Individual claimants com-monly asserted continuity through time by insisting that they "had and inherited" land from fathers, grandfathers, and ancestors. Alongside these claims, petitions frequently asserted that an owner had possessed land "quietly and pacifically" and "without contradiction" throughout the period asserted.[41]

Taken together, these phrases represent the legal grammar of a claim to continuity in possession. Under Spanish law, no claim to property was immune to lapse of time if an owner abandoned land. According to *Las Siete Partidas,* any person obtaining land in good faith and holding it in possession for ten years could acquire ownership, even if the land had once been owned by another.[42] Thus, claiming possession for at least this period, as amparos so often did, was a way of staving off competing claims to the same parcel. Ultimately, the problem lay in proof, of course, but since the amparo was an administrative and nonadversarial proceeding, the evidentiary hurdles were lower than in litigation, where claims clashed head on. As Solórzano y Pereira summarized the principle in the mid-seventeenth century: "[P]ossession, and particularly when continued for some years, is so powerful that one must be protected and maintained in it even by apparent title alone, and even if it is not conclusive," for a later possession is presumed "violent and clandestine and is thought to be more of an invasion than a possession."[43]

Declarations of possession dating back to *time immemorial* or *our gentility* drew on a different principle, echoing Vitoria's arguments, as well as royal decrees holding that the Indians not be dispossessed of their land by conquest.[44] The idea of connecting the present with a distant past to establish property rights was hardly new. One of the earliest known amparos in 1537 referred to "our fathers, grandfathers, and ancestors" in backing its claim to a certain tract of land. Since this petition was filed less than two decades after the fall of Tenochtitlan in 1521, the phrase sought to root the claim to possession in a past predating Spanish conquest by at least two generations.[45] Similarly, nobles of Cuauhtinchan, in a lawsuit against Tepeaca in 1546–47, argued that certain lands belonged to them because they had owned them "from time immemorial," citing boundary markers set in 1466–67.[46] The ubiquitous presence of this language in the amparos from the early 1590s suggests that native petitioners thought of these words as having power in legal contexts, even when disconnected from any concrete claim to continuity with pre-Hispanic times.

Finally, the oft-repeated phrases *quietly and pacifically* and *without contradiction* played critical roles in disputes over property, for both spoke to the issue of continuity itself. A claimed possession of thirty years, interrupted by another group's occupation of the same land for a decade between the fifth and the fifteenth years, and then contradicted by a lawsuit in the twenty-fifth year amounted to little more than a fragmented and momentary holding that did not constitute *quiet* possession.

The centrality of *quietness* was embedded in the very act of posesión. One of the crucial and dramatic moments of a possession ceremony came when the judge looked to the assembled witnesses, often involving the residents of entire villages, as well as local Spanish landholders, and asked whether anyone wished to speak against the proposed possession. Silence was tantamount to a presumption of legitimate possession, for one who later raised an opposing voice would always face the argument that failure to speak when given the opportunity to do so estopped him from objecting at a later time.

While actual possession gave anyone who could claim it a distinct advantage in court, documentation played a vital role in grounding petitions for protection of property. Amparo petitions from the early 1590s frequently invoked *títulos* and *recaudos*—titles and other documents—regarding possession of this or that piece of land. A petitioner might allege that a parcel "belonged to him by sufficient documents [recaudos]," or that a plot's boundaries could be known from a document presented to the judge. Petitions often referred explicitly to mercedes, judicial orders of possession, notarized affidavits memorializing acts of posesión, wills and testaments, or bills of sale.[47] All of these documents held some probative value. Few could settle a claim once and for all.

As with the argument from continuity, Indian litigants and petitioners appear to have had long experience with documents by the end of the sixteenth century. Painted maps purporting to establish pre-Hispanic lineage and boundaries were presented in lawsuits between Indian towns as early as the 1530s and 1540s.[48] By 1600, documentation had become so important in legal settings that indigenous litigants commonly resorted to unscrupulous tactics in their efforts to prevail in court. Parties might submit forged titles for judicial review, or a challenger might attempt to swing things in her favor by stealing or forcibly taking the títulos on which another party planned to rely in seeking an amparo.[49]

Alongside continuity-in-time and documentation, declarations of productive use stood as the third pillar buttressing claims for protection of land. Petitioners might state that they had been "sowing and plowing" or "sowing and benefitting" the land long before a challenger showed up. Or they might point out that the land in question was used "to sustain themselves and pay their tribute."[50] Although such claims appeared less often in the petitions of the early 1590s than continuity-in-time and documentary evidence, they represented the firmly rooted idea, especially prevalent in the New World, that those who held land were obliged to make productive use of it.[51]

Proven cultivation amounted to a prima facie case of possession. This is what the residents of Chayuco understood when they filed a petition for amparo in 1590.[52] They did not identify a particular threat to their land. Rather, they sought a preventive order to ensure that no one enter the land and take it from them. The parcels in question "had many good uses and improvements [*aprovechamientos*]," stated the petition, such as palm trees, coconut trees, rare woods, honey, fisheries, and fields, "with which they sustain themselves and pay their tributes." Since the petition did not cite time of possession or refer to any documentation, this recital clearly aimed to ground the claim to possession in the fact of productive use.

These legal principles—continuity-in-time, documentation, and productive use—were not static categories. Through the seventeenth century they underwent subtle but important shifts in emphasis. It is generally agreed, for instance, that the argument from ancient possession—*time immemorial* and *since our gentility*—declined over the seventeenth century.[53] While petitioners continued to advance the claim through the 1650s, and even into the 1680s, my sample of amparos tends to support the view that over time it weakened in the same measure as the appeal to documentation strengthened.[54] This stands to reason: by the mid-seventeenth century, connections to pre-Hispanic times had in most cases become quite tenuous as people died or moved in large numbers and as land changed hands, often without legal formalities. Moreover, native commoners who had come to possess land could not credibly claim ancient possession, since before the conquest they had not been permitted to hold land as their own. The argument from continuity did persist, though more narrowly as a claim to hold land by direct inheritance.

As the argument from ancient possession waned, the number of land transactions—sales, transfers by will, rental agreements, donations—grew with time, as did the number of documents drawn up to memorialize them. In this context, papers carried an enormous legal and perhaps even psychological weight, as though the mere presence of an official document could change an entire situation. For instance, the village of San Francisco Cheran, Michoacan, complained in 1630 that the son of an alcalde mayor had shown up and moved a boundary marker from one place to another, "on his own authority with the staff of royal justice."[55] The young man appears to have understood that this was against the law, for he then tried to force village officers to sign certain papers ratifying the change. When they refused to do so, he mistreated them "by deed and by word." The officers rushed to Mexico City, "so that they not lose their right" to the land. In effect, by their actions, both sides acknowledged the power of *títulos* and *recaudos* in legal disputes over property. The young Spaniard knew that without documentary evidence he probably could not succeed in what was almost surely a planned usurpation of Indian land. Village officers knew that signing the document thrust at them could only imperil their possession.

The trope of productive use also came into common use during the seventeenth century. Where amparo petitions had only occasionally referred to tribute during the 1590s, they did so often from the 1630s forward, alleging that roaming herds of cattle destroyed "the fruits with which [villagers] pay their tributes and sustain themselves," or that loss of community land would mean that villagers could no longer grow the wheat "with which they sustain themselves and pay tribute and do the other things necessary for their community and republic."[56]

As they would do consistently, in diverse legal contexts, indigenous petitioners expressly acknowledged, even embraced, their nonnegotiable status as tributaries in order to advance their causes: without land they could not contribute to royal coffers and do the other things befitting proper vassals. This was the gist of a petition filed by the gobernador, officers, and residents of San Juan Sitaguaro in 1656. Spaniards seek to take "our lands and those of our community which we have inherited from our ancestors," complained the petitioners. We have held these lands "in quiet and pacific possession" and from them "we sustain ourselves and pay our royal tributes and services to your Majesty." They closed by asking for protection so that they "not be disturbed in our possession." The Juzgado agreed and issued the order.

Like so many others, this petition did not confine itself to a single argument, but combined several: inheritance, quiet and pacific possession, payment of tributes, and recognition of vassalage. Crucially, it was framed in the first-person plural and did not bear the name of a procurador, hinting that these phrases and the ideas behind them had been widely internalized by the mid-seventeenth century, part of the vocabulary with which indigenous property holders faced a world in which land was so often in play. By appealing to the king's name and asserting their tributary obligations, they broadcast a clear message—anyone who interfered with their possession was meddling in the king's business.[57]

This idea found expression in the amparos through the notion of *uso y aprovechamiento*—use and the act of making good use of a thing. From the 1650s forward, petitioners argued that a usurpation of land, or a taking of water, or unshepherded flocks of sheep or herds of cattle were "impeding their *uso y aprovechamiento*" of the resources necessary for cultivation and paying tribute.[58] Petitioners might ask that possession be protected because their use of property benefited "the Spaniards and residents of Acapulco," or "resulted in utility for New

Spain." The Juzgado generally answered in kind, ordering that petitioners not be "disturbed" in their *aprovechamiento* or *uso*. Taken together, and in the broader context of royal decrees favoring the Indians as tributaries, these words conveyed a distinct sense of the relationship between social usefulness and land.[59] They also evoked a broader political principle, what Solórzano y Pereira, discussing the Indian obligation to pay tribute, called the "common utility and . . . the stability and firmness of the republic."[60]

While indigenous people understood their relationship to land in many different ways, the idea of possession seems to have been a dominant one in legal situations. By the late sixteenth century, native concepts and categories appear to have receded into the background of property law in the New World. At least in Nahua areas, early wills and testaments made by Indians did not employ pre-Conquest terms of land tenure. Instead, they used Spanish concepts and ideas regarding inherited land (*patriomonio*), bought land, lands granted by *merced*, or lands belonging to a community (*tierras de comunidad*).[61]

There is some evidence in seventeenth-century wills that testators tended to use *posesión* as a loanword from Spanish when referring to the legal act of taking or giving possession. Thus, in a testament drawn up in San Sebastián Homaxac Huehuecalco, Coyoacan in 1607, Luis Tapia's wife and children were recorded as saying in Nahuatl that they wanted to be "given *posesión*" of inherited lands, where *posesión* appears as a Spanish loanword in the Nahuatl text. Decades later, don Juan Montesinos's 1680 will described how his son "took [land] with *posesión* given to him by the gobernador" of San Andrés Calpa. Although the number of such wills is relatively small, they hint that use of the word *posesión* in circumstances requiring legal precision may have been a deliberate choice. This is not to say that Nahuatl speakers gave up Nahuatl equivalents for *posesión*. In a few wills, *posesión* appears in the Spanish translation but not in the Nahuatl original, suggesting that Nahuatl speakers distinguished between more casual references to the possession or having of property and legal situations calling for the more technical term *posesión*.[62]

A further sign that *posesión* came to be accepted and used among Nahuatl speakers in legal contexts comes from a 1660 document memorializing an act of *posesión* in which residents from the village of Santa Ana, near Zultepec officially took possession of lands belonging to them.[63] They complained that a local Spaniard had, "in the course of time," taken all their lands. According to the official document of possession, the alcalde mayor took village leaders by the hand and led them around the land. With an interpreter's help, he read out the amparo order: "Come here my sons, know that his Majesty commands in his royal decree to give you *posesión,* which I give you of all your lands, so that you can divide them among the residents so they can sow them and sustain themselves and pay the royal tributes."[64] Throughout the original Nahuatl text, the Spanish word *posesión* appears as a loanword to describe the act of transferring land and the condition of holding it. Whatever other ways Nahuatl speakers had to discuss landholding, the Spanish *posesión* appears to have figured centrally in their legal understandings of property and possession.

Those understandings could only reflect the fact that amparos offered no guarantee regarding pending or future litigation. This was the gist of the formulaic language concluding the vast majority of early amparo orders—*without prejudice to third parties.* In effect, the amparo set the burden of proof squarely on the shoulders of those who would challenge an actual possessor. Evidence could rebut possession's presumption at law, so the court's door remained open. But anyone who went through it to claim land possessed pursuant to someone else's amparo order did so knowing he had to present a solid case. In practical terms, an amparo stood as a legal obstacle to outright usurpation or fraud. In legal terms, it did nothing more than protect possession until someone filed a lawsuit asserting a competing claim. On that day, the holder of the amparo would be assured a hearing before a court rendered judgment regarding the land—but nothing more.[65]

Amparos were the Indians' first and chief recourse in disputes over land. But amparos did not aim to stop Spaniards from accumulating property; they sought only to make sure that Indians not lose land against their will. As contemplated in the amparos, then, possession appears to have been less than secure ownership but more than mere tenancy at the mercy of usurpers—a legal idea rooted in the New World reality that property could never be grounded in untroubled dominion. This was hardly a novelty in Spanish law—as *Las Partidas'* distinction between *property* and *possession* testifies. But it was newly problematic in Mexico, where the uncertain legality of conquest cast the very idea of property into shadow, where the crown legally claimed vacant lands, where indigenous people continued to hold land as their own but were willing to alienate it, and where the conditions of a conquest society tended to reward those with the means to opportunism. Willingness to seek an amparo—with its costs in time and money—might be understood as a means by which Indian landholders signaled to potential usurpers that they were firmly committed to the defense of their possession.

Possession, as it emerged in New Spain, might thus be thought of as a legal category that aimed to contain the vagaries of landholding in a colonial society that had fostered a kind of rolling chaos in property relations through the sixteenth and into the seventeenth century. Not merely a legal abstraction projected onto the world, it was simultaneously a reality that forced itself on legal principle. For as the amparos suggest, Indian landholders had no choice but to fight for land in relationship to the idea and experience of possession as something less than full, untrammeled ownership.

IDEALIZED PROPERTYSCAPES,

DISORDERLY LANDSCAPES

For St. Thomas it was lawful for men to own property because "human affairs are conducted in more orderly fashion" and "a more peaceful state is ensured to man if each one is contented with his own." *Las Partidas* recognized the same idea. God had created "all things very perfectly" and "each in its proper place." This principle stood as one of the mainstays of wordly justice—that to each man must be given "that to which he is entitled." In no area of law did these precepts speak quite so intuitively as to the division of property. With regard to a "field, a vineyard, a house, or any other immovable property," the legal demand was clear: every owner should "state specifically where it [the land] is situated, and mention its landmarks and boundaries."[66]

The notion that land tenancy should ideally contain each unto his own was nowhere more eloquently expressed than in *pinturas*—painted maps—used in land cases, submitted as evidence or drawn up at the end of a case. From the sixteenth century forward, such maps often figured in land disputes.[67] The dominant idea in so many of the pinturas was to represent the land in question as fitting seamlessly into the surrounding propertyscape.

For instance, in 1613, the village of Tilapa, Yzucar, "in His Majesty's name," asked the viceroy to grant a merced for two pieces of land petitioners insisted already belonged to their community. Witnesses, Indians and Spaniards alike, testified that the village had always "possessed and worked" these lands and that villagers had nowhere else to grow crops, because so many other Spaniards had received mercedes in the area. Tilapa's application was opposed by the local Dominican convent. Having seen the land and considered the testimony, the judge wrote up a description stating markers and boundaries and ordered a pintura to be made depicting the situation. The viceroy's legal adviser penned an opinion saying the viceroy could award the merced to Tilapa.

Fig. 2 suggests exactly what *Las Partidas* contemplated—clear boundaries. The two lots in question can be seen just northeast of the central town (east is at the bottom of the map), marked by streets and the presence of the church, where the map says *"lo que se pide"*—"what is asked for." It is bounded on the east by a farm belonging to the Dominicans, on the south by a road dividing the land from the farm of another Spaniard, on the west and the north by hills. The other piece in question is south-south-west of town, bounded to the east by a road on the other side of which is the Dominican estate, to the west by a river and land owned by another convent, to the north by unlabeled land that appears not to have been owned or worked by anyone (perhaps swamp or other unuseable land). In both instances, the contested parcel figures as a puzzle piece fitting snugly into the overall picture of property in this area.

Similarly, in a case litigated in 1643, a Spanish widow seeking possession of land offered a pintura representing her claim to a merced (Fig. 3). It consisted of nothing more than two concentric circles with the figure of a forking river running through the middle of the inner circle, where the land in question was alleged to be. Between the two circles ran a band of text reading: "This whole big circle all the way around is the lands and hillocks where the Indians of these villages make their fields." According to the text within the circle, the closest field stood at least one and a half leagues from the widow's site.

The question at issue was whether doña Francisca de Rojas would be allowed to found a sugar mill and plant cane on a piece of land lying in the valley through which ran the Santa Ana and Tzontecomatlan rivers. To succeed, she needed to make a legal showing that doing so would not prejudice the Indians. According to witnesses, residents of the surrounding villages had always preferred to plant their crops on the mountainsides and higher ground rather than on the flats near the river.[68] In the face of this testimony, officers of various Indian villages offered no objection to the widow's pretension, and the tribunal allowed her to found the mill. Obviously, this map did not seek to represent the physical geography of the dispute. It sought instead to portray in clear lines the legal principle at stake: the idea of a well-bounded space that did not impinge upon any Indian lands, as required by law.

A pintura originally drawn by indigenous litigants around 1690 suggests that this idea was widely shared, at least in legal settings (Fig. 4).[69] Compared to the 1643 pintura, which offered an abstracted vision of the local situation, this map conveys the density and patchwork quality of possession so common in New Spain. In the middle of this crazy quilt, however, the land in question is neatly tucked among bordering claims, just

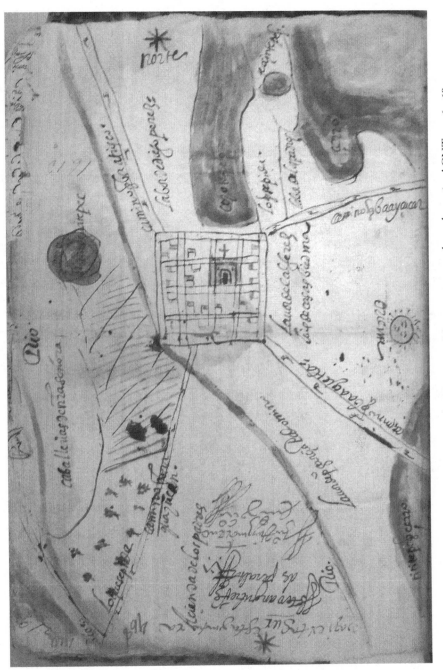

FIGURE 2. Archivo General de la Nación, Fondo Hermanos Mayo, concentrados sobre 563. AGNT 2756.468r.

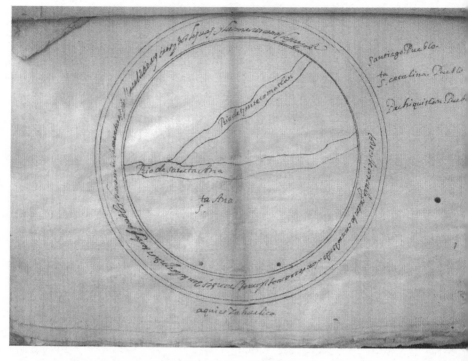

FIGURE 3. Archivo General de la Nación, Fondo Hermanos Mayo,
concentrados sobre 563. Mapa 2029 (AGNT 2756.168r–187r).

east of the Royal Highway (the map is oriented with west at the top), north
of a property line defined by trees and a cross, west of a river, and south
of a shorter property line likewise marked by trees and a cross. At least on
the map, each neighboring plot is distinctly separate from all others.

In all three of these cases, maps represented idealized propertyscapes.
Agreeable parties, as in the latter two cases, had no particular reason to
question that representation. For them, accepting the maps as workable
depictions of complicated realities contributed to local peace and quiet.
By contrast, in the first case the viceroy favored the residents of Tilapa
over the Dominicans. The record is silent on the fathers' reaction to this
loss. Perhaps they refused to reconcile themselves to the outcome, though
they appear not to have pursued any further remedy before the audiencia. Perhaps they decided to work locally to secure the land, though there
is no record that the residents of Tilapa complained to the Juzgado in

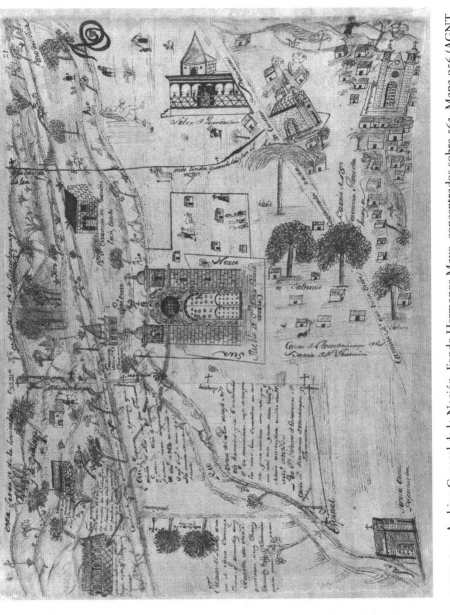

FIGURE 4. Archivo General de la Nación, Fondo Hermanos Mayo, concentrados sobre 563. Mapa 956 (AGNT 1206.1.cuad 2).

later years. Perhaps they had known all along that they were unlikely to succeed, given that the convent already possessed a great deal of land and the Indians had no other land to farm, as Spanish and Indian witnesses testified. Regardless, the map in that case, as in the other two, produced judicial closure by painting a propertyscape in which each party was in its *proper place* without potentially disruptive overlaps or uncertainties. And yet, the fact that the Dominicans did not register their acquiescence to the ruling in 1613 serves as a reminder that the thick and complex textures of land tenure might defy judicial efforts to render a smooth and untroubled canvas for New Spain's landscape.

In part, this was because the possession of land in postconquest Mexico always signified more than mere having. Land figured centrally in sustaining communities at a time when so many springs of identity and survival had dried up. Control of land could mean the difference between life and death, collective survival or disbandment. It could also be the difference between the timely payment of tributes and living under the pressure of chronic shortfalls. One town's search for a measure of stability and a margin of survival might be another town's despair and trouble. In such circumstances, struggles over property easily became debates over basic issues of political organization within Spain's empire in the New World.

In September 1629, two Indian communities near Antequera, Oaxaca, appear to have come to a tense settlement over the possession of certain lands.[70] Capulalpa, head town of the jurisdiction of Yztepexe, had been claiming that the smaller San Pablo Quelatao had possessed and worked certain acreage from "time immemorial and without contradiction." Yztlan, head town of the neighboring district, had insisted that the residents of Quelatao merely rented their land from Yzatlan for six pesos a year. In the middle of this lawsuit, Quelatao agreed to settle the case, more or less by acquiescing to Yztlan's terms. Under the agreement, Quelatao would have the use of water and wood from the land in exchange for a payment of six pesos a year to Yztlan. Quelatao further agreed to attend the annual festival of St. Thomas in Yztlan and bring flowers for the church. According to the understanding, any village leader of Quelatao who tried to file a later lawsuit regarding this arrangement or used "impudent words" would be fined, flogged, and sent to jail for eight days. The very fact that such a clause had to be included at all suggests that the accord was a fragile one.

Though the immediate property issue might appear to have been settled, the dispute ran to a deeper source, for Quelatao spent the next three years in a battle of suits, countersuits, and even criminal accusations over the same land. In August 1632, the leaders of Yztlan obtained two viceregal decrees purporting to settle the matter in their favor. Taken together, these orders held that Quelatao was subject to Yztlan's jurisdiction, that its residents had only rented the land from Yztlan, and that Quelatao's lands belonged to Yztlan. Citing these two decrees in May 1633, the leaders of Yztlan and several named residents of Quelatao joined in another settlement agreement which, unlike the earlier one from 1629, explicitly characterized recent lawsuits and disagreements as a contest over jurisdiction. The agreement specifically stated that the Indians of Quelatao had sought to secede from Yztlan in order to be ruled by Capulalpa, the head town of Yztepexe. The document called for the viceroy's orders to be executed in Yztlan's favor, regardless of any other decrees Quelatao might have obtained during this time. "For it is the custom among the Indians who have lawsuits before the justices of their districts," noted the agreement, "to seek amparos without mentioning those lawsuits and they even get decrees from the Juzgado de Indios to be protected." To avoid any further litigation, and in the interest of "peace and quiet," the parties to the agreement stated that Quelatao would henceforth recognize Yztlan's jurisdiction, pay rent on the land it occupied, and bring flowers for the church during fiesta time, an unmistakable sign of Quelatao's subjection to Yztlan's jurisdiction.

Even this document did not quell the dispute. Less than a year later, in early 1634, the leaders of Capulalpa, for themselves and on behalf of the residents of Quelatao—without naming any individuals—filed a petition for amparo at the Juzgado, requesting that the 1633 settlement be set aside. "From time immemorial" and "without contradiction," they insisted, the residents of Quelatao had held and worked the land in question. They, like the residents of Capulalpa, had always been subject to Yztepexe's jurisdiction, not Yztlan's. The 1633 settlement, argued the petition, was invalid because the signers from Quelatao—"private individuals and commoners"—lacked proper authority to act for the community. Moreover, asserted the petition, they had signed under compulsion, for the alcalde mayor of Yztlan, an interested party in the case, had thrown them in jail to ensure their compliance.

These were heavy charges, and the viceroy seems to have decided simply to put an end to the melée, perhaps fearing that further litigation would only sharpen tensions. Barely acknowledging Capulalpa's argument regarding the 1633 settlement, the Juzgado ruled once again in Yztlan's favor, awarding it the lands "in property." According to maps and witnesses, stated the Juzgado's order, Quelatao's lands had from "ancient times" belonged to Yztlan. And though the people of Quelatao originally hailed from Capulalpa, said the ruling, they had occupied the land with Yztlan's consent.[71] Quelatao's residents were to be informed of the decision and given the opportunity to continue working the lands. If they chose to stay, they would have to pay the yearly rent of six pesos. So long as they did so, Yztlan could not evict them. If they chose to stop working the lands, Yztlan could not compel them to stay. Capulalpa would be allowed to continue collecting tribute from its subjects living in Quelatao, provided its officers did not raise their staves of royal office upon entering town.

Although this case began as a simple quarrel over the possession of certain lands, it became far more in the course of litigation—a battle over jurisdiction, the foundational political category of Spanish rule. Though legal contests over head-town status were common during the seventeenth century, this case reveals the volatilities and stakes of land disputes: three Indian towns, two of them head towns, their elected officers and private citizens, Yztlan's alcalde mayor, the corregidor of Tecuicuilco acting as a special judge by viceregal commission, the Juzgado, and even the viceroy came together at law to hash out this fundamental issue in a local context.[72]

The case says something as well of how adept indigenous litigants could be in such situations. Long experience at the Juzgado, keen awareness of the system's bias favoring settlement agreements, alliances with local Spaniards, an ability to navigate local situations, and exquisite timing in the use or threat of coercion proved decisive for Yztlan and its leaders. Capulalpa fought back with similar weapons, but always lagged a step. Quelatao was caught in the crossfire. Some of its residents may have sided with Yztlan, though they may simply have been coerced, as Capulalpa argued. Others may have taken up with Capulalpa, perhaps hoping to improve their tribute situation by switching jurisdictions.

The case is a reminder of the irreducible complexity of land tenure in New Spain. Yztlan may have won the day, but its claim was hardly free and clear. Quelatao's residents were said to have "possession" of the land that belonged to Yztlan in "property." They, rather than Yztlan's leaders, would decide whether to continue using the land, and Yztlan was legally barred from denying Quelatao's access to the land. Capulalpa lost all jurisdiction over Quelatao, but its tribute collectors could still enter Quelatao to collect from its subjects. Within these communities there was still abundant opportunity for discord, as was the case in so many other places.

On the morning of October 14, 1654, the officers of the towns of Santa Catalina and San Pedro Tlahuac, province of Chalco, were set to take possession of a substantial piece of land called Texapalco.[73] The local alcalde mayor was present, as was an interpreter and a notary, pursuant to an amparo the officers of Santa Catalina had received from the viceroy. According to the record, the Indian officers and Spanish officials went about the land, recognizing boundaries and placing markers. As alcalde mayor captain don Joseph Antonio Altamirano was about to grant possession in the land to the leaders of the two towns, a Spaniard by the name of captain don Francisco Brito spoke up and "contradicted" the measurement and possession. Some of the boundary markers were wrongly placed, said Brito, as a consequence of which portions of his land were about to be usurped. The alcalde mayor suspended the act of posesión and ordered the markers left in place.

Later the same day, Brito filed a petition with alcalde mayor Altamirano. Lands he and his legitimate predecessors had "possessed quietly" for seventy years had been included in the acreage sought by the Indians, he insisted, "in prejudice of the right [I] have acquired in said lands." To avoid future lawsuits, "and so that each party claim only what is properly its own," Brito asked that the land be remeasured and that alcalde mayor Altamirano review all *títulos* (titles). "The Indians are rich and suspect," he noted, while pointing out that Indians often resorted to this tactic of trying to do things without giving proper notice to affected parties.

With these statements, the gauntlet had been thrown and the duel was on. The alcalde mayor ordered all parties to exhibit their títulos. Don Sebastián Mateo, gobernador of San Pedro, and several other officers responded by presenting two viceregal orders supporting their claim, one from 1568 and one more recent against a local Spaniard. Don Sebastián also presented a number of viceregal orders in which a local Spaniard's application for a merced was denied as "prejudicial" to the town's land, the kiss of death for any land claim, if the prejudice could be proven. Brito relied on a merced originally awarded in 1583 to a Spanish woman, doña Elvira de Paredes. That merced had passed by inheritance to the wife of Juan Gonçales de Nava, who had passed it to Brito's wife.

In early December 1654, the officers of the towns offered a series of witnesses to back their claims. Six stalwart Spaniards, citizens of nearby San Francisco, acknowledged the two viceregal orders and testified that the two Indian towns had long possessed the lands in question. These witnesses noted as well that two or three years earlier a viceregal decree had ordered that a house and other structures belonging to Spaniard Matheo Hernandes be torn down for encroaching on the lands in question. Brito offered no witnesses. He chose instead to hope that a new survey of the land would reveal discrepancies between the towns' titles and the actual boundaries.

At 8 A.M. on December 14, the land was remeasured, this time with all parties "and many Indians and Spaniards" in attendance. A judge under viceregal commission, Luis Gómez de Escobar, was also present to oversee the process. Two surveyors performed the measurements, one appointed by don Mateo and his officers and one chosen by the judge. Having watched the procedure, judge Gómez prepared to grant the amparo of posesión to Santa Catalina and San Pedro Tlahuac. He had already drafted the order stating that gobernador Mateo and the other officers had torn up weeds, thrown rocks and toured the land "quietly and pacifically." It lacked only signatures to make it legally binding. At the last second, Brito stepped forward and asked that the order be suspended pending further judicial review.

Having temporarily stopped the act of posesión once again, Brito laid out his case for denying the amparo altogether. In his brief to Gómez, he advanced two main points. First and foremost, the document of posesión that alcalde mayor Altamirano had drawn up was wrong on its face, because it had failed to refer to a certain hill that was crucial to establishing proper boundaries. Second, don Sebastián and the other officers were "very rich" Indians who had been meddling with the property rights of local Spaniards for some time. They had snuffed out Matheo Hernandes's merced application by arguing that the land and the trees growing on it were "useful" to them. Their influence was so great that they had suborned the Spanish witnesses who had testified on their behalf. Brito asked judge Gómez not to proceed with the amparo and instead to reexamine the property and to peruse the titúlos and the map one by one. At best, stated Brito, the Indians might own the land that Hernandes had wanted, but not the rest, which was covered by the royal merced Brito held. Finally, warned Brito, if Gómez continued with the act of posesión, he would appeal to Mexico City.

Over the following year the parties wrangled before the audiencia. The nub of the issue was the existence or nonexistence of a particular hill crucial to the drawing of lines separating San Pedro Tlahuac's land from Brito's. Tlahuac's leaders named the hill in their filings. Brito claimed, in essence, that the Indians had conjured the hill out of thin air, and by referring to it had sought to usurp his property. Judge Gómez tried without success to find an unambiguous answer to this dispute, asking people who lived on the land about the hill and examining a painted map that hung in the stairwell of the local Franciscan convent. Neither witnesses nor the map could establish the hill's presence or absence with certitude. Indeed, Gómez ordered a copy of the stairwell map made (Fig. 5) and issued an official ruling that it did not contain the details necessary to settle possession, an acknowledgment of the ground

FIGURE 5. Archivo General de la Nación, Fondo Hermanos Mayo, concentrados sobre 563. Mapa 1155 (AGNT 1631(1). Cuad 11.96).

fog of uncertainty and confusion that lay thickly over the legal terrain in this case.

Perhaps this is why in early January 1656 the parties came to an arrangement. According to a document of *concierto*—concert and agreement—don Sebastián and his officers, on behalf of their communities, recognized "now and forever" that the merced on which Brito relied was "good and true." They agreed that there was sufficient land for Brito to "enjoy and possess" without causing "prejudice" to the surrounding Indian towns, on condition that the Indians be able "freely to sow" the land for so long as Brito shall own it, without his cattle causing any damage to their fields. Once the harvest was taken in, the land would revert to grasslands for Brito's cattle, until the following planting season. Brito would also be able to graze his cattle on other uncultivated Indian land, including around the lagoon and up the hills. The Indians, in turn, would be allowed "freely to take advantage of [*aprovechándonos*]" all the magueyes on Brito's land. All of this, stated San Pedro Tlahuac's don

Sebastián in the agreement, was in "recompense" of Brito being able to graze his cattle on the Indians' land, from which will follow *"grandes aprovechamientos"* [great advantages]. And finally, if Brito should decide to sell the land, the Indian communities would have a right of first refusal to buy it. All parties signed and judge Gómez accepted the agreement.

In many ways this case was unusual. San Pedro Tlahuac's don Sebastián and his officers appear to have dominated the local situation. They had a powerful ally in alcalde mayor Altamirano, who seemed ready to support them over the objections of a small-time Spanish cattle rancher who needed land, and they had the influence to line up six Spanish witnesses to testify against another Spaniard. Blocked at every turn, Brito did what Indian litigants so often did in such circumstances, he headed for Mexico City to escape a tightly controlled local arena. Subsequent litigation only intensified the battle. Judge Gómez reviewed the documentation and interviewed Indian farmers in an effort to clarify the matter, but could not cut the Gordian knot of local geography. Faced with this vagueness, the parties found common ground in the idea of productive use. Brito appears to have had no greater ambition for the land than to graze his cattle on it. The communities wanted to plant crops and cultivate the magueyes, but cared little for how the land was used once the harvest had passed. The Indians recognized the legality of Brito's merced, but they guaranteed their access to the land and assured that it would not be sold out from under them in the future. Although the record is silent on the matter, it seems plausible to think that both parties came under considerable pressure to work things out while they were before the audiencia.

Outcomes such as this were common. Royal law encouraged parties to settle their differences, especially if doing so promised to keep land producing for the Indians' sustenance and payment of tributes, even if it meant leaving legal issues dangling which might later result in litigation. For all the apparent clarity of the resulting agreement, the situation was one of uncertainty with regard to the contested property. Brito's ownership remained contingent and precarious, in part because the communities of Santa Catalina and San Pedro Tlahuac retained documents claiming rights to the land covered by Brito's merced. Both parties were savvy enough to know this, and they had concluded that it was better to put such issues aside for the moment and get on with the business of grazing cattle and growing crops.

In this case, as in the Yztlan case of 1629, possession remained convoluted even after litigation. Brito gained recognition of his merced. Yet the land in dispute became the stage to a seasonal choreography of crops and cattle, and Brito's posesión depended on sticking to the script. Nor could Brito sell the land without first offering it to the Indians, which meant that his options for its future use were limited and the Indians' options far greater than they might otherwise appear. The placid map from the convent stairwell might seem to reflect a happy situation in which everything was in its place, but its brushstrokes effaced a deeper and more troubled reality.

EPISODES OF STRUGGLE

Given the slow-rolling, "cumulative usurpation" of indigenous lands following conquest, it is hard to avoid the impression that many, perhaps most, Indian villages lived in a state of constant alert regarding property through the seventeenth century.[74] If up through the 1570s, land contests among Indian communities were the rule, after 1600 "the more characteristic disputes occurred between Indians and Spaniards."[75] Villages and individuals could be subject to a wide variety of pressures, including usurpations accomplished "with spears and lances and other arms."[76]

Such blatant cases tailed off over the seventeenth century, giving way to subtler tactics. Spanish ranchers or sheep farmers might release livestock on targeted land, claiming it was open to public grazing. If crops were trampled several years running and if residents fled, a usurper might claim the land as vacant or abandoned. Another ploy involved taking land in rent from Indian villages, cultivating it and years later claiming the same land outright as having been held from "time immemorial." Alternatively, opportunistic tenants might conclude a rental arrangement orally and hope that actual possession and cultivation would later win the day in court when the owners could not offer proof that they owned the land. A would-be usurper might steal an adversary's documents proving a property claim. Or he might seize the land and then try to force or dupe parties into signing documents to ratify the taking. Indians interested in establishing a claim against a local Spaniard might sneak out in the middle of the night and erect structures on disputed land and then argue that the structures proved their possession. The possibilities were endless.

In so many of these cases the goal was the same: to convert an illicit taking into a legal confrontation. The reason for subterfuge is clear: direct usurpations, in which one party forcibly ran another off coveted land, lacked any basis in law. For Spaniards, successful accumulation increasingly demanded at least the color of legality, especially after 1650, when land was no longer as freely available as it had once been and composiciones had supposedly quieted Spanish titles. Under such circumstances, litigation became the instrument of choice in disputes over land.

Once a matter had been brought to court as a lawsuit, a fairly strict set of rules came into play. Complainants stated their grievance and asked for a remedy. The judge or tribunal ordered a preliminary investigation and deposed three witnesses. The opposing party then filed a response. After procedural wrangling, often involving questions of jurisdiction or standing before the court, parties to the litigation submitted evidence to substantiate their claims—documents tending to show rightful possession, such as bills of sale, testaments, donations, royal mercedes, and amparos. Witnesses gave statements by responding to interrogatories written by procuradores and approved by the presiding judge. These questions generally offer the clearest sense of each side's theory of the case. Once all the evidence was in, the court issued a ruling, stating only which party had prevailed. Many, perhaps most cases never got this far, settling out formally or informally somewhere along the procedural path.[77] Although no two cases were exactly alike, for the most part this procedure was followed quite closely regardless of time, place, or legal issue.

Despite procedural regularity, litigation over land was fraught with peril and uncertainty for litigants. No case was airtight. At best, one side might have intimations of how an opposing party planned to argue its case, what witnesses it would call, what documents it would rely on, and how much time and money it could afford to spend. To undertake a lawsuit, or be forced into one was to join one's fate to a contingent process of considerable complexity and only partial control. As close attention to the cases shows, litigants, just to have a chance of success, required a willingness to face adversity, a realistic understanding of the law, a discerning eye for chicanery, and perhaps above all perseverance.

In early June, 1691, the gobernador, officers, and residents of the village of Tesayuca, Texcoco, arrived in Mexico City. They sought out Juan Félix Galves, a procurador for the Juzgado, and told him how local Spanish farmers were trespassing on their land. Specifically, Gerónimo de Guzmán had taken their land and kept them from the water, "disturbing their possession." As a result, they could not grow their crops, with which they paid tribute. They offered two documents to back their claim. The first was a viceregal order held in their community chest since 1552, which they claimed granted them a piece of land called Tetitlan, near their village. The second, an amparo dated 1641, protected their use of water running in the river Papalotla. They suffered "vexations" because their property was not properly marked and others routinely trespassed, leading to sharp disputes and many lawsuits. They asked to present evidence identifying the property contained in the 1552 order and proving their right to use the water, in keeping with the 1641 amparo.

The viceroy and audiencia judges ordered that three witnesses for Tesayuca be deposed. With these statements on the record and having seen the two documents, the audiencia issued the amparo ordering the alcalde mayor to set markers and establish property lines. Guzmán, having been notified of the proceedings, filed a motion to suspend the order. Claiming to have a merced as well as another "title of dominion," in addition to "finding myself in actual possession," he insisted that "the lands relate to me and are mine."[78]

Meanwhile, the Tesayuca litigants found that Guzmán had been busy at the local level. The alcalde mayor, to whom the amparo had been directed was uncooperative, claiming he had other matters to attend to. The audiencia renewed its order on July 21 and gave the alcalde mayor two days to execute it. He sent his lieutenant to inspect the land. That officer, finding that the land Tesayuca claimed was in fact possessed and cultivated by Guzmán, promptly suspended the amparo granted to Tesayuca, telling the gobernador and his officers that they were free to seek legal relief. He also denied them any part of the water, concluding that since their land lay in the valley they got plenty of water anyway.

And so the battle was joined. What had begun as an effort by the leaders of Tesayuca to establish the boundaries had become a full-blown lawsuit. The legal arguments began to fly thick and furious. Procurador Galves, for Tesayuca, continued to push the audiencia to enforce its amparo. Guzmán, through his own procurador, claimed that doing so would usurp his land. By October 1691, things had begun to heat up. Tesayuca filed a countersuit, arguing that Guzmán had offered no evidence supporting his claim to the land. They asked that he be forced to show his titles and specify which ones he planned to rely on. Guzmán responded, claiming that he did not know what land Tesayuca was referring to, since the name *Tetitlan* did not once appear in Tesayuca's 1552 order or in the 1641 amparo regarding water.

In the context of this struggle, the complex circumstances of this piece of land began to emerge. Tesayuca claimed to have owned Tetitlan "from time immemorial." In the early 1550s Tesayuca and nearby Texcoco had litigated over the land. The result was a settlement that left Texcoco with two-thirds of the land and Tesayuca with one-third. In the early 1600s, when the land had been flooded, a Spaniard by the name of Juan García Ponce had begun to buy up small plots from Indians in the region. During this time, García had also obtained mercedes to lands within the boundaries of the village of Tesayuca. In 1641, Tesayuca had obtained an order granting it access to water for irrigation. Witnesses' statements and documents indicate that in the mid-to-late 1650s two other Spaniards may have occupied Tetitlan, one of whom hanged himself in the context of a debt dispute involving the land. Residents of Tetitlan may have worked the land as renters during this period. At some point after that, perhaps in the mid-1660s, Tetitlan appears to have been abandoned, as renewed floods rendered the land unfit for cultivation. Indigenous residents had left their houses and moved to Tesayuca. Like surrounding communities, Tetitlan had also seen "much plague," which had depopulated it and kept people away for some years. At around the same time, a Spaniard by the name of Pulido bought the land from Juan García's son, and sought to take possession of it. Some residents of Tesayuca had shown up at the ceremony of posesión to contradict him, but the alcalde mayor had waved them off, insisting the land belonged to Pulido. Pulido allegedly sold the land to Guzmán in the mid-to-late 1680s though, according to witnesses for Tesayuca, Guzmán had never celebrated a proper ceremony of posesión.

The legal crux of this dispute involved two sharply opposed questions: whether "ancient possesion" and the 1552 order adequately grounded Tesayuca's claim or whether Guzmán's claimed possession from previous owners was legitimate. Both sides advanced powerful arguments. Tesayuca, through procurador Galves, argued that the 1552 order constitued indisputable evidence of the community's possession. Guzmán retorted that the order made no mention whatever of Tetitlan. True, Tesayuca had referred to the land as *Tetitlan* in its petition. But Texcoco's petition had used different names to refer to the land, and the audiencia had relied on Texcoco's labels in issuing the 1552 order. Tetitlan, thus, nowhere appeared in the official legal record. In responding to Guzmán's argument, Tesayuca noted that the ceremony of posesión giving possession to Pulido had been faulty and that Guzmán himself had never conducted a proper act of posesión. Pulido, therefore, could not legally pass the land to Guzmán, and Guzmán could not claim legitimate possession.

In closing statements, each side advanced these arguments and pressed several procedural points. Tesayuca insisted that its twelve witnesses outweighed Guzmán's nine, and confirmed what the 1552 order made clear—that these lands had belonged to Tesayuca from ancient times. Nor had Guzmán presented adequate documentary proof sustaining his claim. At some point the lands must have belonged to the Indians, and Guzmán had not shown that he had acquired them legitimately, as royal law demanded. For his part, Guzmán's procurador sought to impeach

Tesayuca's witnesses as speaking solely from hearsay, since they all claimed only "to have heard" about the land's tortured history. Hearsay was admissible in Spanish law, but counted for less than eyewitness testimony.[79] Guzmán also argued that Tesayuca's case made no sense, since the land they claimed rested at the center of his estate. Last, Guzmán's procurador raised a new point: Tesayuca's petition in 1552 referred to *Etetitlan* not *Tetitlan,* and because these two names were different, there could be no certainty that they referred to the same parcel.

In early 1693, after considering the evidence and the arguments, the audiencia ruled in Guzmán's favor on the land, but ordered that both parties have the "use and benefit" of the water. Faced with this loss, the leaders of Tesayuca took on a new procurador, Alexo Verdugo, and appealed. In a long brief, Verdugo characterized Guzmán's argument about the difference between *Etetitlan* and *Tetitlan* as "repugnant to all reason." There may have been some confusion in spelling, he said, but the fact is that after the 1552 settlement order had been issued, Tesayuca had remained in possession of the land that had given rise to the lawsuit. Indeed, continued Vergudo, Tesayuca had not presented the 1552 order as the legal basis for its claim, but only to show that the village had possessed the land in question from before 1552. Tetitlan had been Indian land prior to conquest, and Guzmán had not been able to show with what title he had acquired it. In response, Guzmán's procurador simply reiterated what he perceived to have been the winning arguments, though he did ask that the decision granting both parties access to water be reversed.[80] The audiencia affirmed its earlier decision in a curt order. The leaders of Tesayuca clearly were not happy with the outcome. They continued to press the matter, asking the audiencia to vacate the 1693 order and raising new arguments, until finally the audiencia imposed a "perpetual silence" on them in June 1695.

Because judges were under no obligation to produce written justifications of their decisions, we can only speculate as to the reasoning behind this outcome.[81] Both sides seemed to have advanced persuasive evidentiary and procedural points. But given the fractured nature of land tenure in this region, the fact that Tetitlan was not explicitly mentioned in the 1552 order may have given the audiencia judges pause. If it accomplished nothing more, Guzmán's documentation hinted at how complex and changeable land had been here, especially at the beginning of the seventeenth century. Another point that may have swung judgment in Guzmán's favor is a particular view of the testimony offered by Tesayuca. One of Guzmán's central arguments was that Tesayuca's witnesses spoke chiefly from hearsay. Over and over again, these witnesses stated that *they had heard some residents of Tesayuca say* that Tetitlan had always belonged to them or that Guzmán had run them off the land. The vague quality of these statements appears to have weighed heavily on the mind of someone at the audiencia, who repeatedly underscored the phrase *he heard it said* in the transcripts of the witness testimony offered by Tesayuca. What appears to be the same hand also underscored the statement by one of Tesayuca's witnesses that "he had never seen the Indians of Tesayuca enjoy or plant the land of Tetitlan . . . nor graze cattle on them." In short, judgment may have hinged, in part, on the audiencia's sense that Tesayuca's witnesses were not credible for evidentiary purposes.[82] Guzmán's witnesses, on the other hand, reported from personal knowledge that they had always known Guzmán to own the land, to have succeeded in it legitimately, and to have cultivated it continuously.

This last point may have been the clinching argument in a decision to cut through the knot of claims and counterclaims: Guzmán rather than Tesayuca had actual possession and was making productive use of the land. The alcalde mayor's lieutenant who saw the land reported corn and wheat fields and spoke to Indian *gañanes* living on site who claimed that they had always worked for Guzmán and considered the land to be his. By contrast, some of Tesayuca's own witnesses stated that the residents of Tetitlan had years ago left for Tesayuca because of flooding.

Here was the central lesson of this litigation: in so tangled and unstable a property regime, actual possession and use stood as the strongest argument in any dispute over land. Judges did not enjoy the luxury of eternal vacillation. Disputes required resolution, and barring some sort of agreed-upon outcome judges had to favor one party or the other. When Guzmán finally produced documentation to back up his claim, he could show some evidence of his "title of dominion," but not proof positive. And since *dominio* was an all-or-nothing proposition, the audiencia judges fell back on the principle of actual possession, which amounted to a legal presumption of rightful possession, an ancient rule of Spanish law that found new relevance amid the riotous uncertainty of land tenure in the New World. In a case otherwise undecidable, he who had actual possession would prevail.[83] And given the crown's desire to ensure productive use of land, actual possession was most easily established by pointing to crops in the ground.

It seems unlikely that the litigants in this case were unaware of this rule or at least of its sense. Indeed, knowledge of it, and concern for its implications, may have been the spark that kindled this legal blaze. If Tesayuca's witnesses were correct that Guzmán had begun to cultivate the land only two or three years earlier, then Tesayuca would have had every incentive to challenge Guzmán in order to stop him from establishing actual possession. According to witnesses for Tesayuca, residents from Tetitlan had farmed the land without trouble from neighboring Spaniards until floods in the mid-1660s. During those years Tetitlan's residents had fled to Tesayuca. At that point, Pulido probably saw an opportunity and sought to snatch Tetitlan. Former residents of the site came out to oppose him at the ceremony of posesión, but were dismissed by the alcalde mayor. These residents dropped the matter, and Pulido had done nothing with the land.

By the late 1680s the waters had receded, and in the early 1690s Guzmán, who claimed to have bought the land from Pulido, began to farm it. So long as the land had remained unsown, neither Tetitlan's residents nor Tesayuca's leaders had seen a compelling reason to establish its boundaries. Once Guzmán began to cultivate it, they realized something needed to be done. And so they went to the Juzgado with a petition to mark all of what they thought of as their property, including Tetitlan. But by that time, Guzmán had wheat and corn fields on the land and workers living at the site. Once the lieutenant reported this fact, Tesayuca became an adverse claimant against an actual possessor and ultimately could not overcome the presumption in Guzmán's favor.

The outcome of this case may not have surprised the Tesayuca litigants. They may have sensed that their case was precarious, given Guzmán's possession and given that they were speaking for descendants of a small group of Tetitlan residents who had abandoned the land nearly thirty years earlier. As Guzmán's procurador pointed out in pleadings, if the residents of Tetitlan had wanted to challenge earlier claimants—García and Pulido—they should have brought lawsuits decades ago.[84] They had not, said the procurador, and so Tesayuca could not now do so on their behalf. Here lay the dilemma inherent in the defense of possession and property. Obliged to constant watchfulness, communities had to be ready at a moment's notice to pursue inconvenient and expensive litigation and be prepared to sustain it over long periods. Having just lost their land to floods and survived an epidemic, Tetitlan's residents in the 1660s may have decided not to take up a lawsuit over land that could not feed them or pay their tribute—a decision that came back to haunt them thirty years later.

Communities that took the long view were generally the most successful in defending possession. Individual lawsuits came and went, sometimes resulting in settlements that calmed things down for years, sometimes in judicial rulings that awarded land to one party or another. Such situations were always changeable. The death of parties to a settlement might awaken an issue that had slept for decades. Sale of a piece of land might cause an earlier dispute to spring back to life. An issue forgotten, or left to one side in the interest of local peace and quiet, might be recalled. As Tetitlan's experience suggests, a flagging of zeal in the defense of land could result in its loss. On the other hand, communities attentive to opportunity and threat might succeed in keeping land—if not on terms initially contemplated.

The officers of two Tlaxcala towns, Santa Ana Acolco and Santa Barbara Tamasulco, in the jurisdiction of Ocotelulco, found themselves before the Juzgado in March 1682.[85] Through their procurador, they presented documents in Nahuatl and witnesses stating that the towns had possessed certain lands and had passed them down through several generations. According to the petition, the towns had been in actual possession of the land, cultivating it, until Spaniard Juan Moreno de Acevedo, owner of an obraje in Puebla, bought the adjoining hacienda. Since then, as an Indian witness put it, "he entered the land all the way to the doors of the church and the cemetery, divesting the natives on his own authority of possession in which they had been for many years."[86] After reviewing translations of a series of bills of sale and testaments stretching from 1597 across the seventeenth century, and after considering over a hundred pages of testimony, the Juzgado issued the amparo, ordering the jurisdiction's alcalde mayor to ensure the towns' possession.[87]

In May, the alcalde mayor accompanied representatives of the towns into the countryside, gave them an amparo, and performed a ceremony of posesión. At the crucial moment, Moreno showed up to contradict the claim, "one times, two times, three times and however many more times the law would permit." Notwithstanding this objection, the justice proceeded with the amparo and ceremony of posesión, awarding the land to the towns, "so that they not be dispossessed without being heard."[88]

In August, Moreno filed a petition complaining that the amparo had been incorrectly awarded to the Indians. Since he had been in possession for over a year they were not the actual possessors and so could not have the legal benefit of an amparo. In effect the amparo had wrongly dispossessed him, and he wanted his land back. The Juzgado turned him down, so he took the matter to the audiencia. There his procurador made a subtle, almost diabolical, procedural point. The amparo of posesión, he argued, stated that the Indians should have what they actually possessed. Because he actually possessed the land, they in fact had nothing. But since they had nothing, the amparo had been improperly granted and should be rescinded. The audiencia should therefore return his land without hearing the Indians. In December, the towns responded. Their procurador seemed to have understood Moreno's gambit. He answered that in failing to appeal the amparo itself, Moreno had declined the only "legitimate recourse" open to him. He was therefore estopped from raising any other objection to the amparo.

The procedural heart of the matter was clear. To appeal the amparo would have required Moreno to recognize that the Indians were in actual possession of the land and therefore had a right to be heard. By denying their actual possession, which was the legal premise of the amparo, he sought to keep the towns out of court. He was arguing, in effect, that the justice who had gone ahead in the face of Moreno's contradiction had acted unlawfully, and the Indians should not be allowed to benefit from his mistake. Because Moreno, rather than the towns, had been in actual possession at the time of the amparo, the order could not properly run against him. The procurador for the towns retorted that this amounted to a naked request for restitution without legal process. The Juzgado agreed with the towns and in March 1684 confirmed the original viceregal amparo, leaving Moreno to pursue whatever legal remedies he chose.

At this point, leaders and residents of Santa Ana and Santa Barbara may have heaved a sigh of relief. They had won a major battle that had hinged on whether they would be heard in court. With the presumption of actual possession in their favor, they doubtless hoped that the matter was behind them, at least for a while.

Whether he initially thought the matter not worth pursuing any further or was merely biding his time, Moreno waited until mid-1686 before finally filing a lawsuit against the towns' property. He may have felt quite strongly about the case, for he wrote a vehement petition directly to the king, laying out his case.[89] From that point forward the litigation unfolded along conventional lines. Both sides filed interrogatories and deposed witnesses. Documents were copied and reviewed. Moreno's witnesses, all local Spaniards, staunchly backed his claim to have purchased the property from the heirs of the previous owner, who had "possessed and cultivated" the land in question as a part of his hacienda "in full view, acknowledgement, and tolerance" of the towns' residents. They agreed as well that the towns were not *pueblos* but *hermitas,* small communities without jurisdictional status and thus not covered by laws protecting lands belonging to *pueblos de indios.*[90] The witnesses for Santa Ana and Santa Barbara, all Indians from surrounding communities, echoed the questions framed for their response: the towns were in fact pueblos, and had always been; the land in question had always belonged to the Indians, falling within the 500 *varas* (roughly 1,000 yards) radius to which all indigenous pueblos were entitled by law; and

Moreno had entered on their lands with "force and violence." As was typical of dueling witnesses, the positions could hardly have been more starkly opposed.

With the evidence in, the audiencia awarded Moreno possession and property in the land in July 1687. It is almost impossible in this case to know what led to the ruling. One possibility is the greater weight—one to six—accorded Spanish witnesses as against Indian witnesses. This did not always matter in cases such as this, but it might have here. Another possibility is that three of Moreno's witnesses said that they personally had worked the land in question, as managers of Moreno's hacienda, or as renters. From the towns' perspective, such testimony was obviously biased. But the same could be said of Santa Ana's and Santa Barbara's witnesses, all of whom were leaders of nearby Indian communities who were probably anxious about the status of their own land in the face of potential usurpers.

The towns appealed, alleging procedural irregularities in the original sale on which Moreno relied and pointing out that one of Moreno's own bills of sale had referred to the towns as *pueblos*. To no avail, for in August 1687 the audiencia affirmed its earlier decision. The only solace for the towns in all of this was when they asked for permission to pull up crops they had planted after the 1684 order granting them the land. Moreno, they insisted, should not enjoy a windfall from the decision. The audiencia agreed, recognizing that the towns' residents had "spent much money and work" cultivating the land, and allowed them to harvest the crops as their own.

Despite this loss, the towns were not done. In May 1688, they filed a petition pursuant to a new royal decree declaring that all Indian pueblos were entitled to land in a radius of 600 varas around their villages. Without the land Moreno had taken, alleged the petition, the towns no longer had any means of sustaining themselves or paying tribute. Moreno had so squeezed them that his holdings now came up to the exterior wall of the church, even encroaching on the cemetery. Residents were leaving. Moreno opposed the motion, arguing that a later decree could not upset an earlier judgment. The procurador for the towns responded by noting that the question of 600 varas was a new issue pursuant to a new law. Awarding land under the decree, he claimed, rested entirely within the audiencia's discretion.

In early 1690, the towns petitioned again. When Moreno went to take possession of the land pursuant to the 1687 order, he was accompanied by a royal notary charged with conducting a proper ceremony of posesión. Upon arriving at what Moreno claimed to be the proper spot, alleged the towns' petition, the notary had refused to proceed with the

act of posesión. The land covered by the audiencia's order was somewhere else, concluded the notary, and the land Moreno had indicated
was not that contemplated in the audiencia's order. So as not to "burden
his conscience," this honest notary left Moreno standing in his field,
without possession.[91] According to the towns' petition, Moreno had to
find another notary willing to do the deed without asking questions.
This is the first hint from the towns that Moreno might have been playing both sides of the legal street. At that point the audiencia ordered that
neither party plough the land, so that neither side be able to claim actual
possession. In practical effect this was addressed to Moreno, who held
the land pursuant to the audiencia's order of August 1687. According to
the towns, Moreno violated the prohibition by preparing the land for
planting. Santa Ana and Santa Barbara then produced a statement from
a local priest who swore "in God's name *in verbo sacerdotis*" that the
towns were pueblos for purposes of royal law. The audiencia's legal adviser then wrote that the Indians should be allowed to seek their defense,
without Moreno being able to claim that the matter had been settled.

Here the record stops, without resolution—until 1706, when the audiencia issued a brief order that Santa Ana and Santa Barbara be allowed to measure their 600 varas.[92] Twenty-four years after they had
first sought to mark their lands, they finally succeeded, though not in
exactly the way they might first have imagined. Such an outcome was
possible only because the towns, their leaders and residents, never gave
up on the possibility of prevailing. Their persistence can only have been
the result of a community-wide effort and commitment, for over the
course of twenty-four years many leaders and residents would have
come and gone. It was also the result of the fact that the law did not
shut them out, indeed it kept encouraging them to come back to argue
their case. In the course of this long struggle, they had won, then lost,
and then won again; and who knows whether they might later be challenged anew. We can imagine that even after the measurement of 1706
they knew themselves obliged to constant wariness, for their experience
would have told them that no arrangement regarding their relationship
to land was safe for all time.

These are only two of hundreds, even thousands, of cases in which land
disputes found their way to Mexico City's legal arena. In these deadly
serious struggles, procedure and process figured as a constant. The local
circumstances of a contest might vary from place to place, but would-be
usurpers and those forced to defend their lands fought with similar weapons on roughly level ground. Advantages of forethought, money, status,
reputation, and the competence of procuradores all weighed heavily in

the making of outcomes. But these were not predetermined. Process, procedure, and the law itself appear to have played the dominant role on the stage of these cases.

There were exceptions, cases in which irregularities overwhelmed the formalities of procedure. For instance, in a bitter 1682 dispute between San Pedro Tonayan and San Joseph Miahuatlan, two Indian villages in Jalapa, northwest of Veracruz, a Spaniard appointed first to act as a procurador for one side and then to act as interpreter in the case, removed himself from the proceedings entirely, because "I knew of the passion the notary has" for one party over the other.[93] He had originally acted as the procurador for San Pedro, but after interviewing many witnesses, had come to realize that the notary intended to make the Indians of San Joseph lose the case. When he learned that the leaders of San Pedro had bribed the notary he refused any further involvement: "I am a Christian and do not want the devil to take me because I feel in my conscience that these Indians of San Joseph Miahuatlan are left without any land on which to grow crops." The case went ahead without him, San Joseph alleging further irregularities. San Joseph had originally asked that the land be split evenly between the two communities—seemingly an offer of compromise. Testimony, however, suggested that in doing so they were claiming more land than they were entitled to. When all was said and done, the audiencia ordered that all of San Joseph's lands be measured and that they be awarded that which was properly theirs.[94]

There is no way to determine who was right and who was wrong in this case. San Pedro may well have bribed the notary. But San Joseph may just as likely have been angling for more land than it could properly claim, disguising their ploy as a willingness to concede a fifty-fifty split. At the end of the day, the law did not concern itself with rightness or wrongness at this level. It sought only to determine who had the strongest claim in any particular case. Of course, this meant that struggles over land remained morally ambiguous, for parties seeking land possessed by another could always claim—and even believe—that they were in the right, and parties forced to defend what they thought of as their own risked a judgment that they had wrongly claimed lands belonging to another.

～

Between the mid-sixteenth century and the end of the seventeenth century a massive transfer of land from Indians to Spaniards took place. In the thick chaos of usurpations, squatting, fraud, and manipulation, indigenous landholders looked to the law as their chief defense. In the amparos and in litigation, they rested their claims to possession and ownership on two broad ideas: documentation and productive use. Yet they knew from experience that no claim was proof against challenge: land unused for decades might suddenly be taken from them, forcing a village to register an almost forgotten claim; a merced granted decades earlier might be challenged and revoked; bills of sale dating back years might be ruled too vague to identify the property in question. Although such instability burdened Indians more heavily than Spaniards—for Indians seldom recovered lands once they had been lost—Spaniards also knew that their ownership could be challenged at any time.

In other words, precarious possession rather than a settled right to hold land appears to have been the norm in New Spanish property relations, at least during the first two centuries of colonial rule. Title, in its strictest sense, might best be thought of as an ideal attained only exceptionally throughout this period, perhaps especially among indigenous people. Some grade of possession, always tenuous, was more often the case. Posesión, thus, stood as a capacious and plastic idea that lent a semblance of order to a notoriously muddled property regime. The idea that land ownership was unstable in colonial Mexico is hardly a new one. My concern has been to suggest something of how Indian claimants confronted the shifting mosaic of property through the ambiguities of *posesión* as a central category of legal experience.

It was in this context that productive use became so vital an element of legal disputes over land, because documents rarely proved the single decisive factor in a case. Cultivation of land became a kind of insurance against seizure by another, though no guarantee. For indigenous litigants, this implied a willingness to embrace their status as tributaries responsible to the king's treasury, at least in legal contexts. At a deep level, this meant that every land dispute represented a struggle over the most basic terms of the Indians' engagement with Spanish rule. Land was not just a matter of private property; it was also inherently public and political. Possession, rooted in the idea of productive use, reinforced pre-Conquest notions of land tenure as inherently social and public in the context of a colonial regime that stressed production as a value at once political and economic.[95] What distinguished the two periods is that under Spanish rule, the meaning of land was inseparable from the universal struggle over it.

CHAPTER FIVE

Liberty, Not Servitude

In a scrubby river valley in the far northern province of Conchos, Franciscan friars founded a mission in 1604. The native people of the area were hunter-gatherers interspersed with part-time farmers. In the next five years, the convent at San Francisco de Conchos gathered as many as 4,000 Concho Indians at the mission, evangelizing them according to what by now were time-tested methods. Large numbers of Conchos stayed at the mission, siding with the Spanish during the Tepehuan revolt of 1616–17. By 1622, 2,000 Conchos had settled permanently at the mission, and the convent had become an important recruitment point for Indian laborers who worked on nearby haciendas and in the mine and ore-processing center in Parral, twenty leagues south.[1] During the following two decades, demand for Indian laborers grew. As a formal hiring and distribution system took shape, workers found themselves under increasing pressure from local officials, Spanish and otherwise.

In the summer of 1641, two Concho caciques, Juan Bautista and don Phelipe, set out on the long road to Mexico City, 200 leagues distant, a month-long journey on foot. Upon arrival they contacted Bernardo López de Haro, a procurador at the Juzgado General de Indios. After talking to the two caciques, López de Haro drafted and filed a petition with the Juzgado on their behalf. It opened by noting that the Conchos, since accepting the Catholic faith, had "given obedience to your Majesty and have never had an uprising or disturbance, rather when there have been uprisings in Nueva Vizcaya they have helped the gobernadores of the province in everything."[2] Indeed, stated the petition, the relatively few Conchos Christians had done their best to "conserve in peace" all of those who had settled in the area, including a large number of unconverted Conchos from as far away as eighty leagues toward New Mexico. These caciques had undertaken the "innumerable travails to come ask for justice" from the viceroy because their gobernador, don

Joseph Mulato, had compelled the Conchos to work far beyond what custom and law permitted. He barely gave them rest, making it almost impossible for them to attend to their houses and fields or go to church. Instead, he sent them to labor in Spanish haciendas and mines, paying them a peso and a half a day, and then only in overpriced sackcloth and silk rather than cash. He had also rounded up many of their children, declaring them orphans, and put them out to serve in the homes of Spaniards, even selling some older children as slaves. As a consequence, said the petition, people no longer wanted to work and unbelievers were refusing to "reduce themselves to our Holy Faith"—"why should they be Christians if they and their children are just going to be made into slaves?" Moreover, as a mulatto, don Joseph was legally barred from holding the office of gobernador in an Indian community.

The petition closed by asking that the Conchos be allowed to elect a new gobernador from among their own people, and that local justices "protect them" by ensuring proper pay for work rendered, "put in their liberty" any children in the service of Spaniards, and proceed criminally against don Joseph. In the formulaic response characteristic of amparos, the Juzgado agreed, inserting two paragraphs of a royal decree issued in 1609, one of which stated that the Indians were "by their nature free like Spaniards themselves." In a separate order issued the same day, the Juzgado called upon village leaders to meet and elect a new gobernador.[3]

At its core, the Conchos's petition sought redress for a situation dangerously out of kilter. From their own experience under Spanish rule, petitioners knew that don Joseph had crossed a line in his use of their labor. In recounting his abuses, they were cueing the viceroy to restore a balance between exploitation and protection. The petition described the aggrieved Conchos as obedient to the king and integral to Spanish efforts to secure the northern reaches of empire. By imputing the question *Why be Christians if they were going to be made into slaves?* to the unbelieving Conchos, the petition simultaneously vouched for the converts' loyalty to Spanish rule, reminded the viceroy of Spain's precarious purchase in those wild lands, and held out the veiled threat of recantation among those who were still relative newcomers to the faith.

In one sense, the petition might be understood as a quid pro quo in a spiritual and political economy. It served notice on the viceroy that upon his willingness to protect them from don Joseph and his ilk depended these Conchos's continued willingness to remain good Christians and obedient vassals. And whether petitioners actually intended to frame their situation so crudely, the point was probably not lost on viceroy Conde Villena. Knowing how important the province was to silver mining, conscious of the fact that the population remained sharply divided between converts and heathens, aware that twenty-five years earlier the Indians had risen up against their Spanish masters, he had every reason to rein in an errant mulatto gobernador.

But the petition may well have gone beyond coarse calculation. For while it is true that a jeremiad of suffering played well against a lyric of the Conchos's spiritual and political virtue, we are left with the poignant query regarding Christianity and enslavement. While procurador López de Haro may have posed this fretful question himself, one more element in his rhetorical strategy, within it runs a current of honest sentiment generated from the Conchos's own circumstances. Collectively, these petitioners had accepted Christian faith and opted to live within a Christian polity. Though that choice—the aggregated decisions by thousands of people over three and a half decades—had been made under Spanish duress and influence, it had been a choice nevertheless, for many Conchos and other indigenous people had done otherwise, and continued to do so. That the petition should have made a point of reporting the doubts of those who would not work or believe bespeaks the frustrations of people burdened by the weight of their religious and political commitments. In the context of growing abuses by the likes of don Joseph, and facing what the petition referred to as the "exasperations" of the unbelieving many, the petitioners were now having to answer for the contradictions of a faith and a law that promised liberty yet allowed people to be made into slaves. So, while these converted Conchos attributed the penetrating question to their unbelieving brothers, it seems likely that in repeating it they were also voicing doubts of their own.

That they did so by comparing their situation to enslavement suggests how pervasive notions of liberty had become in New Spain. And by seeking redress in distant Mexico City, they indicated just how widely the acceptance of legal process had spread. People colonized and converted less than four decades earlier had found their way to the center of Spanish legal and political power, much as litigants did in the south, where by the early seventeenth century life had settled down to a kind of routine.

By including the 1609 decree in its order, the Juzgado sought to remind these who wielded local authority, as well as those subject to it, that even in the faraway Conchos legality held sway, and liberty was not to be trampled. Broadly, the law sought to regulate Indian labor—especially personal service and the repartimiento, or distribution of Indian workers to haciendas, households, churches, mines, and obrajes. The central problem, stated the decree, was that Spaniards acted exclusively out of "private profit or convenience" rather than for the "common good." Indians should labor for the "common utility" of the king-dom and, given the "repugnance they show for work," might even be compelled to do so. But they were not to be treated as slaves. They could not be sold, traded, donated, or made the subject of a will, contract, or conveyed along with land, "for they are by nature free [*libres*] like Spaniards themselves." Their pay should be equal to others', "even if for this reason the profits of miners, landowners, and other employers should be reduced." Personal service, except where explicitly permitted by law, was to be abolished, as were all "involuntary" labor arrange-ments. To this end, the king's decree commanded the viceroy to "favor and secure their [the Indians'] *libertad* in such a way that they not suffer violence or compulsion of any sort," "for even if this should result in some inconvenience to the Spaniards the liberty and conservation of the Indians . . . weighs more."[4]

The Juzgado's 1641 order favoring the Conchos petitioners did not reproduce the entire decree, which easily would have run to over a dozen pages even in a tight notarial hand. Instead, it carefully cited chapter fourteen, which asserted Indian liberty and insisted that the Indians' work be voluntary, and chapter sixteen, which spelled out the penalties against all who sought to obtain Indian workers illegally. The tribunal, no doubt, was acting prudently, citing the relevant portions of the law so that the justice charged with enforcing it would know what was being asked of him.

This coming together of grievance and law—the convergence of the petition's ironic juxtaposition of Christianity and enslavement with an explicit legal reference to the Indians' liberty—suggests that libertad could be a matter of contention and aspiration for rulers and ruled alike. Nor was this case an isolated instance. Hundreds of amparo petitions requesting that libertad be protected were filed between the 1630s and the 1680s.[5] In many ways, these are quite similar in tone and language to amparos concerning land, local elections, or abusive alcaldes mayores and gobernadores. But by explicitly invoking libertad, they distinguish themselves and intimate a deep conversation about liberty and its mean-ing among indigenous people and between them and their rulers in a place where the very idea of liberty might seem at best an arid abstrac-tion and at worst a cruel joke.

FREE MEN, NOT SLAVES

Whether or not the Conchos understood the full implications of the question linking Christianity and enslavement, they had pressed on a tender political nerve in posing it. The issue of the Indians' status had been a bone of contention from early on. During the first two decades after Columbus stumbled across the New World, the Spanish monarchy struggled to understand its moral and legal relationship to the creatures that had come to be known as *Indios*. It did not speak with a single voice. In 1503, for instance, Queen Isabel issued a decree ordering that the Indians be treated "as the free people they are, and not as serfs." By contrast, a special junta of jurists and theologians convoked just a year later by King Ferdinand concluded quite unceremoniously that the Indians "should be given" to the Spaniards, implying an almost complete disregard for the question of their liberty, Christian or otherwise.[6] During subsequent decades, Spanish monarchs addressed themselves repeatedly to the question of Indian liberty. A 1526 decree held that the Indians were to be treated as "free men, not slaves." A decade later, the pope stated in his 1537 bull *Sublimis Deus* that the Indians could not be forced to become Christians, for they were "truly men" and "desired exceedingly" to receive the faith. Rather, "they may and should, freely and legitimately, enjoy their liberty and the possession of their property" and should not be "in any way enslaved."[7]

These propositions regarding Indian liberty were thrashed out in the context of sixteenth-century debates over the theological and political challenges presented by discovery of the New World and its people. Following Aquinas, Vitoria and other scholastics concluded that the Indians could not be dispossessed of their "things" or reduced to slavery by Spanish conquest merely because they were infidels.[8] Las Casas sought to put Vitoria's point into practice, arguing vehemently against the encomienda. Holders of these grants, insisted Las Casas, treated the Indians as slaves. In so doing, they had made the king into a "tyrant" regarding the Indians, rather than a "true lord." True lordship required that one of two conditions be met. Either the people of a land subject themselves freely to the king's jurisdiction, or a king might assume rule over them but only for their benefit. The encomienda's brutality, argued Las Casas, was proof enough that it was not in the Indians' benefit. And since native peoples had not spontaneously accepted Spanish rule, their de facto enslavement by the encomenderos endangered the king's just title to govern the New World. The sole answer to this problem, asserted Las Casas, was to abolish the encomienda and declare the Indians free men and not subject to enslavement.[9] This was the gist of the New Laws of 1542, which formed the substrate for all of the crown's future efforts to protect the Indians.

At mid-century, amid the political tensions that sharpened after the New Laws' failure, Las Casas and jurist Juan Ginés de Sepúlveda disputed the Indians' status. The crux of their debate—whether it was lawful for the Spanish king to wage war on the Indians before preaching the faith to them—hinged on whether the Indians were "natural slaves" whose inferiority required that they be ruled by the Spanish monarch for their own good. Sepúlveda presented the brief in favor of "natural slavery." The Indians, he asserted, had not lived by natural reason and had abided by noxious customs, especially human sacrifice. They could not be left to govern themselves, but needed to be ruled, for their own good, until they could learn better habits. As a result, just war could subject them to Spanish dominion, though this did not imply a legal taking of property or a forfeiture of fundamental human liberty. Las Casas rejected Sepúlveda's argument from inferiority, claiming that the Indians were born equal to other men. They were not natural slaves and could only be persuaded to adopt Christianity and accept Spanish rule voluntarily. War, therefore, could not justly be used against them.[10]

Las Casas's and Sepúlveda's famous exchange does not exhaust the complexities of the debate over the Indians' status. The matter exercised many of the best minds of its day, as jurists and theologians struggled to articulate Aristotelian theories of natural slavery to the presence of newfound peoples deemed capable of conversion to Christianity. For Aristotle, humankind had been divided between those who by belonging to themselves were their own masters and thus free, and those who were "natural slaves" because they were by their very nature the instruments of others. The subjection implied in being a natural slave did not deny humanity so much as it simply determined the political relationship men would bear to each other—who was to rule. Natural slavery, thus, was not slavery pure and simple. Nor, in principle, did it expose the natural slave to the caprices of the free. Rather, for those who were by nature slaves, the condition of being ruled for their own good was both "beneficial and just."[11]

All who took up the question of natural slavery in the sixteenth century were forced to grapple with this formulation. The great riddle for these scholars was how to reconcile the inherent inequality of Aristotle's conception, which extended to the soul itself, with the Christian axiom that all humans were equal before God and therefore endowed with natural liberty.[12] For most, the answer involved a shift of emphasis. Where Aristotle had relied on discernible differences between bodies and souls to distinguish free men from natural slaves, Spanish treatise writers left the soul aside, since under a Christian conception all souls were equal, and focused instead on whether some human beings, regardless of their souls, were less intelligent and less civilized—i.e., less rational—than others. Different writers came to disparate conclusions on this question, depending on the relative weight they gave to the Aristotelian heritage or Christian imperatives. This was certainly true of Las Casas, who stressed Christian equality against Aristotle's narrow view that all non-Athenians were natural slaves, and Sepúlveda, who was more concerned to follow Aristotle to the bitter logical end.

The argument over Indian liberty was paralleled by the closely related question of whether Spanish conquerors or Indian survivors held *dominium* over the New World. For Vitoria, the Indians were "true masters" of themselves, and therefore not "natural slaves." As a consequence, "they cannot be robbed of their property," including "rights of ownership over their own bodies and possessions." Domingo de Soto ventured even further in connecting dominium to liberty. He defined *dominium* as "a faculty or right" that a human being "has over anything, to use it for his own benefit," with stress as much on the *faculty* as the *thing*. "Dominium," he concluded, "is founded in liberty."[13]

In the final analysis, the debate over the Indians' liberty was not a purely theoretical one. The varying conclusions reached by these writers cannot be separated from the facts of conquest itself. In 1550, the king had called a halt to all conquest activity while the legal and theological ramifications of Spain's presence in the New World were pondered and debated. Perhaps because the stakes were so momentous, the panel assembled to consider the merits of Las Casas's and Sepúlveda's arguments reached no definitive decision. The options simply were not palatable: either Spain had to relinquish its grip on the New World and wait for the Indians spontaneously to accept Spanish rule, and withdraw if they refused, or it had to impose its will through naked force regardless of justification. One point was not contested: despite their differences on the broader question, both Las Casas and Sepúlveda fundamentally agreed with Vitoria and most other scholastics of this time, that the Indians enjoyed human liberty and could not be reduced to actual slavery, a position from which Spanish kings never departed.[14] In essence, the crown extended to the Indians the long-established legal principle that *libertad* was a supreme good. *Las Siete Partidas* were clear on this point—"all laws ought to favor [liberty] when they can do so in any way, or for any reason." To this end, "it is a rule of law that all judges should aid liberty, for the reason that it is a friend of nature, because not only men, but all other animals love it."[15]

There is no denying that the sixteenth-century defense of the Indians against slavery served political purposes. Friars, whose impassioned pleas were so crucial in framing the issue of the Indians' treatment, sought to dilute the encomenderos' power over the Indians' bodies as a way to assert authority over their souls. Similarly, the crown's stand against Indian slavery was indissolubly linked to a concern for its own power in the New World: an Indian slave could not be a royal subject. Widespread enslavement of the Indians would have sacrificed a public and political relationship between lord and vassals to one of private ownership between masters and slaves; the king would have been left without any subjects in the New World beyond Spaniards themselves.[16] Not only would crown coffers have suffered, for only free subjects could pay tribute, but the king would have had no leverage at all against conquistadores who by controlling people and land might have been all but unanswerable to royal command. This political dilemma largely accounts for "The Ordinances on the Good Treatment of the Indians," issued by Charles V in 1529, in which the king expressed his desire that the Indians "be treated like our other vassals."[17] In essence, the sixteenth-century discourse of liberty in Mexico flowed from juridical and theological disputation regarding Spain's claim to the New World and from political contests over whether Indians would be the private property of ambitious Spaniards or "free men" under the jurisdiction of a king who had only limited means of checking local challenges to his authority.[18]

Even as the debate over Indian liberty raged, indigenous people were frequently employed in forced labor. During the 1530s and 1540s, Indian lords as well as Spanish encomenderos held Indian commoners in a form of indentured servitude dating to pre-Conquest times.[19] Native nobles referred to such people as *tlacotin*. They worked as field hands, as house servants, as porters, as corn grinders, and as spinners and weavers. Spaniards referred to them straightforwardly as *esclavos*—slaves. Although in the fluid situation of immediate postconquest society *tlacotin* and *esclavo* were often used interchangeably, important differences existed between them. Chief among these was that the children of tlacotin did not inherit their parents' status; they were born free.[20] In other words, according to indigenous conceptions, a slave population could not reproduce itself. This distinction faded quickly under Spanish rule and in the face of growing labor needs. By the late 1540s, the European notion of a slave as the absolute property of a master had taken hold. This made it easier for Spaniards to employ Indian slaves in productive enterprises such as mines and sugar mills.

Yet no sooner had out-and-out Indian slavery taken root than it began to wither as a formal institution. Protective legislation, the drumbeat of condemnation from Las Casian friars, and the crown's efforts to conserve its new vassals appear to have had an effect.[21] In 1550, Mexico's first viceroy wrote to his successor Luis de Velasco, alerting him to the fact that Indian slaves had begun to file lawsuits seeking liberty and that he should see to them, as the law demanded.[22] The king's own instructions to Velasco directed him to pay close attention to such lawsuits and to put any Indians working in the mines "against their will" "immediately in liberty so that they may do what they want." Virtually identical concerns were expressed in royal instructions to several later viceroys up to 1590, suggesting that Spanish kings remained aware of the problem even as they had a very difficult time ensuring their will was done.

Distance and the absence of a strong bureaucracy contributed to this problem. At the same time, many Spaniards in the New World may have sensed a fundamental tension in royal solicitude for the Indians: in one breath the king ordered the viceroy to protect natives from mistreatment, in the next he noted that the Indians were "by natural inclination friends of idleness" who could be compelled to work.[23] There was no direct contradiction here. From the crown's perspective, it was simply balancing competing needs—to keep Indians from abuse and at the same time ensure that they contributed to the common good through their labor. To the ears of New World Spaniards eager to avail themselves of indigenous workers, however, the king's statements may have sounded like an enabling equivocation.

This ambivalence cloaked two closely-related forms of forced labor after the decline of formal slavery in the mid-sixteenth century—personal service and repartimiento. Personal service derived from the general sense that the vanquishers were entitled to benefit from the labor of the vanquished. As common as it was, personal service did not reflect crown policy. On the contrary, royal decrees and instructions to viceroys repeatedly condemned it, particularly after promulgation of the New Laws in 1542.[24] In principle, Spaniards were only supposed to use Indian labor when doing so served the common good. In practice, encomenderos, friars, corregidores, ordinary Spaniards, and rich Indians pressed native commoners into service. The repartimiento, or labor draft, represented a more formal mechanism for appropriating labor, ostensibly for public ends. At least on paper, the repartimiento was carefully regulated throughout the sixteenth century. Royal decrees specified how and under what circumstances Indians could be distributed to haciendas, mines, churches, and obrajes.[25] On the ground, powerful Spaniards and Indian nobles often recognized few limits on the exploitation of native laborers. To many ordinary Indians, repartimiento must have seemed all but indistinguishable from slavery.

As long as these two labor arrangements persisted, indigenous workers found it extremely difficult to complain of their treatment. Even establishment of the Juzgado in the early 1590s availed the Indians little with regard to liberty. Up to the 1630s, most amparos aimed to protect land. Only a relative few raised labor issues. None mentioned liberty as an operative legal term. From the 1630s forward, however, amparos specifically concerned with liberty became quite common. What changed from earlier times was that the crown finally saw fit to abolish the repartimiento. Through the latter decades of the sixteenth century and into the seventeenth century, when the Indian population had declined precipitously, workers had been at a premium. Corregidores responsible for apportioning Indian workers controlled the bottleneck of a viceregal economy strapped for labor power. Not surprisingly, corruption and favoritism were rampant.

After 1600, Spanish land owners, especially those holding large haciendas, had begun to resent the power corregidores held over the workforce. As the native population reached its nadir, hacendados with cash flow began to see advantage in the idea of wage labor. The Indians, they argued, should be "free to work for whomsoever they pleased and in any activity they chose, and to go to those employers who offer them the best conditions."[26] A royal decree in 1601 called for an end to the repartimientos, so that the Indians, who were "by nature free [libres]" might come into the public plazas and offer their labor to anyone willing to pay them, "whether Spaniards or other Indians." The decree was comprehensive, addressing itself to all forms of coerced labor whether in obrajes, sugar mills, haciendas, or fisheries. It berated Spaniards for being "full of greed and empty of the fear of God, [for] they have converted many parts of the Indies into societies of perpetual slavery, against all reason and justice."[27] Mines were exempted from the prohibition, as were ecclesiastical properties, though Indians who worked in those places were to be paid and held no longer than the law allowed. The tenor of the 1601 decree was confirmed in the 1609 decree cited by the Conchos, though that law somewhat narrowed the scope of the earlier proscription of forced labor. At this early stage, liberty was being defined in terms of the Indians' relationship to the labor market.

A 1603 case involving the residents of San Juan and Santiago, indigenous neighborhoods of Mexico City, indicated what was at stake during the earliest years of labor reform. Although it is not clear how the matter came to pass, the viceroy commissioned a judge to regulate and administer the hiring of Indian labor in the markets held in the plazas of the two barrios on Tuesdays and Wednesdays each week. The judge was charged with protecting Indian laborers in their "free choice [elección] and will to be hired and to hire themselves out themselves freely" to the "republic of the Spaniards."[28] Not more than one quarter of a barrio's people were required to appear in any given week, so that the others might have time to rest and tend their own crops. Those hired were to be properly paid, and the judge was to punish any "excesses" and "protect [the Indians] and defend them and compel them to come into the plazas to hire themselves out and lend their help to the republic of the Spaniards"—a statement, which from the perspective of our remove several centuries later, neatly reveals how tricky a coin the wages of liberty could be.

This case appears to have been an isolated one. In general, the decrees of 1601 and 1609 languished for nearly two decades without enforcement. Finally, in 1632, the king chastised the crown attorney in Mexico City for his failure to enforce the many laws regarding the good treatment of the Indians. On January 1, 1633, after a long political struggle, King Philip IV finally agreed to suppress the repartimiento of agricultural (but not mine) workers. It had served no benefit, stated the decree, and instead had encouraged the "oppression and inhumanity" of the judges charged with managing labor allocations. All repartimientos must therefore be abolished in order to "conserve the Indians and to relieve my Royal conscience." Four months later the king reaffirmed his "repugnance" for personal service, which had caused so many Indians to be held "as slaves, or worse." Such practices ran against the royal desire that the Indians "enjoy entire liberty and serve me as do the rest of my vassals." In light of all the reports that laws were not being enforced, he ordered the viceroy to "raise and remove precisely and inviolably such personal services wherever and in whatever form they may be found."[29]

As the new legislation took hold, financially flush hacendados were able to attract workers more easily than those lacking cash flow and access to credit. Struggling to keep workers on, many marginal hacendados reacted by attempting to coerce Indians into staying, often by striking bargains with local corregidores who, having been cut out of a lucrative monopoly over local labor, were eager to oblige. This was the moment when Indians began to cite the law and invoke the term *libertad* in amparos as a means of avoiding forced labor. As long as personal service and repartimiento had sheathed corrupt and illegal practices, Indians had had little recourse. With the formal disappearance of these practices, and the expansion of work for wages, forced labor could finally be seen for what it was. Indigenous petitioners seized their chance. Several decades of experience protecting their lands through the amparo led them to broaden its ambit to questions of liberty. Between the 1630s and the 1680s, nearly 500 indigenous petitioners, both individuals and collectivities, appear in the record seeking amparos to protect libertad.

AS IF THEY WERE SLAVES

Liberty in seventeenth-century New Spain had no single face. What jurists and theologians referred to as *libertas humana,* human liberty, was a varied and multiform idea, made more so by the New World's social and political fluidity. Christian liberty, the freedom of will God had granted all men to reject evil and choose obedience and service to Him, was increasingly at odds with political liberty, understood as the freedom of human beings in political communities. Alongside the polemic over whether Indians could be enslaved, Roman notions of liberty as freedom from dependence on others converged with an anxious concern among Spaniards to protect personal liberty from encroachment by what many saw as an increasingly powerful monarchy. Some worried that too much liberty might undermine the foundations of obligation on which the edifice of political life had been erected. *Las Siete Partidas'* avowal that "all the laws in the world constantly favor liberty" and that "All Judges Should Aid Liberty"—Rule I of the final section entitled "Concerning the Rules of Law"—was ever in tension with impositions upon the New World's lower orders, from Indians to blacks to castas.[30]

Given the long history of legal and learned discourse on the importance of protecting Indians from enslavement, it hardly seems fortuitous that amparo petitions for libertad so often framed their complaints in terms of slavery. In case after case, native petitioners came before the tribunal to complain that they were being treated *as though they were slaves,* or *oppressed as if he were a slave,* or that some powerful person was acting *as if he wanted to make a slave of someone who is free.* As often as not, petitions pointed out that such treatment was *in contravention of royal decrees touching on the liberty of the Indians* or more explicitly referred to laws regulating Indian labor. Others went further, specifically citing the 1609 decree invoked in the Conchos case. A few quoted the decree itself, both the phrase that the Indians "are as free as Spaniards," and the proposition that such treatment must be stopped "because though it be inconvenient for the Spaniards the liberty and conservation of the Indians which must so assiduously be sought has greater weight."[31]

By the mid-seventeenth century, this was uncontested legal ground. Solórzano y Pereira mapped out the terrain in the *Política indiana.* Referring to *Sublimis Deus,* to a passel of royal decrees from the sixteenth century, to the writings of Las Casas, Vitoria, and others, Solórzano left no doubt that the Indians possessed the "natural faculty of a man to make of himself and/or to do with himself [*hacer de sí*] what he wishes." This meant, among other things, that the Indians could not be subjected to personal service. Fray Alfonso de la Peña Montenegro, though writing about Peru, reinforced the point in 1663, insisting that the Indians were "free by nature, like all men in the world." Noting that the first Spaniards had treated them "much worse than if they had been slaves," he concluded that it was the Indians' right to live as "free vassals" and counseled confessors not to absolve encomenderos who by "drinking the blood and sweat of the Indians" deprived them of "liberty, the most precious gem that nature gave them, which is worth more than all the treasures of the world." These same points were enshrined in the compilation of laws published in 1680, which in the section entitled "Of the Liberty of the Indians" held that the Indians were "free and subject to no slavery."[32] Slavery, thus, served as a gravitational metaphor that drew attention to the Indians' plight. Petitioners never claimed that they had actually been reduced to slavery, only that they had been treated *as if they were slaves.* Slavery, they knew, was a legal status from which Indians had long been immune, not merely a fact of work conditions, physical confinement, or harsh treatment. Spaniards, from hacendados to mine owners to procuradores and judges knew this as well.

And yet, so common was mistreatment of Indians in the seventeenth century that perhaps nothing short of equating their adversity to slavery would have gained them the sympathy of the powerful, for by doing so petitioners played on a distinction crucial to Spanish notions of self. Widely varied authorities speak to this point. *Las Siete Partidas* had characterized servitude as "the vilest and most contemptible thing that can exist among men," and slavery as worse yet, because the slave "has not even control of his own person." Sixteenth-century scholastics, by the fervor of their polemic, indicated how crucial the contrast was between being by nature free and being by nature a slave. Covarrubias's 1611 dictionary offered as a first definition of *libertad* "that which is opposed to servitude [servidumbre]," for the "free man has as his opposite the slave." Saavedra Fajardo, in his widely read *Emblemas* of 1640, opposed liberty to servitude and insisted that all men possessed not merely Christian liberty but the liberty to "live for oneself."[33]

Faced with the demands of the moment and clutching at a coarse authority, Spaniards and others empowered by the inequalities of colonial reality, may have found ways to forget or ignore the king's laws protecting the Indians. By likening their treatment to slavery, Indian petitioners sought to remind Spanish procuradores, judges, the viceroy, and even the king himself that not only the law but the integrity of underlying normative commitments to human dignity, as well as the royal conscience, were at stake when "miserable" folk came to claim their liberty.

A powerful corollary to this notion can be discerned in cases claiming that petitioners had changed their minds about living and work arrangements. In 1641, Juan Agustín of Coyotepeque, Guautitlan, nearly fifty leagues outside Mexico City, stated that as a lad he had gone to the mines at San Luis Potosí to work for miner Francisco Gómez.[34] He later married María Magdalena, a native of San Luis, "and now does not want to work for him [Gómez] because the arrangement that he has does not suit him [*no es a su propósito*] and [Gómez] compels him with great rigor to serve when it is not his will to do so, and has his wife locked up . . . and a one-year old child." Juan Agustín asked the Juzgado to remedy his situation "so that he might enjoy his liberty serving whomever he likes." The viceroy agreed and issued an order favoring Juan Agustín.

Referring to many earlier viceregal orders regarding the Indians' libertad, the amparo commanded the local alcalde mayor to do "what is necessary in favor of his liberty" and allow him to "serve whom he likes" in that jurisdiction. Above all, the alcalde mayor was to ensure that he not be compelled to serve Gómez, which is "against his [Juan Agustín's] liberty and natural right and decrees of his Majesty," because Gómez only wants him to "serve against his will as if he were a slave." Juan Agustín, his wife, and their child were therefore to be allowed to "live and be where he will" without Gómez or his servants disturbing him, "in keeping with the great number of royal decrees which demand the good treatment, protection, and conservation of the miserable Indians." The tribunal warned that it would send a *receptor* to adjudicate the matter if the alcalde mayor failed to comply with the order.

As this case suggests, the amparo represented one means by which the formality of law could avail Indians in their informal negotiations with employers. People in Juan's situation did not hold the upper hand in haggling over terms. But Gómez and others who commanded land, influence, or office, could not always do just as they pleased. They often had "to tread quite softly" in their dealings with dependents and employees.[35] Juan Agustín had made a decision to move to San Luis to serve a particular Spaniard with whom he had reached an arrangement regarding the terms of service. Several years on, having married and had a child, he wanted a change. Perhaps as a husband and father he felt the dangers of mine work more keenly. Perhaps he had asked for better terms from Gómez and been refused. Perhaps he simply wished to move for purely personal reasons. Regardless, his situation with Gómez no longer "suited" him—the word of a man who knew himself to have some leeway. Gómez's reaction of confining Juan's wife and child was typical of the time and place. Mining in San Luis had declined 50 percent between

1630 and 1641, and the labor shortage in the region was severe. In such circumstances, a miner might do almost anything to keep his workers, even lock them up and hold their families.[36] But workers were not without recourse. So Juan Agustín had journeyed to Mexico City to assert his will against Gómez's, something no slave could have done.[37]

Although we cannot know precisely how Juan understood his situation, the phrase *so that he might enjoy his liberty serving whomever he likes* offer some clues. Juan had not petitioned for the absolute liberty to do as he pleased. Neither the 1609 decree nor treatise writers contemplated this sort of liberty. Rather, the liberty he sought was the ability to haggle over the terms of his employment. Labor in New Spain had become increasingly fluid and contested by 1600 in response to depopulation and structural scarcity. Workers like Juan could often bargain over wages, place of abode, and freedom of movement. Some bosses were more amenable than others, but few could simply dictate terms. In most instances, people in Juan's position first sought to strike a deal with an employer. Typically they went to court only if these negotiations failed and the employer resorted to coercion, as in Juan's case.[38] In short, tight labor markets and the possibility of legal redress favored dependents in bargaining over the terms of their work lives. Liberty, for Juan, meant preserving this power to negotiate. While the phrase *enjoying liberty to serve whomever he likes* may ring contradictory to modern ears, it expresses the dominant idea that liberty existed only in relation to the obligation to advance the common good by working according to one's place in the social order.

It is worth noting in this connection that pre-Conquest Nahua labor regimes had accepted similar notions. All commoners had been obliged to perform unpaid work on behalf of the commonweal—repairing roads, building temples, tending common fields. The fact that they were under compulsion to do so—those who refused could be punished—in no way infringed on their status as free people. Beyond communal labor, the Nahua had also recognized a continuum of obligated labor that fell short of outright slavery in the European sense of the word. Under this arrangement, a person might put himself out to work for another, most commonly for a period of time, though in principle there was no bar to selling one's labor for life. Alternatively, a debtor might be obligated to a third party in order to satisfy the debt. While employers were entitled to coerce those who did not perform as promised, such workers remained free persons for all legal and social purposes.[39] In other words, even from the perspective of pre-Hispanic Nahua tradition, there was no contradiction in the idea of being free and also being compelled

to work. Elements of this understanding carried over to the postconquest period. Debtors in sixteenth-century Tlaxcala, Puebla, or Cholula
might sell their services to an obraje for a period of years, or be obliged
to by judicial order, without thereby becoming slaves.[40]

How would the likes of Juan Agustín have learned of their right to
liberty? In many instances, procuradores doubtless supplied the phrase
as if they were slaves, calculating the effect such a statement might have
on Spanish judges, particularly in the Juzgado, explicitly charged with
protecting the Indians. This is no reason, however, to assume that petitioners were oblivious to the advantages of invoking slavery in their
defense of liberty. By the mid-seventeenth century, the crown had issued
dozens of decrees regarding the Indians' libertad. The 1609 law may
have been the most oft cited of these, perhaps because Philip III had
ordered it to be publicized by crier in all of the provincial head towns
(*cabeceras*) of Mexico, "so that news of it will reach everyone and they
will know what for their good and utility has been ordered."

The Indians did not have to await a crier to learn of the king's legislation. Many acted on their own initiative to find out about laws affecting them. In October 1633, the indigenous residents of Coyuca and
Tistlantzingo, in Acapulco, requested and were granted a copy of the decree issued in Mexico City just ten months earlier abolishing the repartimientos and "leaving the Indians in their liberty." The record does not
indicate what prompted them to do so. There is merely a marginal nota-
tion opposite the document testifying to the viceroy's execution of the
law indicating the request and that it was granted. In 1655, the Indians
of San Francisco Ystaquimastitlan noted in their petition that decrees
"touching on our protection, ordering that nobody mistreat or bother
the Indians" had recently arrived in their village.[41]

Official sources may have been the least common way Indians found
out about laws favoring them. Liberty was so fundamental a concept
that tidings of laws touching on it must have circulated widely through
informal networks of communication.[42] One successful case in a given
town or village would certainly be news in surrounding villages whose
residents, knowing of the outcome, might be emboldened to file a petition of their own at some later time. Moreover, the very fact that native
petitioners from all over Mexico converged on the capital for legal business guaranteed that they would learn as much from other litigants in
the city's abundant *pulquerías* (local taverns), in its numerous markets,
at the inns where they stayed, at the restaurants where they ate, as from
their procuradores.[43] Having finished in the great metropolis, they returned to their villages and undoubtedly told anyone who would listen
of what they had learned during their adventures.

This begs the question of how the Spanish concept of *libertad* was communicated. Those who understood some Spanish would have been able to recognize the word itself, without translation. Indians who had traveled to Mexico City, conversed with a procurador, filed a petition, and received a written order would almost surely have come away with a working understanding of the word, even if they could not read the document they had obtained. But in talking to others, they may often have done so in native tongues. In Nahuatl, for instance, *libertad* does not appear in lists of accepted loanwords for the seventeenth century, which means that in day-to-day conversations with each other Nahuatl speakers likely used a Nahuatl word to convey meaning. The Spanish-Nahuatl section of Molina's bilingual dictionary gives as a first translation of *libertad* the Nahuatl *tlaca xoxouhcayotl,* which in the Nahuatl-Spanish section of the dictionary Molina rendered back into Spanish as the "liberty of the one who is free and not a slave."[44]

We must be extremely cautious in reading Molina's translations. The Spanish definition of the Nahuatl runs very close to the definition of *libertad* given in Covarrubias's dictionary of Castilian, and Molina's biases and ignorance in translating Nahuatl terms cannot be completely untangled or accounted for. Even so, the centrality of slavery as a controlling metaphor for both terms is arresting. It strongly suggests that there was no necessary gap in understanding if and when Nahuatl speakers used *tlaca xoxouhcayotl* to talk about what they were doing in seeking an amparo to secure their liberty.

Pre–sixteenth-century indigenous and Spanish slaveries were distinct, but shared important characteristics. Both involved the legal subjugation of some people to the will and power of others. Both understood the slave as one who performed socially degrading work. Seventeenth-century Spanish legal notions of slavery may have bloodlessly defined the slave as one under the jurisdiction of another, rather than one's own.[45] *Las Siete Partidas,* however, characterized the slave's condition as "servile" and "contemptible."[46] Pre–Conquest Nahuatl speakers shared this sense. In Olmos's *Metaphors,* the "slave" (*esclavo*) is described in Nahuatl not only as poor and malleable, but also as living "in the place of urination, the place of excrement" and as "fated to urine and excrement." Molina's dictionary suggests the same link: the Nahuatl word for freeing someone from servitude was *cuitlatlaça,* where *cuitlatl* was the word for excrement. The "servant or vassal of someone," by contrast, was characterized in the *Metaphors* as the instrument or utensil of another, but without a scatalogical attribution and without the sense of fatedness defining the slave.[47]

How much of this sensibility survived into the seventeenth century is anyone's guess. Much changed in the everyday lives of Mexico's indigenous people in the century and a half after the fall of Tenochtitlan. Yet such things do not quickly fade from language and thought and may linger longer in the gloaming of psyche. Many Indians experienced first hand the degradation of slave-like treatment, or witnessed the rough handling of black slaves, especially on haciendas or in the mines. Both would have tended to reinforce a strong sense that the slave's lot was one of degradation, allowing older meanings to retain currency. If so, then at a deep level ancient Nahuatl's linking of slavery and scatology hints at deeper motivation: that in seeking amparos to protect liberty, petitioners may have been responding not only to a legal category and the fact of abuse, reasons enough to pursue a remedy, but as well to psychological cues regarding the social meaning of their situation. Through half-remembered intimations as much felt as understood, they must have been as concerned for their dignity and integrity as human beings as with the unfortunate and painful facts of their treatment.

LIBERTY IN PLACE

Whatever the underlying motivations, petitioners' struggles for liberty were circumscribed by colonial realities. Solórzano y Pereira clarified the bounds within which petitioners had to act. By law, Indians enjoyed libertad because, no less than other men, they possessed "the natural faculty a man has to do with himself as he wishes." But, he concluded, quoting Tacitus, they "cannot be permitted total liberty, nor made to suffer or endure total servitude." In other words, they could not be enslaved but their liberty was "conditional" on dedicating themselves to some useful occupation, contributing to public works, paying tribute, attending mass, and discharging other obligations befitting their status as the "feet of the republic."[48] To enjoy libertad was to be a vassal of the king, subject to his protection but obliged to commensurate duties on behalf of the common good.[49]

In practical terms, the amparos suggest that one of the most common understandings of liberty was keyed to the idea that indigenous petitioners should be allowed *to be and to live where they will in keeping with your Majesty's royal decrees*. Of course, the expression could vary slightly from petition to petition, but the essence of the request was the same wherever it appeared—that petitioners be able to choose where to live. This did not imply they could choose just anywhere. Rather, petitioners invariably asked to be allowed to return to their homes or villages, to live there without being "disturbed" (*inquietados*).

In 1653 Francisco Martín, an Indian resident of the pueblo of San Nicolás, Tlaxcala, asked the tribunal to allow him to "go live in my village, where I pay your Majesty's tribute and have my house and my lands and my wife and a son." During several years, he had been serving a certain Spaniard to work off a debt. When his employer died, those who came into possession of the estate had subjected him to "much injury and vexations and bad treatment." He asked that the tribunal allow him to pay off the remaining debt immediately—implying that up to that time his work on the hacienda had not been entirely coerced—and move back to his home village so that "the said Spaniards not disturb me and allow me to live freely [*vivir libremente*] . . . as his Majesty commands." The tribunal agreed, ordering the Spanish governor of Tlaxcala to grant his request and ensure he was not bothered by any person.[50] Hundreds of other cases advanced similar pleas.[51] Most were framed against the abuse of labor arrangements by Spaniards or less commonly by Indian gobernadores.

The language of the petitions and the amparo orders indicate how petitioners may have understood their options. A 1654 case helps crystallize the point.[52] Petitioner Juan Tomás, from Santiago Tecali, complained through his procurador Agustín Franco that "forcibly and against his will" he was being made to serve Spaniard Pedro Martín without pay "as if he were a slave." Juan asked that he be allowed to "live where he will in keeping with his Majesty's decrees." The tribunal agreed, ordering the local corregidor to let him "be and live freely in his village."

It is unlikely that Juan perceived any gap between what he had requested and what he was granted, for he almost surely had not thought of himself as asking to live just anywhere in requesting *to live where he will.* Even if he had not known before venturing to Mexico City to file his petition, he would surely have understood after the fact that he did not have full liberty of movement. Among "other kinds of people and vassals there is this liberty" to move about unfettered, as Solórzano y Pereira noted.[53] The king's indigenous tributaries, however, were a different case. For them, the liberty *to be and to live where they will* implied a freedom from being forced to live in places outside their home towns. Juan, in other words, had the liberty to choose to live in his own village and not somewhere else. While this may seem confining, it distinguished the Indians from slaves, who had no legally enforceable choice of where to live.[54]

For many Indians, perhaps most, life was inseparable from their obligations regarding the place they lived. As with the amparos more generally, acknowledgment of tributary and religious obligations furnished petitioners a means of claiming the king's protection. Villages and groups of Indians appear to have been especially likely to advance this type of argument. A whole village alleging an inability to pay tribute pressed more deeply than did an individual on a royal conscience never forgetful of fiscal concerns. The tone of such cases varied. Petitioners might allege plainly that certain Spaniards favored by the local alcalde mayor were making it impossible for the Indians to pay tribute. Others might rail against the practice of distributing Indian workers to haciendas and households and plead that they be allowed to meet their tribute quotas and "be put in liberty so that we may hear mass and do all the other things of Christian doctrine." In certain instances, petitions could make the point less directly, but no less powerfully. The Indians of the village of Metepeque and its environs brought their woes to the Juzgado, asserting they had been forced into personal service "against their will" and in contravention of royal decree. Spaniards had literally thrown money at their feet, proclaimed them in debt, and then used the debt as a pretext to put them to work without pay. As a consequence, stated the 1658 petition, people were fleeing the village.[55]

Of course, there was an inescapably instrumental quality to these and other cases in which petitions asserted tributary duties. But there is no reason to conclude that this convergence was empty of significance beyond a tight-lipped resignation to an ineluctable fate. Indian petitioners understood that there were political implications to the unavoidability of their obligations. They knew from long experience that everything depended on tribute. Indeed, payment of tribute might be thought of as a barometer of colonial relations. Tribute met in a timely fashion signaled that a local situation was more or less stable. This did not imply an absence of frictions, only that neither internal disagreements nor external abuse had reached a crisis point. It may even be that over the seventeenth century petitioners came to see the untroubled payment of tribute as a proxy for basic legal order. We might even suppose that tribute and liberty became paired ideas, realities that figured as contested principles to live by, embodying a vital hope for liberty as freedom from abusive arbitrariness.

Nahuatl speakers may have had an independent linguistic basis for entertaining such a hope. Molina's dictionary offered as a second equivalent to the Spanish *libertad* the Nahuatl word *tlacaconemiliztli,* which when rendered from Nahuatl into Spanish gave "a secure, pacific, and calm life." This rendering of *libertad* must be approached with care. An obvious concern is definitional asymmetry: Molina gave *libertad* as *tlacaconemiliztli;* by contrast, *tlacaconemiliztli* from Nahuatl to Spanish did not give *libertad.* Although Molina almost surely did not act out of a self-conscious ideological motive, this incongruity suggests he was aware of the potentially disruptive power of *libertad* and sought instead to emphasize the more bucolic notion of liberty as a *secure, pacific, calm life*. Yet, there is no a priori reason to dismiss the possibility that Nahuatl speakers could connect *tlcaconemiliztli* to *libertad*. The amparos did not seek *libertad* in the abstract, but *libertad* as a locally and spatially defined liberty to be in a place, free of forces from within and from without, that would drive residents away from their villages. From this perspective, and for all the toils of meeting tribute exactions, villages were often havens where Indians could find a burdened and ever-tenuous promise of security, peace, and calm—the liberty of being where they belonged and where others might be prevented from disturbing them.

A petition filed in 1664 by an Indian family from Pachuca brings this more general claim into sharp focus.[56] According to the petition, Augustín Phelipe, his wife Pascuala María, their son and his wife and daughter claimed they had been raised in the service of widow Luisa Vázquez, who for many years had seen to their needs, as they had to hers. Upon her death, the executor of the estate had given Augustín and his family over to Spaniard Sebastián Roldán in satisfaction of a debt Augustín owed the widow. Roldán had then moved his entire household, including all his servants and slaves, from the Pachuca mining district to a hacienda near San Augustín Tlaxco, a village in Tlaxcala, more than fifty leagues from the petitioners' homes. There, alleged procurador Luis de Lezeña Matienso on the petitioners' behalf, Roldán had put the men to work in the fields and the women in his home, "against their will because he took them from their homeland [*patria*] and nature [*naturaleza*] where they were born and raised." He had kept them there eight months, but at the first opportunity they had fled back to Pachuca, where they had built ranches and erected houses. They feared Roldán would come after them and take them back to Tlaxcala "with violence and against their will and in contravention of his Majesty's decrees and orders from the government . . . which allow the Indians to live where they wish." They asked that their *libertad* be protected, so that they might choose for whom to work and where to live. The tribunal agreed and issued an order allowing the petitioners "to be and to live freely in their village."

Petitioners were not denying that they could be required to move. The law was clear on this point. The king could demand that his vassals, including the Indians "free though they might be," leave their villages and homes to move elsewhere, but only "so long as it is understood that this must be for public utility, better government and conservation of his [the king's] state."[57] Their point, rather, was that no private person could do this. Sebastián Roldán's actions thus offended on three counts. First, by removing the Indians, as he had done once and petitioners feared he might do again, he had usurped the king's authority. Second, he could claim no legitimate public reason for having done so. The text of the decree suppressing the repartimientos in 1633 precluded any such argument by explicitly noting that the repartimientos had "resulted in no convenience, utility, or benefit to any farmer." Third, by taking Augustín and his family away from their homes, he was interfering with the libertad of five of the king's most defenseless vassals. Augustín was not asking to be removed from Roldán's power, for he had already escaped of his own accord. He sought instead an order that would prevent Roldán from storming their homes and spiriting them back to the hacienda. By referring to their *patria* and *naturaleza*—the only case I have come across using precisely these words—Augustín signaled that he wished to live where the king's law gave him the liberty to live. In this light, Roldán's efforts to force Augustín and his family to live elsewhere were revealed for what they were—actions motivated by purely private and therefore arbitrary ends, or at least that was the legal conclusion Augustín's petition pressed upon the tribunal.

THE INJURIES OF LICENSE

While *as if they were slaves* and *to be and to live freely* succinctly evoked the tribulations of petitioners' lives and offered a kind of answer to their woes, they alone were not always sufficient to the narratives of harm petitioners wanted to tell. For though the former anchored legal claims that a person's will was being overridden and the latter grounded the most commonly requested remedy, neither conveyed the depth of outrage aggrieved petitioners often felt at their treatment or revealed the nuances of power relations within which they had to figure a stance for their humanity. In such situations, petitioners and their procuradores often turned to another formulation to frame their complaints.

In 1653, Juan García filed a petition with the Juzgado claiming that he had been serving on a Oaxaca hacienda for over nine years. The land had changed hands several times, passing from the original owner to his wife, to her new husband, and finally to a buyer, don Rodrigo de Lucera. Don Rodrigo had died and somehow his mulatto slave Nicolás had taken charge of the place. According to the petition, Nicolás "with a powerful hand made bold by the death of his master" had compelled Juan to serve him, causing Juan "vexations of word and deed and whipping him cruelly, as he has done other times." To make matters worse, Nicolás had forced a twenty-five peso debt on Juan to keep him from leaving the hacienda. All of this contravened his Majesty's decrees "which are so attentive to the protection and good treatment of the natives of New

Spain," to the point that Juan was prepared to lodge a criminal complaint against Nicolás if something was not done so that he could "live freely"[*vivir libremente*]. The tribunal agreed on every point, ordering that the abuse stop, that Juan be allowed to live where he wished, and that Nicolás be prosecuted.

Juan's bitterness over his situation breaks through the blandness of the petition. He was being forced to serve on an hacienda against his will by a slave who flogged and insulted a man who by law could not be enslaved. But where a Spanish master might lash an Indian in order to keep him working, Juan's petition hinted at a deeper hurt. For Nicolás's *powerful hand* had been "made bold" by his master's death.[58] The implied harm was a double one: not only physical duress, which was obvious enough, but also the psychological pain of being so ill treated by a mere slave. The phrase *de obra y palabra*—by deed and by word—was a telltale. A term of pleading art, it bespoke an injury not only to body but to honor and reputation as well. We cannot know from the record exactly what Nicolás said. *Cabrón* (cuckold) and *perro* (dog) were two insults commonly hurled at Indians. We can suppose that whatever epithets Nicolás chose, he spat them out as he struck Juan. Nor can we know exactly how the beatings took place, though Juan may have been restrained in some way and at the end he would have been on the ground in pain, a visible inversion of hierarchy, as a slave stood over a free man. In a society soaked in the language and gesture of status, this might have been unpleasant enough from the mouth and hand of a Spaniard, who had a claim to deference, however undeserved. Coming from a slave it must have been positively infuriating and particularly degrading because ordinary people, including slaves and Indians, had clear notions of honor and were extremely sensitive to personal slights.[59] They could not always respond, given their constraints. When they did it was often with violence, as with Nicolás, or through the law, as with Juan.

While few other liberty amparos involved so dramatic a social reversal, many seem to have expressed a type of righteous indignation over treatment that went beyond the simple appropriation of labor. No one petition tells the whole story. But as a mosaic, liberty amparos reveal a clear sense of inner wounding and resentment.[60] In 1654, the residents of San Francisco Ystaquimistlan complained that a mulata servant of the local priest was obliging them to spin and weave without giving them anything to eat, in essence subjecting them to someone who, if not a slave just as easily could have been. In 1656 in Guexotzingo, several petitioners complained that an hacienda steward and a black man stole into their homes in the dead of night, tied them up, and took them to

work on the hacienda, *as if they were slaves,* threatening to kill them
if they tried to escape. In 1661, Diego Martín told the tribunal that an
hacienda steward would enter his house in the middle of the night, take
him by force to the hacienda, and tie him to a tree and whip him like a
slave.

Olmos's *Metaphors* offer some sense of how deeply Nahuatl-speaking
petitioners may have felt the injuries alluded to in these cases. Metaphor
XVI opens with a Spanish gloss: "I live the life or I live with fatigue
lacking what I need I walk offended."[61] The Nahuatl text beneath has
been rendered into English as follows:

> Still I carry myself, I shelter myself.
> I consume my face, my heart, my spirit.
> You honored ones appear, you see my plight.
> My midnight sustenance, my morning sustenance
> Appear not, are not seen.
> Inside another's house, in another's corner
> Still I breathe in shame and longing.

The tone here is one of heart heaviness at being in the power of another. Unnegotiated dependence implied not only having to carry and
sustain oneself, but knowing that those with power recognized one's
plight and did nothing to remedy it. The Metaphor suggests as well how
morally powerful a claim *to be and to live freely in their villages* may
have been, for the closing lines conjure the image of a person cowering
in the corner of someone else's house, yearning for escape to his or her
own home. Across the long stretch of time separating the writing of the
Metaphors from the filing of amparos in the mid-seventeenth century,
this hints at deep emotional stirrings beneath the hard surfaces of legal
language.

In this connection, it is striking that *maquixtia,* Nahuatl for *to save,*
literally meant "to remove (someone) from the hands (of others)."[62]
Molina's dictionary gave forms of the verb *maquixtia* as translations for
to rescue (rescatar or *redimir)* as well as for *to save (salvar).*[63] Indians
may have heard the word most often in a religious context—in a sermon
or in the confessional. Molina's 1569 bilingual confession manual for
priests, written in Nahuatl and Spanish, also equated the two, coun-
seling confessants to uphold the ideal of Christian liberty by "freely
serving, fearing, and having reverence for and obeying your one and only
Lord God so that you may be saved."[64] Nahuatl religious plays from the
sixteenth to the eighteenth century also translated *rescue, save,* and *re-
deem (rescatar, salvar, redimir)* as forms of *maquixtia.*[65] In the sixteenth

century, Christ had been more often portrayed as a savior than as a judge, and in Nahuatl religious texts it was common to use forms of the verb *maquixtia* in connection with Christ acting as a rescuer of captives, "freeing people from the hands of demons."[66] Molina's manual represented this issue graphically. In two different instances, a woodcut depicts a woman kneeling before a priest, hands clasped, in an attitude of penitence. A demon stands behind her, one hand on her head, the other on her chest, mind and heart enslaved—the perfect representation of what it was to be in the hands of a demon.[67]

Resemblance of this picture to the language of the amparos is striking. Figuratively, petitioners wanted to be "removed from the power" of those who held or hurt them (demons) so that they might "live in *libertad*" (be saved).[68] Although the association is necessarily tenuous, indulging it might allow us to see a special poignancy in the close metaphorical parallels between *powerful hands* as a description of the problem Indian petitioners faced and *maquixtia* as a solution rich in the meaning and promise of salvation.

Libertad as salvation aimed not merely at freedom from slave-like conditions but also freedom from the arbitrary power of others. The distinction is subtle but important. Indians could not be enslaved because since the sixteenth century Spanish law had held they could not. Complaints of being treated *as if they were slaves,* were petitioners' way to ask the tribunal to uphold the principle that their labor not be taken without their consent. The gravamen of the claim was the insult to their legal status as men who by law could not be reduced to servitude. By contrast, when petitioners alleged that *powerful hands* had subjected them to *mistreatment by deed and by word* and when the tone of their narratives of harm stressed the indignities of abuse, they were seeking to confine the exercise of power within the bounds of legitimate and recognized hierarchical relationships.

Although there are resonances here with Roman and seventeenth-century notions of liberty as that state countenancing neither dominion by nor subjection to another person, these cases seem to be articulating an understanding of liberty growing specifically out of the interaction between Spanish legal principles and the circumstances of Indians' lives.[69] When individual native petitioners came before the Juzgado begging protection in their liberty, they were not asking to do just as they wished. From their perspective the problem was that so many others did precisely that, with grievous consequences for so many Indians. This is what they wanted stopped. Even without having read the *Política indiana*, Indian petitioners could have agreed with the idea behind Solórzano y Pereira's claim that "the most important liberty is that we all be ser-

vants of the law." Perhaps more acutely than Spaniards, Indian commoners would have understood what might happen "if everyone were to
take license to proceed at their free whim and will," because they were
so often on the receiving end of just such license. In essence, they sought
the liberty of living in a world where everyone else would be bound by
the laws as they were so that they might be free of the intrusive liberty of
others and subject only to the legitimate power of the king's law.[70]

COMMON LIBERTY

Villages might also dispatch members to Mexico City in search of amparos to protect liberty understood collectively or at least corporately.[71]
These petitions expressed village identity by referring to the *gobernadores, alcaldes, común y naturales*—governor, councilmen, common,
and residents of this or that pueblo—making it clear that the request was
not an individual one. Corporate personalities were hardly new in
seventeenth-century Mexico. Pre–1521 Aztec society had borne a distinct corporate cast, in landholding, in political structure, and in spa-
tial organization. Yet village identities asserted in amparo petitions were
not merely holdovers from ancient times. They came to life where fading
memories of the pre-Hispanic past met the dislocations and changes of a
century of conquest. As amparos indicate, shared work, shared suffering,
shared festivities, and shared subjection to powerful others defined these
identities—as had always been so. But from 1600, the shared experience
of legal process contributed crucially to sustaining them. Law, in other
words, did not merely protect collectives. It also helped villages articulate
a sense of unity to themselves. Petitioners might seek relief so that villagers could "repair their church and do other things necessary to the republic," or recover "goods belonging to the community." Petitions framed
in the first person plural referred directly to "our village," "our obligation," "our land," and "our community."[72] At the same time, claims
to community were neither permanent nor emblematic of a communitar-
ian idyll. The very instabilities of colonial life prompting villages to seek
protection also ensured that affirmations of community would be fragile
at best.

One faction within a village might purport to represent the community but find itself accused of acting for purely private ends. Residents
of three villages in Tepexpan, for example, complained to the viceroy
in 1638 that the Indian leaders of the *cabecera,* "with the color of the
community," compelled them to gather at the head town and sent them
off to work in Spanish houses and haciendas for eight to ten days at a

time, without pay. As a consequence, petitioners were unable to tend their community fields.[73] The case bears close scrutiny for a couple of reasons. First, petitioners identified themselves in the vaguest possible way as the *naturales*—native residents—of the affected villages, without mentioning gobernadores, justices, or alcaldes. It is impossible to know whether these officials went unnamed because they were reluctant to go against cabecera leaders, who may have been well connected among local Spaniards, or because they opposed the petition. We cannot discern, in other words, whether the petition enjoyed the tacit support of unmentioned local officials or enacted a small rebellion against them. The ambiguity may have been deliberate on petitioners' part: by denying elected officers an explicit role in the proceedings, the petition deftly palmed the question of whether this was a jurisdictional dispute between cabecera and subject villages or an internal challenge to local authority, either of which could have made the matter much messier for the tribunal than it appeared to be on its face. While this does not resolve the question, the very fact of ambiguity is telling, for it indicates how deeply situational claims to community could be.

Second, petitioners were advancing a collective interest against cabecera leaders who sought to cloak their actions *with the color of the community*. The implication this charge was meant to convey is clear: while leaders at the cabecera claimed to be acting on behalf of the community, they were in fact pursuing purely private ends, their own and those of the Spaniards with whom they were in league. We have no words from cabecera leaders, but they surely knew of the recent law abolishing repartimientos and personal service. Petitioners certainly knew of the king's decree, citing it in their petition. Leaders at the cabera had undoubtedly been parceling workers out to Spanish haciendas and houses for years. Faced with the petitioners' challenge and the 1633 decree's prohibition, they had probably sought to justify the practice by accusing petitioners of shirking work on behalf of the wider community. The case is important, for the dispute at its core reveals not merely a contest over resources, in this case labor, but a conflict over what was to count as the relevant community for legal purposes and who was entitled to speak for it.

If cases of this sort were not uncommon, neither were they the rule. In many others, especially when Indian petitioners had a clear grievance against a Spaniard rather than an Indian, there is a strong sense that a case filed by *the gobernador, justices, councilmen, común, and naturales* expressed something like village unity in the face of adversity. In these, the interests of local indigenous power brokers more often tended to coincide with those of commoners. For all the pressures weighing it down, the idea of community thus figured as an inescapable focus of attention, competition, and yearning for those who lived in Indian villages during the seventeenth century.

When villagers sent representatives to Mexico City seeking liberty for their communities, they mostly wanted the same thing individuals did—relief from repartimientos and personal service—and used the same language. The *común y naturales* of Patlanala for example, sent a delegation to Mexico City in spring 1640, a 200 league trip each way. They wished redress for abuses by the head bailiff of the Xilacayoapa mines, who routinely ordered one of the village councilmen to send seven Indian men and women to serve him, the notary public, and other Spaniards each week, claiming that he did so by order of the alcalde mayor. None of the Indians was paid more than two reales, and they were constantly "mistreated by deed and by word." They asked that the alcalde mayor be ordered to enforce the king's decrees prohibiting personal service so as to "protect them in their liberty."[74] The tribunal agreed and issued the order, adding that they were not to be made to work "against their will."

The lexicon of *libertad* in these cases was the same as in petitions filed by individuals: *as if they were slaves, against their will, mistreatment by deed and by word, powerful hands,* references to the 1609 decree, and statements highlighting obligations to pay tribute and go to church. To this extent, amparo petitions seeking liberty in a collective or corporate register seem unremarkable, a simple extension of a language worked out first for individuals.

From another perspective, however, their collective emphasis runs counter to the trends of the period. Contemporary Spanish notions of liberty were increasingly in tension with the idea of a collective or corporate right to liberty. Covarrubias's definition of *libertad* was decidedly individualistic, opposing liberty first to servitude or captivity, and following with a Latin definition of liberty as the natural faculty to do as one willed within the limits of what was prohibited. He then offered various illustrations of liberty—as a lack of emotional attachment to others who might cause injury (citing Ambrosius), as a freedom from the "miserable slavery" of vice (citing Erasmus)—and closed with a reference to liberty as the freedom of conscience sought by Protestant heretics. Solórzano y Pereira at mid-seventeenth century echoed Covarrubias, quoting Aristotle for the proposition that liberty was "the natural faculty of a man to do with himself as he wishes." This understanding appears to have been quite stable over time. The early eighteenth century *Diccionario de autoridades* offered a virtually identical first definition, with no hint of a corporate sense of liberty in any succeeding entries.[75]

This was in sharpening contrast to established notions of liberty. In medieval Spain, *libertad* had been understood less as liberty for the individual qua individual than as the liberty of the person within the plenitude of his relationships to other men as well as to God. Each person formed part of one or more corporate entities, such as guilds, or municipalities, or other special jurisdictions (e.g., military brotherhoods, religious orders). Liberty did not inhere in the individual—except with regard to Christian liberty and in the threshold sense of not being a slave—but in the circumstances of the individual's place in the greater whole of interlocking corporations and collectivities.[76] By the seventeenth century, this meaning had become quite threadbare among many Spaniards. Saavedra Fajardo, for instance, feared that in the context of Spain's seventeenth-century moral crisis, men in "living each for himself" would forget that they should also "live for everyone else."[77] According to Spanish historian José Antonio Maravall, liberty in Spain's Baroque culture had to do with choice and election by relatively anonymous individuals, with the sense that ordinary people not tied to the structures of power could exercise their will—their *libertad*—in the world.[78]

Libertad could not have this meaning for the vast majority of Mexico's Indians. True, individual indigenous commoners had greater opportunities to influence the terms of their labor than ever before, to possess land, and to participate in local government. But in great numbers they remained part of villages defined collectively by their tribute obligations. As fray Miguel Agia noted in his legal opinion on the 1601 royal decree regulating personal service and repartimiento, it had not been "his Majesty's intention . . . to give general liberty to the Indians that they serve or stop serving if they choose, rather he orders and commands the opposite . . . which is that they be occupied, and serve in what they should, and are obligated as his Majesty's vassals to serve . . . (though without any hint of slavery, or other subjection, or servitude other than what as vassals they owe, etc.)"[79] At the same time, Spaniards and many others, including some native commoners, enjoyed room for maneuver and opportunities for gain that most Indians did not in this place where kingly power was inconstant and at times faded to a thin mist of authority clinging to the hard objectivity of daily life. Readily cloaking their deeds in a pretense of law, or at least knowing that legal actions often could not be distinguished from illegal ones, those with money, position, and influence held sway here and might bend the world, or a corner of it, to their will and interest.

Bound as they were to the king's lawful demands and subject to the illicit impositions of so many, most indigenous villagers were in no position to imagine they might act upon the wider world strictly as individuals. This was why so many Indians experienced libertad as an infliction. From their perspective, others' ability to act with liberty, so often in disregard of the law, amounted to little more than unchecked latitude. Many Spaniards recognized the problem and worried. Solórzano y Pereira, who acknowledged that the Indians had "experienced absolute and perpetual domination" by Spaniards, feared that liberty might too easily become license, as it so often and evidently did in the New World, putting order itself at risk.[80]

Rather than abandon the idea of liberty, as they might have, native petitioners appear to have come to their own understanding of libertad, one that even for individuals was deeply rooted in the unalterable circumstances of their lives as village dwellers who often farmed communally and were subject to tribute obligations that burdened whole communities. And while in some ways this conception of liberty recalled medieval notions, especially with regard to the relationship between individuals and corporate entities, its source as law ran back to the controversies regarding treatment of Indians as colonial subjects.

Sixteenth-century debates over the Indians' place in colonial society and the protective legislation that followed defined indigenous people by their collective political status as subjects, furnishing them a potential corporate identity. Early in the sixteenth century, Vitoria had argued that Indian communities, wherever they might be found, were sovereign republics entitled to rule themselves.[81] In principle, they could not be exploited for the benefit of people alien to the community, and they had the right to defend themselves against others, even to declare just war if necessary (hypothetically speaking). Tribute, therefore, was not an arbitrary exaction; it was the way indigenous villages contributed to the common good, a responsibility they bore as the king's vassals. Of course, such high-minded notions did not stop the Indians from being exploited, but these tenets remained operative, if largely in abeyance until the seventeenth century.

In the 1640s, casting about for a way to understand Indian villages formed under the reduction and congregation policies of the sixteenth century, Solórzano y Pereira settled on the Roman "municipality" as a model. Municipalities, according to authorities cited in the *Política indiana,* enjoyed a special legal status because they could only be established for some useful or beneficial purpose pursuant to the common good. In New Spain, this good amounted to promoting evangelization, facilitating tribute collection, easing labor distribution, and ensuring agricultural production. Furthermore, a municipality could be distinguished from other political communities by the fact that its inhabitants were not free to abandon it.[82] In theory, Indians could not leave their villages, barring exceptional circumstances, because that was where they were registered to pay tribute. The crown reinforced this sense of obligation to place by prohibiting anyone but Indians from living in native communities. As the *Recopilación* stated the matter in 1680: "So that [the Indians] might live with more liberty and peace it was ordered that no Spaniards, blacks, mestizos, or mulattoes live in the villages . . . Nor should any Spanish traveler stay more than two days, or any peddler more than three."[83] In effect, Indian villages were made into legally defensible collectivities grounded by the idea of place. Their libertad was not the liberty of "free cities," which enjoyed political autonomy, but the liberty to be free of arbitrary encroachments and to fend off those who would take unlawful advantage of them.[84]

Doing so represented a constant challenge, as the defense of liberty always is. And it was not something learned all at once. Some petitions seeking relief on behalf of villages from the 1630s and 1640s explicitly mentioned libertad, but just as many did not, suggesting that neither Indian petitioners nor their procuradores automatically thought of libertad in a collective context, at least early on. Petitions might mention a harm, complain that their *wills* had been overridden, refer to tribute, discuss things *necessary to their republic,* request payment for work done—and not use the word *libertad.* Yet in these same cases, the Juzgado itself might respond by ordering that petitioners be protected *in their liberty.*[85] By the 1650s, the word libertad was routinely invoked in any case complaining of labor abuses. Legal process had taught petitioners and their procuradores not only how best to frame their pleadings but also to think of almost any outside interference with village life as an invasion of community liberty.

A number of petitions suggest that the idea of libertad may have come to be associated with a strong sense of economic autonomy rooted in village life. In part, this was a result of the focus of protective legislation. Decrees regulating personal service and repartimientos spoke of libertad in very practical, economic terms: the Indians could not be compelled to work against their will, they were entitled to work for whomever they chose, and they had to be paid for the work they did. By the 1630s, amparos had begun to push the boundaries of libertad to encompass other sorts of economic activity beyond labor.

In 1633, two residents of the pueblo of Los Reyes, outside Chapultepec, complained that Indians from a nearby village had invaded *maguey* lands they had worked for twenty years. They asked the Juzgado to protect their lands and requested that the Indians in question pay restitution for the magueyes lost. Though the petition did not use the word *libertad,* the tribunal ordered the other Indians to leave petitioners' magueyes "free [libres] and clear" of interference. A few years later, two Indian farmers from Tezayuca asked the Juzgado to restrain a Spanish landowner who was "impeding" them and other Indians of that jurisdiction "from selling [their produce] freely" in local markets. The tribunal agreed with the tenor of the petition, but did not echo the oblique reference to libertad. Similarly, the "gobernadores, officials of republic, *común*, and *naturales*" of neighboring towns in Guautitlan complained in 1649 that certain provincial officers were levying a tax on the sale of produce at markets they held within village limits. Petitioners asked that they be allowed "to sell freely [libremente]" and to "hold their markets freely," for without what they earned they could not pay tribute.[86]

Strictly speaking, none of these amparos referred to libertad as such— no one was being forced to work, no one's will was being overridden, no one was being unlawfully held, no one was being kept from returning to their village. Rather, the reference was metaphorical and by extension: interference with magueyes and with local markets impinged on petitioners' individual and collective lives in ways that seemed like more direct and familiar infringements on liberty, enough so that the idea of *libertad* could make sense as an adjective or adverb dignifying and elevating an otherwise mundane narrative of economic harm.

Throughout the seventeenth century, Indians appear to have filed more amparo petitions than any other group in New Spain. In part this reflected demographics: even at the low point of the indigenous hecatomb around 1620, Indians outnumbered Spaniards and castas by four or five to one; by the end of the seventeenth century, they still overbalanced all others by at least two to one. But demographics do not tell the whole story.

In many ways, amparo petitions filed by Spaniards and castas differed little from those filed by Indian petitioners. Spaniards often sought protection of land, much as Indians did, or to gain royal mining concessions. Castilian elites commonly resorted to amparos in settling questions regarding noble status or in disputes over office.[87] Poor Spaniards and castas also filed petitions, though much less frequently than elites. An aggrieved party might request an amparo to stop a third party from interfering with individual economic activity, the making of charcoal, say, or a Chinese barber might ask to be protected in his business. Widows claiming poverty might seek to protect their property against creditors. In rare instances, Spaniards and castas complained of abuse by local officials, as when a priest and several others asked to be protected against the "malice" of the alcalde mayor who by his actions had forced them to bring many lawsuits, which sapped their meager funds and kept them away from their farms for long periods.[88] In form and in language, all of these were identical to the amparos sought by and granted to indigenous petitioners.

Indian amparo petitions were notable in two ways: for the frequency with which they filed petitions on behalf of corporate entities and for the frequency with which they sought liberty. Except in property cases involving religious institutions or jurisdictional disputes, Spaniards filed few amparo petitions asking for protection on behalf of a corporate entity. Among indigenous petitioners, by contrast, villages were almost as likely as individuals to seek amparos. And even when a convent spoke on behalf of members, as Indian petitions spoke of residents, the reference reflected more a sense of legal-institutional necessity than of shared ownership and involvement.[89]

As to *libertad,* amparo requests suggest Spaniards and castas came across the word chiefly in cases of jailing, noble status, and of slaves seeking emancipation.[90] In incarceration cases, petitioners would ask the court to grant libertad, either permanently, or temporarily, while other proceedings were conducted. Noble status did not become much of an issue until the end of the seventeenth century and beginning of the eighteenth century. At that time, there was a rash of petitions seeking recognition of the "exceptions, privileges, and liberties" of being *hijos-dalgo,* which would have allowed successful claimants to avoid arrest for failure to pay debts—a telling contrast with indigenous petitioners, for whom libertad implied the liberty to work and pay tribute in their own villages.[91] The other circumstance in which Spaniards might have heard the word *libertad* in a legal setting involved amparos filed by blacks and mulattoes asserting their liberty as free persons, either slaves who claimed they had been freed, or free people who insisted that Spaniards and others wrongly took them for slaves.[92] Such petitioners drew on notions similar to those articulated in Indian petitions, though they differed from those petitions in being exclusively individual. Assertions of liberty in corporate and collective terms reflected the Indians' unique legal status under colonial rule—free individuals who were bound by law to live in certain places and discharge certain collective obligations to the king.

As with the general run of amparos, enforcement of those favoring libertad remained uncertain. The Juzgado had at its disposal the same arsenal to enforce its orders as it did for amparos not involving liberty. Petitions themselves suggest that the tribunal may have been more likely to threaten to send *receptores* in cases of gross abuse, especially when people were locked up against their will, as happened so often on haciendas and in obrajes.[93] Yet time and again petitioners came to court seeking execution of orders previously issued, complaining that *different decrees and orders* have *not had effect* and that abuses were happening *despite being prohibited by royal decrees,* a phrase that became almost a mantra, suggesting that the law was often violated.[94]

It might be tempting to conclude from this that the amparos were a failure as law. After all, the petitions complain of much the same thing in the 1690s as in the 1620s. It seems there was no progress, that over the seventeenth century amparos did not rein in the runaway abuse of the alcaldes mayores, hacendados, village gobernadores, and the many others who rode the ordinary indigenous people so hard. The only way to make sense of this situation is to see the amparos not in splendid legal isolation, but as part of the weave of a much larger and more intricate fabric of law and daily life, as we might, say, the relationship between law and crime. Laws do not exist to eliminate crime so much as to deal with the ineluctable fact of crime within particular social arrangements. Given the Indians' status as free men who were nevertheless subject to manifold obligations, given the gulf between the exercise of local power and the tenuousness of royal authority, given the alcaldes mayores' enormous powers of passive resistance to laws and orders emanating from Madrid and Mexico City, abuse of the Indians may have been no less inevitable in the grand scheme of things than crime was in society more generally.

If so, Indian petitioners may have sought from the amparos what benefit they might derive. They knew there was no guarantee that a given order would resolve their problems and that filing a petition was just one element in an ongoing negotiation over the terms of their lives as the king's tributaries. From the perspective of the petitions, the problem was not *that* they were tributaries, but that *as* tributaries they were open to abuse in a context where so many people with brief authority could act with impunity. Their daily experience told them that arrangements with the locally powerful had to be worked out on the ground, informally, often regardless of the niceties of law. They went to Mexico City when those arrangements were violated or when circumstances changed. As viceroy Juan de Ortega y Montañés wrote to his successor in 1696: the Indians are "so observant of customs that even judging a thing to be petty corruption, they do not shout nor do they complain . . . unless the alcaldes mayores or justices add . . . something that their predecessors did not do, and then they complain saying that the custom has been exceeded."[95] Customs were established through bargaining and accommodation, a process in which the amparos played an important role by giving Indians the law as a resort when negotiation had broken down. From this vantage, the point of the amparos in practice was not so much to enforce the letter of the law, much less end the abuse of Indians, as to secure an environment within which accommodations could be reached that would promote social peace.

The case with which this chapter began offers a cautionary tale along these lines. In filing their petition in 1641, the caciques of the Conchos noted that in all the time since they had been "reduced" to Christianity they "had rendered obedience to your Majesty and had never had any uprising or disturbance," rather they had helped the king against others who had rebelled. The viceroy, agreeing with the tenor of the petition, ordered the justice to whom it was presented to enforce the 1609 decree against personal service, and "put in their liberty" all Indians deposited in the homes of Spaniards. A separate order removed don Joseph from office. We do not know how these orders fared, whether petitioners found a justice to execute them or whether don Joseph found a way to neutralize them through his own local influence—he was, after all, very far away from Mexico City. Nor do we know if petitioners were forced to make the long trip back to the capital to ask that the orders be enforced. And even if both orders were properly executed, we cannot know precisely to what effect. While the tribunal quoted the 1609 decree, the amparo as such did not specify what should be done. The tribunal's point in quoting from the decree without explicit prompting from petitioners, may not have been to enforce the letter of the law so much as to exhort don Joseph's successor to reasonableness by reminding him that the law could not be ignored altogether. Such a reminder would have furnished the Indians a lever with which to negotiate locally.

Even if that lever was long enough to move the likes of don Joseph toward compromise in an individual case, it appears to have been wholly inadequate to propping up a lasting social peace in remote Nueva Vizcaya. For in 1644, the Conchos, converted and unconverted alike, were swept up in rebellion. Facing a prolonged drought and a much wider set of revolts in the province, Conchos Indians attacked the mission at San Francisco de Conchos, killing the friars and burning the church. They did the same at another Conchos mission, San Pedro de Conchos. We do not know what role complaints of the sort raised in the 1641 petition played in all of this, nor what stance the community of Christian Conchos took in the face of violence. At a minimum, we can suspect that their frangible mediational role vis-à-vis the unconverted, hinted at in their petition, finally crumbled, leaving them betwixt and between, likely forcing many individuals and communities to choose sides. We do know that Nueva Vizcaya enjoyed little peace during the succeeding three decades. The Franciscans did not return to Conchos for nearly forty years, and even then the missions continued to be attacked until a presidio was established in the mid-1680s.[96]

It would be too much to suggest that amparos, if properly and conscienciously enforced, could have prevented such a rebellion, much less ended the oppression of the Conchos and other indigenous people in Nueva Vizcaya or New Spain for that matter. They were not designed to do so. Like all law, they came into existence under particular circumstances to meet particular needs. At their best they offered individuals and communities a measure of protection in concrete circumstances. In many, perhaps most, cases they did precisely that—though not without travail and never permanently. But during the broad economic transitions of the seventeenth century—decline of the encomienda, emergence of the hacienda, abolition of repartimientos and personal service, the widening of wage labor—the Juzgado's amparos became a means by which those most vulnerable to the excesses of Spanish colonialism could reach out to a distant king and make the idea of liberty their own. What had begun as a limited resource for the defense of land had become a capacious idea touching virtually every facet of Indians' colonial lives—labor relations, contracts, tribute, abuse of personal power, liberty, local governance, and community autonomy. This process of legal expansion and rhetorical refinement continued until roughly 1680, when the *Recopilación* effectively codified the previous century of New World law. By that time, Spaniard and Indian alike knew how a changed economic and legal terrain lay. The amparo gave indigenous petitioners a powerful shield (and also a weapon), but its limits were obvious to all: royal decrees could accomplish nothing more to promote the "good treatment of the Indians" without subverting their status as "the feet of the republic."

In some ways it seems odd to speak of liberty in the context of Spanish rule in the New World. Spain conquered the natives, destroyed their religion, and put them to work. What could liberty possibly have meant in such circumstances? Certainly, it was neither the liberty of Roman senators to be free of the state nor the later Enlightenment notion of the individual's freedom to do as he pleases. It was, rather, the colonial *libertad* of Indians ever at risk of oppression to be free of arbitrary encroachments on their persons and their communities. Where Spaniards, and perhaps many castas and even well-placed Indians, faced the apparatus of governance and saw limitations on their opportunities, libertad as submission to the king's protection represented a bulwark for ordinary people against the opportunism of the powerful and greedy. This protection was premised on the notion that the Indians did not live just for themselves alone. As tributaries, they also were unavoidably responsible to the common good, unwitting exemplars, in a way, of Saavedra Fajardo's maxim— "To live in benefit to the republic is not servitude, but liberty."[97]

As such, the legal discourse of libertad in the amparos was neither idle talk nor mere ideological cover for colonial domination, nor simply a tool to pursue immediate interests. Taken together, the amparos tell a story of how Indian petitioners from across Mexico found room for maneuver within tight constraints and came to imagine a liberty for their own circumstances, one that appears to have resonated deeply in the lives of Indians throughout the seventeenth century, and beyond.

Libertad, they had been repeatedly told, was a birthright of all people. The king's laws had been clear on this from the sixteenth century forward, as their petitions revealed. By the late seventheenth century, this notion was widely diffused in New Spanish society. On the afternoon of Sunday, December 6, 1682, an unnamed priest asked the faithful of Santa Catalina Martyr, Chalco, whether God had ordered that they make bricks without straw from sunup to sundown, as the Isrealites had been forced to.[98] Had God stood over them with lash in hand, raining blows on their backs, as the Egyptians had done? "Are you in some sort of captivity? Are you not in the *libertad* of the children of God? Are you not in your father's home?" Of course, in invoking liberty this way, the good priest was concerned primarily to ensure that his Indian flock obey the laws of so generous a God. But the Biblical parallels and the father's earlier statement that "to cast upon the poor man all of the law because he is poor . . . and to release the rich man from all law because he is rich, is not the law of God" almost surely resonated for Indian parishioners long familiar by 1682 with the law's tenuous promise to protect libertad.[99]

And these parishioners may have had deeper reservoirs upon which to draw in imagining their liberty. Against the image of huddled Israelites and in light of the phrases *as if they were slaves, forcibly and against their will, mistreatment by deed and by word,* and *powerful hand,* there is something poignant in Olmos's Metaphor XLVI, which opens with the Spanish gloss "In my hand it is to be good or bad" and follows with a brief verse in Nahuatl:

> It is only by my hand, by my face, my heart, my spirit
> That either I will wither, or I will bloom,
> I will become as green land, as tilled earth,
> I will germinate, I will sprout.[100]

Suggestive as these words are of a deeply human yearning, would it be too much to suppose that the seventeenth-century's amparos favoring liberty were a means by which native petitioners could choose to *bloom* rather than *wither* in the New World created by conquest?

CHAPTER SIX

Of Guilt and Punishment

≈⟩

Sometime around 1600, a "half-*ladino* Mexican Indian" vented his frustrations in a bilious "Romance" against the "scoundrels" who had stolen three roosters from his house.[1] In nineteen four-line verses bearing the confusions and mistakes of one for whom Spanish seemed a taxing second language, the partly hispanized Indian of the poem speaks of having bred the roosters for a ceremony of posesión regarding some land he had acquired from his "cousin, the marquis." In a gesture of goodwill, he had meant to offer these roosters at a banquet for those who would be his new "vassals." Hinting that the thieves did not wish him well in his new status as a landowner, he yearns for a noose and a knife with which to punish them. If they ever fell into his hands, he fumes, "by the life of don Felipe"—the king, either II or III?—he would spill their guts. But four verses on, he has changed his mind. "It is better if I am patient," he says. "I will go to the judge / and lodge my complaint / so that he will favor me / against the culprits" and give me a letter excommunicating the "rogues" so the Devil will take them. But having cast his lot with the law he feared "no justice on this earth / would hang these scoundrels."

The irony of what might seem the raw emotion in these verses is that an Indian probably did not write them. Romances of this sort were common literary fare in New Spain around the turn of the seventeenth century, typically penned anonymously by Spaniards or perhaps mestizos. Authors often assumed invented personae to comment satirically on some aspect of everyday life. In this case, the poem subtly mocked an Indian character who claimed to have a "marquis" for a cousin, who referred to land he was to acquire as an "estate" and the people on it as his "vassals," and who despaired of the fact that people would not use the honorific "don" before his name, even though his wife was a good Christian.[2] The poem's value as a legal-historical source, therefore, is not what it reveals about the author. What stands out from its narrative is the depiction of an Indian's reaction to being the victim of a crime. A powerful sense of hurt sparks a fantasy of vigilante justice which ultimately gives way to a decision to be "patient" and let a court handle things. This is precisely how the law was supposed to work. And yet, the protagonist's concern that justice might miscarry suggests how fragile law's hold on the imagination could be. In other words, regardless of who wrote this "Romance," its compressed verses made plain the law's power and limitations in the everyday lives of indigenous people.

No less crucially, these stanzas express the conundrum at the core of criminal justice: how to transform the personal desire for revenge into an outcome that could be widely seen as "just." Spanish jurists framed the issue in broadly political terms. As with the law more generally, criminal law sought not private utility but the common good. Though occasioned by private harm, a criminal accusation implied a breach of public peace. As *Las Siete Partidas* put it: an accusation "is of great benefit to all the men of an entire country, for by means of it, when it is proved, the malefactor is justly punished, and the party who sustained injury is avenged."[3] "Punishment is reparation for sin," meted out by judges to chastise the guilty and give others "notice and warning to avoid doing wrong through fear of punishment." For this reason, claimed Solórzano y Pereira, criminal causes were in principle more important than mere civil or pecuniary ones. Only through law oriented to the public good, argued Domingo de Soto, and through the fear and awe of law, might the "virtuous" live calmly and in peace.[4]

The poem tracks this sequence from private grievance to acknowledgment of law's public role: the protagonist sticks his head out the window of his house to catch the evening breeze, sees that his roosters are gone, vents his anger, fantasizes a personal revenge, and ultimately decides to complain to a judge and hope justice will be done. Even through the distortions of a mocking tone, the protagonist's rage, humiliation, pride, hope, and despair stand out, while a sense of deep engagement with law in action remains discernible. The anonymous Spanish poet could ridicule his protagonist's pretensions to status, but he could not mock his commitment to legality, indicating that Spaniards and Indians alike drew on a deep aquifer of attitudes toward the law.

This is what allowed criminal process to work in seventeenth century Mexico. Without a basic agreement regarding legality's role in the social order, law could not have mediated some of the rawest conflicts among and between Indians and Spaniards. Litigation required the participation of a considerable dramatis personae. Spanish and Indian victims and witnesses testified in order to persuade a judge either to punish or acquit a defendant accused of a crime. Procuradores helped mold testimony according to broad principles of law familiar to the judge. Judges heard and read the resulting record and, in light of applicable law and the dictates of conscience, decided which story "best coincided with the facts" and ruled accordingly.[5] It was a highly interpretive, deeply casuistic process. Not only judges and procuradores, but ordinary witnesses crafted words and shaped narratives in light of law and conscience. This was how wrongs experienced as personal and private took on wider social meaning.[6]

Criminal procedure set the limits within which this process unfolded. Who could be a witness, what counted as evidence, when torture was permissible, how cases were to proceed—all were governed by rules spelled out in *Las Siete Partidas,* in royal decrees, and in reference works, such as Hevia Bolaños's widely used manual of procedure, the *Curia Philipica.*[7] A case began with the decision of whether to pursue a dispute as a criminal or a civil matter. Spanish law sought to draw a bright line between the two. According to the *Curia,* a criminal matter had to touch on "public vindication and utility" and was distinguished by the possibility of corporal, as opposed to merely pecuniary punishment—at least in principle.[8] Not surprisingly, relations between Indians and Spaniards in the New World warped and shaped law at the level of practice. For instance, Spaniards accused by Indians were almost always punished by fines: it would not do for Spaniards to be flogged, imprisoned, or sent to the galleys or *obrajes* on the word of Indians. On the other hand, owing to the many royal laws protecting Indians from abuse by Spaniards, almost any harm a Spaniard might cause an Indian, to body, property, or honor, could be construed as a matter of public utility, which meant it could be framed as a criminal accusation. The choice of whether to pursue a matter as a civil or criminal case was generally up to the aggrieved party. While it was not uncommon for judges or royal prosecutors to take a case *de oficio*—where the crown assumed the role of complaining party—most criminal actions began with private petitions. Criminal proceedings, in other words, were inherently public in nature but hinged on the willingness and energy of private individuals to bring matters to justice.[9]

This willingness depended fundamentally on procedural regularity. Solórzano y Pereira insisted that rulers could do no better for their subjects than to "administer and distribute justice impartially, cleanly, and in keeping with holiness." *Las Partidas,* which both Solórzano and the *Curia* frequently cited, gave meaning to this broad idea, noting in prefaces to long sections on legal procedure, that justice had to be "dispensed methodically" and in an "orderly manner . . . by each person demanding and defending in court what he believes to be his rights." Only in this way would criminal justice "remove by severe punishment the disputes and tumults which arise from the evil deeds committed for the pleasure of one party to the injury and the dishonor of another."[10]

The idea seems to have been that punishments meted out pursuant to procedural regularity would enjoy public respect precisely because they were not arbitrary. Witnesses testified under oath. Judges were to rule not just as they pleased but in accord with those who "approached nearest to the truth."[11] This was no guarantee that witnesses would speak truthfully and judges act dispassionately. But it did mean that witnesses, judges, and parties were bound within a set of formal constraints that operated more or less impartially to reduce the sphere of caprice.

A criminal complaint was a stripped down affair. It alleged a harm, accused a particular person, and asked that he or she be punished. Once a complaint had been filed, the justice or judge would write up a *cabeza de proceso,* or head of proceeding, detailing the complainant's allegations. He would then order a *sumaria* or *información.* This brief investigation involved deposing three witnesses under oath to corroborate a complainant's story. If the witnesses were Indians, the court would appoint two interpreters. When these statements had been taken, the judge could order the accused person to be arrested—if he was not already in custody—and sequester his goods. The aggrieved party could then offer further evidence, typically more sworn testimony, to bolster the charge. Once these depositions had been completed, a complainant filed a formal *acusación,* or accusation. At this point the defendant was allowed to respond. If poor, as Indian defendants often were, the judge assigned a procurador to handle the matter free of charge. Petitions to be released on bond generally followed.

It was then up to the accused and his procurador to mount a defense. This usually involved deposing witnesses identified by the defendant—typically not more than ten—to answer a court-approved *interrogatorio* (interrogatory), a series of questions drawn up by the procurador regarding allegations made in the sumaria. The interrogatory was administered by a notary or a specially charged judge. Each witness responded under oath. During this phase, and sometimes before, the defendant might offer a *confesión,* which was not an admission of guilt but simply his own statement of what had happened. Meanwhile, the complaining party would ask that her witnesses ratify earlier testimony, changing or adding anything they thought necessary. All of this could be done through a notary and interpreters, with little direct involvement of the judge, though a judge could choose to be more active in the evidentiary phase of the case. With the interrogatories on file, the accuser and his procurador would ask that the case be accepted for decision. Both parties typically submitted what amounted to closing arguments in writing, summarizing the evidence in their favor, pointing out inconsistencies among the other side's witnesses, and advancing points of law and procedure.

The process was conducted almost entirely on paper, and there were no public hearings. Only in rare cases did defendant and accuser acutally meet in court. Away from the capital, a judge might consult a Mexico City lawyer for a legal opinion on guilt and then issue his ruling in the form of a *sentencia,* which either convicted or acquitted the defendant. A convicted person had the right to appeal an adverse ruling to the audiencia.[12] Punishment, when it came, was carried out by a court officer acting in the king's name. Because criminal jurisdiction rested entirely with the crown, ecclesiastical judges had no power to punish ordinary crimes.[13]

"To guilt corresponds punishment," stated Sebastián de Covarrubias in defining *culpa*—guilt—in his dictionary of Castilian.[14] Few ideas in law seem as straightforward at first blush and as confounding upon close examination. Straightforward because the notion that one who is guilty of a crime should be punished is so readily accepted. Confounding because it is so often unclear precisely what constitutes guilt in any circumstance. The work of criminal law and procedure is to satisfy the impulse demanding punishment for crimes but to ensure that in any given case guilt not be too easily arrived at, lest the law slip into a monstrous arbitrariness. The tools of this work in seventeenth-century Mexico were general principles of law, routines of procedure, the conscience of the judge, the cleverness of procuradores, the stories of witnesses and, most crucially, the concrete circumstances of the act in question. But once law's work had begun, a case might be altered, diverted, or changed, for there was no one path to resolution. Each case, in other words, from its "facts" to its trajectory through legal process to its outcome, was *sui generis.*

CRIME STORIES

On Tuesday morning June 2, 1626, just as mass was ending, don Nicolás de San Miguel, gobernador of Malinalco, and his alcaldes, approached the chief deputy of the province, Spaniard Juan Osorio, and the local Spanish notary, Juan de Barrios. In grave tones, they told of a crime that had been committed the previous night: Juan Agustín had been hit in the head with a rock and lay severely wounded in his bed. Osorio and Barrios, followed by don Nicolás and his men, hustled off to Juan Agustín's modest house. Both Spaniards spoke Nahuatl, so they knelt by

Juan's side and asked him to say who had done this, and why, and who else was present when it happened. Barrios then administered the oath required of all witnesses in criminal proceedings and Juan Agustín made the sign of the cross on his forehead and began to tell his story.[15]

At about eight or nine o'clock the previous night he had been walking down a street in town when he was accosted by an Indian who was obviously drunk. This man, who Juan Agustín knew quite well as Juan Clemente from nearby Zacualpa, asked Juan Agustín who he was. Juan Agustín had answered, "I am your brother, don't you know me?" Despite the greeting, and without warning or reason, Juan Clemente had thrown a rock that hit Juan Agustín in the temple, knocking him to the ground, unconscious. After coming to, covered in blood, Juan Agustín had stumbled home. According to his statement, no one else had been been with him at the time. Asked whether he wanted to press charges, Juan Agustín answered that he did not and would rather "forgive [Juan Clemente] of his free will, so that if God decides to take him from this life because of this wound he will forgive his sins and grant merit to his soul."[16]

Having taken this statement, Osorio immediately set the procedural wheels in motion. A surgeon examined Juan Agustín's wound and swore out an affidavit concluding that the injury was life threatening. On June 8, don Luis de Olibares, Malinalco's alcalde mayor, assumed the prosecution of Juan Clemente in the king's name, since Juan Agustín was in no shape to press the case himself. There was no need to issue an arrest warrant, since Indian officers already had Juan Clemente in custody. Interpreters were appointed, a Spaniard and a mulatto. Spaniard Domingo de Ábila was designated to serve as Juan Clemente's procurador. That same day, alcalde mayor Olibares took the defendant's statement. Juan Clemente testified that he knew Juan Agustín well, since they were from the same town and were good friends, but denied his story, saying he knew nothing of what happened. On June 13, Juan Agustín passed away.[17]

What had been an assault became a homicide. Olibares ordered that the conditions of Juan Clemente's imprisionment be tightened. That very day, Olibares also began the preliminary investigation—an información—by deposing three witnesses. Two of them testified that it was "public and notoriously known"—*público y notorio*—that Juan Agustín had died from the wound given him by Juan Clemente. A third witness, Baltazar Agustín (no relation to Juan), stated that he had been with Juan Agustín on the night in question. Baltazar had dropped by Juan Agustín's house and suggested they go out and catch some flying ants as a late-night snack. On their stroll they had encountered Juan Clemente, who was falling-down drunk. He did not acknowledge their greeting. Instead, he demanded to know what they were doing in his barrio and then threw the stone that brained Juan Agustín. At that point, according to his statement, Baltazar had fled, fearing for his safety.[18]

On June 20, Juan Agustín's mother and wife, filed a criminal complaint of their own against Juan Clemente. Pleading that they knew nothing of lawsuits, they asked Olibares to handle the matter on their behalf. The judge was now also an advocate for one of the parties.

Juan Clemente's procurador Ábila responded to the información with a series of procedural and substantive points. He argued that Juan Agustín's mother and wife had no standing to bring the suit. He also advanced a peremptory challenge to the entire case, arguing that there was no proof against Clemente other than Agustín's deathbed statement, in which he had declined to press charges. Moreover, Clemente had been somewhere else on the night Agustín was attacked, as witnesses would show. Finally, claimed Ábila, Baltazar's statement should not be believed. His account was internally "inconsistent" and Agustín himself had not mentioned Baltazar.[19] Baltazar had testified only because he was "induced" to do so by others.

Ábila's next step was to depose six witnesses on Juan Clemente's behalf.[20] In response to interrogatory questions, the first two offered the defendant a solid alibi: he had been with friends, not drunk in the street. According to Juan Miguel and his wife, Agustina María, Juan Clemente had worked all day in Juan Miguel's corn field, against the promise that "another time they would help him." At sundown, they had repaired to Juan Miguel's house, where they had eaten and chatted until about ten o'clock at night. After supper, Juan Clemente had gone "straight home," with one child in his arms and another holding his hand and his wife at his side. They had passed no one on the street. According to Agustina María, she and Juan Miguel had stood in the doorway of their house and watched their guests amble home. Juan Clemente's wife had carried a torch, so it was easy to see them. A third witness, María Gerónima corroborated the story of the evening, adding that she accompanied Juan Clemente and his wife and slept at their house that night. Once inside, they had all lain down and she had heard nothing further until the following morning, when men came to arrest Juan Clemente. Three further witnesses cast doubt on Baltazar's testimony. A Spaniard, the Indian gobernador of Malinalco, and another officer of the town council all claimed that they had heard Juan Agustín's relatives try to persuade Baltazar to testify against Juan Clemente. Don Nicolás, the Indian gobernador, stated that at one point he had cautioned Agustín's mother not to pressure Baltazar to tell untruths.[21] As had the earlier three, these witnesses stated that they knew Clemente to be a "quiet and peaceful Indian, and good Christian."

These depositions were completed on June 25. On July 10, Olibares ruled on the case, acquitting Juan Clemente of any part in Juan Agustín's death and releasing him from jail.

How did Olibares decide? In a way, he did not. Although he signed the order acquitting Juan Clemente, the decision on the merits was made by a degreed lawyer in Mexico City, Licenciado Juan de Fuentes. Olibares appears to have been in some doubt as to how he should handle such jarringly different stories—*Juan Clemente violent drunk prowling the village at night* versus *Juan Clemente model villager who helped others in the community from a sense of moral reciprocity and enjoyed the quiet companionship of friends and family.* The judge's position was more complicated still, because technically he represented Juan Clemente's wife and mother. So he sent the record off to Mexico City for a learned legal opinion. There, Fuentes examined the testimony and proposed a verdict which Olibares signed as his own. Olibares paid Fuentes four pesos for his pains.

Though judges were not required to explain their decisions, the record in this case offers clues to how Fuentes approached the matter. By law, the accuser bore the burden of proof.[22] From this perspective, procurador Ábila may have had the better of the argument, for there were holes in Juan Agustín's deathbed account of the assault. To begin with, crucial elements of his statement did not square with Baltazar's supposedly eye-witness account. The alleged time of the incident varied: Agustín had said eight to nine o'clock, Baltazar nine to ten. More significantly, Agustín had insisted he was alone, whereas Baltazar claimed to have been with him when Juan Clemente showed up. Nor were Juan Agustín's other witnesses much help, since they could only testify to "what was said among the Indians." Hearsay could be heard by a judge but it carried less weight than eyewitness testimony.[23]

This was where Juan Clemente's witnesses seem to have made a crucial difference. They did not merely say that they were with Clemente at the hour of the alleged attack. They said that he was with them at dinner, after a long day in the fields and "tired from all the work." They did not simply note that he went home at ten o'clock. They made a point of saying that he went "straight home" with a child in arms and his wife at his side, and stressed that they knew this because they had stood in their own door and watched them go with a torch lighting the way.

These were likely not the witnesses' spontaneous observations. A "story" of this sort does not exist fully developed before a witnesses' telling. Legal narratives emerge in the course of witnesses' participation in the legal process itself.[24] Juan Clemente's witnesses came to the legal encounter with what they claimed to have seen and what they claimed to know. They doubtless spoke among themselves about what had happened. They may have talked to Ábila before deposing. He may have told them what he needed to hear or at least have asked them questions signaling the answers he sought: *Yes, Juan Clemente went home after dinner. But did he go straight home? How do you know he did? Wasn't it dark? How did you see? Did he have a torch to light the way? How do you know he went all the way home? Did you stand in your doorway and watch them go?* Ábila would have known that the weight and credibility of witnesses' testimony depended on the details of how they knew what they claimed to know—whether it was night, whether there was light, whether they actually saw a thing happen.[25]

Even if they had not met with Ábila before hand, the interrogatory questions themselves could have guided witnesses in testifying. Each question framed a basic answer and invited witnesses to expand upon that answer from their own knowledge. Each response began with the phrase, *as to this question this witness said that what he knows is that . . .* The second query, for example, asked deponents "if they knew" that Juan Clemente had gone to work in Juan Miguel's corn field, following which their two families had supped together until nine or ten o'clock, after which Juan Clemente had gone "straight home" carrying one of his children, with his wife by his side. Assuming that Juan Miguel and his wife favored Clemente in this matter—because they knew he was not the sort of person to do such a thing—they would have had every reason to follow the questions closely and embellish their answers with detail to make them more credible—as when three of the witnesses added that in exchange for Clemente's help this time, Juan Miguel had promised to help him "another time," and Agustina María stated that she and her husband had stood in their doorway and watched their friends go home, which they could do because Juan Clemente's wife had carried a torch. In short, witnesses could be intimately involved in shaping a legal narrative on whose credibility and persuasiveness an accused's fate might depend.

Legal process, in other words, was not just the *how* of what was done, mere background to the substance of the case. It was tangled up with the very essence of *what* was said. Juan Agustín's initial statement that a besotted Juan Clemente had thrown the rock that injured him forced Ábila to respond with an opposing narrative. He thus designed an interrogatory to counter Agustín's deathbed declaration. It was Ábila's job to listen to what the witnesses had to say and then frame questions whose answers would constitute Clemente's defense. By answering them under oath, the witnesses were telling a story to the judge, whose duty it was to make a decision that could free Clemente or condemn him to corporal punishment, banishment, or even death.

Witnesses must often have suspected and procuradores known that clean accounts fared better with judges than testimony marked by doubts, evasions, and ambivalences.[26] The making of such accounts was not a crudely instrumental process. Some witnesses lied and knew themselves to be lying. More commonly, witnesses testified with the understanding that a person's—often a friend's—future might hinge on what they did and did not say. At the end of the day, they knew, a judge had to choose one side over the other. Procedure, in other words, tended to produce sharply contrasting story lines. Nowhere, perhaps, was this more rawly obvious than in criminal proceedings, where punishment or acquittal pivoted on accusers' and defendants' competing narratives.

Procedure alone does not explain the stark contrast between stories in this case. Legal proceedings can only mirror the broader social and cultural context in which they take place. What is striking about the dueling images of Juan Clemente—drunken Indian versus model villager—is how closely they reflected widely held notions regarding Indians in colonial Mexico. From the earliest times, Spaniards had thought of the Indians as drunkards and idlers. Viceroys, from the late sixteenth century through the early seventeenth century, frequently wrote that Indians were "great friends of idleness" and therefore given to "vice."[27] So deeply ingrained was the image of Indian drunkenness that even those who praised the nature of the Indians admitted that they were often very drunk. Solórzano y Pereira, while insisting that Indians possessed sufficient nobility that their honor could be injured, observed that they "easily become drunk." Of course, to the stereotyped idle, drunken Indian corresponded a simple inversion, the idealized Indian who, according to viceroy and archbishop Juan de Palafox in the 1640s, was liberal with friends, committed to family, helpful to his community, industrious and skillful in craft work, and peaceful and obedient in daily life.[28] It is not pure happenstance, thus, but an expression of how deeply this latter image had penetrated colonial society by the early seventeenth century that testimony for and against Juan Clemente portrayed him in precisely these ways.

For "character" as well as the "facts" were in play in any criminal proceeding. The last question in Ábila's interrogatory asked witnesses to say whether they knew Juan Clemente to be a "quiet and peaceful Indian and a good Christian." Such questions, and their responses, were formulaic. But they may have held particular importance for Indians constantly exhorted to sobriety by parish priests. Pulque production had been commercialized across wide swathes of Mexico between 1580 and 1620, and viceroys, alcaldes mayores, and priests in the early seventeenth century worried constantly about Indian drinking. Indians knew this. One of the most commonly used confession manuals instructed priests to tell Indians that they should not drink "wine of Castile, or of this land," and that they should not become "vagrants for lack of work in what is necessary to you." Otherwise, it would not be possible to "live among your neighbors in peace, kindness, and calm, so that at no time you have occasion to break the peace." Tellingly, "drunkard" (*borracho*) was one of the insults mostly commonly hurled at Indians—by Spaniards and by other Indians—and one to which they took great umbrage.[29]

Given the inconsistencies of Juan Agustín's witnesses, it is not so hard to imagine that the nigh-perfectly framed narrative of Juan Clemente as model villager influenced Fuentes's disposition toward the defendant, removed as he was from the concrete realities of the village. Judges, no less than parties to a dispute, their procuradores, and witnesses, were—and are—constrained to reproduce mainstream values and norms of what was proper.[30] This is not to say that Fuentes's mind was completely determined by the constraints of the normative world in which he lived—only that in making a decision with legal effect he could not avoid being affected by them. The crisp and seamless testimony of Clemente's witnesses, compared to the evasions and uncertainties of Agustín's, and suspicions about Baltazar's statement, almost certainly played an important role in his decision. On strictly logical grounds, however, they could not dictate the outcome, for testimony on the record did not answer all questions.

If Juan Clemente's witnesses were right, Juan Agustín was either mistaken about Clemente's identity or he lied about Clemente's role. There is no way conclusively to rule out a mistake, yet nothing in Juan Agustín's testimony suggests he was in doubt. So did he lie? Possibly, but why implicate Clemente falsely, only to pardon him with the next breath? Moreover, Juan Agustín was on his deathbed and concerned for the state of his soul. When asked, he said he wanted to forgive Clemente. Does it make sense to think that he would have committed a sin by lying even while hoping for God's favor in the afterlife?

On the other side of the balance, the alibi provided by Clemente's witnesses was not airtight. Juan Miguel and wife Agustina María agreed that Clemente had stayed at their house until around ten o'clock. But María Gerónima, Clemente's house guest that night, had reckoned their departure closer to nine o'clock, a time nearer to the one Agustín had testified to. They had dined together, yet no mention was made of whether they drank, which would not have been at all unusual. María Gerónima said that they all lay down to sleep and that she heard nothing more until the following morning. Is it altogether implausible to imagine that they did drink and that Clemente left his house unheard to wander the streets until he bumped into Juan Agustín? Hevia Bolaños's *Curia* held that an accused whose defense hinged on his absence from a place had to be very specific about time and location.[31] Yet the record says nothing of how far Clemente's house was from the place where Agustín was assaulted and whether he might have made it there by the time of the attack, even if the witnesses had seen him enter his home. The fact is that none of the witnesses claimed any direct knowledge of what happened after everyone had gone to bed. Olibares, a procurador but also a judge in this case, did not notice this discrepancy—a genuine failure of advocacy on his part.

There is no way to know if this scenario occurred to Licenciado Fuentes as he formulated his legal opinion. If it did not, it may well have been because procurador Ábila took care to craft a story that would efface the seams in the testimony and raise doubt in the judge's mind—precisely what any good advocate would try to do—and because the witnesses understood how to participate in the telling of that story. Thus, Juan Miguel's and Agustina María's testimony did not simply tell the facts; they related a whole narrative that had begun earlier in the day, one that by portraying Clemente as a "quiet and peaceful Indian" seemed to foreclose certain questions and tamp down doubts about his character and credibility. The possibility that Juan Miguel, Agustina María, and María Gerónima cooked up an alibi for Clemente cannot be discounted. Even if they did not lie outright, their zeal to help a close friend could have led them to shade the night's events in his favor, extending the time he was at their house, perhaps adding the bit about standing in the doorway, which seems almost too convenient, and emphasizing the fact that he carried one of his children which, strictly speaking, was irrelevant to the legal issue of where Clemente was that night but an important evocation of the kind of man the law was less likely to suspect and more likely to protect.

Judgments, according to *Las Siete Partidas,* were of "great benefit," for by means of them "controversies which men have in court are terminated, and each one obtains his rights."[32] Juan Clemente certainly had reason to be pleased with the outcome of these proceedings. He and his witnesses had told their stories and the judge had agreed with them. Juan Agustín's mother and wife, who had entrusted the prosecution of the case to alcalde mayor Olibares, were less satisfied. They too had told their side of things—and lost. As losers, they might seethe privately, but they could not, within the community of those entangled in the legal culture of New Spain, simply assert malfeasance and expect to be listened to. Parties were entitled to tell their stories. But once a decision had been rendered, they were legally mute. Legal process worked by hushing the clamor of dispute to the silence of legitimized acquiescence in judicial judgment.[33]

Punishment represented one of the chief means of quieting the "disputes and tumults" arising from criminal acts. As a "reparation for sin," punishment metaphorically righted the balance of justice back in favor of an aggrieved party, thereby stilling the rancor that might otherwise follow from an unrepaired crime. In principle, punishment also deterred future disorder.[34] Early seventeenth-century jurist Gerónimo de Cevallos characterized punishment as having "the effect of lightning, which, striking to punish one, frightens many; and so with one blow, it serves as example and punishment."[35] From Mexico City's *zócalo* to village commons scattered across New Spain, the *picota*—pillory, gallows, and whipping post—was the rod that drew the lightning of punishment to individual culprits, a concrete symbol of the law's legitimate violence.[36]

On just such a post, after being flogged for some time by village leaders, Jacinto Manzano finally agreed to reveal where he had hidden his pregnant wife's body. They cut him down and he led the assembled party a short distance beyond the town limits of Santiago de La Loppa to a place roughly a quarter of a league from the Royal Highway toward Yace, in Villa Alta. Over an embankment and down a steep slope they scrambled and there, among some boulders at the edge of a stream lay the swollen body of María de Bargas, strangled with her own *huipil*, or shawl.[37] By all accounts, twenty-two-year-old Jacinto and his wife María had gone out the previous night to light candles at a nearby convent to augur a good birth for their child. Jacinto had returned. María had not. The following morning suspicious eyes turned immediately to Jacinto.

Three days later, on April 16, 1657, Madalena de Bargas filed a criminal complaint with the village gobernador, accusing Jacinto of murdering her daughter. Witnesses deposed for the opening *información* testified that Jacinto had been having an affair with another woman for four years, with the approval of Jacinto's parents, no less. He had often beaten his wife, they said. Gobernador, don Juan de la Crus, testified that he had arrested Jacinto almost immediately after María de Bargas had gone missing. He and several other officials had flogged him so that he would tell them what happened. Initially he denied knowledge of María's whereabouts, saying she must have run off, as she had done before. But after more blows he finally confessed his crime and led them to the body. Crus and the other officers then strung him back up on the picota and asked him why he had done it. At the beginning, Jacinto replied only that he had been tempted by the devil, as he had been for four years. After more strokes, he said that María Sánchez, his paramour, had put him up to it. Crus had then sent for alcalde mayor don Diego de Villegas. While waiting for Villegas to arrive, Crus and his officers arrested María Sánchez. After much lashing, she corroborated Jacinto's statement that she had asked him to kill María de Bargas.[38]

Two days later, Villegas had drafted a *cabeza de proceso* and begun to depose witnesses. Moving quickly, he appointed local Spaniard Francisco López de Orosco to act as the king's prosecutor. He rounded up interpreters—both parties spoke Zapoteca—and appointed Juan Manzano Chaves to represent Jacinto, as well as his parents, who had been charged as abettors, and María Sánchez, as an accomplice. He then took the defendants' statements. Jacinto's mother denied any part in the affair and referred to her son as a *"bellaco"*—a scoundrel. His father testified that Jacinto and María de Bargas had looked "content and in peace together" when they went to light candles. María Sánchez simply raved, a response Villegas interpreted as an effort to fake madness.[39] Jacinto was asked whether it was true that he had taken his wife out on the pretext of lighting candles and then strangled her to death and cast her body into a rocky pit. He answered that when he had left the house it had been with the best of intentions but along the way the devil appeared and fooled him into thinking that she was pregnant by another man, which caused him to strangle her. Asked why he had done it, he answered that he was tired of his wife going to the gobernador to complain about him, because the gobernador always flogged him afterwards, and it was the memory of this that allowed the devil to "boil his blood." Nor did María Sánchez put him up to it. He had earlier blamed her but that was because he was being flogged at the time.

Manzano then filed a petition on Jacinto's behalf.[40] Jacinto did not deny killing his wife. But the circumstances were not those testified to by earlier witnesses. In fact, argued the petition, María de Bargas had frequently been away from home, sometimes for months at a time. Jacinto had once been forced to obtain a viceregal order commanding the alcaldes of the village of San Pablo Nexixa, outside the city of Oaxaca, to release his wife to him. Already pregnant by another man, she had not wanted to return home. So she circulated the rumor that Jacinto was having an affair with María Sánchez, a false and "treacherous" accusation. Witnesses who said they had been lovers were all María de Bargas's friends and disliked María Sánchez because she was an "outsider" (*forastera*). Contrary to what witnesses said, Jacinto's parents had not abetted his supposed affair with María Sánchez. Her presence at the house was easy to explain: she had often taken tamales to Jacinto's parents when they were sick, because they had no relatives in the village.

Manzano then deposed witnesses for the defendants.[41] Responding to interrogatories, Jacinto's father testified that María de Bargas was never home, rarely cooked, fought with her husband, and had gotten pregnant by another man, a fact that was "public and notorious" in the community. Jacinto Pérez, the church organist, agreed that María de Bargas was always away from home. That was why Jacinto beat her not, as her witnesses claimed, because he was having an affair with María Sánchez. Indeed, María de Bargas herself had started that rumor to excuse her own sins and cast blame on Jacinto. To make matters worse, she used this lie to persuade the alcaldes to whip him often. And yet, when the alcaldes investigated the matter, concluded Pérez, they found no evidence of an amorous relationship between Jacinto and María Sánchez.

Prosecutor López, on behalf of Madalena de Bargas and for Royal Justice, closed the evidentiary phase of the case, arguing that Jacinto's witnesses should not be believed.[42] They had alleged that Jacinto mistreated his wife because of her adultery and not because of his affair with María Sánchez. Yet Jacinto himself testified that he had killed his wife because he was tired of her complaints to the alcaldes. Nor was it true that Jacinto had tried to get María de Bargas back when she fled to the other village. She went to the gobernador there to seek protection from her husband's fists and stayed for a whole year without Jacinto making any effort to fetch her.[43] As to María de Bargas's supposedly adulterous child, she and Jacinto had appeared before the gobernador and alcaldes, where they had been reconciled and signed safe conducts.

With all the evidence before him, Villegas convicted Jacinto, as well as his parents and María Sánchez in the death of María de Bargas.[44] "Because of the guilt that results against her," the judge sentenced María Sánchez to two hundred strokes at the picota and exile from La Loppa for a year. Jacinto's parents were condemned to ritual public shaming and costs. Jacinto was to be put on a donkey, with a rope around his neck, hands and feet tied. He was to be paraded through the streets of town to the picota, a crier going before him to proclaim his crime. There he would be hung by the neck until dead. His body would be put into a sack with a live dog, a live snake, a live monkey, and a live capon. With its mouth sewn shut, the bag was to be tossed into the deepest part of the river near the place he had killed his wife. Jacinto's procurador appealed the sentence to "the king our lord." The prosecutor opposed the appeal in so heinous a case of uxoricide. Lacking money, Manzano was unable to travel to Mexico City in time to file the appeal. The sentences were carried out on September 21, 1657.

Once he had led village officials to the body, there was little doubt Jacinto would be convicted of killing his wife. The only open question was whether circumstances might mitigate punishment. Competing story lines portrayed very different versions of Jacinto's and María de Bargas's relationship. The prosecution made Jacinto out to be an adulterer and wife beater who had driven María de Bargas to seek protection far from La Loppa. Witnesses testified to Jacinto's brutality and claimed that his parents had encouraged him in his illicit and sinful relationship with María Sánchez. Jacinto had feigned reconciliation with his wife, they said, so that he might more easily lure her to her death. The candle lighting was no more than a cruel ruse. Here was a complete narrative of perfidy and deceit aimed at abetting private pleasure over the public obligation implied in matrimony.

Jacinto's witnesses, by contrast, made the defendant into a man beleaguered by his harridan of a wife. She shirked domestic duties, was away from home for long periods, and was pregnant with a bastard child. She accused him falsely before the alcaldes, exhorting them to flog him for no reason, injuring both body and honor. She had spread the false rumor that Jacinto and María Sánchez were having an affair. True, Jacinto had killed his wife, but only because the devil had made him remember the abuse he had received at her hands. In short, she had at every step of the way pursued her own private pleasure over the public obligation implied in matrimony.

Although the case ultimately was handled by the Spanish alcalde mayor, its direction and tone were set by the actions of village officers in immediate response to the crime. Ignoring regulations limiting the use of judicial torture, they had taken matters into their own hands and flogged Jacinto into confessing.[45] Though statements obtained by torture were recognized in law as potentially untrustworthy, Jacinto led officers to the body, something only the murderer could have done. These men were obviously horrified by what had happened. They had long experience with Jacinto's and María de Bargas' turbulent marriage. Indeed, María's murder may not have come as much of a surprise. For some the killing may even have been a death foretold: María's mother and a friend had urged her not to go with Jacinto to light candles, fearing he would kill her on the way.[46]

Once Villegas came on the scene, procedure took over. Because there was no real doubt about Jacinto's guilt, the question uppermost in everyone's mind seems to have been *why* it had happened. Ten witnesses, evenly split between prosecution and defense, produced sharply divergent stories about Jacinto's motives. The distinction between Jacinto's killing María de Bargas because of his affair with María Sánchez, as prosecution witnesses claimed, and killing her because of her faithlessness and mistreatment may seem a fine one, but establishing it represented Jacinto's only wisp of hope. His procurador understood that Jacinto had no clear exculpatory principle on which to rely. This was not the justifiable homicide of a husband who finds his wife and her lover in flagrante in his own home, or a case of insanity, which could excuse his actions. Nor was it a case of diminished capacity, which might at least have softened the sentence.[47] It was, according to witnesses for the prosecution, a case in which Jacinto had lured his wife on false pretenses to a dark place at night when, as *Las Partidas* put it, "many dangers and evils may result." Jacinto, thus, needed to admit his act but deny responsibility for it. His claim that the devil had tempted him suggests that even under the duress of being whipped he understood the dilemma.[48] Demonic possession represented an imaginative, if desperate, solution to a legal riddle. It allowed Jacinto to claim himself a victim, first of his wife, who had treated him so badly over the years, and second of the devil himself, who had preyed on the weakness of one so mightily abused. To accomplish this, the defense needed to paint María de Bargas in lurid tones.

But this was not just a legal dispute. The proceedings were also a collective performance by the community, one that began when local officials arrested and flogged Jacinto on their own initiative. Since everyone understood that the death penalty was a genuine possibility, witnesses for the prosecution had every reason to depict Jacinto in unforgiving terms; so severe a punishment called for legal clarity and righteous indignation, not the nuances of what appears to have been a very complicated relationship.[49] Moreover, local officials had gone out on a limb by flogging Jacinto and surely felt their actions were vindicated by the black heartedness of a husband who could kill his pregnant wife, whatever else she might have done.

Villegas, thus, may have had relatively little leeway as judge. Jacinto's crime was undeniable, and local action had set the scene long before the alcalde mayor's arrival. Besides, significant elements of the community were outraged by what had happened. Jacinto's family and friends could testify on his behalf, but they could not deny what he had done. This was, at the end of the day, a participatory proceeding. The brutal theatricality of the sentence appears to have been aimed at satisfying María de Bargas's family and silencing Jacinto's—but also at awing the wider community. Jacinto the wife murderer would ride through the public streets while the crier called out the horror of his crime. He would be hanged, fighting for his last breaths as his wife had done. Inside the sewn bag, perhaps a metaphor for the womb where a child had died, the animals would maul each other and Jacinto's broken body—a reminder, perhaps, of what happened when men became as beasts—in the very water where he had left his wife's corpse. According to the acknowledgement of execution, the sentence was carried out precisely as ordered, while several prominent citizens of the town, Spaniards and Indians alike, and many Indian commoners looked on.[50]

Criminal proceedings did not invariably produce tidy resolutions of acquittal or conviction. The stories told by witnesses and shaped by procuradores, rather than reduce a conflict to its essence, might magnify and multiply disputes in ways that taxed process and decision making. In such circumstances, the universal availability of procedure, far from dampening tensions, could throw a community into turmoil.

On June 29, 1641, a calm, early summer Saturday morning in Ocuila was shattered by the report of an arquebus. The entire town had been at church up the road in Malinalco. Mass was done and the priest was having hot chocolate with two other Spaniards when a villager burst in, urging the father to come administer last rites to an Indian boy. The priest hurried off, everyone in tow. A short time later, he bent over teen-aged Rodrigo, who was on the point of death, half of his skull blown off. Unable to confess the lad, the father annointed him with oil and commended his soul to God.[51]

As this was going on, Diego Vásquez, the Indian gobernador of Ocuila, was hearing from townspeople that Rodrigo had shot himself with the gun of Francisco Torres, a Spanish tribute collector who had stopped in town to hear mass. On his way to church, he had left his baggage and gun at the house of don Nicolás, gobernador Vásquez's brother. Vásquez immediately went to don Nicolás's house where he found a gun that had been recently fired, a fact corroborated by two Spanish witnesses. Knowing that it was against the law for a Spaniard to bring a loaded arquebus into an Indian village, Vásquez returned home to fetch his staff of justice, the symbol of his office and of his judicial authority over local matters. With an impromptu posse, he set out to arrest Torres. Catching wind of this, Torres jumped on his horse and fled, narrowly escaping the angry crowd who wanted him jailed until matters were clarified.

Captain Francisco Soltero, the alcalde mayor for the area, began an investigation at once. He ordered Juan de Eguigurén, his chief bailiff, and a notary to despose witnesses, examine the body, and arrest Torres and anyone else who might have been involved, if they could be found. Two Spaniards who claimed to have accompanied Torres to Ocuila, said they did not remember seeing him with an arquebus. One of them suggested that perhaps the boy had fallen from a tree and hit his head, since he had been found outside among magueyes and trees. By contrast, several Indians reported that it was commonly said among the villagers that Rodrigo had shot himself with Torres's gun. Torres had hitched his horse at don Nicolás's house and left the gun inside with don Nicolás's nine-year-old son, Nicolás Jr. At the time, don Nicolás was away at the market in Toluca and his wife was at mass in Malinalco, so young Nicolás was home alone. Rodrigo lived just up the road. These witnesses speculated that Rodrigo must have come to visit and, playing with the gun, accidentally shot himself in the face. Rodrigo's mother, María Salomé did not dismiss that possibility, but also suggested that young Nicolás may have shot Rodrigo.[52]

On July 2, bailiff Eguigurén asked María Salomé and Agustín Juan, her husband and Rodrigo's stepfather, whether they wanted to press charges against Torres. They responded that they had no one to prosecute because they did not know who had killed Rodrigo. It was, rather, *"una desgracia"*—"a misfortune." They wanted a judicial order directing Torres and don Nicolás to fund masses for Rodrigo's soul, "and with that they would be content and would not ask anything else."

Two weeks later, María Salomé had changed her mind. On July 18 she and her husband went before a notary to draw up a criminal complaint against Torres, which she filed with the alcalde mayor. The document was written in Nahuatl and bore their signatures, suggesting that they had been to see the Indian notary of the village. Reading in the first person, the document argued that Rodrigo would not be dead but for the fact that Torres violated the king's order prohibiting Spaniards from bringing loaded guns into Indian villages. They had "come to ask for our justice, that he be punished and that he pay for the death of my son." The words *justicia* and *rey*—*justice* and *king*—appeared in Spanish. And though the husband's name was on the petition, we know that this was largely María Salomé's doing, because certain Nahuatl usages in the document indicate that a woman was speaking.[53] A later filing also accused nine-year-old Nicolás Jr. in the death and charged don Nicolás with breaking his son out of jail, "violently and with a powerful hand."[54] The couple then petitioned the viceroy to order that father and son be arrested secretly. They feared a direct order might not be carried out, because don Nicolás was "favored and protected by the justice and the ministers of that jurisdiction and by powerful people." In late September, they asked the viceroy to command Bartolomé de Pineda, defender and bailiff of the Indians in that jurisdiction, to arrest don Nicolás and his son without warning.

On October 11, accompanied by a small group of Spaniards, Pineda went to Ocuila to execute the arrest warrant. After father and son had been taken into custody, Diego Vásquez, gobernador of the town and don

Nicolás's brother, confronted Pineda. Accounts of what happened then
varied. Pineda testified that gobernador Vásquez tried to raise a mutiny,
calling Indians to intimidate him from carrying out his order. Vásquez
denied the allegation under oath. He had only asked to see Pineda's order
authorizing the arrest. Pineda produced it and, having seen it, Vásquez
had done nothing further to interfere. Pineda was not mollified and filed
criminal charges against Vásquez for attempted insurrection.

By mid-October, the matter of Rodrigo's death was tied up in legal
knots. María Salomé still wanted to bring Torres to justice, but he was
long gone. She had succeeded in having a nine-year-old boy locked up
for his alleged role in Rodrigo's killing—he was later released to Joseph
de Çeli, his court-appointed procurador, pending the outcome of proceedings—and had obtained a viceregal order to arrest don Nicolás
for allegedly interfering with the processes of local law enforcement.
Bailiff Pineda had carried out that order and, in a fit of pique, filed suit
against Vásquez for insubordination. Don Nicolás, sitting in jail, lodged
a suit of his own against Torres, as the chief author of the crime, and
a countersuit against María Salomé and her husband for "accusing me
with evil design and against the truth" because they were jealous of his
position in town.[55] At that point, alcalde mayor Soltero was out of his
depth. On October 17, having seen the competing claims, he shipped the
entire record off to the Juzgado for the viceroy to rule on. He sent the
royal notary to take it in person, because he suspected that some of his
earlier dispatches had not reached the tribunal—"It would appear that
there has been some malice" on Pineda's part in not wanting the matter
to be decided by the Juzgado.[56]

In early December, De Çeli, the defendants' procurador, asked the
Juzgado to approve three separate interrogatories on his clients' behalf.
An order bearing the viceroy's signature accepted them. The brawl of
suits and countersuits looked to be on the point of escalating. New
witnesses were about to be forced to speak on delicate matters, possibly even be compelled to choose sides in a tangled dispute involving a
Spanish alcalde mayor, a Spanish bailiff, an Indian gobernador and his
brother, an aggrieved mother, and a fugitive Spanish tax collector. In a
clever bit of lawyering, procurador De Çeli upped the ante by threatening to involve more Spanish judicial officials. To this point, the case had
been confined to the towns of Ocuila and Malinalco, both subject to a
single alcalde mayor. De Çeli's proposed interrogatories requested that
two other alcaldes mayores, responsible for the towns of Quautlatlauca
and Tenango, also conduct interrogatories in their respective jurisdictions, because they might have some helpful information.

It is precisely at this point that the record peters out. No witnesses ever responded to De Çeli's proposed interrogatories and no official resolution of the case appears to have been reached. It is difficult to determine what happened. One obvious possibility is that influential people, in Ocuila and Malinalco, but also in Mexico City, began to fear the case might be spinning out of control. Far from calming the interpersonal chaos produced by Rodrigo's death, legal process seemed to have produced only rancor. The confusion was a direct consequence of Torres's absence from the proceedings. María Salomé and don Nicolás both agreed on Torres's role in the incident, and both filed suits against him. Whereas stories differed on young Nicolás's part in Rodrigo's death, all of the witnesses agreed that Torres had violated the king's law by bringing a loaded gun to town. Had Vásquez nabbed Torres right after the crime, María Salomé likely would not have had any reason to go after a nine-year-old boy. Had young Nicolás not been jailed, don Nicolás would probably not have responded as he did, and María Salomé would not have had him arrested. And if Pineda had not had to arrest don Nicolás, he would not have had a run in with Vásquez.

But Torres was absent. The entire case unfolded according to the story-warping logic of that absence. A mother's pain and anger brought out latent tensions within the community and led people to lash out at one another. Like a collective narrative denied its villain, the story of Rodrigo's death shattered into small shards of a larger whole, which everyone acknowledged but could do nothing to recompose. María Salomé, whose initial testimony admitted but did not dwell on the possibility that young Nicolás had shot Rodrigo, shifted guilt to the lad once it became clear that Torres was not going to be found. Perhaps feeling the helplessness of a parent who has lost a child, she also railed against don Nicolás's power to save his own son from jail and scattered broader accusations that he was a mestizo who enjoyed *the favor and protection of powerful people* in the community. Forced on the defensive, don Nicolás accused María Salomé of testifying falsely and of wishing him ill because of his position at the church. Her witnesses, he alleged, were liars. As if this were not enough, by arresting don Nicolás, bailiff Pineda provoked a misunderstanding rooted in his fears of Indian rebellion and an Indian gobernador's concern to protect his authority against instrusive Spaniards.

In all likelihood, María Salomé was persuaded to drop her case against young Nicolás and his father. She may have repented of trying to substitute a boy's head for Torres's on the pike of her anger and was willing to settle for a few masses on behalf of Rodrigo's soul, which had been her request in the first place.

This may not have been an unreasonable outcome under the sad circumstances of this affair. María Salomé's case against young Nicolás was never very strong: her later claim that the boy had shot Rodrigo was inconsistent with her first statement, which had said nothing of the sort. Moreover, young Nicolás himself testified that Rodrigo had come to the house, had taken up the gun and, while banging its stock on the ground, had accidentally shot himself. María Salomé's early testimony that Rodrigo's face was covered with gunpowder agreed with this account and was at odds with her later statement that young Nicolás had shot Rodrigo from a distance. Given the straightforwardness of young Nicolás' account, and in light of the discrepancies of María Salomé's testimony, it seems unlikely that a judge would have punished a nine-year-old boy. According to the *Curia,* children younger than ten-and-a-half could not be tried for criminal offenses, and a single contested witness did not constitute "proof" sufficient to convict on a criminal charge.[57] Besides, the entire village seems to have been convinced that Rodrigo shot himself. Nor did María Salomé's suit against don Nicolás, owner of the house where Torres's gun had been fired, seem any likelier to succeed, since it appears to have been little more than a gesture of irritation and frustration at Torres's absence. Don Nicolás and his wife had been away when Torres showed up: regardless of whether Rodrigo shot himself or was shot by young Nicolás, they had played no part in the shooting and could not have prevented it.

When all was said and done, procedure had played a deeply ambiguous role in the affair that began with Rodrigo's death. It had allowed various parties to tell their stories. Yet these stories, deformed by Torres's absence, quickly became destructive to the community at large. This was the subtle politics of Torres's flight and the tacit decision not to hunt him down. The processes and narratives of criminal proceedings, by their very essence, demanded a culprit and his submission to law. Without Torres, María Salomé and don Nicolás had only each other to fight, a struggle that stirred up deep, easily roiled sediments of village life.

UNDERSCORING JUDGMENT

If witnesses' testimony and interrogatory answers represent a relatively straightforward path to recovering legal narratives, judges' decisions defy direct reading. Under Spanish law, judges bore no obligation to expose their reasoning in the rulings they issued. They were responsible only for applying law and conscience to the facts of a case in order to reveal the truth of a situation and then to issue a judgment "in good and suitable language which can be readily understood without any ambiguity."[58] In this endeavor, they were guided by principles of evidence detailed in *Las Partidas* and the *Curia*.[59] Careful consideration of these principles in concrete cases permits little more than a sense of the possibilities judges faced.

Occasionally, however, legal decision makers left a faint trace of how they actually confronted a case—underscoring in the record itself. This appears to have happened most often in two situations: when complainants succeeded in persuading the Juzgado to assert jurisdiction over a local matter or when a local alcalde mayor sent a record to Mexico City for a legal opinion. In the first instance, the Juzgado's chief lawyer took the matter away from a local judge and ruled on the case himself. In the second, a legal advisor reviewed the case and offered a nonbinding opinion on the matter to be decided. Officially, the opinion remained advisory, for the local judge retained jursdiction over the case. Whether Juzgado judge or paid legal consultant, these men occasionally underlined as they read, providing a fine Ariadne's thread of reasoning through the labyrinth of the record.

For fourteen years Juan Ximénez and his wife Cecilia María, and Lucas Juan and his wife María Juana, had been living peacefully, tending their crops and paying their tributes in the village of Malacatepec in the province of Metepec. One Sunday morning, Spaniard don Miguel Bermeo and four roughneck cowboys intercepted them on the road as they were walking to mass with Thomás Juan, Juan Ximénez's father. Brandishing swords, don Miguel and his men tied the two couples up, flung them over horses, and rode off to Bermeo's hacienda. Thomás Juan had been wounded while trying to stop Bermeo. Three days later, on July 20, 1678, Thomás Juan and friends of the kidnapped four were in Mexico City. They spoke to Juan Félix de Galves, a procurador at the audiencia, who filed a criminal complaint against Bermeo in the Juzgado. According to the complaint, Juan Ximénez and Lucas Juan had worked for Bermeo's father, don Juan, long ago. Fourteen years earlier they had cleared their debts and left the hacienda. But don Juan had died recently and his son Miguel insisted that Juan Ximénez and Lucas Juan still owed him money. Having filed the complaint, Thomás Juan stopped by the surgeon's to obtain an affidvait testifying to the wounds he had received from Bermeo during the altercation.[60]

On August 4, Nicolás de Vega, a royal notary, accepted a commission to judge the matter. The complainants had already drawn up a list of witnesses. Vega appointed two interpereters. Although the people of the village spoke Nahuatl, their first language was Masagua, so Vega wanted someone who could speak Masagua, in addition to Spanish and Nahuatl. Francisco Hernández, a black resident of the town knew Masagua quite well and agreed to act as interpreter. Vega proceeded to examine the witnesses, mostly local Indians. Once the información was complete, he ordered Bermeo arrested and his goods sequestered. With complainant Thomás Juan at his side, Vega himself went to Bermeo's hacienda. He ordered a reluctant Joseph Bermeo—Miguel's brother—to unlock all the rooms, so that Thomás could search the premises for the missing four. Then, as Thomás looked on and over the howls of Miguel's sister, who claimed the hacienda by inheritance, Vega inventoried and took legal control of all the land, structures, and fixtures of the hacienda, and ordered the livestock to be rounded up and counted.[61] Neither Miguel Bermeo nor his servants were arrested because they had fled the jurisdiction.

By late August the viceroy was involved. He ordered a manhunt for Bermeo and his men. On September 5, a notary from the Juzgado wrote that he had taken Bermeo into custody. The prisoner gave his statement, denying the accusations. His procurador called witnesses on his behalf. On October 19, the Juzgado's chief legal officer Montemayor de Cuenca condemned Bermeo "for the guilt against him," imposing a 250 peso fine, 25 of which were paid to the complainants, and ordered that Bermeo remain in jail until Juan Ximénez and his wife could be found.[62] On November 14, the couple appeared and went before the Juzgado to testify to their identity.

While a judgment of guilt or acquittal was supposed to be "without any ambiguity," reaching it was never simply a matter of applying static rules of law to straighforward factual situations. Judgments always came down to making sense of competing legal narratives. In this case, Montemayor faced irreconcilable stories. In one, the Indians claimed to have been assaulted by Bermeo after fourteen years of peaceful and dutiful living—"paying our tribute," as they put it. Bermeo and his servants had threatened the group with swords, wounded Thomás Juan, bound four people hand and foot, and ridden off with them. In the other, Bermeo, alone and without servants, simply stopped to talk to the Indians, who did not take their caps off all the while, and reminded them gently of the money they still owed him. Though he never got off his horse or unsheathed his sword, said Bermeo, these Indians rallied a crowd and began to pelt him with stones, forcing him to gallop off in fear of his life. As in other cases, both stories conformed to well-known stereotypes: *dutiful Indians who mind their own business until a greedy Spaniard comes along* versus *honest Spaniards confronted by uppity Indians who not only refuse to pay debts, but fail to doff their hats in respect and then almost mutiny.*

From the underscoring that runs through the record, it is clear that Montemayor, or someone on his behalf, was trying to figure out which side came "nearest to the truth" in their testimony—exactly what *Las Partidas* suggest he ought to have been doing.[63] As he read, he seemed to be testing the witnesses' statements for credibility, probing for inconsistencies. He appears to have begun with the complaint and then to have read the witnesses' statements in the order they were taken. This was no simple linear reading, for he seems to have flipped back and forth in the record to compare disparate accounts. For instance, he underlined the phrase "with four cowboys" in the original complaint, a reference to Bermeo's servants. In later testimony offered by Indian witnesses, he underscored statements that Bermeo was in the company of only one or two servants. Similarly, he underlined sections of the complaint alleging that four people were tied up and taken away and also underscored testimony by eye witnesses claiming that only one or two people had been carried off. The judge appears to have noticed as well that witnesses did not always agree on who was taken and when. Although the complaint and two witnesses stated that Juan Ximénez and his wife Cecilia were tied up and kidnapped, one witness claimed that Juan and Cecilia were not taken until the following day. In the same vein, the complaint alleges that Lucas Juan's wife María Juana was kidnapped during the altercation with Bermeo. Yet one witness testified that she escaped at the last second. Underscoring indicates that Montemayor was well aware of these contradictions. He also seemed very concerned to know the whereabouts of those kidnapped. Most witnesses stated in general terms that they had been taken to Bermeo's hacienda. One witness, however, testified that Juan Ximénez and his wife were dragged off to the mines a Talpuxagua to work off a debt Bermeo owed the mine owner there. After two weeks of work, they were returned to Bermeo's hacienda. The judge underlined all of this, more than half the text on the page.[64]

Nor was the judge concerned only with inconsistencies. In the complaint and in the depositions of seven witnesses, he underlined descriptions of Bermeo's behavior, including testimony that he dismounted, drew his sword, wounded Thomás Juan, and ordered his servants to tie people up. On this the witnesses seemed to agree, a fact the judge noted. He also underscored the statement of a witness who, admitting that he knew nothing of the incident in question, complained that Bermeo was holding his wife at his hacienda and would not let her go.[65] Strictly speaking, such testimony did not bear on the case and the judge could have ignored it as irrelevant. By underlining it, he seemed to accept this statement as adding sinew to the allegations regarding Bermeo's treatment of the Indians.

Montemayor (or an assistant) approached the interrogatories filed on Bermeo's behalf in much the same spirit he did the Indians' testimony. In a question posed to Bermeo during his confesión, he underlined a reference to three servants (rather than one, two, or four), and then underlined Bermeo's statement that he was "<u>alone</u>," because his "<u>two</u>" servants were somewhere else. Ignoring Bermeo's statement that Thomás Juan acted disrespectfully by refusing to take off his hat, the judge underscored lines in which Bermeo accused Thomás Juan of pulling a knife just as many other Indians were arriving. He also underscored Bermeo's denial that he dismounted and unsheathed his sword. In the testimony of Bermeo's witnesses—a mestizo and four Spaniards—the judge seemed concerned for the accuracy of their supposedly eyewitness accounts. He underlined statements regarding how far from the village the encounter between Bermeo and the Indians had taken place—sometimes the distance of a single arquebus shot, sometimes two, though the interrogatory itself stated three. He did not draw attention to a witness' claim that Bermeo had escaped while the Indians were throwing rocks, or a statement that none of the Indians had been wounded. Nor did he appear to have been impressed by another witness's statement that he had heard "various accounts" that the Indians had mutinied, and Bermeo had been attacked with stones.[66]

In closing arguments, Mathias de Xisneros, Bermeo's procurador, pointed to confusions regarding the number of servants, the time of the incident, and the number and names of those taken. He characterized the Indians' testimony as *plena probanza contra producentem*—proof to the contrary of what they alleged. Moreover, argued Xisneros, after their near-mutiny, the Indians had known Bermeo would probably file a criminal complaint against them, so they had anticipated him by going to the viceroy first.[67] Galves too offered a closing argument on behalf of the Indians, though his was briefer. He relied on the "many royal decrees of his Majesty in which he has ordered the good treatment of the Indians" and referred to the gross injustice of Bermeo's attempt to collect a debt that probably did not exist. As to confusions of numbers, time, and people, these were small discrepancies considering the blameless Indian witnesses who had testified and their agreement on so many matters of substance. We cannot know how much credit Montemayor gave these arguments, for he did not run his pen under any part of them. Perhaps he wanted to make up his own mind about the testimony.

In the final analysis, underscoring cannot fully account for the decision in this case. Testimony was problematic on both sides. And yet, as a judge, Montemayor had to choose, and he appears to have thought that the Indian complainants had the better of the argument. It is worth noting that in doing so, he accepted the story of seven Indians, with all their inconsistencies, over the word of five Spaniards, despite the principle that the testimony of one honest Spaniard might be worth that of six Indians.[68] But one can as easily imagine Montemayor coming to the opposite conclusion, stressing the variances in the complainants' testimony. In cases such as this, judges were often hard pressed to separate truth from falsehood, the only accepted basis for punishing one party for acts against another.

What tipped the balance? The sentencia proclaimed the additional factor: an abiding concern that the king's laws be strictly obeyed.[69] In his order condemning and fining Bermeo, Montemayor referred to specific royal provisions regarding the good treatment of the Indians and recalled emphatically that Spaniards who committed crimes against Indians were to be punished more severely than when they committed the same crimes against Spaniards.[70] In this case, the law itself and the king's desire to afford Indians a measure of protection, won the day, representing a broad norm on which Indians might pin their hopes for just treatment in disputes with Spaniards.

No such categorical benefit of the doubt was available in criminal disputes between Indians. Judges faced with opposing testimony either equally credible and consistent or equally suspect and variant were thrown back on the bare presumptions of law, the dictates of conscience, and a rough sense of what was right and proper in a given circumstance. Such a case was one beginning with Catarina María's accusation that Juan Teoia "took my virginity."

On August 20, 1696, Catarina María of the barrio San Nicolás in Malinalco, went before the chief justice of that jurisdiction, don Luis de Lippi, to ask that Juan Teoia, an Indian man of the same town, be punished according to the law.[71] After receiving the complaint, Lippi ordered Juan arrested and his statement taken. Speaking from his cell, without a procurador present, Juan claimed that Catarina María had repeatedly sent him amorous messages with Juan's sister. In these missives, she had taunted him, saying that he was not man enough to come to her. On the night in question, said Juan, Catarina had passed by his house. Seeing him, she had begun to flirt with him—"*lo empezo a provocar con amores.*" She had entered the house, thrown herself on the ground before him, and so he had had sex with her. When it was over, according to Juan, Catarina had said "look what you've done and don't think bad of me because I love you a lot," and then she had gone home. On the same day, Madgalena María, Juan's sister, also testified. Asked how she responded to the allegations against Juan, she admitted being a messenger between Juan and Catarina and otherwise corroborated Juan's story, adding that after their encounter they had both looked "very content."

At that point, Lippi made the unusual move of having Juan and Catarina appear before him together, as neither of them had procuradores yet.[72] Catarina affirmed her complaint and Juan admitted having been with her. But, he hastened, he did not think she was a virgin at the time. Catarina persisted, saying that she did not want to marry Juan and demanded that he pay for her virginity. Having accomplished nothing, Lippi returned Juan to his cell and deposited Catarina with doña Bernabé de Vargas, with orders that she not be allowed out of the house until matters were resolved.

Faced with a classic he-said-she-said case, Lippi decided to consult a Mexico City jurist to help him decide the matter. He ordered the record sent to Licenciado don Joseph de Morales, a degreed lawyer of the audiencia, for his opinion. Meanwhile, Catarina's brothers, fearful perhaps that Lippi would not handle the case fairly, went to Mexico City and filed a petition of their own with the Juzgado. They told a somewhat different story than Catarina had: Juan Teoia, they said, had deceived their sister into giving up her virginity by promising to marry her. They asked that Juan either pay for the damage done or marry Catarina. They also requested that the case be taken out of Lippi's hands and that the whole record be sent to the Juzgado for decision. Having seen it, the secretary of the Juzagdo issued an order to Lippi, telling him to depose all further witnesses and have the record back to Morales within eight days.

With the case back in Malinalco, Lippi appointed Francisco de Herrera to defend Juan Teoia. Juan offered a confesión. His answers to the questions broadly tracked his earlier statement. Two further witnesses testified on his behalf, saying that Catarina María was a known "public woman" who had led Juan on.[73] Lippi then ordered Catarina to present her own witnesses. She declined. The documentation was sent to Mexico City and on November 9, Morales sentenced Juan to 12 pesos of court costs but acquitted him on the charge of taking Catarina's virginity. He further ordered Catarina not to "solicit" or "provoke" anyone else. She should "live well or get married," for otherwise she would be sent to a nunnery in Mexico City for six years.[74]

As with the earlier case, it is possible to follow Morales' decision by the underscoring that runs through the record. Far removed from the heat of the case, Morales coolly dissected the testimony. He underlined Juan's statement that Catarina *"threw herself on the ground."* In Magdalena María's statement he highlighted the lines in which she said Catarina came to Juan's house on the pretext of talking to Magdalena on the day of the encounter. He underlined the words *"she [Magdalena María] found them [Juan and Catarina] very happy together"* after they had been alone.[75] In the transcript of the face-to-face interview they had with Lippi, Morales underscored Juan's phrase *"she was not a virgin"* and Catarina's vehement statement that she did not want to marry Juan. He appears to have paid no attention at all to the brothers' claim that Juan falsely promised to marry Catarina, a statement never otherwise corroborated. In Juan's later confesión, Morales underscored the lines in which Juan said he did not know whether Catarina was a virgin, *"because he had never been with a woman before and had no experience of such an act."* He also drew a quick stroke under Juan's claim that he had been *"misled"* by Catarina's flirtations and messages to him.[76] Although the statement was hearsay, Morales also noted Juan's report that Mateo Clemente, another Indian, had warned him not to get involved with Catarina, because she was not a virgin. Morales appears to have followed this issue through Herrera's closing argument, underlining the words *"she flirted with him"* and *"she lay down for him on the ground."* Following Herrera's argument that the case involved neither "kidnapping nor violence"—a tacit reference to *Las Partidas,* which spoke of men who "force or carry off a woman who is a virgin"—Morales ran his quill under the words *"a simple fornication."*[77] Morales also focused on the claims of two local villagers who stated that Catarina, by *"public acknowledgment"*—*"pública voz y fama"*—was a *"public woman."*

It is fairly clear from the points Morales chose to emphasize what weighed on his mind in acquitting Juan of deflowering Catarina María. Absent witnesses on Catarina's behalf, he defaulted to testimony regarding her character and circumstantial evidence regarding the act itself: Catarina went to Juan's house without being called, she flirted with him, egged him on, called his manhood into question, crossed the threshold of his door on her own initiative, and lay on the ground before him. These were not the acts of a girl concerned for her reputation or anxious to protect her virginity. And even if not all of them were precisely true, taken together they bespoke the acts of a *"public woman"* who either would not or could not muster any witnesses on her behalf. Of course, this did not constitute direct proof that Catarina had not been a virgin at the moment of the sexual encounter with Juan. But under the codes of honor and chastity prevalent at that time and place, it was a reasonable inference.

Indeed, the normative values of sexuality in mid-seventeenth century Mexico not only framed the criminal accusation against Juan Teoia but served as an unacknowledged resource for its mitigation. According to *Las Siete Partidas,* a man found guilty of abducting and raping a virgin was liable to the death penalty. One who forced himself on a woman, regardless of whether she was a virgin, could be banished.[78] Obviously, neither Catarina nor her brothers had ever contemplated such punishments: she wanted to be compensated for the damage done to her honor; they wanted a payment, or for Juan to marry her (though she refused the marriage option).

In a sense, Catarina had trapped herself in a dilemma. She might have had a greater chance of seeing Juan punished had she simply accused him of forcing her to have sex—of raping her—rather than of taking her virginity. On the evidence, the judge might have fined and banished Juan. In accusing Juan of deflowering her, she sought to protect her reputation. By emphasizing her virginity, Catarina made the crime against her compensable but opened the door to allegations that she was a public woman without honor to protect. With no one other than herself and her brothers on the record affirming her chastity—and they had an obvious financial interest in the outcome of the case—Morales looked to the evidence before him. Hearsay, such as witnesses' characterization of Catarina as a *public woman* could in principle be admitted when no other evidence was available, but it constituted only *semiplena probanza*—half proof.[79] And since the burden of proof lay with Catarina as the accuser, Morales appears to have decided that there simply was not enough evidence to convict on the deflowerment charge. In a case that might otherwise have been very difficult to resolve on evidentiary grounds, Morales was able to render judgment comfortably in keeping with dominant norms and expectations because Catarina had not met the burden of proof.

PEOPLE CONCERNED FOR PEACE AND QUIET

The most broadly binding and least acknowledged norm of criminal law was to repair the peace shattered by crime. *Las Partidas* may have spoken of quieting the "tumults and dissensions" caused by criminal acts, but in everyday life the law focused tightly on guilt and punishment. Yet, in any given case, the impulse to judge might be in direct tension with the desire to defuse confrontation. Such situations could arise for any number of reasons. As in the case of Rodrigo's death, they could result from a contingency of the case itself—Torres's absence producing a general legal fracas. Alternatively, a particular crime might trigger rumblings from a deep fault line within a community, or people outside the community might chafe against a strictly legal resolution. In certain instances, parties themselves might prefer or even expect a negotiated settlement over legal judgment. Regardless of how they came to pass, such cases suggest the ways law and procedure could produce legal narratives in which peace, more or less explicitly acknowledged, loomed larger than guilt.

On September 8, 1638, an Indian named Domingo Robles from the town of Ystapa filed a criminal complaint against Juan Agustín, an Indian alcalde in the town, and several confederates, also members of the town's governing council. According to Robles, represented by Joseph de Çeli at the audiencia, Agustín and his men had tried to rob his home and had nearly burnt his house to the ground. They had hurt his wife and children and so badly beaten a family guest that she was at risk of death. The attack had not been a random one, claimed Robles. Three years earlier some of Robles's enemies had obtained an order expelling him and his family from the town for being mestizos; by royal law, mestizos were not allowed to live in Indian villages.[80]

Having obtained the order, these enemies sat on it for three years. In August 1638, Juan Agustín and his men had gone to the alcalde mayor of the jurisdiction of Zacualpa to execute the order. The alcalde, "for private ends" and out of "malice and passion" against Robles, had decided to enforce it. Robles had immediately gone to Mexico City in search of a legal remedy to the situation. Learning of this, the culprits had gathered at Robles's house and perpetrated their "atrocity" which, said Robles, deserved "exemplary punishment." In his criminal filing, he asked that an investigation be undertaken and that all materials relating to the case be sent to the Juzgado. In particular, he did not want the alcalde mayor, his "capital enemy," to have any part in the proceedings.[81] The tribunal ordered the investigation.

A couple of days later, procurador De Çeli deposed three Indians who had traveled to Mexico City to testify on Robles's behalf. All corroborated his story, under oath.[82] Through interpreters, these eyewitnesses described how Robles's wife had fallen to her knees to beg the men "por dios" not to burn down the house and how Juan Agustín and the others had set upon the sobbing woman, her daughters, and a family friend. Bystanders who sought to intercede on the family's behalf were struck. But for the intervention of the town priest, stated the witnesses, Robles's house almost surely would have been torched.

Having seen these statements, the Juzgado, in the viceroy's name, ordered Agustín and his compatriots arrested and commanded that all future proceedings be conducted before the tribunal. At first the teniente in nearby Tenancingo, to whom the order was directed, declined to execute it, perhaps under pressure from the alcalde mayor, who was his superior. Or perhaps he refused because he had some inkling of what lay ahead. Robles had to return to Mexico City for a further order compelling the teniente to obey the viceroy's earlier one. Faced with a second order, and threatened with a stiff fine for noncompliance, teniente don Diego de Leyba complied, but dragged his feet.

There may have been good reason for delay. Sentiment against Robles was running so high in certain quarters of Ystapa that Leyba worried there might be fresh violence. He had to commandeer a house in Robles's barrio to conduct his business, for the priest's house and the royal house were in barrios unfriendly to Robles. Given the deep enmities in play, Leyba took the added precaution of strictly separating the parties, "so that there not be any dissensions or tumults between Robles and his partisans and Juan Agustín, alcalde, and his." He commanded Robles not to leave his house and above all not to go to Agustín's barrio to "persuade people to testify in his behalf" (hinting at a politics of witness inducement). Doing so, he warned, could upset the "peace and quiet" of the town.[83]

Leyba then deposed further witnesses.[84] Asked about the "tenor of the suit," seven Indians recounted what they saw, adding little to the testimony of the first three witnesses. With one exception, they were all from Robles's barrio, Santana. On October 11, Leyba finally swore out an arrest warrant against Agustín and the others. By that time, the would-be defendants had skipped town.

That same day, the gobernador and elected officers of Ystapa presented Leyba with a petition, ostensibly on behalf of the entire town.[85] According to their story, Robles had repeatedly filed false and misleading accounts in obtaining viceregal orders favoring him. He was a mestizo who, in violation of royal law, lived in an Indian village. He and his band of Indian followers from the barrio Santana had some time earlier punished several residents from the neighboring barrio San Gaspar, including Agustín and several of his friends. Witnesses from Santana will lie through their teeth, stated the petition, and so are not to be believed. For this reason "we contradict" the depositions already taken and request that they be declared null and void and excluded from the proceedings.

Caught between the sword and the wall, Leyba renewed his order that the parties keep apart, warning that any Indians violating the order would be flogged. The plot thickened when a local Spanish landowner started to intimidate and beat Robles's partisans in the town's streets. Robles filed a petition with Leyba asking that the harassment be stopped. They were trying to keep him from going to Mexico City, he claimed, in order "to cloud my justice in the criminal matter."[86] Leyba issued the requested order. After this he threw in the towel. With a fragile peace in place, he ordered Robles be given four pesos to travel to Mexico City and take the matter before the Juzgado. Robles did so and on January 1, 1639, he filed a petition asking that he and his family be allowed to live in the village, undisturbed. The Juzgado returned an order telling the alcalde mayor, whom Robles had earlier characterized as his "capital enemy," to investigate.[87]

We do not know what happened after this, for the record ends. Perhaps the alcalde mayor determined that Robles was not, after all, a mestizo and therefore could not be thrown out of town. Perhaps contending parties reached an informal accord: Robles promising not to interfere in village politics so long as Agustín and his crowd were in charge; they pledging not to harass Robles, his family, and his followers. Maybe the alcalde mayor sat on the order, doing nothing and Robles, frustrated and lacking the money to pursue the issue further, simply gave up and left town.

What is so striking about this case, as a legal matter, is that it began as an unadorned complaint regarding heinous crimes—the unprovoked beating of a man's family, the near arson of his house—and ended with a full airing of village animosities. This case was hardly unique. Indian villages, even seemingly placid ones, often rested on deep political fault lines. These were face-to-face communities in which annual elections for office could and frequently did lead to unpleasantness or even violence, as one group vied with another for control of tribute collection, church funds, and labor distribution. Personalities could divide villages—and Robles and Agustín doubtless despised each other—though such hatreds commonly had deeper roots.

The pueblo of Ystapa had a long and unsettled history. It had undergone a congregación in 1593. Together with the adjacent estancia of San Gaspar, Ystapa served as a cabecera (provincial seat) for surrounding areas and received the inhabitants of several other settlements. Santa Ana Sochuca (Santana) was one of these. Santana had initially refused to obey the congregación and had rejected San Gaspar's status as the cabecera.[88] By 1639, Santana appears to have been absorbed into San Gaspar's sphere of influence, though tensions between Robles's and Agustín's factions suggest that older rivalries persisted. Although the case makes no direct comment, it seems likely that Robles was a kind of political entrepreneur who purported to represent the Indians of Santana against the importunities and demands of elected officials from San Gaspar, such as Juan Agustín.

The task of Ystapa's elected officials could not have been an easy one in 1638. As in so many other places, the province of Zacualpa had seen massive death during the preceding six decades. From 1,267 in 1569, the number of tributaries dropped to 269 by 1643. From such diminished numbers, the gobernador had to collect the king's tributes and provide

labor to the nearby mines. At the same time, the non-Indian population grew, as mining drew mestizos, mulattoes, and blacks. Under these
circumstances, it is not hard to imagine that residents of Santana would
have been somewhat suspicious of an alcalde from San Gaspar and that
elected officials of San Gaspar might have had reason—or at least seen
advantage—in accusing Robles of being a mestizo.

Teniente Leyba, commissioned by Mexico City to serve as judge in
this affair, quickly understood that he was not dealing with a simple
criminal matter. Local peace was at stake. Both sides had followers, and
both had proven themselves willing to use violence. And yet, Leyba could
not simply ignore Robles's case; once a complaint was filed, certain formalities had to be observed. So he ordered the groups apart and stressed
the need to keep a lid on things. Robles's antagonists—the gobernador
and other officials as proxies for Agustín and his followers—responded
by trying to keep him out of court. They knew the law would not countenance their actions, and they did not want to face charges of wan-
ton violence against women and children. So they argued that Robles
should not be heard because he was a mestizo. It was a weak response,
for even if it were true that Robles was a mestizo, an allegation never
proven—and by allowing him to file a claim, the Juzgado seems to have
taken him for an Indian—the fact did not excuse or mitigate the crime
against Robles's family and property. Leyba thus could not just dismiss
the matter. His position was more delicate still, for he had been tapped
to deal with the issue because Robles felt that the alcalde mayor, Leyba's
immediate superior, would surely side with Agustín.

Once a reluctant Leyba had assumed the role of judge, procedure became his instrument and defense. He proceeded cautiously, sensing that
little was to be gained by insisting on the letter of the law. Robles's witnesses were persuasive, and there was no testimony to counter them—
Robles's wife and children had the bruises and cuts to prove the point,
and the family friend hovered between life and death. Perhaps this is the
chief reason the petition from San Gaspar's gobernador and officers
framed the problem so starkly—they understood they had little hope of
prevailing on the merits. By arguing that Robles's witnesses should not
be heard, they were defying Leyba to rule in what amounted to a faction
fight. Faced with this dilemma, Leyba demurred. He issued arrest war-
rants and deposed Robles's witnesses, as the law required. But he did
not rule on competing petitions.

Content to let both parties float in a limbo of legal indecision, Leyba
seemed to sense that pressing the case to conclusion would clarify nothing—and might further unsettle the village. Fearing open violence might
be a small misstep away, he forbade Robles from going to San Gaspar

to drum up more witnesses. Agustín and the others had already fled, so there was no one to punish anyway. Even if the matter went forward, Leyba may have reasoned, witnesses for the defendants would doubtless be influenced by the gobernador and his officers, and possibly by the Spanish estanciero (landowner), who remained a shadowy presence throughout the proceedings. Better to let the Juzgado sort things out. With Agustín on the run, Robles in Mexico City trying to settle his status in the village, and the estanciero under orders not to interfere, perhaps things would calm down. Local peace, in other words, appears to have brooked larger in Leyba's mind than discerning the narrow "truth" of the incident—which in barest terms, was pretty clear to begin with. And, Leyba may have thought, if Robles obtained the order he sought, his family would probably be satisfied, and Agustín would have no legal recourse against him, which might allow the dust to settle.

This was not an uncommon scenario in criminal cases growing out of dissenssions between Indian factions. If the law demanded that the guilty be punished, the spirit of the law sought first to pacify and reconcile contending parties. Given tensions in Ystapa, it is unlikely that Robles's case could have been resolved in splendid isolation from local rivalries. Crime and criminal law, in this context, were politics by another name. By filing a petition to have Robles declared out of court, the gobernador and officers of San Gaspar, were telling Leyba and indirectly the viceroy, that they could be pushed only so far. Implicitly they seemed to be saying that truth, guilt, and punishment strictly by the book might do more harm than good. Leyba seems to have taken their message to heart. Robles's wife may have continued to fume over the way she and her children had been treated. She may also have recognized that it was far more important for her husband to obtain the order he sought, a goal which may have been strengthened by the fact that his family had been so horribly mistreated and his justice denied.

Although not used in Robles's case, Spanish law recognized a procedure for ending a criminal suit without a legal conclusion about guilt. According to Hevia Bolaños's *Curia,* complainants could withdraw—*apartarse*—from criminal cases, as long as they met certain conditions.[89] Parties could file *apartamientos* for any number of reasons. Perhaps most often they did so in recognition of private settlements.[90] Bringing a criminal complaint was a way of exerting pressure against another party and, once proceedings had begun, the threat of guilt served as a lever in negotiations. If parties agreed to some outcome other than conviction and punishment, the apartamiento signaled the accusing party's surrender of any right to further redress. A party might also withdraw from a criminal proceeding for lack of funds. Particularly if a case had been filed to soften another party's negotiating stance, the point of diminishing returns might be reached earlier than if principle or pride were on the line. On occasion, a party might withdraw for lack of witnesses or for other evidentiary concerns.[91]

Apartamientos appear also to have been used as part of a process by which parties were reconciled to one another or, at least, by which complaining parties were persuaded to end criminal proceedings in order to secure local peace. In early May 1641, in the Villa de Cuyoacan, not far from Mexico City, widow María Ana accused Juan Hernández of burglary and mistreatment. Hernández and several other men dressed only in loin cloths, she told the local justice, had knocked down the door to her home late one night. They had tied up and abused her family and friends, ransacked the house, and trussed her up from a beam and cut her with knives and needles for spinning wool. They had stolen some expensive clothes and, threatening to kill her and the others, had forced her to reveal where she had hidden fifty pesos, part of which was hers and part of which she was holding for others.[92] The local justice interviewed three of the victims. With these statements on the record, María Ana filed an angry criminal complaint demanding that Hernández be punished and that her property and money be returned. She then granted power of attorney to Pedro Salazar, a Spaniard, to act as her procurador. Through Salazar, she called several more witnesses and asked don Andrés de las Ynfantas, chief justice of the jurisdiction, to have Hernández arrested.

The arrest was made, and Ynfantas immediately named Sebastián Adame, another resident of Cuyoacan, to be Hernández's defense attorney, because Adame was "a person capable and intelligent for that job."[93] On May 27, Ynfantas took Hernández's statement.[94] Through two interpreters, Hernández identified himself as a gañán for a local widow. Asked what he had to say about the events at María Ana's house, Hernández did not deny having been there. But, he said, he had been drinking much of the day with a friend, Juan Miguel of Puebla, and several other men he did not know. They had agreed to go to María Ana's tavern that night to drink some more. He slept the rest of the day. At night Juan Miguel and the others woke him and, according to his testimony, all but dragged him to María Ana's. When the other men entered the house, he had remained outside the door, so he had neither seen nor heard what went on inside. He denied tying people up, or stealing anything. When the others finally came out after about an hour, they had shoved a sack of clothes into his hands, and fled. He had wandered over to a neighbor's house to sleep, saying that he had quarreled with his wife.

María Ana clearly was not satisfied with Hernández's story. She filed a formal accusation, asking that he be tortured until he revealed the names of his accomplices. Though judicial torture was only rarely used in such cases, it was a recognized technique of truth finding in Spanish law and María Ana was within her rights to ask for it. By law, torment could be ordered only if all other means of determining the truth of a matter had been exhausted.[95] There was a plausible argument to that effect in this instance: Hernández had testified that he did not know anyone's name other than Juan Miguel's, and María Ana's witnesses had recognized no one else. Torment could also be ordered if there was a presumption of unreliability against the witness in question, which is doubtless why María Ana accused Hernández of being "a known thief in this jurisdiction" who had been jailed many times previously.[96] Ynfantas accepted the accusation and put off a decision on torment, saying he would consider the matter in due time.

Several days later Adame filed an opposing petition, insisting that there was no justification for torturing Hernández: he had no reason to protect the others, since if he was tried alone he would take the fall for them; under the duress of torture, he would almost surely finger the first innocent person who came to his mind; the torment would be greater punishment than he deserved, given that he had not been involved in the most egregious acts against María Ana and her family; and finally, he had lacked any intent to commit the crime, because he had been fooled by the others into going to María Ana's. All of these were framed in terms of the *Curia*'s conditions regulating the use of torment.

After this skirmish, Adame made ready to despose Hernández's witnesses by interrogatory. It is clear from what he submitted for Ynfantas's approval that he and his client planned to argue that drunkenness precluded intent and that *indios forasteros*—Indians from outside the community—had forcibly taken him to María Ana's. One of the questions asked whether Hernández was an "honorable man" of "peaceful and quiet" ways, who would not have gone with Juan Miguel and the others if he had known what they were up to, and had done so only because his judgment was blunted by drink. Meanwhile, María Ana was ratcheting up the stakes. In two petitions, she demanded that Hernández be given the death penalty for his crime.[97] Everything seemed to be moving toward a judicial dénouement.

August and September passed without further legal action. Then, in early October, María Ana abruptly withdrew from the case. Employing formulaic language, her petition noted that although she had intended to see the matter to conclusion, "people concerned for peace and quiet" had asked her to stand down from the prosecution.[98] "To please them and looking to God's service" and out of her "free and spontaneous will, without force or threats nor for fear of not attaining justice," she had agreed to do so. Ynfantas immediately granted her petition for apartamiento and officially took the case on behalf of Royal Justice.[99] Adame then filed a petition asking that Hernández be released from jail. He had been there six months. Ill and near death, he had gone broke defending himself. He should be released, "for the love of God." Two days later, Ynfantas pronounced sentence, condemning Hernández to a twenty peso fine.[100]

We cannot know with certainty what led María Ana to give up the case and acquiesce to a fine in lieu of the corporal and later capital punishment she had earlier sought. One strong possibility, despite her statement that the decision to withdraw had been of her "free and spontaneous will," is that she came under pressure from powerful people in the community. The defendants were employees of prominent local Spaniards who may have wanted to avoid the attention such charges brought. The alcalde mayor was in a position to press María Ana to relent. On the other hand, she appears to have been a no-nonsense woman who had retained her own procurador and never expressed any worry about costs. We might therefore suppose that any pressure brought to bear on María Ana may have been softened by an offer to restore what she had lost, or at least the fifty pesos. Apartamientos explicitly contemplated the exchange of money for withdrawal, though in a criminal matter that exchange might be tacit.[101] Moreover, even if Hernández had been convicted, it is unlikely he would have been put to death, as two of her petitions requested. In principle, a prisoner could be sentenced to severe corporal punishment—including the death penalty—if the evidence was "certain, full, and clear."[102] That would have been a stretch in this case. Of course, Ynfantas had wide discretion, but a death sentence for Hernández would have been out of all proportion, since punishments in such cases usually involved floggings and perhaps banishment from the community for a year or two.

There may have been further legal reasons for María Ana's withdrawal. Though the crime was dire, the case against Hernández was hardly unassailable. Only one witness, twenty-year-old Jusepe, one of María Ana's three sons, had been able to place Hernández inside the house that night. And he offered that testimony only after Hernández had been found with some of María Ana's clothing and after it had become clear that none of the others was going to be caught. All other witnesses testifed only that they heard about Hernández's role from Jusepe—or they said nothing at all. According to the *Curia,* the testimony of a single witness did not suffice to convict: two witnesses testifying from "certain knowledge" were required.[103] Meanwhile, Hernández's procurador hammered away at intent, insisting throughout that his client was drunk and fooled into going, an argument with a solid legal basis. The *Curia* explicitly recognized drunkenness as mitigating ordinary punishments and it is almost certain that Hernández could have found witnesses to testify to his inebriated state that day. By alleging that he stood outside the door, he sought to exculpate himself from the more brutal side of the crime. In doing so, he put direct stress on the case's weak link—the fact that only a single witness claimed to have seen him inside the house. To make matters worse, María Ana's other two sons, Pablo Cruz and Juan Hipolito, falsely accused an Indian named Juan Matias. They claimed to have seen Matias wearing a shawl stolen from their mother. Matias was arrested and thrown in jail for six days while the matter was sorted out. The judge ultimately tracked down the weaver who had sold a shawl to María Ana. This woman stated unequivocally that the one she had made was very different from Matias's. In short, the brothers were dead wrong—whether by mistake or for less honorable motives is unclear. Although we can only guess, it would not be surprising if this incident began to cloud Ynfantas's mind to the credibility of Hernández's witnesses. The judge may even have wondered whether perhaps María Ana and her sons were too desperate to pin the crime on someone.

Whatever the private reasons for María Ana's withdrawal, the invocation of unnamed "people concerned for peace and quiet" and the insistence that she was doing "God's service," was a way in which the case could be brought to a close without one side or the other having to lose face publicly. There were no obvious factions involved here, as in Robles's case. But tensions may have been running high after María Ana's sons dragged two other townspeople into the legal fracas. Hernández undoubtedly had supporters, as the interrogatory suggests. Had their testimony been taken, more witnesses would have had a stake in the outcome and Ynfantas might have faced a difficult choice. Finally, by October, Hernández had been in jail for six months and by all accounts had been sick much of that time. If María Ana could not have the satisfaction of seeing him broken by torment or punished for his crime, she could at least know that she had caused him to suffer and had bankrupted him. No less plausibly, her bright anger had dimmed and she had come to see Hernández with greater compassion—a compassion that dovetailed with what powerful others may have urged her to do.

The language of "peace and quiet" in María Ana's apartamiento reflected the fact that criminal cases in indigenous communities frequently tapped into the deeper structures and arrangements of local life. Crimes were not isolated incidents affecting only individuals. Through accusations and witnessing, they involved whole relational webs of family, friends, and even patrons. This was perhaps particularly so in affairs of honor, especially with regard to accusations of deflowerment.

On July 12, 1674, don Juan Diego, Indian fiscal—church steward— of the town of Chiconautla, jurisdiction of San Cristóbal Ecatepec, ten leagues from Mexico City, brought charges against Matias Nicolás for deflowering his daughter, Margarita Angelina.[104] It was a fairly typical case. In a few scant lines, the complaint accused Matias, Josepha María, his mother, and his brother, Bartolomé Andrés, of "ruining" Margarita— *"echándola a perder."* Witnesses interviewed for the sumaria testified that Josepha had lured Margarita to their house, where Matias had had sex with her, whether forcibly or not was never clear.

Matias told a different story in his statement. With his mother serving as go-between, he had invited Margarita to the house to ask her if she would come away with him. She had accepted the invitation to talk, but had refused to elope. Nothing more had happened. After their conversation, Matias had left the house. Hours later he and his brother Bartolomé were arrested by don Nicolás, the Indian alcalde of the town. They were shackled and shuffled off to jail. Shortly after, don Juan Diego, Margarita's father, showed up at the jailhouse, to have "words" with Matias.

Hearing of this, don Lorenzo Asaldo, the Spanish corregidor, began to worry. He knew that the threat of violence hung over such disputes. As a precaution, he ordered don Juan arrested, to prevent an "outrage" that might cause "some misfortune or deaths."[105] The next day Matias's mother filed a countersuit. Don Juan had not merely talked to Matias, he had severely beaten her other son, Bartolomé, who had been arrested with Matias. Don Juan responded to the countersuit by denying the allegation and stuck to his story that he had gone to see whether Matias was willing to marry his daughter.

On July 14, just three days after the initial complaint, the two parties filed a joint petition asking that criminal proceedings be suspended. "People desirous of God's service . . . and who want to conserve peace and amity" had asked them to do so, stated the petition in the formulaic language of apartamiento. And since Matias had agreed to marry Margarita, there was no reason to continue the litigation. The corregidor released Matias and ordered him to reappear in a month, with proof that he had married Margarita. In the meanwhile, "everyone must preserve peace and amity." To ensure the order was carried out, don Lorenzo ordered Matias to post a bond against his later appearance. He also released don Juan, requiring him to post a bond to guarantee the health and safety of Bartolomé. He would get his money back once the marriage had taken place and upon presentation of proof that Bartolomé was unharmed. In other words, he was being warned against breaching the peace. Lacking necessary cash, don Juan asked "the whole town" to post bond on his behalf, which was done.[106]

Here procedure made possible the negotiated settlement of a volatile personal situation that threatened public consequences. Determining which of the competing stories was true proved less important, to both parties, to the corregidor and to town representatives than working out a mutually agreeable outcome. If criminal complaints were a sign that peace had been breached, settlements followed by apartamientos were one important way of sealing that breach. Don Juan's initial complaint and sumaria allowed him and his family to show they meant business. Josepha's countersuit made clear that she and her family would not be bullied. The measured tones, restraint and straighforwardness of procedure during the three days of legal contest was in sharp contrast to Matias's alleged subterfuge and don Juan's alleged violence at the jail. The complaints, witnesses' statements, and responses became the basis for an off-the-record conversation between the two parties, one that resulted in a private settlement backed by community sentiment.

In an attenuated but meaningful way, this conversation was mediated by a distant king. Both parties filed their complaints "before Captain don Lorenzo Ansaldo alcalde mayor on behalf of his Majesty." Most of the orders in the case, and each of the last three—the ones that in effect memorialized the agreement reached—were issued by don Lorenzo "for his Majesty." Because these orders had legal effect, they had to have been read out to the affected parties, either in Spanish or translated into Nahuatl, so that the parties would have heard the king mentioned repeatedly in the context of the settlement they had hammered out. There was nothing unusual about this language. As a formula, it represented a ritual of routine acknowledgment of royal authority over judicial matters—one more way in which those who participated in legal proceedings might have come to a sense of the royal presence in their lives.[107]

❧

"Men cannot all be sufficiently virtuous," wrote Domingo de Soto in his *De la justicia y del derecho*.[108] Thus was the law necessary that communities might live in peace and even the unvirtuous be pacified. This was likely no greater a mystery to indigenous people than to Spaniards in seventeenth-century Mexico. Over decades of litigation and complaint, Spanish criminal law became familiar, concrete and quotidian. Criminal procedure, more viscous or more dilute depending on circumstance and geography, coursed through innumerable lives in Indian villages during the hundred years after 1600. Ordinary Spaniards could be tapped to represent Indian defendants or complainants. And if some Indians knew little about how to pursue a criminal case—Juan Clemente's wife and his mother, for instance—others had clear ideas, as when María Ana decided to go after those who had broken into her home. Most complainants and defendants, as well as most witnesses, cited to testify seemed to have had at least a basic idea of what was expected of them and of what might be at stake. Far from an abstraction, guilt paraded itself through the streets to the picota in towns and villages across Mexico.

Guilt was far more than a simple outcome of procedure. It represented as well a metaphor of proper conduct, which allowed ordinary people to embody and express notions of right and wrong. The Nahuatl word most often used as a translation for the Spanish *culpa* (guilt) appears to have been *tlatlacolli,* a word that also meant "sin" (*pecado,* in Spanish). Molina's Nahuatl-Castilian dictionary is symmetric in this regard, giving *tlatlacolli* as the equivalent of *pecado* and of *culpa,* and vice versa.[109] His sixteenth-century confession manual also used the same translation, suggesting that Indians heard the word *tlatlacolli* in religious and legal settings.[110] The anonymous Spaniard who wrote the "Romance" seemed aware that Indians might equate guilt and sin, for the Indian of the poem hopes for a judicial order that will "excommunicate" the scoundrels who had stolen his roosters—a technical non sequitur. But the comic charge of attributing this mistake to the Indian—*see how dull these Indians are, they think that a judge can excommunicate*—suggests a further possibility: that for most Spaniards *culpa* and *pecado* were more tenuously linked by the seventeenth century, more sharply distinguished as belonging to separate legal and religious spheres, than for Indian complainants. Put another way, the dual meaning of *tlatlacolli* hints at a deep normativity underlying the legal notion of *culpa* for Nahuatl speakers, one Spaniards may not have shared quite as powerfully with them by the late seventeenth century.[111]

Witness testimony tended to reproduce dominant norms and became true as people deposed. Witnesses shaped and shaded what they said and how they said it. They did so in light of legal consequences and of broader community expectations. Despite the fact that none of these proceedings was conducted in open court, thus, the stories told by individual witnesses were collective narratives. Few Indian witnesses did not refer at one time or another to *pública voz y fama*—what was publicly said—and things that were known as *público y notorio*—publicly and notoriously. This is why criminal procedure often seemed as concerned with discerning a community's collective sentiment as with "truth" in the abstract; there was no truth separate from witnesses' entanglements with their communities. The Spanish legal system tacitly recognized this, for I have found no cases charging witnesses with perjury, even though witnesses often disagreed on the evidentiary crux of a case: whether Baltazar had been with Juan Agustín that fateful night; whether Bermeo had been alone, dismounted, and brandished his sword; whether Juan Teoia had forced himself upon Catarina María or she had given herself to him. By law perjurors could be punished.[112] In practice they almost never were.[113]

For complainants, criminal procedure represented a powerful instrument of control over lives disrupted by the momentary anarchy of crime. They could go before the alcalde mayor, swear out a complaint, and within relatively short order see the person they had accused be arrested and his goods sequestered. This was one of the instances in which Indians could legitimately cause Spaniards considerable discomfort, as when Miguel de Bermeo was thrown in jail pursuant to a criminal complaint, and Thomás Juan stood alongside Nicolás de Vega and watched him inventory Bermeo's hacienda while Bermeo's sister screamed. Of course, this power could cut both ways. In disputes between Indians, criminal accusations could express personal animosities or, when factions were involved, they could amount to a form of politics, one reason lawsuits so often bred countersuits within Indian villages.

Although defendants were coerced participants in criminal proceedings, they knew that they were entitled to a defense and to tell their story. With regard to cases that got as far as Mexico City, the system seems to have been more or less true to its spirit, for defendants did generally have court-appointed procuradores. Their quality varied, of course, but once a case had passed beyond the boundaries of local village justice, defendants had a legitimate expectation of something like a full proceeding—unlike Jacinto, who was tortured by local officials until he confessed his crime.

Procedure did not guarantee outcomes—punishment, acquittal, or settlement. At best, it promised only that matters would be handled so that parties would be heard. In doing so, it allowed people to take part in a process that could extend beyond this or that small village or town, to Mexico City and, figuratively, Madrid.[114] It implied that individual participants had the ability to demand that someone in power take account of a situation. It also meant, of course, that someone else was at risk of falling into what sixteenth-century Nahuatl speakers had known as the "trap" or "maw" of the law.[115]

Ordinary people in ordinary circumstances, by filing suits and countersuits, witnessing, crafting answers, aligning with one side or another of a dispute, or just trying to stay out of things, took part in criminal proceedings, alongside local officials, alcaldes mayores, notaries, interpreters, procuradores, Mexico City legal advisers, even the viceroy, and fictively the king. During the seventeenth century, through cases like the ones discussed here, Indians across Mexico built up an expectation that they were entitled to participate in this way and to force the powers that were to answer their grievances. Defendants came to assume that they could not be punished arbitrarily or at least not without process—even if at times that is precisely what happened. Participants were not always satisfied; legal contests, after all, tended to produce winners *and* losers. But it did mean that under the most difficult circumstances, when emotions ran highest, and even while despairing of the law, they rarely thought to do anything other than lodge a complaint—like the "Romance's" Indian, who decided that it was "better if I am patient," even though he feared no judge would rule as he wanted.

CHAPTER SEVEN

Voices in the Republic

Governance represented a central problem for all who lived in sixteenth- and seventeenth-century Mexico. With the fall of Tenochtitlan in 1521, Indian communities were forced to consider how they would be ruled. What was now known as New Spain had been a congeries of *altepetl*— kingdoms, tributary provinces and military colonies—dominated in the fifteenth century by the Mexica emperor. Local rulers held sway within their jurisdictions, answering to Tenochtitlan for tribute and obeisance.[1] As this structure crumbled and morphed during the decades of conquest, altepetl retained local jursidiction, leaving indigenous communities to assume their own stance in relation to the Spanish invaders. For Spain, the New World posed the question of how to establish and maintain "a political government, prudent and competent" over so vast a land in which Indians vastly outnumbered Spaniards.[2] In a more theoretical vein, the crown faced the challenge of creating a political structure true to the legal and theological principle that Spain's rule of the New World was justifiable only if it benefited the Indians.[3] Though discussion continued long afterwards, the Spanish crown answered this question in 1555: as long as they paid tribute and did not actively oppose evangelization, Indians would rule themselves at the local level and keep their own "laws and good customs that in ancient times they had for their good government and politics."[4] Indian communities, fractured by ethnicity and political rivalry before the Spaniards' arrival, and decimated by disease and war after, effectively assented by choosing survival over utter disintegration.

By 1600 this did not mean that each Indian town ruled itself autonomously according to ancient practices. Conquest and disease had strained native communities and stretched older traditions to the breaking point. Self-rule meant, rather, that Indian villages and towns chose their own leaders, in much the same way Spanish towns chose theirs—by elections conducted among notable citizens once a year.[5] These elected officers, in turn, formed part of the hierarchy that began with indigenous justices and gobernadores at the village and town level, continued with Spanish tenientes, alcaldes mayores, and corregidores, rose to the judges of the audiencia and the viceroy in Mexico City, and culminated in the king himself. Indian governance thus was a question neither of strict local rule nor of strict subordination, but of how fluid local situations flowed into the complex hydraulics of colonial power and vice versa.

One of the crucial changes wrought by Spanish rule in the New World bore on the relationship between indigenous rulers and commoners. Until the Spaniards' coming, lines of authority had been fairly clear. Altepetl rulers had, in principle, direct and uncontested power over the *macehuales*, or commoners. With the advent of Spanish rule, this authority became more clouded and ambiguous. For while the crown relied on native caciques and principales to rule at the local level, it also held that Indians, regardless of preconquest status, were vassals of the Spanish monarch.[6] In other words, indigenous leaders faced a novel political situation in which those they had ruled enjoyed new possibilities for redress and action. Over time, as commoners and others learned to negotiate a changed political terrain, new currents of conflict appeared within and among native communities.

Channels of legal dispute contained opposing pressures but also intensified the resulting turbulence. Parties raised civil, and more often criminal, suits against each other in contests over local political power. Contenders for a governorship might accuse each other of electoral irregularities. An Indian governor might take on a corrupt Spanish corregidor for abusing his power over labor. Village alcaldes might charge their own gobernador with heavy handedness in the exaction of tribute. Aggrieved commoners might push to have the king's decrees enforced. In all of these cases, legal arguments drew on pivotal ideas of Spanish rule: the Indians' right to forge local political arrangements, the centrality of Spanish authority within Indian towns and villages, the hierarchical relationship between these villages and the institutions of Spanish power, and the ideal that all who wielded public power were in principle accountable to the common good. If these ideas never received full due in practice, neither were they completely ignored in the hurly-burly of colonial life. They defined, rather, the rules of engagement for personal and political contestation among actors at every level of the Mexican polity.

TO ELECT WHOM THEY THINK BEST

Day to day, year to year, Spain's governance of Mexico from the late sixteenth century to the eighteenth century, rested upon the outcome of

elections held in Indian towns and villages—*repúblicas* as they were generally called in legal papers, *republics* or *commonwealths*. In these elections, Indian voters, chiefly principales, caciques and other local notables, chose members of the community to fill important posts, including
gobernador (governor), alcalde (justice), *regidor* (councilman), *alguacil*
(bailiff or constable), *escrivano* (notary), *tequitlato* (tribute collector),
and mayordomo (responsible for managing community labor obligations), as well as religious offices such as fiscal (church steward) and *can-
tores* (church musicians and singers). By law, Indian voters in any given
jurisdiction gathered annually in the cabildo, or town hall, to elect new
officers. With minor differences, the same provisions governed these
meetings as did the election of officers in Spanish towns.[7] Ordinary Spaniards were barred by law from taking part in, or even being present at,
Indian elections.[8] Elegibility to vote hinged principally on local tradition
since Spanish law remained silent on the issue. In many communities, only
those of *tlatoque* or *pipiltin*—that is, noble—status could vote, a pre-
Conquest practice.[9] Nahua communities had long chosen their own
leaders. Elections conducted under Spanish rule differed from earlier
ones principally in their frequency—preconquest elections had been
held to choose a new leader when an old one had died, rather than every
year. Local custom also determined who could stand for election, with
the caveat under Spanish law that no one serve successive terms, a pre-
scription as often violated as honored.

On a local stage, elections settled who within a community would
bear the responsibility of ensuring tribute collection, distributing labor,
enforcing church attendance, and keeping justice. From the perspective
of Spanish rule, the men wanted for this task were to be "virtuous and
propertied."[10] Of course, this meant that elected Indian officials might
wield enormous coercive powers vis-à-vis Indian commoners and have
considerable opportunity to benefit themselves while acting for the republic. A gobernador, together with his alcaldes, could protect a town
by meeting tribute quotas without exceeding them, or they could wring
excess payments from a jurisdiction's people. Elected officers could
try to create a balance of labor exploitation, just enough to keep local
hacendados happy and public projects going, or they could effectively
force people to work on nearby haciendas and in distant mines.

As the first link in the judicial chain, gobernadores and alcaldes were
in a position to arrest, flog, or exile those who refused or opposed them.
Their power within Indian republics, for good and for evil, derived from
the fact that colonial rule depended on their role as go-betweens and brokers. Not surprisingly, their actions often aroused deep resentments on
both sides. Spaniards suspected native officials of serving themselves at
the expense of royal tributes and strapped employers. Indian commoners

frequently accused their gobernadores and alcaldes of aligning too closely with dishonest Spaniards who ignored royal laws protecting the Indians.

Local elections brought a jurisdiction's elite together on a yearly basis. With outgoing officers in attendance, caciques and principales voted to determine who would bear the royal staves of justice—the *varas de justicia*. Winners who took the varas in hand generally promised to "act with entire justice" and for "the good of the republic" during the coming year.[11] The number of *personas vocales*—vocal persons, or voters—taking part in any given election depended on the size of a jurisdiction and on local political alignments. In 1561, 220 electors voted in a Tlaxcala election. The winning candidate for gobernador garnered 120 ballots. In a sharp, three-way contest for the governorship of Tenochtitlan a century later, a total of 129 votes were cast, 79 for the winner, 49 and 1 for the two remaining candidates. In smaller jurisdictions voters might number a few dozen. Thirty-four voters took part in Cuauhtitlan's election in 1676.[12] At times the number of voters varied inversely by size of the pueblo. In a large town, such as Patzcuaro, Valladolid, a dozen notable citizens might dominate elections, whereas in tiny Tlacotepec, in the same jurisdiction, all forty heads of household might take part in the election of an alcalde.[13]

Not all contests boiled down to counting votes. Elections might involve no individual balloting at all. Instead, the assembled electors discussed and sought consensus. In Nahuatl, the word often used to describe the outcome of such a gathering was *pepena*, connoting an act of choosing that might or might not be determined by voting.[14] In certain instances, a smaller group of notables might preselect a slate of officials before gathering to vote. Even so, by the seventeenth century, most Nahuatl speakers with any political experience would have known the words *elección*, *elector*, and *voto*, whether or not they spoke Spanish, for they had been accepted as loanwords into Nahuatl by the 1550s.[15]

Electoral disputes hint that commoners were, at times, present during deliberations and voting, acclaiming and applauding a particular slate of officers, or grumbling at a controversial choice. In some contests commoners cast votes, though their doing so might provoke a lawsuit over the legitimacy of the outcome. Or elections might be conducted in secret. A legitimate slate of candidates fearing a challenge from outside their ranks, could meet, vote themselves into power, and present the town or village in question with a fait accompli. Challengers might meet secretly to vote themselves into power and then hustle to Mexico City, where Juzgado officials ill equipped to detect electoral chicanery might be duped into approving the choice. Outmaneuvered parties generally filed complaints, asking the viceroy to disallow errant results.[16]

While disputed elections brook large in the archive, we must recall that hundreds of towns held yearly elections throughout the seventeenth century. Most never made the historical record, because the vast majority of elections proceeded without incident. Juan de Palafox, the bishop of Puebla between 1639 and 1649 and also, briefly, the viceroy in 1642, held a generally favorable impression of indigenous elections. In his essay "On the Nature of the Indians," he wrote that the Indians, "(if left to themselves)," tended to elect the "most deserving" candidate, usually someone who knew how to read and write, or a noble, and always of a "good aspect and bearing."[17] Palafox doubtless overstated his case, for many elections were bitter, hard fought, even violent, and candidates could be anything but noble.[18] Though the raucousness of these melées tends to drown out the quiet of peaceful elections, they command close attention, for the details of accusation and counteraccusation reveal how intensely contested local power—the cornerstone of colonial rule— could be.[19]

In principle, elections represented a village's right to conduct its own affairs within the limits of its political subjection to Spanish institutions. At the same time, elections frequently gave rise to struggles over local power, which unsettled communities and set people, barrios, and whole villages against each other. Disputed outcomes led to lawsuits, typically criminal accusations of wrongdoing. In these cases, there was no stark split between Spaniards and Indians, for while indigenous litigants routinely charged Spaniards with electoral mischief, they complained as bitterly of other Indians. Indeed, election disputes reveal how tightly geared the *república de españoles* and the *república de indios* were to each other and how that gearing could be made to drive disparate interests.

Certainly, Spaniards commonly interfered in local elections. In 1640, the "gobernadores, alcaldes, regidores, and other officers of the republic of the pueblo of Acambaro, province of Michoacan," filed a petition with the Juzgado alleging that the Spanish alcalde mayor and the village priest were using a rich Indian as a cat's paw for controlling town government. Alternatively, an alcalde mayor might refuse to ratify an election presented to him by the successful slate of candidates, "because he wanted to name a mestizo who is devoted to him and who he favors." Or a local encomendero, using the *powerful hand* of his office, might subvert a local election to appoint his own candidate for gobernador, "with whom he is in league."[20]

Indian petitioners typically responded to such intrusions by requesting that their elections be confirmed or new elections held. Sometimes they asked the Juzgado or the audiencia to dispatch a receptor to investigate the alleged wrongdoing and then conduct a "legitimate and juridical election."[21] In doing so, they resorted to the language of amparo and asked that royal edicts be enforced in their favor. "We the residents in common of the pueblo of San Francisco Ystaquimastitlan . . . with heavy hearts," began a 1655 petition written in Nahuatl, say that we held an election in "our cabildo," choosing as gobernador don Diego Periañes. The alcalde mayor and the parish priest have ousted Periañes, saying he is too old to serve. They have installed don Miguel García in his place, "much to the displeasure of all the residents," because when García served as gobernador once before he took advantage of us, "against the decrees of his Majesty." Some time ago, continued the petition, we received royal decrees and orders "touching on our amparo" and commanding that no one mistreat or bother us. To no avail. Now some Indians of the town had joined the priest's gang and had begun to burden the rest of us with illegal levies. People were fleeing the village. The petition concluded with the request that the properly elected officers be restored to their positions, or that new elections be held, prohibiting don Miguel from participating.[22]

What these and many other cases show is that even when Spaniards meddled in electoral disputes, Indian petitioners complained chiefly of power configurations in which Spaniards and other Indians conspired or acted in parallel. As much as they might have liked to, alcaldes mayores and other Spaniards could not assert direct control of pueblo life. They had to rely on Indian collaborators to take up the mantle of gobernador or alcalde, however thinly disguised the manipulation may sometimes have been.

Consequently, Spaniards did not always play the lead in the theater of disputed elections. In the face of depopulation and the fragmenting of communities, villagers as often fought among themselves over the spoils of local government.[23] Elections frequently brought deep tensions within a community to the surface. For instance, villages subject to a single cabecera, or head town, commonly forged arrangements to secure an always-precarious political peace. These might involve the yearly rotation of office among several pueblos, or they might touch on agreements barring villages or barrios from meddling in each others' elections. With time, such arrangements came to bear the weight of *costumbre*— established custom. Population changes, the appearance of a new alcalde mayor in a jurisdiction, or the emergence of new political constellations within pueblos might strain such understandings. Election season often brought these strains to a breaking point.

In 1642, a group of petitioners identifying themselves as the principales and caciques of barrio Olac, a village subject to the town of Tlayacapa in the province of Chalco, asked the Juzgado for an order allowing them to elect their own gobernador and alcaldes. They claimed to have received an earlier viceregal decree, which had become the "costumbre," allowing each barrio of the jurisdiction to choose its own officers. After seeing the decree, the Spanish alcalde mayor had ordered the other barrios to obey it. But, claimed the petitioners, he had kept the decree and now had it hidden, "so that it could not have any effect." Meanwhile, the other barrios of Tlayacapa had held elections, during which they had tried to arrest don Nicolás de Tolentino and other candidates for office in Olac on trumped up charges.[24]

Don Francisco de San Juan, gobernador of Tlayacapa, for himself and the other officers of Tlayacapa, saw it differently.[25] For fifty years, stated his petition, barrio Olac had never held its own elections. With fewer than thirty souls to its name, Olac simply did not have enough people to field candidates and elect its own officers. Instead, according to what had become "settled custom"—*costumbre asentada*—the more populous barrios of Tecpan and Tepetete had always chosen a councilman for Olac at election time. Now, in 1642, don Nicolás de Tolentino and his followers, had offended custom by seeking to elect themselves on Olac's behalf. Their ploy should not be allowed, argued San Juan, for aside from the fact that they had violated costumbre, Tolentino should not be able to hold office until he had answered for certain misdemeanors. Therefore, concluded the petition, the alcalde mayor should "not consent to any kind of innovation in the custom."

The Juzgado acted according to pattern. In response to the initial petition, it ordered the alcalde mayor to enforce the decree cited by the Olac petitioners. This may have heartened don Nicolás and his men, but in fact the tribunal had committed itself to precisely nothing in a dispute that was still unfolding. The decree cited by don Nicolás, dating to 1622, made no mention of Olac. Rather, it spoke broadly of the king's desire to buffer native elections from the meddling of interlopers, pointedly admonishing parish priests and royal justices not to interfere with whatever "usage and custom"—*uso y costumbre*—the Indians had in conducting their elections. No one, concluded the king's order, could "take away" the Indians' "liberty" to "elect whom they think best."

The Juzgado's dilemma is obvious—both sides were appealing to costumbre. Realistically, the situation favored gobernador San Juan and the officers of Tlayacapa. They, after all, were duly elected officers of republic, while don Nicolás and his men arguably were upstarts whose actions had stirred up the jurisdiction. And where don Nicolás's appeal to the 1622 decree suffered from a kind of fatal vagueness, the Tlayacapa officers stated clearly that the custom in that region had been for Olac not to elect its own officials and argued forcefully that don Nicolás was a ne'er-do-well unqualified to hold a royal staff of justice. At the end of the day, the tribunal commanded the alcalde mayor to keep gobernador San Juan and his officers in their posts and to do nothing that would "consent to any alteration in the *costumbre*."[26]

By coming down against don Nicolás, it might seem that the Juzgado made a decision to favor the party of the establishment, as it were. Legal principle may also have been involved. According to the early eighteenth-century *Diccionario de autoridades*, *costumbre* could be understood as "unwritten law," with the same force and effect as written law, so long as: (1) good followed from it; (2) its exercise was public; (3) all or a majority of people in the affected region subscribed to it; and (4) it did not contravene written law. There was nothing new in this formulation; the enumerated points distilled *Las Siete Partidas*'s section defining usage and custom.[27]

Because these principles would have been widely familiar to lawyers and judges in the seventeenth century, it is worth considering the Juzgado's decision in their light, even though they were not explicitly invoked. Although the law assumed that villages benefited from electing their own leaders, it was not clear from the situation what good might have followed from don Nicolás serving as Olac's gobernador. He might have been speaking for Olac's thirty residents, or he might have been making a power play at villagers' expense. Much depended on don Nicolás's character. Gobernador San Juan's allegations of criminal misdeeds were aimed at this soft spot in the Olac petition. The second criterion might have been more or less a toss up, because both customs—that villages be allowed to elect their own officials and that larger barrios had always chosen a *regidor* for an underpopulated Olac—were alleged to be matters of public knowledge. Number three could well have been decisive and consistent with favoring the establishment over upstarts. Don Nicolás spoke at most for thirty people—a number not contradicted in the record—whereas gobernador San Juan and his officers were the elected officials of large barrios. To favor don Nicolás over the Tlayacapa officials would have been to subordinate the custom recognized by the residents of the other two barrios to a highly dubious claim to custom on behalf of tiny Olac. The fourth point might have been don Nicolás's strongest, for the refusal to allow Olac to choose its own leaders arguably contravened the spirit of the 1622 decree, as his petition insisted. The most plausible response for the Tlayacapa officers would have been to argue that the decree in question did not address the issue at hand: it aimed to prevent Spaniards and other outsiders from interfering in village elections, not to resolve disputes within villages or among Indians themselves.

The Juzgado's concern that costumbre not be tampered with bore heavy implications for the governance of indigenous republics. Indian self-government stood as a fragile political compromise. Royal and vice-regal decrees maintained a loose scaffolding of support for a structure that refused Indian communities full autonomy and denied Spanish rulers full control. The resiliency and durability of this structure rested, in part, on the notion of costumbre as an emblem of a well-ordered society. According to jurist Covarrubias, "custom makes law" when nothing contradicts it. "To change a custom is as bad as death," he argued in 1611, because *"consuetudo est altera natura"*—custom is another nature.[28] In Mexico, where Spanish law overlay pre-Hispanic traditions and local practice varied from place to place, costumbres evolved as a kind of "other" nature to fit a complex and changing environment.

The concern for custom thus betrayed a fundamental conservatism at the foundation of Spanish rule: if costumbre could be kept, if innovation could be minimized, peace would be assured. In bringing lawsuits, power brokers in indigenous villages might affirm the conservative premise underlying the idea of costumbre. In 1677, the elected officers of Cuautitlan filed a complaint against certain "residents" who had tried to hold an election before the accustomed date. Petitioners pointed out that elections had never been held until February of any given year, when terms of office expired. Because "disturbances [had followed] from changing the *costumbre*," insisted the petition, the custom should be kept.[29]

In many instances written law itself became a kind of costumbre in the minds of Spanish judges and Indian litigants alike. The elected officials of the pueblo of Huitlapa in Orizaba, complained in 1657 that an Indian by the name of don Joseph de Luna had usurped the office of fiscal (church steward), with the connivance of the parish friar.[30] With the "hand and favor he enjoys," don Joseph had been able to subject Huitlapa's residents to grave mistreatment, "losing respect for the gobernador and alcaldes" and becoming drunk in public. Not content merely to recount their woes, the Huitlapa petitioners submitted copies of royal decrees and provisions dating to 1560, 1570, and 1571. In the first, King Philip II commanded the viceroy to ask the archbishop of Mexico to forbid parish priests from appointing *fiscales* in Indian towns. A decade later, the king renewed his order, addressing himself to all of Mexico's bishops and provincials of regular orders: "we beg and charge each and every one of you" not to appoint fiscales in Indian villages, as the 1560 decree had asked. The archbishop retorted that priests had always appointed fiscales, and that the 1560 decree had been obtained on the basis of a false and "sinister" report suggesting otherwise. A thing so long done "should be tolerated and left to its good use and custom," concluded the bishop. Responding in 1571, the king did not agree. He recognized the principle that custom should not be disturbed, but he again "beg[ged] and charge[d]" the bishop to keep and enforce the 1560 prohibition.[31] Though we do not know whether this decree had any immediate effect, by the seventeenth century it had become customary for Indian villages to elect their own fiscales. In any event, nearly eighty years later, the Juzgado, faced with the king's decrees, ordered Orizaba's alcalde mayor to enforce the prohibition against outsiders appointing fiscales in Huitlapa.

Exactly how the Huitlapa petitioners came to know of these early royal orders is unclear. Their procurador, Juan Pérez de Salamanca, may have inserted them into the record, hoping to bolster his clients' case. No less likely, petitioners came to Salamanca complaining that in foisting a fiscal upon the community, the priest had violated custom and established law. Indian communities often kept copies of royal edicts gained in earlier litigation for use in later disputes and local power holders were keenly aware of laws that could be used to shore up their authority. After all, had they been ignorant of the law they could not have known to complain. Perhaps it makes most sense, therefore, to suppose that in situations such as this one, procuradores and petitioners frequently had the same idea about how best to present a case, for over time law itself evolved into a costumbre backed by the power of intentional legislation.

AN ACTIVE VOICE

Late in the summer of 1641, Joseph Huexolotl and several comrades conspired to have themselves elected gobernador and alcaldes for the pueblo of Malinalco—by illegal means.[32] Or at least that is what the sitting gobernador of the town alleged in a criminal action against Huexolotl before the Juzgado. According to a witness for gobernador don Juan de Escovar, Huexolotl and his followers had sown "hatred and enmity" within the town, "disturbing the republic and its residents." By splitting the town into "partisan bands" they sought to persuade residents to elect them to office, "so that with the powerful hand of gobernador they could do what they wished." All of this, stated the witness, had interfered with the collection of tribute and constituted the "principal cause of so much ruin." Other witnesses for Escovar corroborated this view, referring to Huexolotl as *"gente de mal vivir"*—a person of disruptive and immoral habits—and a "friend of quarrels in the republic." All who testified for the *información* agreed that he and the others should be banished from the community.[33] The tribunal ordered the alcalde mayor to jail Huexolotl and his men, pending legal proceedings.

Arrests were made and depositions taken in early September. Huexolotl had skipped town by that time, so his statement does not appear in the record. The others flatly denied charges of unsettling the village. Juan Caunochil, one of Huexolotl's allies, insisted that they had not sought to disrupt community life. Rather, they had raised lawsuits against Escovar "so that Your Excellency [the viceroy] would remedy the excesses and vexations that the pueblo's residents receive from the said gobernador." It is not true, continued Caunochil, that they had refused to pay tribute or attend mass. Rather, Escovar had made these false accusations to punish them for "following their justice, which he seeks to impede."[34]

With these statements on the record, the tribunal ordered both sides to present their cases. Escovar, through his procurador Joseph de Çeli, submitted a long document refuting Huexolotl's and Caunochil's accusations on procedural and substantive grounds. Three Spaniards and an Indian principal, testified that they knew Escovar to be a good gobernador. One Spaniard noted that he always acted "for the good of his republic as a loyal and lawful minister," a statement echoed by an Indian witness, who said Escovar "had particular attention for the common and public good of the pueblo." These witnesses dismissed allegations of Escovar's abuses.[35] At this point, the record tails off, without Huexolotl or his men putting up a defense or offering any witnesses of their own.

Like so many others, this case seems frustratingly unresolved—a whirl of accusations and counteraccusations with no judicial determination. Yet, this lack of resolution may not have been arbitrary or accidental. Huexolotl and his partisans were not alone in opposing Escovar. In late August, another band of Malinalco residents had traveled to Mexico City to file *capítulos* complaining of the "many offenses" they had suffered at Escovar's hands. By early October, these men wanted to return home to tend their crops. They filed a petition alleging that "honorable persons" had entreated them to "suspend" the case. They had agreed to do so, provided that neither Escovar nor his compatriots "mistreat by deed or by word any resident of the pueblo" for having brought suit, and so long as Escovar "quietly and peacefully" served his remaining three months in office.[36] The tribunal rejected the suspension, ordering petitioners to remain in the city. Twelve days later Escovar's last witness deposed and the record stopped.

While this incompleteness might suggest that nothing had happened, careful consideration of the situation illumines another possibility. Clearly, Malinalco was embroiled in a summer of discontent. A contingent of residents had trooped off to Mexico City with capítulos against Escovar, even as Huexolotl and his men were politicking among ordinary residents in a bid for elected office. These were not unrelated activities. Escovar himself claimed that there was "malice" between Huexolotl and the capitulantes.[37]

This explains the timing of crucial sallies in the litigation. The capitulantes went to Mexico City and filed their complaint against Escovar on August 30, 1641. Escovar lodged his local criminal complaint against Huexolotl less than a week later, on September 5. The reason seems obvious: Escovar went after Huexolotl because there was nothing he could to do stop the capitulantes. They were already in Mexico City and any effort on his part to interfere with them would have made him look worse before the Juzgado. Huexolotl was another story. A macehual "holding meetings" could easily be arrested for disturbing the peace and quiet of the republic. Escovar may thus have hoped that jailing Huexolotl and his men would intimidate the capitulantes. From this angle, one might suspect that Escovar had wrung the case's suspension from the capitulantes and that he, not they, had won the day. And if it had been a suspension pure and simple, that conclusion would be hard to avoid. But the petition's language is clear: "we" will suspend "our" action "if Escovar behaves himself for what remains of the term of his office." Otherwise, stated the petition, we will be back to renew the lawsuit. Far from laying down their claim, the capitulantes appear to have been offering the town and, crucially, the Juzgado, a compromise. If Escovar could be made to agree, the issue would resolve itself without the tribunal having to render a decision in which one side would prevail legally over the other in what had become a volatile situation.

So why did the Juzgado reject the suspension? Perhaps because the tribunal's jurists wanted to hear from Escovar before deciding what to do. They knew Escovar's witnesses could be deposed quickly. With those statements on the record, Escovar would be unable to claim he had not been heard. The record's abrupt break suggests what probably happened then. With the petition for suspension in hand spelling out the capitulantes' terms, the tribunal would have been able to admonish Escovar to go back to Malinalco and clean up his act. The judge would have warned him, as happened in so many other cases, that he risked the full rigor of the law if the capitulantes returned to complain. For their part, the capitulantes and Huexolotl would probably have been happy for matters to end this way. Escovar had only three more months of his governorship to serve and with the capítulos already filed in Mexico

City, he would likely behave and have a tough time succeeding himself, which was against the law anyway

One of the lasting impressions this case leaves is of just how fluid power could be in local political contests. Both Huexolotl's band and the capitulantes appear to have been macehaules: they did not claim to be principales or caciques, an opportunity rarely missed by those who were (and some who were not), and none of their names was preceded by the honorific *don*. They were just ordinary people who mounted a broad political and legal challenge to an abusive gobernador. The fact that Huexolotl had gone about talking to people, promising to help them in exchange for their support implies a politics of capillary influence, just as sentiment within the community was running strongly against Escovar. This seems to be what galled Escovar and his officers more than anything else. Their initial complaint and the testimony of several witnesses stressed that Huexolotl and his followers were macehuales, an attribution none of the arrested men disputed. From Escovar's vantage, such people were not supposed to be involved in local elections, since they could neither vote nor run for office. He was hardly alone in his frustration at Huexolotl's temerity. Village elites—principales and caciques—complained routinely during the seventeenth century that Indians who were "nothing more than macehuales . . . interfered in local politics."[38]

This reaction bespeaks an anxiety among those who had long dominated indigenous communities. As villages gained greater and thicker contacts with the world beyond their borders, and specifically with the structures of Spanish rule, commoners discovered new ways of affecting their circumstances. While the details of how they did so remain obscure, people who could make no credible claim to be principales or caciques might take over the reins of local government, to the chagrin of local elites.[39] Once in power, they might lighten the weight of impositions on commoners' backs, as the capitulantes and Huexolotl insisted they wanted to do. Just as often they acted no differently from so many others who succumbed to the temptations and opportunities of office. Such was the case in the pueblo of Tepeacacualco, Villa Alta de San Yldefonso, in 1657. Principales, in the name of the residents of the village, alleged that the gobernador and his officers were all "macehual Indians of low rank" who, with "trickery and artifice," had taken office. They were mistreating the Indians and "with violence" had managed to have themselves "elected and reelected" by forcing voters to promise their support.[40]

Given these manipulations and machinations, what could elections have meant within Indian villages during the seventeenth century? From a purely practical point of view, elected officers bore considerable responsibility. Not only did they collect tribute and meet a town's labor obligations, they also administered lands, managed funds, organized fiestas, and made decisions about when to file lawsuits to protect the community against outside intrusions or internal dissensions, or to encourage them. Elections, in principle, determined who would be entrusted with seeing to a pueblo's survival as a community. The great challenge, as the cases indicate, was that opportunities for self-dealing were all but infinite.

Despite corruption and fraud, elections appear to have held deep significance in Indian communities. By choosing their own officers from within, pueblos asserted a fundamental right to exclude outsiders. According to Spanish law, only Indians were to live in Indian villages and stand for election to community office.[41] This did not stop non-Indians from aspiring to and gaining office—especially mestizos and mulattoes, whose racial backgrounds could be so uncertain. And as long as things went well, there was little occasion for a lawsuit. A gobernador known as a mestizo might govern a village peacefully for years, even have a loyal following among local indigenous residents. But when matters became contentious enough to spark litigation, former supporters might turn against a leader they had long accepted and just as easily accuse him of being a mestizo who "meddle[d] in everything, including the cabildo and the elections."[42] Such charges did not guarantee victory. Judges knew how elastic the terms *mestizo* and *mulato* could be. Yet with every assertion of exclusivity, Indian litigants were reminding themselves, their opponents, and the judicial system that indigenous villages were entitled to a measure of autonomy from outside interference.

This principle of exclusion could be scaled and stretched to meet different circumstances. Litigants and witnesses might characterize individual Indian opponents as *advenedizos*—newcomers or outsiders— who had no right to participate in local affairs.[43] Whole villages might be similarly faulted. For example, don Lorenzo de Velásquez, gobernador of Guautitlan, gathered the other "officers of republic" and sped to Mexico City in 1677 to seek ratification of their recent election.[44] A competing slate of candidates had conducted an unlawful election, alleged Velásquez, by allowing nonvoting macehuales and principales from other villages to vote for officers in Guautitlan. In a petition prepared by procurador Mathías de Cisneros, Velásquez and his officers argued that "the other villages intruded" upon the cabildo's autonomy, "alter[ing] the *costumbre*" dictating that each village's election be held so as to "exclude the other villages, as has been usage and custom from time immemorial, each village voting for its own gobernador and alcaldes without those of one village voting in the elections of others." In agreeing to confirm petitioners' election, the tribunal noted that "the majority of the principales of that jurisdiction acclaimed don Lorenzo Velásquez as their gobernador and that the election was legitimately conducted," indicating the Juzgado's willingness to insulate the village from outsiders.[45] Even the location of an election could be the basis of a complaint. The law specified that elections be conducted in a community's cabildo building. This was what grounded the 1641 lawsuit filed by the officers of Guexutla, who asked that a "false election" be voided because it had been held "secretly, outside the community without any of the officials of republic being able to vote as the ordinances of the viceroys say they must."[46]

The notion that Indian pueblos were entitled to exercise a measure of control over their relationship to the outside world could also be expressed in a different but familiar register—*libertad*. With no procurador's name on the petition, the "*común* and residents" of Nopaluca in Tepeaca complained in 1642 that they were sorely "oppressed" by an Indian called Juan Andrés.[47] With "trickery and favors," and in league with the alcalde mayor, he had succeeded in derailing an election and arresting the gobernador, so that he could assume office instead. They asked the viceroy to issue an order allowing them to "conduct their election freely," that they might "escape this slavery and enjoy their liberty." Other cases employed the same language, insisting that elections be held *libremente* (freely), in *keeping with the ordinances of government*, and in accordance with the *free will and applause of the electors*.[48] In one petition, the gobernador, caciques, and principales of San Andrés Atzala, Xalatzingo, told how don Pedro Cortez had succeeded himself in the governorship, "without having been legitimately elected." Although they had a viceregal order approving their slate, petitioners refused to go before the alcalde mayor, fearing he would not enforce the order. Referring to a moment when don Pedro had threatened all who opposed him with 200 lashes and had arrested the notary and another resident who had gone to Mexico City to seek help, the petition stated that the común had "all together acclaimed the gobernador in order to escape the tyranny and slavery in which don Pedro Cortez held them." The Juzgado agreed, ordering don Pedro to leave the jurisdiction for as long as the petitioners remained in office.[49]

To what end did Indian litigants seek to hold their elections freely? After all, elections produced frictions and factions, "conflicts and frauds" that might have been avoided without them.[50] The answer, I believe, rests in the sense of autonomy and self-rule implicit in the idea that a village was entitled to choose its own officers of republic. As several cases make clear, by the mid-seventeenth century, the inability to conduct free elections had come to be understood in terms of *tyranny* and *slavery*. *Libertad* was at stake. As with all mechanisms of political choice, elections represented a field of action for opportunists. But villages' persistence in exercising their right to elect officers, and their willingness to litigate against those who interfered with the practice, shows that the idea of elections was deeply prized within these communities.

A couple of exceptional petitions late in the seventeenth century offer a tantalizing vision of the stakes for petitioners and litigants. In 1685, Antonio Pérez asked the Juzgado for an order confirming his status as a cacique and principal of Tlaxcala. His recently deceased wife had been a *cacica* and principal, and he wanted to succeed her in titles and position, because according to "laws and ordinances he was entitled to exercise the right to have active and passive voice and vote in all the cabildos and elections and meetings of government in that city." The tribunal granted the request. Sixteen years later, in 1701, the *"común* and residents" of the three barrios of San Gerónimo Tlacosaguaya, Oaxaca, insisted that long-established costumbre held that all of the residents should meet once a year to choose officers for each barrio. According to the petition, drafted by procurador Fernando de Galves, the caciques and principales at the cabecera had altered the custom, thereby "usurping the active voice my clients have had in their elections." Petitioners wanted the costumbre to be kept and asked that all three barrios be allowed "to hold their elections freely." The tribunal agreed.[51]

Through the filter of procuradores' words, we can discern a tangible sense that petitioners understood precisely what was at issue in elections: it was the ability to speak—to have voice. Spanish procuradores may have drafted the documents, but it is no strain at all to suppose that these phrases reflected Indian sentiments fairly directly. After a century of adapting to Spanish rule, Indians understood how important it was to be able to choose local leaders. And while technically only caciques and principales actually spoke as voters—*vocales*—commoners too might have a "voice" in elections, for their willingness to listen to upstarts, acclaim a gobernador who was being challenged, and applaud or grumble as lawsuits were brought could set the political context within which elected officials governed.

The 1701 case provides a glimpse of this effect in the list of offices over which petitioners expressed concern. The three barrios were not lobbying to choose a gobernador in their own right. That happened at a higher level. Settled custom did permit them to choose those who would occupy lesser posts—councilman, bailiff, ward officer, tribute collector, and local justice. Lesser, but not unimportant, for these were the offices with the most immediate impact on day-to-day life. Men who held them could arrest, punish, judge, collect tribute, and impose labor obligations. This is what the *"común and residents"* of San Gerónimo Tlasocaguaya understood—they could not afford to surrender the "active voice that they have had in elections" to outside pressure, lest they lose a crucial measure of control over their everyday lives.

LOOKING TO THE KING'S STAFF

As with Spanish alcaldes mayores and corregidores, Indian officers, from tribute collectors to gobernadores, embodied a local power tenuously connected to a distant king. Their legal authority derived from royal power, embodied in the structures of Spanish rule, radiating outward from Mexico City. Every pueblo, in principle, was the king's pueblo. Every gobernador and alcalde the king's man. Every Spanish farmer and Indian macehual the king's vassal.

The most concrete symbol of this authority was the *vara de oficio*— staff of office. By law, every elected officer bore a vara. Royal decrees required Indian gobernadores and alcaldes, like Spanish corregidores and tenientes, to carry *varas de justicia* when in public, "for it is the insignia by which they will be known as judges." According to Solórzano y Pereira, the vara was a proxy for the royal scepter, from which all officers received their jurisdiction. For Covarrubias, vara—literally a branch cut from a tree—was a metaphor of rule itself. A horse, he noted, is "governed" by a vara. In contemporary Spanish society, stated Covarrubias' *Tesoro*, the vara served solely as an "insignia and warning to the people," so that even the lowliest officer could say, "Here is the king." Among colonial Nahuatl speakers, the word *vara* had been recognized as a loanword by the 1560s. *Vara* could also be rendered into Nahuatl. Molina's dictionary translated *vara de justicia* as *justicia topilli*, where *justicia* was also a loanword from Spanish, and *topilli* meant a staff borne by pre-Hispanic indigenous leaders.

In Spanish law, one who held a vara was authorized to speak with an official voice. Officers of indigenous villages typically fetched their varas before acting in an official capacity. Nahuatl recognized the same basic idea, for only a *tlatoani*—the Nahuatl word for *ruler*, which literally meant *speaker*—had been allowed to carry a topilli. The metaphorical qualities of *vara* may also have resonated with Nahuatl speakers familiar with the word. Olmos's Metaphors XIII and XXIX chose a wooden branch or staff cut from a tree—variations on the word for *wood* (*quauitl*) as the image for the act of scolding, correcting by word, or punishing so as to "cause someone to be good." This understanding closely paralleled Covarrubias, who noted that the vara, "always cut from barren trees," had in ancient times served as an instrument of punishment.[52]

To hold a vara was presumptively to hold or possess *oficio*—office. In 1630, for instance, an Indian church steward from the pueblo of Tlacuehuaya appeared before the Juzgado claiming that a fellow villager had conspired with the alcalde mayor, the local vicar, and the bishop to deny him the "use and possession" of his office by taking his vara away. Similarly, a litigant who claimed to be the legitimate gobernador of Metepec complained to the tribunal in 1643 that a competitor, through the "artifice" of a false election and in league with the alcalde mayor, had taken "possession" of the governorship. The imposter should be removed and the alcalde mayor fined, insisted the petitioner, so that the tribunal might grant him his vara and "put him in possession of his office." Other petitions complained when Spanish officials refused to bestow the vara upon legitimately elected officers, instead giving "possession" of the vara to "someone of their devotion."[53]

The word *posesión* in these cases is striking, for it is the same language found in land disputes. During the seventeenth century, *posesión* appears to have become a common expression by which holders of local office claimed precedence over pretenders and usurpers. Seventeenth-century Spanish law recognized the metaphorical qualities of posesión asserted in this way. Office was an abstraction and as the *Diccionario de autoridades* noted, "incorporeal things, properly speaking cannot be possessed." To possess an office thus was to possess it metaphorically, to "have it for oneself" as one might have land or some other "corporeal thing"—such as a vara. Of course, a vara was also a metaphor, "an insignia and warning [that] represents royal authority." Outside the context of office holding, vara was nothing more than a stick. Its symbolic power derived from its status as an emblem of an officeholder's connection to royal authority. Vara and office were linked metaphors expressing a legal and political relationship through the idea of posesión.[54]

This convergence of legitimized authority and a possessive sensibility made local office a flashpoint of personal and political struggle within indigenous communities.[55] Gobernadores and alcaldes routinely charged commoners with *speaking impudently*, of *losing respect*, and of *speaking with disrespect*. They complained acidly of villagers who *spoke words of offense*—as when Miguel Juní publicly called the gobernador of Mizquiaguala a cuckold, "without looking to the office he represented"—indicating how tightly office and personal honor were bound up.[56] The ease and frequency with which such accusations were hurled bespeaks the fragility of a public authority derived from a distant monarch but exercised locally as a prerogative of personal power.

Varas figured centrally in these small, intense dramas. Indian officers whose authority had been snubbed would accuse macehuales, mestizos, and even Spaniards with failing to *look to the staff of the king*. When tempers flared, it was not uncommon for a gobernador or an alcalde to complain in court that someone had seized his vara and broken it. Juan Antonio, the gobernador of the pueblo of San Mateo, Coyoacan, alleged in 1650 that Diego Hernández, a principal of the town, had "dashed to pieces the staff of justice that the gobernador held in his hands in the presence of many people, Spaniards and Indians."[57] Gobernador Antonio claimed to have done nothing more than remind Hernández that he had been elected to office and needed to take possession of his own vara and get on with his work. According to Antonio, Hernández called him a "drunk dog," screamed that he had had enough of elected office and did not want a vara and had then grabbed Antonio's staff of office and broken it. Witnesses agreed with the gobernador's account, stating that Hernández had "shattered the staff of the king." Hernández's wife, attempting to justify her husband's action, maintained that the gobernador had once entered their home and had insulted the couple, calling her a whore and her husband a cuckold. Her testimony came to naught. Ignoring the personal insult to focus on the affront to Antonio's authority, the Spanish corregidor who heard the case sentenced Hernández to fifty lashes at the picota. The order was carried out before several Spanish witnesses "and many Indian men and women." It was a punishment symmetrical to the crime, which had occurred "in the presence of many people, Spaniards and Indians," one meant as a symbolic revindication of the privileges of local office and its connection to royal authority.

As an emblem of office, the vara often carried a greater charge locally than at upper levels of Spanish officialdom. In 1643, outside the village of Guautitlan, mestizo Diego Velásquez assaulted Juan de Mendoza, Indian tribute collector. During the ensuing scuffle, with drawn swords, Mendoza continually exhorted his attacker to "go with God" and to "look to the staff of the king," which Mendoza waved continually in Velásquez's face. Velásquez did not heed this invocation of royal authority and fled the scene empty handed only when Mendoza's two Indian companions showed up. These two, one of them a village alcalde, corroborated Mendoza's story, pointedly noting Velásquez's failure to "respect the staff of royal justice" that the victim "held in his hands." In the course of proceedings, three further witnesses, two mestizos and a Spaniard, told of an earlier encounter in which Velásquez had been surprised in flagrante at the house of a "suspicious woman." Then too, stated all three witnesses, "respecting nothing" and "without looking to the king's staff," he had drawn his sword against native officers of the law. Despite the witnesses' focused attention on the varas, the royal prosecutor filed a three-and-a-half-page long brief against Velásquez without once mentioning the king's staff. For the prosecutor, Velasquéz's attack on Mendoza had been a case of attempted highway robbery pure and simple.

A divergence of perspective is hardly surprising. Higher echelons of Spanish rule obsessed through much of the viceregal period over vagabondage and brigandage.[58] From this vantage, Velásquez's sword-wielding attack on a tribute collector posed a far greater threat than the fact that he had failed to respect the royal staff of a lowly alguacil (bailiff) accompanied by two Indian commoners. The three witnesses, on the other hand, saw with local eyes. They knew of Velásquez's previous run-in with the law and they seemed worried that this surly ruffian who lived among them had twice persisted in violent confrontation when faced with the king's vara. They knew as well that the vara held by each officer represented the only visible source of authority available to those charged with collecting tribute, enforcing labor arrangements, and otherwise compelling commoners to live up to their obligations under their compact with a distant king.[59] They could not do other than seek to protect what this stick symbolized.

THE MIRROR OF AUTHORITY

The aura of royal authority that emanated from the vara might also be contested in legal proceedings, perhaps most commonly between Indian officers of republic and the Spanish alcaldes mayores who so frequently failed to "administer [justice] equally and hear everyone with mildness."[60] On September 12, 1662, Indian alcalde Nicolás Martín was with the gobernador of Atocpa. Returning from a routine tribute-collection trip, the two men ran across mestizo Juan de Mendoza. As their eyes met, Martín recognized Mendoza as the man who three years earlier had killed Martín's son.[61] Mendoza had fled the jurisdiciton before he could be arrested. Face to face with him now, Martín and the gobernador wrestled the killer down and took him into custody, an act well within the scope of their authority.[62] They then headed immediately for Ysquiquitlapilco to turn him over to teniente Francisco García while Martín made arrangements to have Mendoza transferred to the jail in Atocpa, the jurisdictional cabecera.

Three weeks passed before Martín appeared in the chambers of alcalde mayor captain Agustín Gutiérrez in Atocpa. On October 5, 1662, he presented to Gutiérrez a petition he had drafted himself. "Nicolás Martín, ordinary Indian alcalde for his majesty of the royal crown," read the document, "I ask and supplicate your excellency that justice be done for me and that you order Francisco García teniente to render Juan de Mendoza, delinquent, so that he may be brought to jail." He closed his request by asking "with divine deference" that he be granted a copy of Gutiérrez's order so that he might pursue his justice when and where he saw fit.[63]

After reading the petition, the alcalde mayor looked up and asked Martín whether he was aware that the prisoner had escaped the makeshift jail teniente García had set up in Ysquiquitlapilco. Hearing this, Martín lost his cool. For when Gutiérrez then asked why he had delayed so long in bringing the case to him, Martín exploded. According to Gutiérrez's testimony, the man retorted "with rashness and disrespect that what did it matter whether he had come if there is no justice nor is justice done." With those words still hanging in the air between them, Gutiérrez tossed Martín in jail and ordered his property impounded and deposited with a local Indian resident of Atocpa.

Gutiérrez had been personally slighted by Martín's outburst. Worse, his authority had been publicly diminished. Wasting no time, he immediately charged Martín criminally, deposing witnesses to back his story and taking Martín's statement. In his confession, Martín denied saying what Gutiérrez accused him of. He claimed, rather, to have asked "why should he come when the father of the prisoner [Mendoza] had told him that it did not matter whether he complained to the local justice or not." Either Gutiérrez misheard him, stated Martín, or he had not made himself understood in Spanish. Faithful to the mechanics if not the spirit of procedure, Gutiérrez appointed a local Spaniard to serve as Martín's procurador. Juan de Anaya appears to have done the best he could under difficult circumstances. By insisting that the alcalde mayor heard wrong, Martín had thrown down the gauntlet. But in taking his guard he backed himself into a corner, for Gutiérrez was not going to retreat before an Indian commoner. Anaya tried to negotiate between these two hardened positions by picking up on Martín's statement that perhaps he had garbled the Spanish. "With his limited capacity and bad language he switched his words and the meaning sounded differently from what he wanted," wrote Anaya in his brief. This may have been too much for Martín, for while he had opened the door to the argument, Anaya's interpretation of it made him sound like an idiot. After this, Martín refused to cooperate with Anaya in his own defense, deliberately refusing to name witnesses who would have been willing to testify to his shaky Spanish. On October 24, Gutiérrez—simultaneously the aggrieved party, the prosecutor, and the judge in this matter—convicted Martín to a fine of 20 pesos. He warned him, both in Spanish and in Nahuatl, "so that he not feign ignorance," that henceforth he "speak with all modesty and composure and with all the respect and attention owed to all ministers of justice . . . and Spaniards." If he could not civilize his tongue, he would be striped with 200 lashes and sentenced to four years in a quarry or an obraje.

Through all of this, Martín had not been idle. Somehow or other, word of his plight had reached Juan Peres de Salamanca, one of the Juzgado's procuradores. On November 3, barely a week after Gutiérrez issued his sentence, Salamanca filed a petition with the Juzgado on Martín's behalf. He recounted the sordid tale of Mendoza's two escapes—the one three years earlier and the more recent one—implying that teniente García may not have been entirely innocent in the second instance. Martín further accused Gutiérrez of locking him up just because he had had the boldness to ask for a testimonio of his petition so that he could go to Mexico City to pursue his justice. The tribunal sympathized and commanded Gutiérrez to release Martín pending further investigation. A month later, the viceroy issued an order absolving Martín of any guilt and rescinding the fine Gutiérrez had ordered him to pay.

The case had begun when alcalde Martín and the gobernador of Atocpa exercised their jurisdiction to arrest a known criminal. García's carelessness (or worse) and Gutiérrez's disdain cut Martín to the quick as the father of a son dead at Mendoza's hands. In a moment of pique he forgot himself and uttered dangerous words. Whether he actually said "there is no justice nor is justice done," as Gutiérrez claimed, or only that "the father of the prisoner had told him that it did not matter whether he complained to the justice or not," insinuating that the fix was in, the effect was the same—he had challenged Gutiérrez's authority as alcalde mayor and impugned his personal integrity. It was an offense Gutiérrez could not ignore. And yet, Martín was far from helpless. While Gutiérrez conducted a procedurally correct if substantively farcical proceeding, Martín sought his remedy in Mexico City. We do not know whether Martín ever had the satisfaction of seeing Mendoza punished. We do know that he prevailed in a contest over the limits of an alcalde mayor's authority, upholding his rights as a person and as an officer for his republic and "for his majesty of the royal crown"—because he knew the system as well as Gutiérrez did. Perhaps better. For we can imagine the look on Gutiérrez's face upon reading the viceroy's order releasing Martín and reversing the sentence and fine. Royal authority did not run in only a single direction.

That authority, according to Solórzano y Pereira, should be so inclined that the king's subjects might see themselves reflected "as in a pure and crystalline mirror." Framed in dignity, the people would govern themselves "concertedly and prudently"—in the sense of living according to the king's law and its spirit—as befit rational creatures. In New Spain, this meant that the Indians had to be "preserved in peace and justice," so they might have reason to see themselves in the looking glass of the king's and his officers' "modesty, moderation, and habits." When this is done, Bartolomé de Góngora wrote reassuringly in 1656, "good government preserves the Republic . . . and preserves the natives in their villages, so that they adhere to the Holy Catholic faith with greater devotion and pay the royal tributes which they must offer to his majesty with greater zeal."[64] In this pithy formulation lay the foundational ambivalence of Spain's presence in the New World: church and tribute represented both the wages of domination and the emblem of right rule. Indigenous litigants played endlessly on this ambivalence, opportunistically or in pursuit of a semblance of good government, or both simultaneously, depending on circumstance. Authority's mirror, in short, could reflect Indians who sought themselves in it, but only through the imperfections of a surface cracked and clouded by the harsh social and political climate of colonial life.[65]

In everyday legal usage, the word *authority*—*autoridad* in Spanish—spoke with more than one voice. Jurist Covarrubias gave "esteem, gravity, eminence" as a first definition for *autoridad*. To *authorize* a thing, stated another entry, was for a "man with credit to approve it." The *Diccionario de autoridades* offered a somewhat fuller characterization. *Authority* implied "excellence" and "eminence," but it also meant "power and jurisdiction to do or order some thing," as in the prince's "supreme authority."[66] At least in theory, *autoridad* was a name given to legitimately exercised power.

In actual legal disputes, this meaning seems often to have been reversed. The odd amparo petition recognized authority's positive sense, referring to a thing properly done as being with "all the necessary favor and authority," or with the "authority and intervention of justice."[67] More commonly, the word *autoridad* appeared in the amparos to describe acts performed by those who abused their power or position *with a powerful hand*. Indian principales, alcaldes, and tribute collectors and Spanish alcaldes mayores and landowners might be accused of compelling labor, taking tribute, or seizing land "on their own authority" or, more fully, "on their own authority without proper title or other right."[68] Legitimate authority, especially the viceroy's and the king's, remained implicit in these formulations, tenuously and speculatively, if hopefully against the power of local authority misused.

In 1615, "the *común* and residents of the pueblo of Otucpa," filed capítulos against their alcalde mayor don Juan Cano Montezuma.[69] Some time earlier, the community had dispatched several representatives to Mexico City to complain of Montezuma's "excesses." The viceroy had heard their tale of woe and given them a letter "reprehending" the alcalde mayor for his actions and "admonishing him to make peace with everyone." Upon their return, officers of the community had presented the letter to Montezuma. After reading it, the alcalde mayor burst into anger and summoned the gobernador and acaldes of Otucpa to the Royal House, where he dressed them down for having gone to Mexico City behind his back. During this rant, claimed the capítulos' first count, Montezuma had insisted that he was the "natural lord" of that province and that the residents of the town should look to him as the rightful heir of that kingdom, because he was a direct descendant of the emperor Montezuma.

Indian witnesses testified in support of the charge. A principal of the town claimed that don Juan erupted "in wrath," asking why they complained to the viceroy and made him write that letter, when he, Montezuma, was "natural lord of all this land and there was no other lord like him in the kingdom and they should respect and help only him." Other witnesses told the same basic story, adding that Montezuma justified his claim to be their natural lord by arguing that he was "the heir of all New Spain and not a newcomer like those from Castile."[70]

There was much more to these capítulos than this single count. The Otucpa litigants presented detailed allegations of Montezuma's other abuses, including threats to the local friars, "lascivious solicitations" of Indian women, arbitrary arrests and prosecutions and trespasses upon land. Through his own procurador, don Juan responded to the accusations, referring to the plaintiffs as "calumniating litigants" whose accusations should not be believed because they were all his "capital enemies." He claimed to have told the officers of Otucpa only that they were obliged to him because of the privileges he held as a descendant of the original Montezuma. Moreover, he argued, the plaintiffs had been encouraged by the provincial notary, a Spaniard called Melchor Gonzales, who was jealous of Montezuma's power and wanted to discredit him in the eyes of the viceroy. (There appears to have been more than a grain of truth in this latter assertion.)

About three months after the case had been filed, the presiding judge, relying on an advisory opinion from a Mexico City lawyer, found for the plaintiffs on several of the charges, but absolved don Juan on the first count. Feeling strongly about this particular claim, the Otucpa litigants asked their procurador to appeal to the audiencia. Five eyewitnesses had testified to Montezuma's statements, said the petition, written by Rafael Díaz de Herrera, a local Spanish resident and known enemy of don Juan's. Before the audiencia could render a decision, the matter was folded into don Juan's residencia, or posttenure investigation, and nothing further was heard of it.[71] This represented a fairly typical outcome for capítulos. The audiencia judge ruled in the plaintiffs' favor on the most tightly framed issues of abuse, awarding 60 pesos here, 13 pesos there. He also saddled don Juan with the greater part of his own salary, forty days' worth, a not inconsiderable sum. But he remained silent on the complainants' principal charge—don Juan's subversion of royal authority.

This silence rang loudly in the litigants' ears. Whether don Juan actually said what they accused him of, the fact that they insisted he did merits close attention. Counts two through seven of the capítulos, as well as two cases that ran parallel to this one, leave no doubt that don Juan had overstepped his bounds.[72] In practical terms, alcaldes mayores were entitled to a certain impunity, as long as theirs were not gross and prolonged infractions. A measure of tolerated malversation was built into the system. Specific complaints of abuse thus did not prompt the filing of these capítulos; Otucpa's leaders had initially sought a less formal remedy through the viceroy's letter to don Juan. They filed the criminal complaint only after the alcalde mayor's tirade. With don Juan's words and his utter disregard for the viceroy's letter still very much on their minds, they listed Montezuma's delusions of grandeur as exhibit number one in their case against him. From their perspective, don Juan's statements loomed as a threat. If he rejected correction by viceregal letter and implicitly challenged royal authority by insisting that he alone was the "natural lord" of the land, there was no telling what he might do. In the shadow of that menace, the Octupa litigants probably feared don Juan's many "excesses" were a prelude to a long season of local abuse.[73]

A Spanish judge might have been expected to sympathize with this concern. Taken at face value, don Juan's statement amounted to a usurpation of royal prerogative. Yet the judge concluded, on the strength of a legal advisory opinion absent from the record, that the charge was "not proven." We can only guess at the reasoning behind the decision. Perhaps the six-for-one rule was in effect: since six Indian witnesses counted for one Spaniard, the fact that there were only five Indian witnesses amounted to a technical failure of proof, nothing more. Had the Spanish witnesses said anything about the capítulo's first count the outcome might have been different. But they did not. One might also suppose that the Mexico City lawyer who gave his opinion understood that nothing could be gained by siding with the capitulantes. To rule the charge unproven risked little. Don Juan could blather all he wanted. The fact remained, as the capitulantes' procurador noted, that Montezuma's ancestors had relinquished all rulership rights to the Spanish king in 1521. Nothing don Juan might say would change that, for he had no means, legal or otherwise, to make his exaggerated claim stick. Simply put, don Juan was no threat, to viceroy or king. To accept the argument from Otucpa, by contrast, would have meant validating a symbolic reversal in which ordinary Indians brought low a powerful ally of Spanish rule, not an outcome the audiencia was liable to accept.

Native litigants had held the mirror of royal authority up to don Juan Cano Montezuma and found much to complain of. By alleging that he had sought to usurp the king's role, they wanted the viceroy to see the ugly reflection they could not avoid. In principle, they had a point—one Solórzano y Pereira could not have quarreled with. But, of course, what one sees in a mirror depends entirely on the angle from which one looks into it. Indigenous litigants and those in power to whom they addressed themselves were both concerned for royal authority. What each side saw reflected, however, varied crucially—less a failure of understanding than an irreducible problem of perspective.

THE DYNAMICS OF PEACE AND DISCORD

A key to making sense of the Otucpa decision may lie in seemingly offhand language contained in the first charge against don Juan. According to the litigants, the letter granted them by the viceroy had exhorted don Juan to keep "peace with everyone." This was neither empty rhetoric by the viceroy nor merely a hopeful gesture on the part of the capitulantes who repeated it. It reflected, rather, a deep principal of Spanish theology and law. *Peace,* according to Aquinas, was "the principal social good," the condition in which men lived alongside each other without "repugnance."[74]

This language of peace saturated litigation over local political arrangements. Local judges, the Juzgado, the audiencia, and the viceroy might order antagonists to have *paz y conformidad*—peace and conformity—with each other, or to hold elections in *paz y quietud*—peace and quiet. Petitioners and litigants also drew on this language. In 1671, for example, the residents and principales of the village of Cutzio filed a criminal suit against their alcalde mayor. In their complaint, drafted initially in Tarasco, these native litigants twice referred explicitly to their desire for paz y quietud.[75]

This idea more often found expression in phrases used to describe those who disrupted peace and to characterize communities lacking peace.[76] Those who subverted paz y quietud were frequently referred to in complaints and by witnesses as *reboltosos, inquietadores* or *inquietos,* and *alborotadores.* In Spanish, these words had fairly precise meanings. Covarrubias defined *reboltosos* as those who "spread rumors and innuendo here and there, and cause enmities and raise doubts." The *Diccionario de autoridades* characterized the *revoltoso* as a "mischief maker, intriguer, or seditionist." An *inquieto,* according to Covarrubias, was "one who has no repose or quiet," the *inquietador* somone who went about disturbing other peoples' quiet and repose. The *alborotador* was a person who "provokes noise and quarrels," so that with just cause people want to "banish him from themselves." Nahuatl was well-endowed with cognates for these terms. Molina offered *teyollococolti* as the equivalent of *reboltoso,* glossing it as "one who promotes wrong or harm among others." He translated *teamamanaliztli,* which he equated to *inquietud,* as the "disquiet or disturbance visisted upon another," and gave *teacomamani* for "*alborotador* of people or a town."[77]

Cases stretching across the seventeenth century suggest that communities suffering such persons in their midst could expect *discordia, disensión,* and *disturbios*—in English, discord, dissension, and disturbances. *Discordia,* according to Covarrubias, numbered among the deadliest of poisons to human communities, for it had "upset and destroyed monarchies, kingdoms, cities, lineages, houses, brothers from the world's very first days." *Disensión* followed from "the diversity of wills and opinions"—what a 1693 case involving a contested election and the breaking of a vara called a "disruption of voices."[78] A *disturbio,* stated the *Diccionario de autoridades,* was the "disruption of peace, quiet, conformity and concord in which people lived with each other, whether of a kingdom, a city, or a family." Here was the tonic to which all of the variations on this language ultimately resolved—peace, quiet, conformity, concord within human communities large and small. Or as the *Diccionario* put it, *paz* could be understood as that state of "calm and good correspondence of people with each other, especially in families; as opposed to *disensiones,* fights, and quarrels."

Paz, in this sense, was less an abstract category of political philosophy than an active metaphor of human community in the context of legal disputes over local governance.[79] No one group monopolized this vocabulary. Spaniards and Indians, macehuales as well as caciques might appeal to it, and parties accused of disturbing a town's *paz y quietud* might just as well respond that the complainants themselves were the actual *inquietadores,* filing *pleitos* and *litigios*—lawsuits—and moving about in partisan groupings known as *bandos* and *parcialidades*—bands and factions. In such cases, opposing sides competed to offer the most compelling account of efforts to keep paz y quietud in a given community, while accusing opponents of promoting discordia. Lawsuits thus expressed a fundamental paradox, for the very fact of litigation bespoke a breach of peace. This is why those accused of wrongdoing so often referred to their accusers as *pleitistas*—people who brought endless, frivolous lawsuits—and why the act of filing *pleitos* was taken to be a mark of the *inquietador*. In short, legal procedure itself, by its availability to all, represented a potential source of discord within indigenous communities.

In June 1644, several principales and residents of San Miguel Hinacuniapco, in the name of the whole village, filed capítulos in Mexico City against Alonso Martín, the gobernador of nearby Sinacantepec.[80] The complaint, written originally in Nahuatl and translated to Spanish, opened by claiming that Alonso Martín, as a "mulatto," was in violation of royal decrees barring non-Indians from holding office in Indian towns. He had been appointed by the local Spanish teniente, "on his own authority and against the will of the residents of said village." Proceeding directly to the first charge, don Andrés Xuárez and several other named plaintiffs accused Martín of renting village Indians out to Spanish farmers in the Toluca valley, where they were "oppressed and mistreated." As a consequence, stated the complaint, those forced to work in this way "have no means or time to attend to the ordinary things of life or to work for their own sustenance and payment of their tributes." Six other charges followed, including accusations that Martín mishandled community funds, drank wine, kept a mistress, flogged residents, and verbally abused people.

On the strength of the complaint and depositions of three witnesses, the Juzgado issued an order forbidding Martín to act as gobernador until matters were clarified. Martín responded by denying he was a mulatto and claiming that Xuárez was a *"macehual revoltoso y alborotador de toda aquella república"*—a commoner, mischief maker, and provoker of quarrels in the whole republic—as were his followers. Several witnesses, caciques and principales all, concurred, noting that Xuárez had the whole town *"rebuelto"*—stirred up—with his lawsuits and intrigues, for the sole purpose of destroying Martín and his officers. With this exchange of accusations, the record stops, except for a brief order from the Juzgado, commanding residents "from both factions in this city" to go home and "have among themselves peace and conformity without discords or enmities." "Be warned," said the tribunal, "that we will proceed with full rigor against those who violate the order." In the meanwhile, Martín was to continue as gobernador and the local justice should protect him in that position.

By issuing this order, the tribunal sought to avoid a more intrusive legal proceeding that might well have churned up the community. By sending the parties home under a strict injunction to peaceful dealings, the viceroy was urging the antagonists to work things out on their own. He weighted those negotiations in Martín's favor, allowing him to retain the governorship and promising judicial protection against challenges to his authority.

From the tribunal's perspective this makes a great deal of sense. Xuárez's case was thin. He had hoped to oust Martín by citing the king's decrees against mulattoes serving as gobernadores in Indian villages. As it turned out, the tribunal barely paused to consider this issue. Martín's witnesses, pillars of the community, testified that they had known Martín from birth and knew his parents and grandparents to have been Indians of the village. Against this solid evidentiary edifice, Xuárez's windy claim and the testimony of his three witnesses, common farmers who did little more than agree with the tenor of the question, had no effect. And while Xuárez's original Nahuatl capítulos charged abuses, the allegations were hazy and unsupported by testimony. By contrast, gobernador Martín enjoyed the support of several caciques and principales who insisted that Xuárez was the *inquietador*. Martín may well have been guilty of some abuses. But his actions, whatever they were, had not yet sparked a reaction from below.[81] In short, whether this lawsuit was Xuárez's ill-conceived attempt to provoke a scandal against gobernador Martín, or a heartfelt expression of indignation at real abuses, or both, he appears to have misjudged local political conditions and failed to take into account the Juzgado's predisposition to favor outcomes promoting paz y quietud.

That the tribunal came down on the gobernador's side in this case should not tempt us to suppose a blind preference for established authority on the part of the viceroy, the audiencia, and the Juzgado. Their barometers could be far more sensitive to the different and oftentimes opposed pressures in the political atmosphere of the kingdom—as sensitive, at times, as indigenous litigants' own.

As soon as mass had finished on Sunday April 29, 1691, don Juan Ramírez Chimal, local cacique and church steward, stood up.[82] Speaking in his native Mayahua, he told the Indian congregants of San Miguel Temascalcingo not to pay tribute until the election for a new gobernador had been concluded and an order from the royal counting house received. Hold it back, he told the packed church, for anyone who paid now would end up paying again later.

When word of Ramírez's little speech reached him, gobernador don Pasqual Chimal fumed. Four days later, he went before Hernando de Perea, the local teniente, who seemed only too eager to help a gobernador whose authority had been undercut. A criminal complaint, officially lodged as a matter of royal justice, accused Ramírez of inciting people to ignore their tributary obligations, "from which could follow many disturbances, anxieties, and seditions [*disturbios, inquietudes y sediciones*]." By May 7, depositions were being taken. Many people had been at mass that day. Three Spaniards, two mestizos, a free mulatto, and a man described as a *lobo* (a mix of black and Indian) testified that Ramírez had indeed said what the complaint accused him of. Those who spoke Mayahua testified from personal knowledge. Others reported that they had heard it said among the Indians.

Three weeks later, Ramírez was arrested and his property impounded. He sat in jail for nearly six months before any further action was taken. In mid-October, alcalde mayor don Diego Ponze de León summoned him to give a statement. In answer to the first question, he admitted having told people to withhold their tribute, but only for three or four days while a new gobernador was elected, at which time they should immediately pay what they owed. Subsequent questions put to Ramírez suggest that don Pasqual and alcalde León thought he was angling for the governorship. One question recalled his bid for gobernador in 1688, suggesting it had failed because the *común* suspected him of corruption years earlier. Another query asserted that he and two confederates had "joined together" to "stir up the village [so that people would] not pay their tributes on time as they should." He denied all of these, sticking to his original story that he had intended only a few days' delay in tribute, pending a new election. Mestizo Pablo Romero, Ramírez's associate, also deposed. The questions to him, framed by alcalde mayor León, indicate that Romero and Ramírez had been agitating in Temascalcingo for several years. The boom was about to be lowered against the two defendants.

Out of the blue in late October 1691, gobernador Chimal and his officers filed a petition with León asking to withdraw from the proceedings. Ramírez's long incarceration had sparked unrest in a community where so many people had family ties (accuser and accused shared the name Chimal). And so, for the "calm, *paz y quietud* of everyone" they asked that Ramírez and Romero be released, promising to "make friends and conserve *paz y quietud*—without disagreements with each other, we request justice." Alcalde mayor León would not hear of it and pushed the case forward on his own. He was doubtless surprised when in mid-November captain don Francisco de la Peña, a Spaniard and knight of the Order of Calatrava, arrived in the town of Istlaguaca to post bond so that Ramírez and Romero could be set free. Obviously, word of Chimal's and Ramírez's reconciliation had reached the audiencia.

Upon their release, Ramírez and Romero set out to wrest the proceedings away from alcalde mayor León, who seemed intent on punishing them. In early February, 1692, they traveled to Mexico City and contacted procurador Juan Félix de Galves. Galves filed an appeal with the audiencia on their behalf, requesting that all orders issued against them by León be revoked. The procurador also asked the audiencia to take the case away from León and instead hear it in Mexico City. The audiencia agreed, commanding León to send the record. More than a month passed before León's eyes swept over this order. On March 13, 1692, with Ramírez and Romero standing before him, he took the paper in hand, kissed it and touched it to his forehead, as was done with all royal orders, and said that he would "obey it with all due respect as a letter of our king and natural lord." He undoubtedly intoned these familiar, formulaic words through gritted teeth. We know of his ire and frustration because in the legal proof of his obedience, a written document filed with the audiencia, he registered his displeasure. He would obey, "though speaking with all due deference [the order] had been obtained on the basis of a false report." This small rebellion notwithstanding, two weeks later the packet containing all the documents reached Mexico City. The affidavit attesting to its arrival is the last page of the record.

Clearly, the audiencia took control of this situation because the alcalde mayor had turned his back on a clear chance to reestablish paz y quietud in Temascalcingo. Opposed parties, who were also family, had been reconciled. Whatever threat there might once have been to tribute collection had passed. Alcalde mayor León's persistence, whether out of a sense of legal duty or because he saw an opportunity to intervene in local politics, could only make things worse. Gobernador Chimal's reason for withdrawing seems straightforward. As the leader of a tight-knit community, he could not ignore the voices raised in Ramírez's defense. Dissension within the village made it more difficult for him to govern and harder to meet his obligations. His hard-heartedness against a kinsman imperiled his standing and authority in the community.

What Ramírez gained from this deal, if anything beyond his release, is open to speculation. His statement in the church suggests that late April, early May had been election season in Temascalcingo and that Chimal was probably trying to overstay his term of office. By law, of course, Chimal could not succeed himself. Ramírez may have felt it was his turn, or he may have backed someone else's bid for the governorship. The crucial point is that he chose tribute as a way of starting an argument within the community—in effect, disrupting the peace. By telling Temascalcingo's residents to withhold payments, he had pressed on one of the tenderest spots on the local body politic. Chimal's response had been swift and severe, harsher perhaps than Ramírez had anticipated. Ill after six months in jail, he may simply have wanted to forget the whole incident and go free. He had not derailed the election, for in August 1691 Chimal was still gobernador. At the same time, Chimal's admission that he was under pressure within the community leaves open the possibility that the two men reached some sort of accord. Both may have worried that their dispute had allowed León to insert himself too deeply in local affairs. And so they chose peace. Amid their discord, they saw themselves framed in Mexico City officialdom's broad desire that indigenous communities live in paz y quietud. The absence of a further record strongly suggests that León understood he could not prevail against this convergence of interests and so abandoned the case against Ramírez.

PERMITTED TO USE THE LAW

Often, the struggle within a community over the terms of paz y quietud unfolded through several legal encounters stretched out over long periods of time. In such cases, a contest touched off by one or more disgruntled individuals might be sustained only by a broader collective effort.

On Saturday, April 9, 1633, Francisco Santiago and his brother Felipe, residents of the village of San Matheo, entered the central plaza of Suchimilco walking alongside Spaniard Diego de Ybarra, 200 Indians in tow.[83] Waving an order that they and "other long-time Indian residents of Suchimilco" had obtained from the viceroy, they marched up to the house of don Francisco Ponze, the teniente of Suchimilco's alcalde mayor. They told Ponze, who was flanked by the Indian gobernador of San Matheo and his alcaldes, that the order contained a certified copy of the king's new decree forbidding Indians from being forced to perform personal service. They wanted it posted in the marketplace, for all to see, and demanded that Ponze officially notify all Indian officials of republic that personal service was to cease immediately. When Ponze equivocated "many voices" were raised, and someone shouted out to the gobernador and his alcaldes "you will pay for the dirty trick you play in selling the Indians."[84] According to witnesses, there may have been calls from among the commoners for Francisco Santiago to assume the governorship, because he had sought to save them from the "vexations" of the gobernador. Others may have called out that the elected officials were all "thieves" and that the teniente himself should be arrested. At that point, Francisco Santiago left the plaza and the crowd began to throw rocks at the Indian official responsible for rounding up workers for the local gunpowder factory.

The gobernador, in the name of the común, immediately filed criminal charges in the Juzgado accusing the Santiago brothers of inciting commoners to "disobedience" and of "violently" interfering with the legitimate distribution of labor in the city. A judicial investigation quickly followed, and a week later don Francisco and don Felipe found themselves in jail. In early June 1633, they responded to interrogatories. Principales both, they denied the accusation and said that they had only wanted the viceroy's order to be posted in the marketplace so that the other Indians would know they did not have to perform personal service against their will. They also denied gathering the crowd. Rather, people had followed them spontaneously upon hearing what they intended to do. Not until July did they get a court-appointed procurador. Melchor López de Haro raised a variety of procedural concerns, but the core of his argument was that they had done nothing wrong. As the brief put it: "There is no crime because my client and the Indians who were with him were and are permitted to make use of the law and it is very common when a principal goes on official business, however minor, for others to accompany him . . . the more so when the matter is of common concern such as the order in question, as a consequence of which he cannot be accused of rebellion or lack of respect."[85] By early August, the men had been released on bond, pending the tribunal's ruling.

That ruling did not come, probably because the Santiago brothers decided to lodge a countersuit. In January 1634, they filed a criminal complaint against their newly elected gobernador, a man called Diego Xuares.[86] Xuares had been an alcalde during 1633 and had now been chosen gobernador. After his release from jail in August, Francisco Santiago had made the rounds in the village, talking to residents and persuading them to contribute money for lawsuits he planned to bring against Xuares. Xuares responded by accusing him of levying illegal *derramas* and being an *"indio inquieto y reboltoso"*—an Indian who stirred things up. Xuares's witnesses agreed, pointing to an incident in which don Francisco, when asked why he wanted to "unsettle the Indians" had responded by "beating his chest" and saying that he was entitled to bring whatever lawsuits he wanted. The record abruptly stops at this point. We do not know what happened to don Francisco. In all likelihood he was released, though his experience may have put him off any further efforts to oust Xuares, or at least counseled greater caution, for his name does not appear on any later lawsuits against don Diego.

In the following years, others took up the challenge the Santiago brothers had begun. In 1640, the *naturales and común* of the villages of Santiago, San Andrés, San Matheo, and Santa Cecilia filed another criminal case against gobernador Diego Xuares, being careful not to name any individuals as complainants.[87] In violation of law, charged the complaint, Xuares had remained in the governorship since 1634 and had gained enormous power over the community. Complainants accused him of forcing indigenous commoners to choose between unpaid day labor on the haciendas of local Spaniards or shelling out 3½ pesos to avoid the duty—clear violations of the king's 1633 decree. To make matters worse, stated the complaint, he even rents Indians out for fifteen to twenty days at a time, without paying them. Three witnesses, commoners all, a woodsman, a farmer, and a muleskinner, offered their testimony corroborating the charge. Once again, the record ends without an official conclusion. Whether the plaintiffs backed off because they could not make their case or agreed to some sort of informal resolution in the hope that Xuares would behave himself is impossible to say.

Whichever it was, the "*naturales* of the village of San Matheo" were back at it three years later.[88] In early 1643, they renewed the charge that Xuares forced them to perform personal service and added an allegation that his mulatto teniente had frequently whipped Indians, almost killing one of them. This time, the Juzgado acted quickly, ordering Xuares arrested. He insisted that he had done nothing wrong; sending Indians to work at various places was simply part of his obligation as gobernador. He alleged as well that recently some Indians had mutinied against him, throwing stones and trying to kill him.

The proceeding moved forward. Witnesses were deposed and the case was made ready for a judicial decision. After much procedural fencing, Bernardo López de Haro on the complainants' behalf found an opening in Xuares's case and lunged hard. He noted that "through the fault and negligence" of Xuares's procurador Augustín Franco, Xuares had missed a crucial filing date. In essence, he had not submitted his proof in time—*adbersus lapsum termini probatorii et omissam probasionem,* as López de Haro put it with a latinate flourish.[89] The tribunal agreed. On June 14, 1644, it ordered the plaintiffs from San Matheo to appear and have justice done. A year and a half later, however, the matter still had not concluded. Apparently, Xuares had managed to dodge the court's orders by the simple expedient of refusing to talk to his lawyer during this time. By then, the tribunal's patience had worn thin. In December 1645, it ruled that Xuares had never executed a valid power of attorney in Franco's favor, which meant he could be personally served. In January 1646, the notary sent to serve Xuares with papers could not find him and surmised that Xuares had "hidden himself." In effect, he had left the jurisdiction in the face of the complainants' legal campaign.

Fearing his absence might be temporary, the Indian litigants continued with the case, lodging a detailed complaint against Xuares in early 1647. Translated into Spanish from Nahuatl, the document recited the many abuses their village had borne over the preceding years. "We cannot suffer any longer," they insisted, and petitioned the tribunal to send a judge to investigate. The Juzgado dispatched a receptor named

Jacinto Ballego. But when the Indian litigants saw Ballego dining with their nemesis, they indignantly asked that he be relieved of his commission. Instead, the investigation was conducted in Mexico City by the Juzgado's legal adviser, don Diego de Barrientos. Six Indian witnesses testified regarding the abuses alleged in the complaint. After that, the record comes to an end.[90]

What makes this series of cases so compelling is the broader context within which it unfolded. When the Santiago brothers spoke up in 1633, they were among the first to demand enforcement of the king's new law against personal service and the labor repartimiento.[91] They were fighting a practice that over preceding decades had become an onerous custom. And while they respected custom when it benefited them, they were attentive to opportunities for positive change. To accomplish it, they had to disrupt business as usual. This is what got them in trouble with San Matheo's gobernador and his ally the alcalde mayor. Up to that time, it had been the gobernador's job to supply Indian labor to Spanish haciendas—and the alcalde mayor's to ensure the gobernador delivered—an arrangement from which both men undoubtedly profited. After promulgation of the 1633 decree, it was no longer legal for Indians to be coerced in this way. As persistent complaints during the 1630s and 1640s attest—and not just in Suchimilco—the law was hardly self-enforcing. It depended for its effectiveness on the willingness of local people to press the matter in Mexico City. Yet those who were accused of abuses, like gobernador Xuares, characterized people like the Santiago brothers as disturbers of the peace and promoters of discord. This is why on its surface and in its language, this case is almost indistinguishable from those more narrowly a matter of personal contests over local power.

But something else was going on. Even if don Francisco and don Felipe acted as they did out of personal animosity toward Xuares, or because don Francisco wanted to be gobernador, as Xuares alleged, the fact remains that the two brothers represented commoners' complaints about labor arrangements. They countered Xuares's accusations by talking up the idea that the king's decree could bring change by the mere fact of being posted in the market for all to see—a sign of hopeful faith in the efficacy of the king's law. So when Xuares challenged don Francisco's right to bring lawsuits, don Francisco thumped his chest and said in a loud voice that he would bring whatever lawsuits he wanted—effectively asserting his right to disrupt community peace if circumstances called for it. And when the Santiagos could not or would not push the matter any further, others picked up where they had left off. Given don Francisco's imprisonment in 1633, they chose to identify themselves collectively rather than to sign as individuals. Through their persistence, Xuares's power to continue operating under the old assumptions gradually faded until it was finally gone. The complainants did not win an official legal finding against him. But by 1647, their willingess to brook discord in order to pursue the law's promise of a more just peace had revealed Xuares for the common bully he was. Of course, the people of San Matheo would have known that at any moment someone else might emerge to disrupt this hard won peace—such was the way of their world.

⤳

Legal disputes over the arrangements of village government were far from strictly local affairs. Much hinged on these contests—village autonomy, collective liberty, the relationship between local and centralized power, the conditions of tribute collection. Indeed, whenever indigenous litigants brought complaints to Mexico City regarding an election, a broken vara, or an abuse of authority, the entire structure of Spanish rule was implicated. For if the *republic of Indians* and the *republic of Spaniards* "are today joined and form a single body in these provinces," as Solórzano y Pereira argued in the mid-seventeenth century, indigenous towns and villages were the enveloping fascia, enclosing and giving shape to the whole organism.[92] Put another way, colonial rule could not escape the reality of Indian communities and the conflicts within and between them. Procuradores, judges, oidores of the audiencia, and the viceroy himself knew this, which is why endless complaints regarding the minutia of local governance received the attention they did in Mexico City.

In 1599, Jesuit scholar Domingo de Soto pointed out that "it is impossible to enclose men in a common society so long as there is no public authority that can control them in peace." Law represented that authority. One of its central challenges in New Spain was to check the power of Indian gobernadores and Spanish alcaldes mayores who saw in the vulnerable only an opportunity. Royal decrees were clear on this point— the Indians were to be allowed to live "together and in concert . . . without oppression" and royal officers from the viceroy on down were to do everything possible to ensure their "good government."[93] Though the injunction was as often violated as upheld during the seventeenth century, Indians understood what it represented in their ongoing negotiation of colonial power. This understanding is what emboldened Alonso Martín to succeed in reversing the alcalde mayor's sentence against him. It is what empowered the elected officials of Huitlapa to cite royal decrees over a century old to insist that they, rather than the parish priest, should appoint the church steward in their town. It is what allowed the Santiago brothers to imagine that posting the king's decree in the marketplace might improve Indians' lives. These and many other petitioners and litigants demonstrated that law could redress an imbalance of power in local affairs. Of course, that same law could also be wielded by Indian and Spanish officials seeking to protect positions and privileges and by ambitious challengers intent on pushing their own agendas. Litigation over questions of local governance, in short, amounted to politics by another name. And thus, litigation, like village elections, played ambivalently on the local stage. Power and hierarchy might be contested but also affirmed. Justice could be pursued, but the very act of filing a lawsuit raised a cacophony of voices in the republic.

Peace within indigenous towns and villages, therefore, could never be a durable accomplishment. Too great were the opportunities to exploit the Indians and too many the willing exploiters for anyone to imagine that something like an idyll might be achieved. Yet, too insistent were local people in preserving dignity and autonomy for the muffled peace of utter resignation and domination to fall permanently over native communities. In villages and towns across Mexico, seasons of affliction came and went, now harsher, now milder, depending on configurations of local power, on personalities, and on the willingness of litigants to risk discord.

As an abstraction, peace represented a desire to balance exploitation against law's promise to protect the king's lowliest vassals. In practical terms, *paz y quietud* could mean different things to different people, according to where each stood in the local scheme of things. For Indian officials of republic, Spanish tenientes and alcaldes mayores, peace generally meant being able to collect tribute in a timely fashion and apportion labor without undue hassle or opposition. They filed lawsuits when people balked at their demands or when they felt their power challenged. For ordinary people and those who purported to speak on their behalf, peace usually involved stopping local abuses, protecting local autonomy, and contributing only what tribute and labor law or custom demanded of them. Communities and individuals might spend years in pursuit of such a peace growing out of change, as did the residents of San Matheo Suchimilco between 1633 and 1647. Tenacity did not assure success, but success could not be had without it. And even if a legal battle ended well for litigants, there was no guarantee that a new storm of discord would not break out over a community, as opponents contested the terms and conditions of lives lived inescapably in common. In any given case, litigants might not know whether they would prevail, but like don Francisco Santiago they were sure of their right to raise their voices.

This meant that local authority itself was far more mutable and far less sturdy than alcaldes mayores and gobernadores would have liked. Law destabilized the power of local office by allowing Indian commoners and others to complain of its abuse. In doing so, however, it created an arena within which competing parties might negotiate the terms of peace and quiet at the village level through their connection to viceregal and even royal authority. Although the process was one of constant adjustment, specific outcomes represented a kind of legitimacy that allowed Indian litigants to bind themselves to the broad tenets of Spanish rule.

Even so, Indian litigants faced formidable constraints. The delicate balancing of peace and discord that allowed them room for maneuver at the local level might be completely irrelevant when indigenous communities found themselves embroiled in political disputes among New Spain's great powers. In 1643, for instance, the elected officials of the village of San Andrés Calpan in the province of Atrisco, on behalf of the entire village, filed a civil lawsuit against the local priest, who had forbidden them to celebrate religious festivities and processions in the *cofradía*—religious brotherhood—attached to the town's Franciscan monastery.[94] Procurador Agustín Franco argued that these celebrations had been "established costumbre" and that by law and conscience the Indians were entitled to choose "freely" which church to attend. Viceroy Conde de Salvatierra agreed with them and issued an order "requesting and charging" the priest to keep the settled custom.

But as the Indian litigants almost surely understood in 1643, their real antagonist was not the local padre. They were up against none less than Juan de Palafox, the archbishop of Puebla, who in 1641 had stripped the Franciscan friars in the archbishopric of Puebla of their jurisdiction over Indian villages they had been ministering to, in some cases, since the mid-sixteenth century. Palafox had ordered secular priests to take the friars' place and had insisted that Indian parishioners leave their old churches behind. This was the opening salvo in a long struggle over the "secularization" of Indian parishes in New Spain—a struggle between the archbishop and the regular orders for control of Indian bodies and souls. The 1643 case by the residents of Calpan sought to test the permanence and reach of secularization in their district. By ruling in their favor, the viceroy indicated his tilt toward the Franciscans, fearing that Palafox would only be a greater threat to viceregal authority once Indian parishes had been fully secularized.[95]

The Calpan litigants faced an uphill battle. Alcaldes mayores might hem and haw over the viceroy's orders, but they could not ignore them. Clergy, by contrast, could openly oppose viceregal authority, which was rooted in nonecclesiastical jurisdiction. The Calpan priest, certainly, was not acting alone. He knew, just as surely as did the Indians, that he was a pawn in a larger game. Thus, Palafox simply set the viceroy's request and charge aside and directed his priests to bar the Indians from attending mass and festivities at Franciscan churches. Throughout the mid-1640s, secular priests and Franciscan friars dueled in the province of Puebla. Priests would hold mass when the Indians would otherwise have been at the Franciscan church, threatening to punish those who were absent. The friars would toll the bells of their empty churches as priests were saying mass, to remind Indians parishioners of what they had lost. Though viceroy Salvatierra did everything in his power to support the Franciscans, it came to naught, for between 1644 and 1646, the Franciscans' governing council in Madrid capitulated to Palafox, ordering the Mexican Franciscans to resign their claims to Indian parishes lost in 1641.[96]

No lawsuit by the residents of San Andrés Calpan was going to change this. The viceroy's power, ordinarily so crucial a part of Indian litigants' possibilities, had been negated. This dispute was worked out at another level, where archbishops, Franciscan priors, and viceroys vied for the king's ear, and even the Pope weighed in. In these upper strata of Spanish government, the voices of Indians who proclaimed themselves the king's "loyal vassals" and hoped to find some exception to Palafox's stern policy, barely rose to a murmur[97]—an object lesson in the limits of their position as colonial subjects.

CHAPTER EIGHT

Rebellious Subjects

On October 17, 1661, at the town of Nexapa, in the bishopric of Oaxaca, an Indian cacique named Fabián Martín, gobernador of the town of Lachixila, climbed the steps to the gallows where he was to be hanged. Attended by two priests, Martín turned to the large crowd of Indians that had gathered to witness his execution and spoke to them in their native Zapoteca. "My brothers," he intoned in a clear voice, "I do not die as a traitor to the King our Lord, nor for disobedience, nor for having led an uprising, but for the repartimientos." The priests then whispered their words of comfort and ministration and watched him hang by the neck until dead. His body was quartered and his limbs posted along the Royal Highways as warnings to any who might follow his example.[1] So ended a central chapter in the rebellions of the province of Tehuantepec, which contemporaries and historians have characterized as among the most important rural upheavals in colonial Mexico.[2]

Historians have offered diverse interpretations of events leading up to and following Fabián Martín's death. The uprising has been seen as a drive for local ethnic autonomy, as an effort to renegotiate interethnic relationships, as a political movement within rather than a rebellion against Spanish rule, and as a millenarian outburst, a brief and dramatic exception to the Indians' acquiescence to colonial hegemony.[3] I have no quarrel with any of these. I wish, rather, to ponder Martín's final utterance as a kind of puzzlement. Here was an Indian gobernador using his last breath to insist that he had neither betrayed the Spanish king, nor disobeyed the king's laws. What was behind Martín's choice to leave these words to his fellow Zapotecas? What could they have understood him to mean? What does Martín's framing of the rebellion say of the possibilities and constraints within which Indians sought to steady their stance in an unbalanced and fractured political order?

The repartimiento Fabián Martín referred to on the gallows was not the labor draft so often the subject of amparo petitions and litigation during the seventeenth century. His words focused attention on the *repartimiento de mercancías,* the system of sales, exchanges, and credit that stood alongside tribute as the chief engine of economic circulation in New Spain's economy from roughly 1600 forward. The repartimiento had been created toward the end of the sixteenth century to alter the terms of trade between Spaniards and Indians.[4] Until the 1580s or so, indigenous villages had often enjoyed highly favorable terms in their commerce with Spaniards. The reason was simple: Spaniards needed the goods pueblos produced—raw materials, such as dyes for textiles, foodstuffs, cash crops, such as cacao, and the material of everyday life, such as pots and woolens—more than Indians needed to produce them. These same products were collected in tribute, but Indians often had surpluses. The repartimiento had two chief aims: to ensure this surplus made it to market where Spaniards could buy it; and to force Indians to spend their surplus in cash or in kind on goods brought into indigenous villages by Spanish merchants. Alcaldes mayores and corregidores generally acted as middle men, controlling the flow of merchandise between the villages and a broader world of commerce.

While the repartimiento de mercancías has often been characterized as an imposition, the system enabled peasants at the margins of survival to purchase goods they otherwise would not have been able to afford. Villages might produce surpluses but often had no way to cumulate them over time to pay for other goods. Repartimiento amounted to a kind credit—at times forced—in which Indians took on debt for merchandise sold to them by Spaniards. Though there was ample opportunity for abuse, as with any system of credit, it seems that indigenous individuals and villages often embraced the repartimiento in "conditions of tremendous risk and imperfect markets," through which "they obtained valued goods and needed income, unobtainable from other sources."[5]

The repartimiento and its burdens were not everywhere the same. In central Mexico the Indians were above all consumers, paying cash for products they desired. In the south and southeast, Indians figured chiefly as producers of goods bought by the alcalde mayor in exchange for cash, which they spent on other goods, typically offered through the alcalde mayor. Unscrupulous alcaldes mayores could gouge the Indians at both ends of the process, underpaying them for what they produced and overcharging them for what they bought. The two regions, central and south, differed primarily in the terms of trade between wages and available goods. Around Mexico City and Puebla a native laborer might work two days on an hacienda and earn four reales toward the purchase of cattle or textiles. In the south, Indians might take months to earn the same amount of money, because they were paid little for what they produced—woolens, grain, and cochineal dye—and faced high prices for what they bought—imported goods, textiles, and mules.[6] The repartimiento thus could become a heavy onus on struggling communities, especially when economic conditions were tight or when the system was badly or dishonestly administered.

In Oaxaca, as elsewhere in the south, the repartimiento economy tended toward a tense and changeable equilibrium between production for local sustenance and production for trade (one of the most sought after trade commodities was labor-intensive cochineal dye—"a good equal to gold and silver," according to King Philip IV in 1621—for Mexico City, Spanish and European looms).[7] At the local level, subsistence and commerce were bridged by overlapping market systems: the official repartimiento, controlled by the alcalde mayor; local Indian *tianguis,* or markets; and itinerant Spanish and casta peddlers who went from village to village buying and selling products.[8] These three circuits mediated the flow of goods, cash, and credit into and out of pueblos, tending to a rough proportion of benefits and burdens. As long as the scales did not shift dramatically, the various participants had little reason to complain. When the balance was upset a whole region might be destabilized.

CHAPTERS OF REBELLION

By early March 1660, drought and crop failure had pushed the native inhabitants of Tehuantepec to the brink of survival.[9] Unlike other regions in the bishopric of Oaxaca, the Indians of Tehuantepec—Zapotecas, Mixes, Chontales—may have been more vulnerable during hard times, as so much land was owned by Spaniards.[10] To make matters worse, the regional trade on which towns and villages had come to depend so heavily had tightened considerably since the arrival of Juan de Avellán as their alcalde mayor. Avellán had been appointed as a reward for his loyalty to outgoing viceroy Duque de Albuquerque.

Like so many in his position during these years, Avellán saw the repartimiento as an opportunity to enrich himself at the Indians' expense. So he had set out to structure the local system to his advantage. In doing so, he disrupted a delicate economic equilibrium in Oaxaca. Specifically, he forbade Indian and non-Indian traders who had once moved freely along the north-south route connecting Tehuantepec, Nexapa, Ixtepec, and Villa Alta from entering towns subject to his jurisdiction. Dozens of villages were cut off from established commercial and credit relationships. In effect, he aimed to monopolize the region's markets. His designs met with local resistance, which he punished with a heavy hand; he once boasted that he had personally delivered over 7,000 strokes of the whip upon Indian backs.[11]

Around midday, March 22, 1660, Holy Monday, a crowd of nearly 2,000 Zapoteca Indians gathered in the town of Guadalcazar, Tehuantepec, to protest Avellán's abuses. He had recently flogged several Indians for failing to meet their repartimiento quotas; a cacique had died under the lash for selling Avellán "badly made blankets." He had also jailed an Indian alcalde ordinario from the pueblo of Mixtequilla. In this last instance, a group of Indians had surrounded Avellán's house, demanding he come out and talk to them. When he appeared at the door brandishing a sword the crowd had chased him to a local church. While he was dashing for the sanctuary's safety, a rock struck him in the head and he fell to the ground mortally wounded. Once down, he may have been further beaten. His slave, a black man, was also killed in the melée. According to viceroy Albuquerque's letter to his successor detailing the episode, the crowd had then dragged both corpses through the streets and dumped them in the main plaza.[12] Dominican priests had tried to cool passions but retreated to their monastery as the crowd torched Avellán's residence, the Casas Reales or royal residence, and raided the local armory, taking arquebuses, drums, and royal banners—the appliances of war.

News of the killing spread quickly up and down the road connecting Tehuantepec and Ixtepec (Fig. 6). In late May, 4,000 Indians converged on Nexapa for Corpus Christi celebrations. On May 28, the gobernadores and alcaldes of the province wrote to bishop of Oaxaca Juan Alonso de Cuevas y Dávalos asking him to intercede with the viceroy on their behalf. They complained of the repartimientos, as had the people of Tehuantepec, and alleged further that the alcaldes mayores frequently imprisoned and beat them—and on occasion killed them. Many Indians, they claimed, had begun to flee their villages and lands. With special bitterness, they noted that the alcaldes mayores' servants had repeatedly attacked them for trying to communicate their grievances to the viceroy.[13]

Taking advantage of the Corpus celebration, the gobernadores and other officers of Nexapa had told their alcalde mayor, Juan de Espejo, that they wanted to discuss the repartimiento agreements. Nervous after events in Tehuantepec, Espejo had already mustered a small troop of Spaniards, mestizos, blacks, and mulattoes and was in no mood to negotiate, fearing that the Indians intended to abrogate the repartimiento. The Indians, too, were afraid, as rumors swirled that "they would be consumed by the rigor of arms."[14] According to Indian witnesses testifying after the

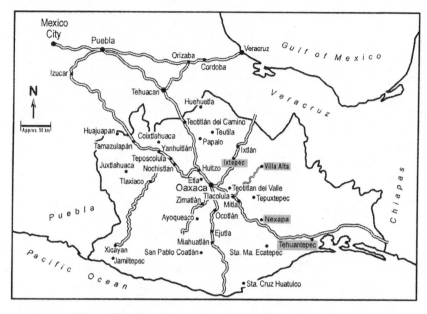

FIGURE 6. The roads of southern Mexico. The principal towns of the
Tehuantepec rebellion—Tehauntepec, Nexapa, Ixtepec, Villa Alta—are
highlighted. (Adapted from Baskes, *Indians*, p. 146.)

event, Espejo and twenty soldiers holed themselves up in the church on
the morning of his meeting with local officials. From there he summoned
the gobernadores and alcades and reminded them in no uncertain terms
what their repartimiento obligations were. They insisted they could not
pay, since there was no fair exchange of value.[15] Espejo responded that
this was not his fault, but the fault of Bartolomé Ximénez, the mestizo
interpreter, who was a "great thief." The Indians then appealed to the
bishop in Oaxaca, who agreed to convey their petitions to the viceroy
in Mexico City.[16] Meanwhile, an uneasy Espejo asked the viceroy for
a battalion of soldiers to quell any further dissensions. A column was
sent from Antequera, and somewhere between 200 and 600 Indians
went out to the Royal Highway to head them off. Shots were fired and
several Indians were killed or wounded. At that point, villagers fled to
the hills.[17]

Tensions remained high throughout the summer of 1660. On August 22, Francisco Álvarez, tribute collector for the alcalde mayor of Ix-

tepec, arrived in the village of San Mateo de Capulalpa to find a ghost town, except for a single Indian *alguacil mayor* (chief bailiff) by the name of Juan García Capitán. Álvarez ordered García to tell Capulalpa's gobernadores and alcaldes to collect the tribute and take it to the cabecera at San Juan Chicomexuchil. The following day García told him that the *cabildo*—village council—had decided to withhold payment, as had been done in Tehuantepec. García warned Álvarez that his life was in danger and suggested he flee. Álvarez brushed off the advice, thinking García drunk. The next day, Álvarez returned again to arrest two fugitives, who had broken out of jail the night before. Unable to find them, he ordered García to arrest the wife of one of the fugitives. García again warned Álvarez to leave town immediately. This time Álvarez believed him and fled on a mule, without García's wife. The residents of Capulalpa came out of hiding and gave chase. About a league out of town they caught up with Álvarez, pelted him with rocks, knocked him unconscious and left him for dead. Wounded, he managed to make it back to the Royal Highway, where a group of Indians told him that his attackers had discovered he was alive and were looking for him. Álvarez borrowed one of their horses and rode to safety. Meanwhile, the rebellious Indians grabbed García and flogged him until other village members interceded on his behalf.[18]

By October Nexapa's officials of republic had heard nothing back from the bishop or the viceroy regarding their petitions. The town was a tinderbox awaiting a spark. It came when the alcalde mayor publicly slapped their gobernador, Pascual Oliver, for complaining about the repartimientos. Townspeople vowed revenge. In contrast to Tehuantepec and Ixtepec, the Nexapa uprising took on a millenarian cast. There, according to don Francisco Montemayor de Cuenca, the Mexico City judge later sent to pacify the region, some Indians alleged that the ancient king of Tehuantepec, Congún (Cong Hoy) had risen from the lagoon where he had been hiding since the Spaniards' arrival a hundred and fifty years earlier. Congún's message was simple: stop obeying the Spaniards. Leaders and residents from twenty-six villages and towns joined the uprising which, by some reports, began to move toward Antequera, the colonial capital of Oaxaca, hoping to "recover their *libertad* and expel the Spaniards from their territory."[19]

These episodes were but chapters in a wider story of upheavals that rolled across the isthmus of Tehuantepec between March 1660 and October 1661. From small revolts rooted in local relationships among villagers, local gobernadores, officials of republic, and their Spanish alcaldes mayores arose a more general complaint in which at least three different ethnic groups—Zapoteca, Mixe, and Chontal—took part. Thousands, perhaps tens of thousands, of people were involved. Not all rebelled.

NEGOTIATING TERMS

Colonial authorities reacted cautiously to these incidents. Several months passed after Avellán's death in March 1660 before the viceroy dispatched oidor Francisco Montemayor de Cuenca from Mexico City to look into matters.[20] Montemayor arrived in the city of Antequera, Oaxaca, on August 13, 1660, when the number of Indian complaints and disturbances was still growing. In his October 1660 report to King Philip IV, Montemayor represented Avellán's killing as an "impudent"and "scandalous" affront to Spanish authority. At the same time, he noted that the "tyrannical arbitrariness" of the alcaldes mayores' "greed" was such that "not even the greatest rapine nor the most inhuman rigor could have dreamt them up."[21]

The gobernadores and alcaldes of Tehuantepec understood that much was riding on these competing, though not entirely irreconcilable characterizations. In a March 1660 letter to the viceroy shortly after Avellán's death, these Indian leaders depicted the alcalde mayor's conduct as violating "the many Royal provisions we have in our archives." This was a crucial move in their efforts to shape the narrative of the uprising. In effect, they were reminding the viceroy that an alcalde mayor who acted out of private motive could not cloak himself in the king's law, a point Montemayor himself made in his October report.[22]

The letter advanced three main points. First, by contrasting Avellán's violations of royal laws with their own faithful archiving of the texts of those laws, Indian leaders were insisting they had meant no challenge to the king's authority. Second, Avellán's death had been inadvertent, the result of a scuffle that began as a legitimate protest against his "tyranny," for when villagers had gone to his house to discuss the situation, he had drawn his sword rather than hear their grievances, as a proper justice should have done. Finally, after Avellán's death, and "[w]ithout anyone to govern us, we met in cabildo and elected a gobernador *in your Majesty's name, so that you not think of us as rebels and as denying obedience to our King and Lord, rather we await your commands as loyal vassals, as can be seen from the fact that this is neither a rebellion nor an alzamiento, the proof of which is that we have not harmed any vecinos, nor afflicted any Spaniards, nor anyone else who lives among us.*"[23]

A minor miracle of concision, this letter framed events in such a way that Spanish officialdom could conclude that there had been no breach in the Indians' relationship to the king: Avellán was an alcalde mayor who, out of personal greed, had broken royal law; his death was not intentional, but accidental; their election of a new gobernador, far from undercutting the king's authority, aimed at bolstering it; and if further token was needed of their loyalty, no other Spaniards had been harmed since.

Montemayor also faced the question of how to understand the up-heaval in Tehuantepec. For him, the issue was whether to approach the Indians as punisher or as reconciler. On one hand, he wrote in an early report to the king, "it is not prudent to approach violent opposition with gentleness." Natural law demanded that the guilty be punished. Yet, to send a military force was "extremely dangerous." War was dicey business, "starting when we want, but not ending when we wish."[24] He knew that Oaxaca had only a few soldiers and that the rigors of its ge-ography counseled against military adventurism; the Indians could too easily flee to the mountains where they could hide indefinitely. Fielding a force big enough to subdue the region would require mulattoes and mestizos, and arming so many of them carried its own risks.

Prudence aside, basic principles of justice complicated matters. Divine and natural law, wrote Montemayor, hold that a magistrate who "acts iniquitously and unjustly" acts not as a judge but as a tyrant who can for that reason be resisted.[25] Avellán had treated his subjects "with less humanity than he would have his own slaves." Nor had there been any help from higher up, noted the oidor. Twice the Indians had traveled 150 leagues to Mexico City to complain. Twice the viceroy—at the time, the Duque de Albuquerque—had turned them back. In making these comments, Montemayor was not condoning the Indians' actions, but he was indicating that a just outcome might not require punishing the Indians collectively. Finally, argued the oidor, there is no practical basis for collective punishment. Either they all sinned, in which case they would have to be punished to the last man and woman, which would require military force, or none of them had, or at least none who could be identified with any certainty. Better, concluded Montemayor, still early in his handling of the situation, "to correct with clemency than with rigor, love being a stronger bond than fear for keeping vas-sals in obedience."[26] Of course, he knew that this was precisely what the king would want to hear, which makes it ring somewhat hollow given what happened later.

Crucially, the word "vassal" was central to both the Indians' and Mon-temayor's framing of the issues. In their letter, Tehuantepec's gober-nadores and alcaldes sought to depict themselves as loyal vassals who had resisted a corrupt alcalde mayor, but had never defied the king's authority. Montemayor, somewhat more ambivalent in his initial re-port, came to roughly the same conclusion. Both sides were drawing on the fundamental idea that political and social order hinged on the relationship between lord and vassal. *Las Siete Partidas* held that vas-sals and lords both bore duties of love, honor, and protection to each other: "And when these obligations are properly observed, each of them does his duty, and true affection increases and endures between them."[27] Solórzano y Pereira noted in the *Política indiana* that lords who subject their vassals to "violent and tyrannical impositions and vexations" and intrude upon their "natural liberty," could be punished with excommunication. By contrast, the prince who lightened the burdens of his vassals could rest easy and conserve peace.[28]

Both parties were constrained to make their points in these terms. Montemayor had no choice but to speak of the Indians as the king's vassals, subject to his protection and free within the limits of their service to him. To have done otherwise would have been to insult nearly a century of royal decrees and learned commentary on the Indians' status.[29] Native leaders also understood how to proceed. They opened their March 1660 letter to the viceroy by "prostrating ourselves at your excellency's feet as the loyal vassals we are of his Majesty." In an April 13, 1660, letter acknowledging bishop Cuevas y Dávalos's imminent arrival to Tehuantepec, the Indians said they would come out to greet him and, "falling at your feet we will yield our persons" in sign of "service to our King and natural lord." From this point forward, they wrote, "we will render obedience," surrendering the drums, banners, and arms that they had taken from the royal armory and putting themselves under the bishop's, and by extension the king's, *"amparo"* (protection). And while the polish of this letter suggests it may have been drafted with the help of someone knowledgeable in these matters, perhaps a Spanish notary, a shorter and rougher note from an individual Indian alcalde to the viceroy promised "much obedience to the alcalde mayor, your excellency and the king our Lord."[30]

An unusual letter from the village of San Pedro de Tlapalcatepec to the bishop shows how intent Indian leaders were in arguing that the bonds of vassalage had not shattered with Avellán's death.[31] The letter begins by noting the presence of several named Spaniards, who in essence vouch for the Indians' loyalty to the king. The document takes the form of a dialogue, with the Indians posing questions to their Spanish interlocutors, and the Spaniards providing brief answers confirming the tenor of the question. The "Indians" begin by asking whether it is not the case that "we" govern ourselves well, with the king's staff in hand, and that "we" faithfully attend church, obey the law, pay tribute, are not risen up, and willingly serve in what "we" are told to do by the Spaniards. "Is this true?" The "Spaniards" respond, "as those who understand the Mexican language, it is true friends, why do you ask?" The "Indians" then say that they have been defamed, for they have not shirked the repartimiento and are preparing to deliver it to the alcalde mayor shortly. "Fearful of a company [of soldiers] which our alcalde mayor has in Nexapa for his protection, because of what has happened in other jurisdictions and nations, we ask for the love of God that you give us a letter certified by your name for our defense." The letter closes with the "Spaniards" agreeing that it is all true: "these *naturales* are quiet and peaceful, without change or alteration, rather they are very humble, like loyal vassals of your Majesty." All of the Spaniards named up front are listed as signing the document.

Nothing of substance in this letter was new. This missive was remarkable chiefly for its form. It purports to be the transcription of a conversation between "Spaniards" and "Indians" sitting in a room together, speaking in native languages, calmly discussing the infamous charges that had been leveled by other Spaniards. In this tableau, there is mutual respect, measured tones—Indians make their points, Spaniards readily agree—and a reciprocal commitment to social peace. Whether the "Spaniards" were actually present is hard to say. It is not altogether implausible to think so, especially as names were given and they appear to have signed. Either way, the letter represented a rhetorical strategy aimed at reassuring Spanish officialdom. Nor was this just any conversation, for the letter mimicked a legal form with which both Spaniards and Indians would have been familiar from litigation—the interrogatory. Witnesses, in this case Spaniards, were asked to agree or disagree with a series of questions framed by the Indians. The Spaniards' agreement amounted to a public acknowledgment of the truth of the points advanced by the Indian questioners.

Of course, the bishop was predisposed to believe the Indians. He had long served as their protector. It is unlikely therefore that this letter alone swayed him. But it could have influenced the tone of his words to the viceroy. In his report from early 1661, he echoed the last line of the dialogue, noting that it is "unimaginable the number of actions of vassalage in which [the Indians] prostrated themselves and knelt, placing their lives and heads in my hands, the multitude offering to give their lives for the King, our Lord, to whom their humble and loyal hearts cried out." [32]

It would be easy to dismiss the Indians' assertions of vassalage. Standing alone, they seem formulaic and instrumental, whether coached or the product of a self-preserving prudence. After all, the bishop had repeatedly urged the Indians to adopt the attitude of proper subjects, so they may simply have been parroting someone whose sympathy they sought. Montemayor too had exhorted the Indians to be good vassals, though his blandishments must be understood in terms of the punitive threat he wielded. Still, there is more here than meets the quick eye.

For those who had taken part in Avellán's death, written signs of willing submission were not just for show. The question for the Indian communities of Tehuantepec was whether Montemayor would treat them as loyal vassals or as rebels. Repeatedly, Indian leaders insisted that they had only protested the odious practices of their alcalde mayor, not risen up against the king or his authority. The bishop agreed. So did Montemayor, at least initially. Events resulting in Avellán's death, wrote the oidor in one of his first reports, appeared not to have been a general uprising—*levantamiento* or *alzamiento*—but an expression of "hatred" for the man himself, as Indian *regidores* claimed.[33] The collective fate of thousands hung on this distinction.

The killing of Avellán pressed hard on a central nerve of social and political order in viceregal New Spain. As Montemayor stated baldly, it "is not for subjects to remove or install alcaldes mayores."[34] All parties acknowledged that the central question was whether royal authority had been subverted. This issue brought close to the surface of political negotiation a deeper principle, one not explicitly acknowledged by Montemayor but implicit in his actions—and one understood by Indian leaders who looked to the bishop, the viceroy, and a distant king for help: the fundamentally reciprocal quality of the relationship between vassals and lords.

Covarrubias's dictionary, after defining a *vassal* in hierarchical terms as one subject to a *lord,* cites *Las Partidas* to say that these two words are "correlative": "because there would be no lord without vassals, nor vassals without lord."[35] Vassals who joined an alzamiento were those who violated a reciprocal duty of love, honor, and loyalty regarding their lord and in so doing removed themselves from his protection.[36] Indians who merely rose up against an unjust and abusive officer were reacting to a manifest injustice and, in principle, were not banished from the king's sheltering embrace. As Montemayor noted, having twice been rebuffed by the viceroy, the Indians may have had no other means of bringing Avellán's "tyrannical arbitrariness" to royal notice.

With Montemayor in Antequera, Indian leaders faced a dilemma. They had to convince the king, the viceroy, and the oidor that they remained loyal vassals while acknowledging Avellán's death. But they knew from experience that even if the king sided with them, his protective arm, though long enough to reach New Spain, was weak against local power. To meet these challenges, they needed a response that could simultaneously dramatize their situation to the king, open up some room for maneuver and negotiation with Montemayor, and make up for the lack of a clear means of enforcing royal will. Their answer, given from their deep understanding of the colonial social order, was flight.

Time and again, letters among Spanish officials expressed concern that the Indians were either fleeing their villages for the *montes*— the wilderness—or were about to. In October 1660, outgoing viceroy

Duque de Albuquerque warned the incoming Conde de Baños that it was not possible to "reduce [the Indians] by force because they retire to the Montes." In 1661, the alcalde mayor who took Avellán's place in Tehuantepec wrote to Montemayor that the Indians of the village of Miztequilla were gathering clothes and corn and heading for the hills. The bishop, always more histrionic in describing the plight of his Indian flock, wrote to the viceroy in early 1661 that people were not only fleeing to the montes, but throwing themselves off cliffs and hanging themselves to avoid the abuses of their alcaldes mayores.[37] With rumors swirling that a military force would be sent to punish the rebels, desperation and fear alone may have been reasons enough for flight. As the bishop pointed out to the viceroy, wherever it was easy to do so Indians were leaving their villages, "fleeing the sounds of war."[38]

There are strong hints that this was more than just a panicked run. On May 18, 1660, unnamed Indian officials in Tehuantepec addressed a letter to the viceroy. In broken Spanish they thanked him for the bishop's presence in their midst and noted that until his arrival people had been fleeing their villages. With the bishop's assurance that the viceroy would pardon them for the sin of killing Avellán, people "want to return from the monte like deer." They closed by pledging "much obedience" to whomever the viceroy and the king should send to be their new alcalde mayor, as "our father the bishop" commands us to.[39]

There is here the suggestion of tacit deal making between the sides regarding the terms on which the Indians would agree to return to their communities. Consciously or not, those who left for the montes were acting on their sense that flight represented a lever against a colonial arrangement that lacked the means to mount a punitive military expedition. The rag-tag militias of mestizos, mulattoes, blacks, and Spaniards sufficed to subdue isolated villages, and were to be feared on that count, but they were not enough to rout people from the wilderness and force them back to civilization. Indian calculations from within their circumstances thus exposed a fundamental paradox of Spanish rule in Mexico: flight called into question the idea that men were meant to live together in political society—the very premise of human life properly understood—and simultaneously revealed the limits of Spanish power in securing that society. Although the viability of a genuinely social and political life had always been at issue in postconquest New Spain, few in Spanish officialdom questioned the ideal. Solórzano y Pereira noted that what had once been separate republics "were now united and mixed of Spaniards and Indians and must help each other as they are able."[40]

Above all, the Indians "helped" by paying tribute—"chief nerve of the republic."[41] Tribute filled royal coffers and financed the Indians' own incorporation into colonial society. In practice, alcaldes mayores, their lieutenants, and interpreters frequently abused their positions to enrich and empower themselves. From long legal experience, indigenous leaders in the Avellán affair understood that they could neither repudiate nor seem to be repudiating tribute: their only defense, echoing countless petitions and lawsuits, was to portray themselves as willing and eager tributaries driven from their obligations by those out for private gain. Flight worked as a tactic in negotiation precisely because it dramatized a social compact broken by the alcaldes mayores' excesses.

Mexico City officialdom recognized the predicament flight had created. In an October 1660 letter to his successor, viceroy Duque de Albuquerque admitted that the Indians' actions had put him in a bellicose mood: "I must confess that I very nearly came to the opinion [that the Indians should be harshly punished] if they had but waited for the company to arrive, knowing that they were leaving and seeing that they went to the roughest terrain in the mountains to the loss of his Majesty's tributes and the administration of their souls."[42] But they did not wait and there was nothing he could do about it. The audiencia came to a similar conclusion, noting that in addition to the "great loss to the Royal Treasury," flight would "offer a terrible example to the other provinces." And once the Indians had vanished into the montes, not even an army of 10,000 with arquebuses would find them, an academic point since no such army existed in New Spain.[43]

The alternative was to give up the idea of collective punishment and instead seek reconciliation. A peaceful approach enjoyed broad, general support. Castillo y Bobadilla, in his widely read *Política para corregidores,* had argued that it was better to resolve discord by "reason and justice," which was "honest," than by "force," which was "brutal and terrible." Royal law spoke to the issue as well. Decrees dating from the 1540s and later enshrined in the *Recopilación* called upon viceroys and the audiencia to confront Indian uprisings "with gentleness and peace."[44]

Indian leaders knew they could not use flight as a direct threat. An ultimatum would have constituted a bare-faced affront to the king's authority and have been at odds with the image of loyal vassals that they sought to project. If it was not for subjects to install or remove alcaldes mayores, as Montemayor had said, less was it for them to make demands of the king. And so, it is no accident that in all their letters and petitions, Indian leaders referred to flight only obliquely, by way of informing someone in officialdom that the villages were emptying out because of abuses. They knew the message would be heard: in a region with dozens of towns and tens of thousands of tributaries, the threat of mass exodus represented a clear and present danger to the realm. In effect, the Indians left the oidor, the bishop, the viceroy, and the king to draw their own conclusions about the meaning of flight. They knew that for people in power, desolate villages meant far more than just a loss of tribute—a threat to the reciprocal relationship between vassals and their monarch portended chaos.

Flight to the montes, then, was not merely an expedient for avoiding harm. It represented a bargaining chip in an ongoing negotiation. Indian leaders appear to have sought a quid pro quo for returning to society. In October 1660, the audiencia cited secret reports to the effect that unless granted "public instruments and a Royal Provision," the Indians would burn their own houses and retire to the montes permanently, "which would be very easy for them to do and result in a great loss to the Royal Treasury."[45] Other officials made the same point, relying always on "secret reports" for their assertions.[46] The source of these reports appears to have been Oaxaca bishop Cuevas y Dávalos.

The bishop was the first Spaniard of any prominence to venture into the region after Avellán's death. His own report reproduced a letter from Indian leaders to him in which they referred to themselves as "lost sheep" who seek to "return to the flock."[47] It is hard to know what to make of this line. At best it was an indirect allusion to the biblical story of sheep who stray from the shepherd's care. At worst it was little more than an effort to curry the bishop's favor by flattering his pastoral role. Ambivalence may have been the point. By letting it be known through the bishop that they sought a "public instrument," the gobernadores and alcaldes of Tehuantepec were signaling their desire to rejoin society's fold and abide by the reciprocal relationship defining lord and vassals. The open question was, on what terms? Ideally, they would have wanted a pardon exonerating all involved. This is what the bishop lobbied for with the viceroy and the king. Minimally, Indian leaders appeared willing to settle for an assurance that Montemayor would proceed judicially rather than militarily and against individuals rather than against whole villages.

It seems likely that Indian gobernadores, alcaldes, and regidores framed their problem in terms of obtaining something like an amparo order. In a letter to the viceroy shortly after Avellán's death, they talked about how the alcalde mayor had flagrantly violated myriad royal provisions, copies of which "we have in our archives."[48] This was familiar legal terrain. In essence, they were asking to be brought within a legal setting, where the king's protective embrace was most likely to reach them. The alternative they feared most was a Spanish captain at the head of a column of armed blacks, mestizos, and mulattoes who would lay waste to their towns and take their land.[49]

The Indian leaders of Tehuantepec were probably under no illusion that a "public instrument" would literally let them get away with murder.

Bishop Cuevas y Dávalos himself reminded them that they bore a "guilt of great gravity worthy of severe demonstrations of exemplary punishment" for killing Avellán.[50] He offered to plead with the viceroy and the king on their behalf, seeking a pardon for them, in recognition of the suffering they had known at his hands. The key to this request, he told them, was that they return the weapons they had taken and be patient as matters unfolded.

We cannot know how the bishop's advice was discussed within Indian communities. They may have been ambivalent, much as were Montemayor and the viceroy themselves. Would the viceroy respond militarily, or would the Indians "reduce" themselves to their villages and peacefully await the outcome of Montemayor's commission? Flight was an alternative to full-fledged rebellion and a measured response to the abuses they had experienced, but a sustained refusal to return to the villages would have placed them beyond the pale of the king's protection. At the same time, the real possibility that the Indians might flee en masse put Montemayor on notice that he would have to labor under the threat that they would take to the montes if they felt a manifest injustice was being done.

By January 1661, Montemayor was ready to take the next step. He had been in Antequera for several months, gathering information and consulting with the viceroy, the audiencia, and the king and his council. Those consultations appear to have resulted in a decision to proceed judicially rather than strictly militarily. Setting off into the countryside on January 11, Montemayor had in hand a blanket pardon. Signed by the new viceroy Conde de Baños and by the secretary of government in the king's name, the document exonerated anyone who might ever be accused of involvement in the Tehuantepec tumults and imposed a "perpetual silence, so that no more be said of [the disturbances], neither in writing, nor in word, as if they had not happened."[51] The pardon was to be translated into all of the relevant indigenous languages, publicized by criers, and posted in towns and villages, so that all might know of it.

It might seem that the Indians and the bishop had succeeded in ensuring the matter would be handled gently rather than harshly. But there was a catch. The pardon was to have legal effect and be published "when and in the form that the appointed minister"—in this case Montemayor—"should think best." In other words, as the oidor made ready to meet those who had risen up, he had in his pocket a document that could forgive every person who might come under a cloud of suspicion. To all intents and purposes, however, its use rested in his sole discretion.

Two and a half months later, Montemayor began to issue a series of pronouncements and letters to lay the legal and diplomatic groundwork for his advance into the countryside. On March 21, he wrote to captain Alonso Ramírez de Espinosa, Tehuantepec's new alcalde mayor, disclaiming any intention of proceeding with armed force. "Neither his Excellency [the viceroy] nor I has ever imagined to go with troops," he wrote, the better to show the Indians "that his Majesty's chief aim, and his Excellency's and mine, is their conservation and amparo."[52] He knew that Espinosa would convey these words to the Indians in his jurisdiction.

The same day Montemayor wrote an open letter to the Indians of Tehuantepec, noting what good vassals they were and how in need of the king's amparo. On March 23, he published an order assuring the Indians that he had not come merely to punish. This order explicitly mentioned the royal pardon, stating that it would be published for all to see. It also indicated that both the viceroy and the king understood that the alcaldes mayores' many abuses of the king's native vassals violated "natural law" and the "law of peoples." Henceforth, said the order, the alcaldes mayores would have to obey royal decrees regarding the good treatment of the Indians. Moreover, wrote Montemayor, the repartimiento de mercancías would be suppressed, so that the Indians might live obediently and peacefully. This and another order "to constrain the alcaldes mayores" were published by crier on March 28 in the public plaza of Antequera, with a large crowd present.[53]

Two weeks later, on April 9, Montemayor dispatched a letter to the gobernadores, alcaldes, and regidores of Tehuantepec transmitting the text of the March 23 order, telling them to put it in their community book, "for it will serve in your defense in the future." Referring to the cabildo members as "good and honorable vassals of his Majesty," he thanked them for the 110 fish they had sent and reminded them that the king's officers were not permitted to receive gifts. This time, however, he would make an exception and happily accept the fish.[54] Clearly, both sides were reaching out to one another in anticipation of a future meeting where people's fates and possibly the stability of one of the empire's far reaches would be on the line.

On the eve of his departure, then, Montemayor's charge had been clarified from the uncertainty of late 1660. He was to bring guilty individuals to justice, document and correct the abuses of the alcaldes mayores, and grant a general pardon. He had issued a series of proclamations—the orders against the alcaldes mayores, the pardon, the assurances that he did not come as an avenger—to allay the Indians' fears.

His efforts had been cautiously reciprocated by Indian officials with whom he would be treating in coming weeks.

The oidor set out from Antequera with his entourage on May 14, 1661. On May 21, he stopped about fourteen leagues from the town of Guadalcazar. He sent messages ahead, telling the cabildo that he was accompanied by a *señor togado*—a university-trained judge—"charged with the pacification, investigation, and punishment of everything." In return, the gobernador and alcaldes stated that they would come out to greet him. He waited the better part of a day. No one showed up. Wary of Indian spies, he crept ahead to the small village of Tequizistlan, just a league from Tehuantepec.

Before entering the village, word reached him that the Tehuantepec council awaited him there. He went before them. It is imperative, he informed the assembled cabildo members, that those who bore any blame for the uprisings be heard "according to justice." He told them as well that they had to return the *varas de justicia*—the staffs of justice—that they had taken on their own authority, allowing that perhaps they had done so "with the intent of pacifying the land and keeping it in peace." And a number of them would have to be arrested, though he promised to "ensure you are done justice in the measure you should have it" and to extend all "appropriate grace" so that "by being taken prisoner you neither be distressed nor afflicted, because you might well be exonerated and be freed from prison." The regidores he named very grudgingly agreed to hand over their varas and be bound. As they were led away, Montemayor reminded them of the grave charges they faced and told them that "satisfaction was required, so that the truth could be determined."[55] He then returned the varas to the officers who had been cast out by the rebellion, thanking them for their loyalty to the king and for suffering under the "tyranny" of the "usurpers." Both sides, it would seem, had decided to conduct themselves according to the familiar protocols of a judicial proceeding, though Manso Contreras's July 1661 report indicates that those arrested were stricken with fear.[56]

After Tequisiztlan, Montemayor and his retainers conducted similar arrests in surrounding villages. Most came off with little fanfare. An exception was Miztequilla. Upon approaching the village, Montemayor found it empty except for six older men. Everyone else had fled to the montes nearby. He sent thirty of his irregulars to surround the area where the villagers might be hiding, ordering them to fire shots into the air as a warning. Then he installed the six men he had found in the village as regidores and told them to inform those in hiding that if they did not return to the village, he would torch their houses and give their land to mulattoes. Those who were to blame in the uprising had to account for themselves, he said, and it was far better that they do so than that "everyone become delinquent." Over the next couple of days villagers began to trickle in and by the fourth day the town was full again.

Events in Miztequilla offer clues as to what may have been going on within Indian villages facing Montemayor's approach. Through most of 1660 and into early 1661, the uprisings appear to have enjoyed a remarkable degree of cohesion among communities separated by distance and even by language and ethnicity. Bishop Cuevas y Dávalos noted that leaders from pueblos all over the province signed their letters and reports to him not as representatives of this or that village, but on behalf of the Provinces of Tehuantepec.[57] In late March 1661, a Spanish witness noted that in one village he visited, no one would fix individual blame for flogging and running their Indian gobernador out of town, insisting instead that the "*común* [common] of the whole pueblo" had lost patience with a local official who, together with the alcalde mayor, had oppressed them.[58] This is not to deny disagreements within villages, for collective responsibility implied collective punishment. But as long as Montemayor had remained in Antequera, the question of how long to shelter rebellion leaders had not crystallized. After hearing guns fired over their heads and being told that their village would be torched and their land ceded to mulattoes, the inhabitants of Miztequilla were forced to reconsider. After some deliberation, they decided to return and rest whatever hopes they had in the operations of Spanish law, though they knew these to be unusual circumstances.

This was one of the chief effects of the decision to proceed judicially rather than militarily: the knowledge that Montemayor was after individual culprits and that they would be handled according to well-known legal procedures weakened the bonds of collective endeavor and grievance forged during the earliest phase of the uprisings. We can only imagine the conversations among village leaders and perhaps even commoners as they decided to give up those charged as ring leaders in the uprising. *I heard that Montemayor published an auto ending the repartimiento de mercancías and forcing the alcaldes mayores to abide by the king's law. But haven't we heard that before? They just won't obey them. But do we want them to come get us, putting our children at risk? Are we willing to stay here in the wilderness indefinitely, scavanging food, vulnerable to whomever might cross our path? And how will we live without land? I can't stand the thought of mulattoes living on our land. I heard that Montemayor has a document from the king that could pardon everyone. How do we know he will abide by it? Well, who dragged us into this in the first place?* And so on.

In making some sense of individual and collective decisions to return, it is not enough to argue that the villagers of Miztequilla, and the inhabitants of Tehuantepec province more generally, went back to their towns in response to coercion. This is true but analytically trivial. Montemayor's strong arm tactics are undeniable, especially the threat to raze their houses and turn their land over to mulattoes. These people may have had few good options, but in weighing them they were conditioned by a sense of their place in colonial society. Indians such as these held land, owned houses, grew their own food, went to market, attended mass, organized fiestas, paid tribute, brought lawsuits, and governed their own communities. Their lives were integrally engaged with the colonial social order. The poverty of their alternatives—and the burden of Montemayor's threat—was the measure of how deep that engagement ran. In the main, rebels had protested a corrupt repartimiento de mercancías; they had not sought to overthrow Spanish domination or consign themselves to the wilderness.[59] Villagers knew there was no army large enough to drive them back to their pueblos. Yet they returned at the substantial cost of surrendering the uprising's leaders to the oidor.

It did not go well for these men and women. In all fifty-three people were jailed, tried, and punished in Tehuantepec.[60] Trials were conducted over the month of June 1661. Little is known of these proceedings except their outcomes. The record indicates that many of the prisoners were deposed and told their own stories, though we do not have their testimony. Manso Contreras's report, always favorable to Montemayor, says only that the oidor proceeded "carefully, maturely and with prudence." In the course of matters, Montemayor determined that the killing of Avellán and the ensuing mayhem had amounted to an "alzamiento and disobedience to the King our Lord"—a finding at odds with his and the viceroy's initial assessment of the situation.

Sentences were handed down on June 27. No appeals were allowed—in direct contravention of recognized legal principle. Five people were executed. Gerónimo Flores, considered the prime mover of the rebellion, was hung and quartered and his body parts posted along the Royal Highway. The person identified as having thrown the stone that killed Avellán was shot on a post, his body placed where the stone throwing happened and his right hand cut off and nailed to the scaffold. Four were condemned to death in absentia. Several others felt the whip, typically 100 strokes through the streets of Guadalcazar, and were exiled from the community for anywhere from two years to perpetuity. Six went to the mines. Half a dozen women had their hair cut off and were flogged and then exiled or sold to obrajes. A woman who had sat astride Avellán's body, insulting and hitting it with a stone, was shorn. Montemayor justified the light sentence in this last case by recognizing the whippings she and others had suffered at Avellán's hands. Another woman avoided the obraje by cutting off her own hands. Finally, Gracia María de la Crespa had one of her hands cut off and nailed to a post at the place she had allegedly set fire to the stables. All of this was done very publicly in one bloody week between between June 27 and July 2, 1661, in the town where Avellán had been killed. According to Montemayor's June report, the Indians were terrified, having never before witnessed a quartering or watched someone's hand be chopped off. The rest of the prisoners were flogged and kept in jail.[61]

It is difficult to know how these people came to their roles in the rebellion. Some, surely, were swept up in the moment, throwing stones and setting fires on impulse, heedless of later consequences. Others may have had a longer history of protest against the abuses of the alcaldes mayores. An intriguing possibility in this regard is Gerónimo Flores, who was identified as a ring leader of the uprising.

The hint we have of this comes from an amparo petition filed in December 1656, three years before Avellán's death. In that year, Juan Martín and several officials from the village of Tepancacualco, in the jurisdiction of Villa Alta de San Yldephonso, accused several Indians, among them Gerónimo Flores, of sowing the seeds of discord within the village. According to the petition, Flores and the others were not residents of the village, but men of "low status"—macehuales—who by "guile and artifice" had insinuated themselves into village politics.[62] By claiming to be local notables and mistreating the residents of the pueblo, stated the petition, Flores and his compatriots had succeeded, "with violence," in having themselves elected and reelected to the governorship of the town. They had acted with so heavy a hand that local residents had abandoned their lands and homes, barely tending crops and fields. Petitioners sought an amparo to stop this campaign of harassment and abuse and to bar Flores and the others from participating in local elections or holding any local offices. The tribunal agreed, granting the amparo.

Because this was an amparo petition, Flores and the other men had no occasion to respond and may have learned of the order against them only when the alcalde mayor served it and threatened them with jail if they did not comply. As a result, we have little to go on in trying to make sense of this situation. At bottom, there are two possibilities. From the vantage of Juan Martín and his fellow petitioners, Flores and his followers were simply interlopers who sought to wrest political control of the village away from the legitimately elected officers by intimidating a vulnerable population. This is a plausible scenario. The repartimiento de mercancías offered genuine opportunities to those willing to work closely with Spanish alcaldes mayores. Flores may simply have wanted to horn in on the action, which meant displacing Juan Martín and his officers. Alternatively, Flores's actions might be understood as an incipient protest against the abuses of the local officials behind the repartimientos. From this perspective, the point of challenging Juan Martín and his officers was to resist the alcalde mayor's growing exactions. Flores and the others might truly have been men of "low status" who had tired of the abuses of local Indian gobernadores at the beck and call of Spanish alcaldes mayores.

There would be little reason to suspect the latter of these two but for the fact that the name Gerónimo Flores gained top billing in the Tehuantepec uprising. Thus, the real question is whether the Gerónimo Flores of the 1656 petition was the same one executed and quartered by Montemayor in 1661. We cannot be certain, but the hypothesis is worth entertaining.

If, as the 1656 petition alleged, Flores was not of Tepancacualco, and if the amparo was served on him by the alcalde mayor of Villa Alta, he almost surely would have moved on, regardless of whether he was protesting the repartimiento or trying to get in on it. If he continued his activities elsewhere along the road connecting Villa Alta to Tehuantepec, he could have ended up in Tehuantepec three years later just as simmering tensions were beginning to boil over. If so, he may have found himself among the visible leaders of a growing protest movement at a moment when only the bold, the reckless, or the truly committed would have chosen a political position. The name and title "Gerónimo Flores, alcalde," appeared as a signer on a letter sent to the viceroy by the gobernadores and officers of Tehuantepec on September 14, 1660, insisting that they had not risen up and were now "in obedience to our alcalde mayor, who treats us as vassals of the King our Lord and not as slaves"—a reminder of how closely vassalage could be connected to notions of liberty in the minds of Indian litigants.[63] We know that this Flores had only recently become an alcalde, for Manso Contreras's report refers to him as an "intruder alcalde" (*alcalde intruso*), one who came in from the outside.[64] According to a letter to the viceroy from Alonso Ramírez de Espinosa, the alcalde mayor who succeeded Avellán, Flores and the other officers were elected to replace the gobernador and officers of Tehuantepec who had abandoned their positions for fear they might follow Avellán to the grave at the hands of an angry mob. Rather than "run the same risk" as the alcalde mayor, they had escaped the wrath of the "plebeians" by hiding in the town church, whereupon these same "plebeians" had named new officers in their place.[65] At that point, Flores's name became one of those most prominently connected with the uprising, earning him the dubious distinction of being the only one of fifty-three to be hung, quartered, and posted along the royal highways.

The oidor understood the effects such sentences might have on a populace still reeling from months of upheaval. They would inspire awe, as they were intended to. They might also provoke resentment. This too was carefully stage-managed. As soon as the punishment phase of the proceedings had concluded, Montemayor announced an Act of Pardon. On the night of July 3, solemn vespers were sung at the Dominican convent and *luminarias* put out. Montemayor ordered a stage built in front of the Casas Reales, which had been torched during the tumult. A portrait of the king graced an easel on the highest step and below it were placed a velvet chair and a table, as though the monarch himself might attend.[66] On either side stood two benches. A stool was set out for the oidor. Soldiers from Montemayor's retinue stood in formation and as the pardon was read hoisted the royal banners and fired a salute. The secretary read the pardon in Spanish, with simultaneous translation into Zapoteca. After this, all prisoners in the village's jail and even the royal jail were released, including several held for their participation in the uprising. Copies of the pardon, in Spanish and in Zapoteca, were posted on the door of the Casas Reales, where they remained all that day and the next. A Spanish copy was then permanently posted in the parish church and a Zapoteca one in the Indians' community hall (*casa de comunidad*). The Act of Pardon concluded with a *Te Deum* and a mass for the long and happy life of the king. The priest's homily emphasized the king's clemency in pardoning offenses so grave as had been committed in Tehuantepec. He exhorted townspeople to peace and obedience and closed by promising them that in the future their complaints would be heard. Then twenty-eight gobernadores and their alcaldes swore fealty to the king. Montemayor ordered that a Day of Pardon be celebrated each year, in which the pardon and the order of March 23 putting an end to the repartimiento be read aloud, so that Indians might know themselves to be "*amparados y asistidos para en lo venidero*" (protected and assisted in the future) "like the rest of my vassals."[67]

We may speculate that many, perhaps most of the Indians who witnessed these events, or heard tell of them, were relieved that normalcy had been restored after a long period of suspense and peril. The Act of Pardon had officially sealed a breach in the social order that opened with the killing of Avellán. There were probably sullen murmurings as well. Montemayor had said he did not come to punish and he had kept his word by not insisting on collective responsibility for the acts undertaken by a few. But some of the punishments meted out to those few had been horrific, and for many even the milder ones may have seemed excessive given the abuses that the Indians of Tehuantepec had so long borne. Indeed, some may have begun to wonder whether the March 23 order outlawing the repartimientos was anything more than a stalking horse for a vengeful and covinous oidor.

PUNISHING NEXAPA AND IXTEPEC

From Tehauntepec, Montemayor made his way to Nexapa. Emboldened by recent successes, he proceeded more resolutely. He wrote to the viceroy on August 23, 1661, that he had spent twenty days in the province, persuading people to come down from the montes and return to their villages. A number of arrests followed, "with all felicity and without any noise." This claim appears to have been generally true, though he did face resistance or indifference in several villages whose people "showed no fear of punishment." The residents of one Chontal pueblo snubbed the oidor, refusing to greet him as he entered town. In two others, gobernadores defiantly disregarded his orders or even ripped them up to his face. In the pueblo of San Martín, an angry crowd gathered when Montemayor went to arrest three villagers. Members of the crowd shouted that they did not want the arrests to take place. When the oidor asked them who said so, they responded that the whole pueblo did "which," he quipped to the viceroy, "is how they seek to cover up their crimes." When asked who the "pueblo" was, they replied that those present were. Impatient with them, Montemayor stood up, struck those who spoke most openly with his vara, and placed them under arrest. They spent a few days in jail and were released. The original three were arrested shortly thereafter.[68] In all, sixty people were jailed for their participation in the Nexapa disturbances.

By mid-August the oidor had begun to depose witnesses. Hearing the testimony, Montemayor deemed Nexapa a more serious affair than Tehuantepec, calling it an "alzamiento general" (a "general uprising" rather than just an "alzamiento") in his report to the viceroy. Uprisings in Tehuantepec had been widespread, but not well coordinated. In Nexapa, leaders who had been in communication with fellow rebels in Tehuantepec signed "letters of convocation" in which Zapotecas, Chontales, and Mixe alike agreed to act together against their alcaldes mayores. By one report, Indians in Nexapa had more than 400 firearms and knew how to use them.[69] The oidor seemed troubled as well by the millenarian tone of some of the Nexapa rebels and the comparative barbarousness of these Indians—especially the Chontales—in contrast to those from Tehuantepec. He wrote darkly of rumors that the mythic king of the Zapotecas, Congún, had risen from his watery sanctuary at the bottom of a sacred lagoon and that Indian witnesses reported seeing a nearby mountain shake, a sign that the time had come to throw off Spanish rule and reclaim their lands. One cacique in Villa Alta, don Melchor, had been elected captain and king and had issued orders to stop obeying the Spaniards, proclaiming that he would die defending the Indians. Montemayor promptly arrested him and spared no effort obliging him his fate.

In mid-October, three Nexapa leaders were hanged, among them Fabián Martín who, like Gerónimo Flores, was quartered. Seven others escaped the noose, sentenced instead to permanent exile from their communities and lifetime service in the galleys at Veracruz. All others were exiled, some for a term, some for perpetuity. Of the sixty arrested and tried, most later avoided punishment under the general pardon, as in Tehuantepec. The oidor also rewarded exemplary conduct. One gobernador who had refused to sign the letter of convocation, and even arrested a rebel gobernador, was exempted from tribute payments for life. Montemayor granted the same benefit to an Indian couple who had notified the alcalde mayor of the growing conspiracy and in so doing helped several Spaniards to escape harm.[70] Bartolomé Ximénez, the interpreter so bitterly complained of by the Indians, was exiled from Nexapa and stripped of office. Montemayor spared him further penalty, as the Indians had burned his house and taken his land.

Like Gerónimo Flores, Bartolomé Ximénez may have had a long history of involvement in the circumstances that gave rise to the upheaval in Nexapa. Amparo petitions from late 1656 and early 1657 suggest that by 1660 he had been a source of irritation among the villages for some time. In 1656 Francisco Ximénez (probably no relation), a leader in the pueblo of Santo Domingo Zontecomatepeque, had gone to Mexico City to complain that Bartolomé was trying to arrest him for a debt. Early the following year, in March 1657, Francisco López, a resident of Lapaguia, Nexapa, charged that Bartolomé owed him money. Fearing the interpreter would abuse him for demanding payment, he asked the Juzgado for protection.[71]

By the time news of Tehuantepec reached Nexapa, Ximénez appears to have been known far and wide for his excesses. Juan de Espejo had blamed Bartolomé, calling him a "great thief," when faced with an angry group of Indians calling for an end to abuses. Many had it in for the interpreter. According to a report after the fact, the Indians who had cornered Espejo in the church had asked that Ximénez be handed over to them so they could kill him for the harm he had caused.[72]

The intimate corruption and personal animus implied here bespeaks a depth of hurt and frustration hard to discern in the documents themselves. Montemayor, not surprisingly, saw matters with a somewhat more clinical (and perhaps cynical) eye. Recognizing that the Indians bore legitimate grievances against their alcaldes mayores, he wrote to the viceroy that "[f]rom what I have seen in these provinces and from what the Indians of Tehuantepec have requested of me, I have come to see how poorly they are governed and this is the principle reason for the altercations."[73] He commanded that the March 23 order he had used in Tehuantepec be published and posted throughout Nexapa. He stressed that in the residencia against outgoing alcalde mayor Juan de Espejo, the Indians must be heard and the abuses of which they complained given satisfaction. But he took no other action against Ximénez.

The final theater of Montemayor's pacification campaign opened in early 1662, mainly in two pueblos, San Mateo de Capulalpa and San Pedro Nesiche, both in the province of Ixtepec. Montemayor arrived in Ixtepec with a clear plan of action. Before leaving Oaxaca, nearly a year earlier, he had interviewed a number of local people: Spaniard Francisco Álvarez, the teniente who had been chased out of town and nearly stoned to death by angry villagers; Juan García Capitán, Indian chief bailiff of Capulalpa, who had always been helpful to Spaniards; and Miguel de Yllescas, Indian gobernador of Nesiche, who had refused to take part in the uprising. Other Indian witnesses were deposed in Capulalpa and Nesiche in January and February 1662, nearly a year later. For reasons which can only be guessed at—a sense that the worst was over, a cocksureness born of earlier successes, the simple luxury of time, or perhaps an accident of archiving—we have a somewhat fuller record of proceedings in Ixtepec than in Tehuantepec and Nexapa.

Montemayor dealt with two separate incidents in Ixtepec. The first involved an attack on Spanish teniente Francisco Álvarez and the unauthorized punishment of Juan García Capitán, the Indian bailiff of San Mateo Capulalpa. The second grew out of an uprising in San Pedro Nesiche in which the duly elected gobernador had been punished by local residents.

In San Mateo Capulalpa, residents' testimony indicates that problems had begun when Francisco Álvarez started to serve as alcalde mayor Joseph Reynoso's lieutenant.[74] In a common arrangement, Álvarez collected tribute and managed the repartimiento de mercancías on Reynoso's behalf, allowing Reynoso to stay above the sometimes brutal process of wringing profit from the Indians. As the record makes clear, the residents of Capulalpa had no shortage of complaints against the alcalde mayor himself. The village had already dispatched their gobernador, don Pedro Ramírez de Gusmán to Mexico City to seek legal remedies against Reynoso. Álvarez, however, was the man on the spot and appears to have been particularly zealous in exacting tribute and enforcing the repartimiento which, since Tehuantepec, had seemed increasingly burdensome to Indians across the region.

Álvarez got himself into trouble with residents of Capulalpa in August 1660. According to Indian witnesses, he and Indian bailiff Juan García Capitán came to barrio Santa Cruz, one of Capulalpa's two neighborhoods, in the middle of the night to arrest Diego Hernández, alcalde of the town, and his son. The two men had escaped from jail the night before, where they were being held for failure to meet repartimiento quotas. Unable to find them, Álvarez had tried to arrest Hernández's wife. Neighbors had rushed out of their houses and wrested the woman from Álvarez and García before they could reach the jail. At that point, Álvarez testified, Indians gathered in the street, playing drums and trumpets and screaming for his death. He had fled. The crowd caught up with him and stoned him, a point corroborated by Indian witnesses to the incident. Though left for dead, he was able to drag himself back to San Juan Chicomexuchil, the cabecera, and inform alcalde mayor Reynoso of the night's events.[75] When Diego Hernández returned to town the next morning and learned what happened, he and Tomás Baptista, another alcalde, arrested Juan García and flogged him until some other residents begged for mercy on his behalf.

The criminal charges in this case were two: the attempt on Álvarez's life and Hernández's and Baptista's unauthorized whipping of García. The record of proceedings indicates that four residents of barrio Nuestra Señora de la Asumpción, Calpulalpa's other neighborhood, testified. Responding to questions put to him by Montemayor, one of the Asumpción witnesses noted that Hernández and Baptista had justified García's punishment by claiming that their gobernador had written from Mexico City blaming García for the abusive repartimientos. A second witness agreed, adding that Hernández and Baptista had insisted that García spied on town residents and told alcalde mayor Reynoso who had grain stashed away. Don Diego de Acevedo, a resident of Capulalpa, testified that he and others attempted to interecede on García's behalf as he was being whipped. Eventually, Hernández and Baptista had relented and let García go.

There is more in this testimony than meets the eye. All of the events took place in barrio Santa Cruz. Yet the only witnesses to testify were from barrio Asumpción. This was almost surely not a coincidence. A close look suggests that the town pursued a cunning strategy in offering the witnesses it did. One of the oddities of the testimony is that Asumpción's witnesses were very careful to insulate their barrio from any participation in the affair. According to the witnesses, residents of barrio Asumpción played no role whatever in the incident, except to plead for García's release: they had not become involved in trying to keep Hernández's wife from being dragged to jail, they had not pursued Álvarez, and they had nothing to do with Garciá's flogging. Superficially, this seems perfectly plausible. Álvarez showed up in Santa Cruz in the middle of the night and tried to arrest Hernández's wife. The closest neighbors, other residents of Santa Cruz, would have been the most likely to respond to shrieks for help, and therefore would have been most likely to chase Álvarez and stone him. Yet something about this story does not quite fit.

While Santa Cruz residents would have been the first to respond to cries for help in their barrio, Asumpción was close enough that three of the four witnesses stated that they and others heard the commotion and ran to the scene (the fourth claimed he was sick). If the witnesses are to be believed, having bolted from their beds in the middle of the night, Asumpción residents then stood idly by as Álvarez tried to arrest Hernández's wife and simply watched as Santa Cruz residents snatched her back and then chased Álvarez. What remains so puzzling about this testimony is the almost hermetic separation between the two barrios. Witnesses made a specific point of noting that the town "was divided into two barrios." Why?

One straightforward possibility is that the village was riven into two factions. It is true that Hernández and Baptista were alcaldes and that both were from Santa Cruz, but there is no other evidence of community antagonism. Alternatively, it might be supposed that the barrios had split over how to confront recent events, specifically the provocations of Tehuantepec and Nexapa. Testimony is clear that Hernández had in recent times become a focal point for local anxieties. He was a known agitator and, according to one witness, went around meeting with people to discuss the repartimientos. In addition, there were rumors that he was plotting with Indians from other villages to kill the alcalde mayor. It is certainly reasonable to suppose that some people would have wanted to distance themselves from someone liable to draw attention from the authorities.

Yet, there are problems with this tale of two barrios. To begin with, one of the Asumpción witnesses noted that the town's gobernador, Pedro Ramírez de Gusmán, had gone to Mexico City to complain about the repartimientos "at the whole town's request," suggesting unity on this crucial question.[76] If so, it is likely that the residents of Asumpción hated Reynoso and Álvarez for their role in the repartimiento every bit as much as those of Santa Cruz. And while it is reasonable to suppose that many in Asumpción wanted to avoid entangling themselves in Hernández's dangerous activities, the same could be said of Santa Cruz residents. But if there was no community rift, why did the Asumpción witnesses consistently cast blame exclusively on the residents of Santa Cruz? And why were there no Santa Cruz witnesses to dispute their testimony?

Here, I think, is where a neat trick may have been turned. There was no denying that Álvarez had entered Hernández's house in Santa Cruz, nor that he had tried to arrest Hernández's wife, a woman of Santa Cruz. Residents of Santa Cruz had chased Álvarez, nearly killing him. Santa Cruz, in other words, was unavoidably implicated in the incident. And by now, villagers knew how things had gone in Tehuantepec and Nexapa. Had the Asumpción witnesses placed residents of Asumpción among those gathered to watch García's flogging, they might have risked drawing greater attention to Asumpción's role in the incident. By focusing attention on Santa Cruz they insulated half of the town from judicial prying.

But they did not leave Santa Cruz out to dry. By refusing to name any individuals and by insisting that the Indians of Santa Cruz, "with the voice and in name of the whole barrio" had chased Álvarez down, the witnesses were playing on the constraints of criminal proceedings, which did not affix collective blame or inflict collective punishment. There is no other way to understand how the witnesses could in one breath say that they were unable to name any of the people involved in attacking Álvarez and in the next that all who did so were from barrio Santa Cruz. The witnesses appear to have been well aware of the line they were treading, for rather than testify from personal knowledge, even though three of four had rushed to the scene, they relied on "what everyone was saying." In effect, they limited themselves to identifying those whose names were already known to Montemayor from other sources and offered as a source of culpability a collective entity which they knew he could not punish judicially. As one witness took care to point out, "he had not heard anyone named as the mover of events, nor of any person who led the rest."[77] Testimony also consistently denied any knowledge of plots to kill the alcalde mayor. With regard to García's flogging, the witnesses confined themselves to Hernández's and Baptista's roles, which everyone already knew about. None of this could have come off without a careful squaring of stories. And since no Santa Cruz residents testified, they did not risk contradiction.

If this was the strategy, it appears to have worked: no one in Capulalpa was punished for chasing and stoning Álvarez. Hernández and Baptista were convicted for García's whipping, a fate they probably could not have avoided given the public nature of their actions. They knew well before Montemayor's arrival what fate might befall them, so they had fled the jurisdiction, forcing the oidor to sentence them in absentia to be hung if ever caught. No one else in Capulalpa felt Montemayor's judicial wrath.

In the village of Atepeque, near San Pedro Nesiche, troubles had been brewing since at least 1659, when don Nicolás Pineda, teniente of the jurisdiction, had arrested two men. Each man held two offices simultaneously—alguacil of the church and alcalde of the pueblo—which violated royal edicts. Pineda had asked them to surrender their staffs of alcalde. When they refused, he had jailed them. After their arrest, a group of women from the neighboring village of Analco gathered outside the corregidor's house, near the town jail, and began to call for the men's release. Pineda appeared, with staff of office in hand, to disperse them. Egged on by the prisoners shouting from the window of their cell nearby, the women began to pitch sticks and stones at Pineda. According to an Indian witness, a woman called Ana La Caxona cried out that the king had not sent Pineda to give them so much work making cotton blankets, soap, and other things. She called on the other women to capture Pineda. Then the women pulled up the makeshift picota Pineda had erected in the plaza and used it to storm the jail—an interesting inversion of its symbolic purpose—freeing the two prisoners. According to one witness, Pineda fled the pueblo and returned a couple of days later, with Joseph Reynoso, alcalde mayor of the jurisdiction. Together they had four women flogged for the attack on Pineda. Two bailiffs who criticized Pineda and Reynoso were also whipped.[78]

The area was still at a slow boil in early 1660 when news of Tehuantepec arrived. By that time, Miguel Yllescas, the gobernador of San Pedro Nesiche, had become a focus of hostility and resentment among many of Ixtepec's Indians. Witnesses testified that he had been extorting money from the repartimiento and putting all the macehuales to work for the alcalde mayor, without paying them, a clear violation of royal provisions against personal service.[79] Pedro Pacheco, also an Indian alcalde at the time, testified that everyone in the pueblo had agreed he should arrest Yllescas and throw him out of the village. Pacheco did so, took Yllescas's staff of office, mounted him on a packhorse, and flogged him through the "calles acostumbradas"—the usual streets—and exiled him permanently from town. He was supported in this by other principales and alcaldes of the village, who said that they were tired of Yllescas' impositions, especially with regard to the repartimiento.[80]

Yllescas told another story. Pacheco resented him because he had refused to plot against alcalde mayor Reynoso, not because of the repartimiento. The occasion of this resentment was two letters from leaders
at Capulalpa (Diego Hernández being one of them) asking the people
of Nesiche to help kill Reynoso, "as had been done at Tehuantepec."
Yllescas stated that he had refused to go along, "because I was a gobernador and had the king's staff, and I was a poor Indian and did not
want to be against the Spaniards." About twenty days later he received
another letter saying that the Indians of Capulalpa had killed Álvarez
instead of Reynoso and that people in Nesiche should be on the lookout
for Reynoso and his family. Still he did nothing. Pacheco arrested him
shortly thereafter, said Yllescas, claiming to have a letter from the viceroy
ordering that Yllescas be hung. When Yllescas asked Pacheco to show
the order, Pacheco responded that the order itself specified that it should
not be shown for any reason. In the end, Pacheco did not hang Yllescas. Rather, just "as is done with one who has been convicted," Yllescas
was flogged through the streets, a trumpeter and a crier proclaiming
his crime—"because he went around with Spaniards and helped them
and had eaten with don Joseph Reynoso."[81]

With these depositions on the record, Montemayor joined the various
cases. He gave those arrested fifteen days to present a defense, with the
help of an appointed lawyer who acted for all of them. Although the defendant's side of the record is thin, the petitions and witnesses on behalf
of Pedro Pacheco and another defendant, Hernando de Santiago, give
some glimpse of how the accused sought to spare themselves.

To escape the charge of imposture of authority, Pedro Pacheco testified that he had never claimed to possess a viceregal letter ordering
Yllescas to be hanged or exiled. He admitted arresting Yllescas, though
"with an eye to the public good." The truth of the matter, he said, was
that the macehuales were angry at Yllescas for his abuses in league with
Reynoso. After the arrest, Pacheco treated Yllescas "in form of justice"
and "with no intent other than to pacify everyone so that nothing would
happen to cause harm or alteration." Witnesses who said otherwise,
he insisted, did so falsely and "siniestramente"—with malice. Pacheco
called three witnesses. One of them contradicted his testimony at a crucial point. The other two did little more than vouch for him as an honorable man. Hernando de Santiago, who was accused of serving as the
crier while Yllescas was being flogged and ridden out of town, denied
the charge. He had done nothing more than try to calm Yllescas down,
so that he would obey Pacheco. "As a good subject," he simply did what
his superiors, in this instance Pacheco, ordered him to do.

Sentences in Nesiche were similar to earlier ones. Pedro Pacheco of
Nesiche received 100 lashes, perpetual exile from Ixtepec, and six years

service in the mines. Hernando de Santiago, Ana de la Caxona, and five others from Nesiche were to be flogged, banished, or given into service at mines or obrajes. Floggings were carried out on March 13, 1662, with Montemayor presiding. As he had earlier in Tehuantepec and Nexapa, he made a point of declaring publicly that the root of the uprisings had been the excesses of the alcaldes mayores and corregidores, for which the order of March 23, 1661, forbidding the repartimiento, was the remedy. Henceforth, the alcaldes mayores and corregidores were to obey the king's many decrees regarding the proper treatment of the Indians.[82] Though they may have been reeling from the severity of Montemayor's punishments, Indians of the villages grasped at the March 1661 order, flocking to the oidor to obtain testimonios for their archives.[83]

Montemayor's disposition of the Ixtepec cases makes it almost impossible to avoid the conclusion that these trials, and the earlier ones in Tehuantepec and Nexapa, were little more than summary justice. While the cases against some defendants are reasonably persuasive on evidentiary grounds—that is, the accused probably did what they were alleged to have done—the proceedings seem to have been radically compressed in time and straitened in procedure. Few defendants' witnesses appear in the record. There is no record for Tehuantepec and Nexapa, but in Capulalpa only four witnesses gave testimony, in Nesiche only three. Most who might have spoken may have held back for fear of calling attention to their role in the altercation; anyone who knew enough to have something to say risked being seen as a participant. In addition, advocacy on behalf of defendants largely failed. In the Nesiche case individual defendants did not have lawyers. One lawyer sufficed for all eight of the accused. It was not uncommon for one lawyer to represent two or three related defendants, but eight unrelated people was unusual, a sign that Montemayor looked chiefly to outcomes rather than process in these cases. Finally, the right to appeal appears to have been completely abrogated for those put to death on the spot, a total of eight between Tehuantepec and Nexapa, or maimed or flogged.

IF ONLY THEIR CRIES HAD REACHED YOUR EARS

Although no consolation to those hanged, the king seems to have been deeply distressed by the severity and high-handedness of Montemayor's actions. In a letter dated August 30, 1662, he chastised the viceroy and the oidor for proceeding too hastily to the most ruthless penalties. Repeated royal orders, wrote the king, had made clear that the Indians were to be pacified "with the greatest gentleness, not burdening them with harsh punishments and not proceeding without first giving an account to my Council and that in any case you be advised to aim for pacification rather than conquest and warfare, as my previous orders set out in great detail." Moreover, fumed King Philip IV at Montemayor and the viceroy, you "acted before receiving my dispatches and I cannot doubt that seeing what I ordered you will [henceforth] proceed with the gentleness that I wish and which is just for those vassals." The king further commanded the viceroy to collect the records of all the cases and send them to the council for review. That submission should detail the reasons and causes for each and every sentence. Finally, the king ordered the oidor off the case and suspended any ongoing legal proceedings against Indians.[84] A year later, the crown attorney concluded that Montemayor had been justified in his actions, "except in the punishments he gave."[85]

Although the king's order and the crown attorney's conclusion probably never reached the Indians, it appears to have converged with some of the Indians' own efforts to remedy the injustices they had suffered at Montemayor's hands. In January 1664, several San Pedro Nesiche defendants found themselves before the audiencia. The original sentences handed down by Montemayor were amended and they were all ordered to an obraje. All eight of them—Marco Figueroa, Pedro Pacheco, Hernando de Santiago, Baltazar García, Juan Ambrosio, Andrés Pérez, Melchor Martín, Ana María la Caxona—appealed this decision to the audiencia itself. They then sat in the audiencia's own jail to await a reply. Eight months later, on August 26, citing the legal opinion of the crown attorney, who concluded that the sentences were inconsistent with an earlier royal decree, the audiencia reversed itself and ordered the defendants freed, on condition that they not return to their home villages.[86]

Here, at long last, was vindication of a hopeful engagement with Spanish justice. In the countryside, with the oidor in command of his own rough police force, and given the immediacy of events, there had not been much Indian villagers could do about judicial fiats. Eight people had been put to death as a result, dozens lashed and exiled. These Nesiche eight had somehow found their way back to Mexico City, where experience told them they had a prospect of altering the fates charted for them by drumhead proceedings.

This successful appeal is only the most salient example of a staunch refusal to give up on the light of justice even during the midnight of Montemayor's judicial terror. Where they might easily have despaired in the face of the oidor's arbitariness, and some doubtless did, others tirelessly sought out the byways of legal recourse. The irony of this is

that Montemayor may have acted as summarily as he did precisely because he knew that Indian defendants would take full advantage of the
law if given the chance to do so. Indeed, through the long months of
Montemayor's commission, and after, Indian letter writers refused to
break faith with the principle that justice flowed downward and outward from the king. A royal officer who acted for himself or in flagrant
violation of the law did not represent the king's justice—such a one,
whether alcalde mayor, corregidor, or even someone like the oidor with
a special commission, became a tyrant. The uprisings were premised on
this notion, as Montemayor himself had recognized in his first report
from Antequera. Thus, while the rebels and residents of Tehuantepec,
Nexapa, and Ixtepec could not avoid negotiating with the oidor, and
while they might not be able to oppose him at any given moment of arbitrariness, they appear not to have confused his actions with the king's
will. The Nesiche eight's persistence in pursuing their appeal stands as
proof of the fact.

This image of reaching justice and being heard is a particularly powerful one for making some sense of the uprisings and for understanding
the Indians' refusal to give up hope in the idea of justice. In an October
21, 1660 letter of inquiry to the new viceroy, Conde de Baños, the audiencia noted that the Indians had been unable to bring their lawsuits
to the audiencia because of the "favoritism"—*valimiento*—the alcaldes
mayores enjoyed at viceregal court.[87] Procuradores refused to plead their
cases because the Duque de Albuquerque's servants and friends had been
everywhere. The problem had become particularly acute in Oaxaca. In
years past the archbishop, under the provisions of a royal decree, had
been allowed to hear Indian complaints and act on them. Shortly before the Tehuantepec uprising, the alcaldes mayores of the region had
obtained a viceregal order stripping the archbishop of this jurisdiction.
Cut off from Mexico City and lacking the archbishop's help, concluded
the audiencia's letter, the Indians of Oaxaca have been almost totally
abandoned to "vexations and oppressions."

The audiencia was not alone in seeing that the Indians had been denied
all legal recourse. Montemayor had raised the issue in an early letter to
the king. In October 1660, two months after arriving in Antequera, and
before setting out for the countryside, Montemayor wrote Philip IV to
offer his first assessment of the situation in Oaxaca.[88] Noting the greed
and inhumanity of the alcaldes mayores—at that time, all appointees of
the oidor's political enemy, outgoing viceroy Duque de Albuquerque—
he noted that the Indians, these "oppressed wretches," had repeatedly

gone to their alcalde mayor to beg relief from the repartimientos, only to have him ratchet up the abuse. Having failed to obtain justice at the local level, two delegations of regidores had trooped to Mexico City to air their complaints at the audiencia, only to be turned back. Porteros did not admit them to the audiencia chambers. Procuradores refused to sign their petitions. Oidores declined to see them. All because the Duque's servants had passed the word that the Indians'claims were not to be recognized.[89] Upon returning home, they faced even harsher punishments and impositions from their alcalde mayor, who seemed to act with impunity.

Bishop don Diego Osorio de Escobar y Llamas of Puebla also weighed in on the matter, noting that in one instance he knew of, a group of 400 or 500 Indians from Metepeque—with chocolate, candles, soap, and other repartimiento goods in hand—had arrived in Mexico City seeking an audience with the viceroy. But since the alcalde mayor of whom they complained was the viceroy's intimate friend, he refused to see them, even though the audiencia had dispatched many provisions in their favor. The implications of these different accounts from officialdom are clear: the uprisings in Oaxaca grew, in good measure, from the Indians' inability to make themselves heard at the local level and in Mexico City. As of late February 1661, as Montemayor made ready for his foray into the countryside, a parade of petitioners from Villa Alta de San Yldephonso had complained before the audiencia that their alcaldes mayores and tenientes blocked the avenues to justice, harassing them whenever they went to Mexico City to file a petition.[90] Oaxaca bishop Cuevas y Dávalos sharpened the point, concluding in his March 1661 report to the viceroy that the Indians believed "that if these things, or the smallest of them had reached your Excellency's very pious ears" Tehuantepec and Nexapa would not have happened.[91]

Perhaps he was right. In a poignant letter just weeks after their May 1660 skirmish with the column from Antequera, in which several Indians had been killed or wounded, and still months before Álvarez's close brush with death, the alcaldes and regidores of Nexapa had asked the bishop, "Should we or should we not go to Mexico [City]. *Once again, no one will help us;* only God and you our sainted Bishop."[92] By early October, when the uprising began in Nexapa, they still had not received word from the audiencia on petitions the bishop had transmitted to Mexico City in May. Against this background, what Montemayor and others took to be an alzamiento against Spanish rule was for Indian rebels an insurrection of involvement with Spanish justice, a desperate struggle against those who would choke off the channels of legal redress so important to the king's most vulnerable vassals.

OPPORTUNISM AND REFORM

Even before he had finished judging the uprisings in Tehuantepec and Nexapa—some have argued that he purposely drew matters out[93]—Montemayor undertook a reform of the tributary system in Oaxaca. Over the last several months of his commission, roughly between October 1661 and March 1662, he went village to village conducting a census of the Indians in the whole archbishopric. He determined that the tribute lists, some of which were fifty, sixty, or even seventy years old, understated the number of Indians in jurisdictions across the province. His efforts yielded a count of more than 11,000 "hidden tributaries," for a total of nearly 22,000 pesos a year above the amount collected on the basis of the extant lists. On his own authority, he ordered new *tasaciones*—tribute assessments—for all the towns and villages in the region.[94]

Many Indians, who had been promised that the abuses of the alcaldes mayores would be addressed and had instead suffered under Montemayor's mockery of judicial process, were incensed. By mid 1662, villages from across Oaxaca had filed an "infinite" number of lawsuits, and some were banding together to make the long trip to Mexico City at great expense.[95] According to the king's treasurer, villages were suspending tribute payments, and many residents were fleeing their pueblos once again.[96]

In light of these conditions, bishop Cuevas y Dávalos wrote one more time to the viceroy on the Indians' behalf.[97] In August, after rehearsing Montemayor's abuses and excesses in Tehuantepec and Nexapa, he noted that the oidor had effectively denied the Indians all legal recourse on the new tasaciones. When representatives from the villages have gone to Mexico City to complain about tribute, he wrote pointedly, their procuradores and agents "became deaf and none have dared write or sign petitions in favor of the Indians, so great is the dominion of your oidor." His actions are particularly aggravating, said the bishop, given that the legal merits of the Indians' complaints were indisputable. Indeed, less than a month after Montemayor had imposed the new count, viceroy Conde de Baños himself dispatched an amparo to one village, ordering that tribute be collected according to the schedule established by the audiencia in 1632, in effect revoking the oidor's new tribute list for that village. This, concluded the bishop in a letter to the king, has been the state of things in these provinces since the arrival of your oidor: "There has been only punishment of the Indians and no remedy of their vexations."[98]

Petitions flooded in from villages across Oaxaca.[99] In late 1662, caciques, gobernadores, and alcades of various pueblos and head towns joined together in a long petition to the king.[100] "It may seem strange, your Majesty, for your royal hands to receive a letter from the humblest, most downcast, wretched [miserables], and persecuted of all the vassals your Majesty has in his kingdom, that is the Indians of New Spain, so ruined by our unhappiness, vexations, extortions and bad treatments, so long suffering and left to submission and silence, that we barely have the breath to formulate complaints, much less declare them in court." The viceroy will not help, they wrote, because Montemayor is his friend. And though the audienca has seen our miseries close up, "they do not want to hear us." Many villages have sent delegations to complain, at times having to beg for food along the road, but they are never received. For all those "interested in the same cause," we come before you "looking for a remedy, and though it seems to come from far away, it is actually close and present, since your Majesty is never too distant for the amparo of his vassals, and especially ones of our condition, because immediately after God we look to you, for those who judge in your place and who ought to care for those your Majesty has ordered them to care for, which ought to be our amparo and relief and liberty, are in fact the knife of our destruction."

As the bishop had done, Indian petitioners prefaced their specific complaints by reprising the events of 1660–62. It is true, they admitted, that some among the *"plebe"* had killed Juan de Avellán. But the violence had stopped there. No other Spaniards were hurt. If the *"alboroto"*—disturbance—in Tehuantepec and Nexapa came to be called an *"alzamiento"* or *"levantamiento,"* it was because the oidor sought to make a name for himself as the pacifier of many provinces. In fact, stated the letter, even the *"plebe"* and the *"seditious"* who were behind the upheavals "contained themselves within obedience and submission to your Majesty," because while they denied the authority of a corrupt alcalde mayor, they had chosen a new gobernador "in your Majesty's name." As to the supposed revolt in Villa Alta de San Yldephonso, they said, it was a fantasy Montemayor dreamed up to take vengeance on the alcalde mayor there, Pedro Fernandes de Villaroel, the nephew of the Duque de Albuquerque, the oidor's sworn political enemy.

From this prologue, petitioners turned to the gravamen of their complaint—Montemayor's new tribute arrangements. By no authority except his own fiat, they charged, the oidor had ordered the priests of Oaxaca's villages to supply him with a confession list of all their parishioners. He compared those lists against the old tasaciones and simply added all new names to the tribute rolls, regardless of age, dependent status, or whether they actually lived in the jurisdiction any longer, grossly overestimating the number of tributaries. Consequences have been dire.

Towns were unable to meet such stiff impositions, and every day people were fleeing to the montes, creating a vicious cycle. "The oidor's intent," charged the letter, mincing no words, "always was to feign a great service and merit at the expense of our blood." They begged the king's "clemency and justice" against the "tyranny" they were living, "when your Majesty's spirit and intention is the relief of his vassals, especially those so unprotected as the Indians."[101]

Many in Spanish officialdom agreed with the Indians and the bishop. In early 1663, royal treasurer Martín de San Martín, wrote from Mexico City to the king, the viceroy, and the audiencia that Montemayor's new lists were wreaking havoc with tribute receipts in Oaxaca. Indians were suspending payment and filing suits with the viceroy, the audiencia, and even the council. The alcalde mayor of Teposcolula agreed that something had to be done. Under the new counts, wrote Francisco Alfonso Diez de la Barrera, one person might be forced to bear the payments of three or four tributaries. As alcalde mayor, he was resorting to threats of force to collect what the law required. This, too, was becoming harder, since the Indians refused to take up local offices connected with tribute collection, understanding how hopeless the job was under Montemayor's new regime.[102]

These, however, were general points. The crux of the Indians' petition involved a highly technical dispute regarding the tangled procedural maneuvering between the Indians and Montemayor. Understanding how taxing this could be, petitioners begged his Majesty's "benign attention, so that that you may know the gravity of what we refer to." Shortly after Montemayor had promulgated the new tasaciones, Indian complainants had brought their cases to the viceroy. After an initial once-over, the files were supposed to have been sent to the audiencia for review. Their transmittal, however, was held up. The delay came at a crucial moment, for Montemayor was able to appear before the audiencia to argue on behalf of the new tribute counts when the audiencia had not yet seen the vast bulk of the Indians' written complaints and petitions. On September 2, 1662, with little basis other than Montemayor's reports, and barely acknowledging the Indians' lawsuits, the audiencia had approved the tasaciones as the oidor had drawn them up.[103] Of course, the order formulaically allowed the Indians to pursue whatever legal recourse they might find most convenient. Native petitioners responded by asking the viceroy for an order certifying that their cases had been filed *before* the audiencia had approved the tasaciones. Once that was established, they planned to ask the audiencia to void its order ratifying the new counts, since their approval had come without a proper hearing on the Indians' lawsuits. This is the point at which the oidor displayed a kind of nefarious legal virtuosity. According to the Indians' petition Montemayor, fearing the audiencia might rescind its order in the face of allegations of foul play, hastened to the Real Acuerdo—a committee consisting of the viceroy and his legal adviser—without notifying anyone. The acuerdo, without hearing the Indians, approved the tasaciones as an executive rather than judicial action.

This, argued the Indians, amounted to a kind of fraud. There was a solid legal basis for their argument. Though the petition did not explicitly mention them, there were strict requirements for conducting tribute censuses, dating back to the sixteenth century. In addition, a 1620 decree had ordered that tasaciones be made by gobernadores, corregidores, and alcaldes mayores, local officials with local knowledge of their territory and its people, rather than by outsiders.[104] Montemayor had bypassed all of these provisions by calling his tasaciones an executive action. But, said the Indians' petition, an executive action could be issued in this way *only* if the petition requesting it had been unopposed. Since the Indians' cases had been filed four months earlier, the oidor's request that the censuses be treated as an executive action had in fact been opposed all along. By issuing an order without hearing them, insisted petitioners, the Real Acuerdo effectively disposed of claims that had not been properly litigated. At a minimum, the relevant parties, including the Indians, should have been cited to appear before the Real Acuerdo to make their argument, as the king's decrees demanded. Instead, Montemayor did little more than parrot the fact that he had increased tribute receipts by 22,000 pesos.

The Oaxaca petitioners then detailed Montemayor's efforts to keep them from being heard in Mexico City. The viceroy had been so impressed with Montemayor's handling of the situation in Tehuantepec that he had appointed the oidor to be his legal adviser at the General Indian Court. In doing so, complained the petition, the viceroy had made Montemayor "the absolute lord of the Indians." From his new position, Montemayor had been able to derail Indian petitions. According to the bishop of Puebla, who wrote a letter in support of the Indians in December 1662, petitioners from Oaxaca had been all but cut off from justice, since Montemayor was now able to dispense with lawsuits at his whim.[105] He also used his position against the Indians' allies and defenders in Mexico City. For instance, Antonio Rendón, a wealthy man and holder of the royal gambling license for New Spain, had tried to help the Indians gain a hearing. Montemayor retaliated by having Rendón jailed on the pretext of failing to pay a debt to an Indian. "This," stated the petition, "is how your oidor serves your Majesty, and no one will dare say it."[106]

Montemayor was able to get away with such maneuvers because he took great care to cloak his actions in the mantle of legality, making him a formidable adversary to Indian petitioners seeking justice. Alcaldes mayores such as Avellán, Espejo, and Reynoso were full participants in the "public business of corruption." Montemayor appears to have operated at a different level, where legality and illegality shaded almost imperceptibly into one another.[107]

Whatever he may have intended early in his endeavors, he wound them up with a manifestation of legalist precision and seeming faith in law's ability to ensure proper behavior. On January 2, 1662, with Tehuantepec and Nexapa behind him and the Ixtepec investigations just under way, the oidor promulgated a series of ordinances ostensibly designed to establish a balance between the Spaniards' legitimate exploitation of the Indians and the Indians' legitimate pleas against those who flouted the law to take advantage of them.[108] The ordinances accepted without question that in the grand scheme of things, the Indians, as vassals of the king, were foremost defined by their obligation to pay royal tribute. The problem in Tehuantepec, stated the ordinances, had been that the alcaldes mayores' profiteering had begun to interfere with the Indians' ability to collect that tribute. Specifically, Oaxaca's repartimientos had grown so onerous in the late 1650s, in the context of a gathering agricultural crisis, that the villages simply could not meet their quotas.

First among the many provisions in these ordinances was a flat ban on the repartimientos, echoing the oidor's order of March 23, 1661. Indians were to have the "liberty," guaranteed by natural law, to engage in commerce with the king's other vassals. Alcaldes mayores who violated this regulation were to be fined and denied office. The Indians were to be given "traslados y testimonios"—notarized copies of orders—so that they might use them in their legal pleadings against those who would violate the law. At the same time, the ordinances reflected Montemayor's deep ambivalence about Indian litigation. Like Spaniards, he insisted, Indians too often filed a lawsuit "in order to profit from it, or to get out of work or to not have to live in their villages, and they pretend to bring it on behalf of the whole community."[109] So, the ordinances required that anyone claiming to act for a community provide a notarized copy of a certificate indicating the bearer's power and naming the group of people on whose behalf he spoke.

Taken together, the thirty-four provisions of this document—and number thirty-three listed thirty-five subparts—amounted to a blueprint of a properly ordered, smoothly functioning colonial society. Alcaldes mayores, parish priests, mestizos, mulattoes, and blacks, Indian gobernadores, councilmen, and alcaldes, ordinary villagers, each had a clearly defined place in Montemayor's scheme. From the long list of parts and subparts, one senses that the oidor was truly shocked by the fiscal disarray of Spanish rule in Oaxaca. The ordinances express an almost naïve faith in the power of written law to order the minutia of colonial social relations. Mestizos, mulattoes, and blacks would be restrained from abusing the Indians, as would alcaldes mayores. Spanish merchants, as well as Indians, would be able to sell their wares without interference from the repartimientos. Friars and priests would not be allowed to extort food and money from the Indians. Indians would live and work in their communities, which would prevent them from becoming idle, wayward, and drunk. Salaries for Indian labor would be fixed according to a clear schedule so that Spaniards not pay less than they should and Indians not ask more than they deserved. To prevent the abuse of women, any gobernador or alcalde who arrested an Indian woman was to refer the matter to the alcalde mayor.

Of course, Montemayor was anything but naïve, and for all the reformist fervor that may have been behind this order, his own conduct suggests that he too worked the system for personal advantage. His statements, especially to the king, indicate that he saw an opportunity to profit from his handling of the Tehuantepec disturbances. Having downplayed the matter initially, he was by the end claiming that the pacification and punishment of the uprisings was "one of the greatest affairs that has happened or can happen in the Indies."[110] Nor did any legalist sensibilities—or his earlier criticisms of former viceroy Duque de Albuquerque's nepotism—lead him to oppose the appointment of the viceroy Conde de Baños's son to the alcaldía mayor of Villa Alta. And Montemayor had a ruthless streak. He had impugned Antonio Rendón's honor because of his close connections to Indian leaders. He did the same to the king's accountant in Mexico City, Valerio Martínez, who wrote to the king arguing that Montemayor's new counts were procedurally defective, contrary to law, and above all fiscal folly, because the Indians could not pay. In response, said Martínez, Montemayor had been circulating a report "little favorable to my person."[111] Martinez's successor, Martín de San Martín, had come to the same conclusions about the new tribute counts and also suffered Montemayor's wrath.[112] We might speculate that with his appointment as the viceroy's legal adviser in the Juzgado, Montemayor had in his own mind become "absolute lord of the Indians" and would not brook trespassers such as Rendón, Martínez, and San Martín upon his domain.

Unimpressed by Montemayor's legalism and undaunted by his heavy-handedness, the Indians' 1662 petition to the king gave impetus to a final push to reverse the new tasaciones across the board. With bishop

Cuevas y Dávalos's help, petitioners managed to gain the support of several prominent Spaniards who saw the imprudence of Montemayor's actions. In petition after petition, the Indians showed how wildly inaccurate his counts were. The wheels of judicial bureaucracy ground slowly. The matter was officially dispatched to Madrid in October 1663. A first response returned in March 1664.[113] Having seen all of the paperwork from Montemayor's Oaxaca campaign, the crown attorney stamped royal approval on the oidor's deeds. Except for the tasaciones. Acknowledging receipt of the letters from the bishops of Puebla and Oaxaca, and from his Majesty's treasurer in Mexico City, Martín de San Martín, the document ordered further study to prove the harm alleged and to show whether the oidor had "exceeded the use of his commission." In May, the matter was sent back to the viceroy and the audiencia for disposition.[114] The crown attorney and the council of the Indies saw the materials in early 1665. The queen regent issued a decree in the Indians' favor in May of that year, directing the viceroy to void Montemayor's tasaciones and default back to the original tribute rolls, in effect ratifying the earlier counts claimed by the Indians.[115] One more time, as with the Nesiche eight, persistence in the face of enormous pressure allowed Indian litigants to transcend local circumstances of abuse and assert their status as vassals deserving the king's sympathy and amparo.

⁀）

Writing to the viceroy in June 1661 as he was concluding his pacification of Tehuantepec, Montemayor said, with unguarded amazement, that "[i]t seems almost a miracle that no irreparable harm has followed from such tyranny, given that other villages and provinces have followed in Tehuantepec's footsteps."[116] This is a statement in some ways no less puzzling than Fabián Martín's, for in the heat and immediacy of confronting the rebellion, the oidor had been less confident. Before setting out from Oaxaca just months earlier, he had burdened the king with a sobering assessment: "That as the harm spreads, a terrible outcome was feared every day, since with the greatest of ease 40,000 Indians could come together."[117] Of course, he had every reason to exaggerate the danger and dampen the king's expectations, against the possibility of failure. Yet, his reference to a "miracle" suggests more than anything that he remained somewhat baffled by the apparent ease with which order had been restored: "A business of greater and graver difficulties and consequences has never been achieved so easily and with such gentleness."[118] Granted, this was before Nexapa and Ixtepec. But, if anything the pacification of those provinces proceeded more quickly because of the experience he gained in Tehuantepec.

It might be argued that this reference to a "miracle" represents little more than a rhetoric of self-congratulation: the king's expressed desire throughout had been that the Indians be handled gently and, in writing to the viceroy, the oidor knew he was best advised to parrot royal will. Alternatively, we could chalk this statement up to the necessary flattery of a lord by his vassal, for Montemayor tells the viceroy that "it is all due to your excellency's good intentions and zeal." Whatever sense of respect and submission Montemayor may have felt toward the man and his office, the fact was that the viceroy had great powers of patronage and reward at his command. Or perhaps we could hear in Montemayor's words the unctuous gloating of one who knows he has defied the odds. None of these has quite the ring of full truth. There can be no doubt that the oidor was puffing up his achievement in Oaxaca—as Indian petitioners had noted in their successful fight against the tasaciones. But neither genuflection nor servile adulation demanded so breezy a characterization. Nor did self-aggrandizing swagger. Montemayor could just as readily have shaped the record to highlight the rigors and risks of his task and credited the viceroy—and indirectly himself—with his manly handling of them. Even playing down the difficulties of his commission, he could have painted a more heroic tableau, one like Manso de Contreras's *Relación cierta y verdadera,* though without the panegyric excesses.

Granting that Montemayor himself was somewhat surprised at the outcome in Tehuantepec, an explanation of this "miracle" begins with the recognition that the unfolding of events had as much to do with Indian communities and the decisions they made, as with Montemayor and the actions he took. The return to order may have seemed a "miracle" to the oidor, but only because he had come to see the disturbances as uprisings that threatened colonial rule in the isthmus of Tehuantepec. While there were some Indians who aimed to reclaim their lands and oust the Spaniards, especially in Nexapa, it appears that most perceived themselves to have a stake in returning to order. The general rebellion despaired of among Spaniards was largely a figment of imaginations fevered by the anxiety of domination, as evidenced by the fact that the threat grew in the telling: where Manso Contreras's paean to Montemayor's Herculean labors had pegged at 30,000 the number of Indians who could have taken up arms, and Montemayor in a letter had said 40,000, viceroy Conde de Baños, in a 1663 missive to the king, put the number at 100,000.[119] In other words, the disturbances were not merely suppressed. Most Indians, despite their situation, had something to lose by remaining outside viceregal society and so were prepared to negotiate a way back in.

Available evidence indicates that the levels of abuse by alcaldes mayores had not always been so great and in 1660 had worsened at a time of agricultural crisis.[120] In reacting to Montemayor's tactics, village leaders and común could remember a time in the recent past when things had been better. Never trouble free, of course. But their benchmark—except at the millenarian margin in Nexapa—appears not to have been a situation of freedom from all exploitation. Even under the duress of their circumstances, Indian petition writers distinguished between alcaldes mayores who engaged in the noxious practices of Avellán, Espejo, and Álvarez, and those who did not, such as Pedro Fernandes de Villaroel, alcalde mayor of Villa Alta, and others who obeyed royal decrees, or at least honored their spirit.[121] On this view, the willingness to rejoin society was a coming down from the montes, writ large. People returned because they seem not to have thought of life in the wilderness as a long-term option for themselves. Such an explanation is intuitively appealing. It is also incomplete, for it begs the question of why they were willing to accept the harsh sentences of their leaders, given that Montemayor had stressed in early communications that he did not come to punish them collectively.

The price for this bargain was that those individuals identified as leaders of the uprisings had to risk punishment in a judicial context. Indian communities, and even affected individuals, appear to have been willing to make this sacrifice. Though the documentary record tells chiefly of those who came under some suspicion of involvement in the uprisings, there are hints that many, perhaps most, people were enablingly ambivalent about their role in the disturbances. Those in constant communication with the bishop and the oidor, and many others on their behalf, doubtless hoped that the bishop's intercession might win a royal pardon that would obviate all punishment. At the same time, Montemayor, and bishop Cuevas y Dávalos himself, often reminded the Indians of how grave had been the crimes committed. We cannot know precisely what gobernadores, their officers, and ordinary villagers expected as these proceedings began. It seems likely they did not realistically think to escape punishment altogether. And yet, they also knew that criminal proceedings very often came to informal settlements aimed at keeping the peace. Regardless, the evidence hints that the people of Tehuantepec and Nexapa were especially shocked by the severity of Montemayor's penal retribution, and they may have felt deceived given the oidor's initial promises of peace and suavity. It is impossible to know whether they heard of the king's later pique with the oidor. But it

seems reasonable to suppose they would have hoped for the king's condemnation of Montemayor's excesses.

This argument accords easily with the notion that people in such situations make rational choices or at least act so as to best serve their perceived interests. But it does little to help us understand Fabián Martín's
last words: "I do not die as a traitor to the King our Lord, nor for disobedience, nor for having led an uprising, but for the repartimientos." This
statement stands in sharp relief against the background of the Nexapa
disturbance. With his final breath, Martín neither invoked Congún nor
lashed out at the Spaniards who were about to execute him. Nor did
he remain defiantly silent. Instead, he professed his loyalty to the royal
person, insisted on his obedience to the king's authority, and proclaimed
his opposition to the illegal repartimientos—and perhaps obliquely criticized Montemayor for his actions. On its face, this statement strongly
suggests that as he died Martín wanted to be seen, above all, as a good
subject who had risen up against the injustice of the alcaldes mayores,
whose abusive repartimientos were not only a plague upon the Indians
but an affront to laws expressing and vivifying the king's amparo.

At bottom, Martín's unapologetic claim to obedience might be understood as an effort to assert the fundamental legal and moral reciprocity
between himself and the king. Heard this way, Martín's scaffold declaration was no mere statement of submission. It was a reminder that the
Indians and the king shared a fundamental interest and concern: to protect those whose mistreatment at the hands of greedy Spaniards augured
the wreck and ruin of Indian communities and hence the kingdom itself.
Because this relationship was reciprocal, Martín could figure himself
within it only by claiming the moral high ground, by being obedient to
the king's authority and expectant of his amparo, in contrast to the Spaniards of whom he and others complained. Of course, he understood that
there was no magical point at which royal protection could be said to
have been definitively secured. Too many and too great were the pressures on the king from those who would decieve and betray him. Like
so many Indians, the king struggled against corrupt officers who did not
act justly. He, like they, had to confront the guile of legal maneuver.
They, like he, had little choice but to proceed on the assumption that
justice remained a real possibility, even if, as with the reversal of the
sentences of the Nesiche eight and the voiding of the tasaciones, it could
be a long time coming.

This does not imply that all Indians naïvely believed in justice or that
they were uniquely law abiding—or even that they agreed unreservedly
with Martín. Rather, for Fabián Martín and others outraged by the repartimientos, law and justice represented a powerful moral resource

precisely because Spaniards had greater access to the levers of political power. Through it they could articulate and insist upon their status as the obedient vassals of a king who, by law, had a special duty to protect the weak and powerless from the strong and powerful. Nothing compelled them to claim this status, and in many instances they did not. But the status of subject was available to them, as long as they were willing to embrace the obligations of being the king's vassals, as Fabían Martín had.

We may be tempted to suppose that embrace was like the reluctant hug a child gives to a distant and ill-smelling relative—an act of resignation in the face of superior authority. In this, perhaps, we would be like sixteenth-century Pedro de Quiroga, who wrote in his 1563 *Libro intitulado coloquios de la verdad,* that the Indians seemed passively acquiescent in their relationship to royal protection: "The king is so far away," he imagined them to say, "that we can't see him and so don't expect any remedy from him."[122] Whether or not Quiroga's characterization was true for the sixteenth century, a hundred years later the Indians of Tehuantepec, Nexapa, and Ixtepec understood that, while it was no easy task to reach the royal person, doing so represented a crucial political act by colonial subjects. Rather than surrender the idea of justice, Indian petitioners did everything in their power to seek and hold the king's attention through the only channel open to them—the law. "Your Majesty is never too distant for the amparo of his vassals," wrote community leaders from across Oaxaca in December 1662, reminding the king of their obedience to him and his obligation to them.

In time and space, the king was remote. Morally he was not. Herein lay the source of the Indians' hope. Four years later, as if to requite this hope, Philip IV's catafalque at the Cathedral in Mexico City bore an emblem entitled "The love and care of the Spanish kings for their Indian subjects." The brief verse referred to the "Indians, Mexican chicks" toward whom "the kings of Spain" had "always been merciful and clement," as befit "paternal affections" for "adoptive" sons become "natural" children.[123] Even in death the king reached out to his most vulnerable subjects—as they reached out to him.

CHAPTER NINE

Summation and Beyond

In 1799, the Spanish official charged with collecting the tithe for the cathedral church in the city of Oaxaca arrived at the town of Tule. He met with local sharecroppers and told them that it was time to pay up. He was taken aback when one of these men addressed him "insolently," arguing that they were all exempt from payment. Much to the surprise and exasperation of the cathedral's representative, this lowly farmer made his case by quoting directly from the *Recopilación* of 1680. How different this moment was from one reported by Pomar-Zurita in his *Relaciones de Texcoco* two-and-a-half centuries earlier. When Zurita asked an indigenous community leader why the Indians had become so litigious, the man answered "because you do not understand us, nor do we understand you or know what you want."[1]

Much had changed in the span between these two conversations. In the sixteenth century, New Spain's indigenous people were still reeling from the chaos of conquest. The ways of Spanish law remained uncertain to them. By the late eighteenth century, Spaniards and Indians had been living in each other's presence for nearly three centuries. Over that time, they had observed each other, fought with each other, and allied with each other, depending on circumstance. Not every farmer or villager was as knowledgeable as this man or as bold in confrontation with a Spanish official. But law and litigation had become an intrinsic part of Indian lives, enough so that a common *terrasguero* could confidently quote the century-old legal compilation that in 1799 stood as the most definitive statement of law available.

While Indians had begun to seek out the viceregal courts during the sixteenth century and litigated tenaciously through the eighteenth century, the process by which law and the pursuit of justice became central to Indian lives unfolded largely during the seventeenth century. In the decades following establishment of the Juzgado General de Indios and with the easy availability of the amparo from the early 1590s forward, Indian claimants came to an understanding of legal process and the role it could play in their lives. By 1700, few would have thought that law was "irrelevant" or "alien" to them.[2] Quite the contrary.[3] By then, law had become a chief means by which individuals and communities defended and contested liberty, land, and local autonomy. It served as the fulcrum for balancing community and individual tensions in criminal and civil matters. It was the weapon of choice, sword as well as shield, in disputes between Indian communities. It bridged distances between Spaniards and Indians, but it also established boundaries. It offered ordinary Indians a means of approaching a distant king whose decrees were all that stood between them and innumerable opportunists.

For indigenous claimants, colonial legality came to represent far more than just an arena of contestation and negotiation. It had become a place from which they could speak. By appealing to the king's decrees, they could lead power to act on their behalf, countering the defenselessness in which they so often found themselves as colonial subjects. In law they found a source of values and moral structure, a resource for seeing themselves in a positive light as people more loyal to a faraway monarch and more vigilant of the common good than many Spaniards.[4] Law's promise of justice allowed them to embrace the empowering dependency of the king's protection and enabled them to make habitable the space of coercion in which they lived, allowing them to communicate with other segments of colonial society, perhaps on better terms than they generally received outside the law.

Those terms came to be crystallized in the word *justicia*. Amparos and motions filed during litigation routinely concluded with the words *pido justicia*—I ask for justice. Parties to legal disputes were under no illusion that they would always prevail: the obvious paradox of litigation is that both parties to a dispute equate justice with victory but recognize that only one of them can win. Losers often felt that injustice had been done. But their private, individual feelings counted for little. Justicia in practice did not guarantee a particular outcome; it ensured only that a dispute would be handled in a particular way—that each party would be able to confront the other legally, that each would be able to tell its story to the judge and present its best case. Decisions regarding the terms and circumstances of their lives might or might not favor them, but those decisions remained subject to the strictures of process.

Within the limits set by procedure, indigenous claimants could speak their minds. They could and did accuse Spaniards and others of abuse and unfair dealing. They recruited Indians as well as Spaniards and castas as witnesses to support their arguments. Alongside their procuradores, they learned to frame their cases in broad normative terms and came to understand the need to articulate their plea for justicia in relationship to the idea of common good. In this, Indians who came before the law enjoyed a distinct advantage—their unavoidable status as tributaries, "useful to everyone and for everyone . . . as all would cease if they were absent."[5] And so, they hurled the accusation of private interest in order to claim their role in securing *bien común*.

Individual legal disputes, in short, formed part of a larger continuum of conduct and conviction that defined the moral possibilities of colonial subjects. Justicia was law's best idea of itself. Without the law, and the idea of justice behind it, Indians would have been cut off from any sense of connection to a normative universe beyond the fact of their subjection. Their litigiousness, far from an act of desperation, represented a very human effort to wrest from the world before them as much sense and order as they could manage. The burden of their hope, so often violated, was an open-ended commitment to the possibility of a social world governed by justicia and shared uneasily with those who would otherwise have been mere dominators.

This hope took shape under a deforming pressure. In the seventeenth century, Indians and Spaniards alike were experiencing an important shift in the temperament of social, political, and personal life. They were living through what we can think of as the transit from "a belief in the steady perfectibility of the social order," that had been the hallmark of sixteenth-century Hispanic political thought, to the seventeenth-century "conviction of [the social orders'] relentless disintegration" in the face of self-centered individual action.[6] In Mexico as elsewhere in the early modern world, human beings were coming to be seen as self-serving rather than self-realizing. Obedience, amparo, and the common good still stood as the pillars of an ordered society, but there was a growing consciousness that cynicism was eroding their bases. The contrast between the old and new views was stark. Where Dominican theologian Domingo de Soto could insist in 1556 that "nature had made man sociable, that is, inclined to live in society in order to be protected by the laws," Bartolomé de Góngora by 1656, speaking from his long experience as a corregidor in New Spain, noted with a Hobbesian tone that "war is man's entire life on the earth."[7]

Spaniards and Indians confronted this change differently. For Spaniards, the world was becoming a place of *aprovechamiento,* an arena for taking advantage of others, because others were out to do the same.[8] It was a world in which hierarchies were seen to be unstable. For those with the means, self-regarding action was increasingly the only sensible response. In Mexico, Indians were an ever-present opportunity. Alcaldes mayores, corregidores, hacendados, mine owners and many others were driven to *aprovecharse,* often abusing position and privilege. For many, law became an obstacle to personal attainment, or at best an instrument to private ends. It was no less true of the New World than of the old that the powerful "trample the laws and do not have the same care for what is just as do their inferiors."[9]

On the whole, Mexico's Indians were in no position to *aprovecharse* through the seventeenth century. Many tried. Some succeeded. Most worked, as they always had, and it was no secret that Spaniards would seek to enrich themselves from the "sweat and work of the Indians," and that castas and not a few Indians might try to as well.[10] For the vast majority of Indians, the conditions of life called forth a response other than a simple desire to *aprovecharse*. They knew themselves to be dependents, subject to tribute payments and work schedules, and too often to the whims of others. The question they faced was the quality of their dependence. Would it be the principled dependence of subjection to the king, premised on willing obedience, a thirst for royal protection, and a sense of how their lives were interwoven with the common good? Or would it be the abject subservience of those whose lives were wholly given over to the greed of people like Juan de Avellán, Juan de Espejo, and Francisco Álvarez in 1660 Oaxaca?

In the mid-seventeenth century, just as the bonds of meaningful subjection were loosening among Spaniards, Solórzano y Pereira continued to insist, perhaps with a desperation born of knowing the battle had already been lost, that the essence of being a subject was to subordinate oneself to power and to find oneself in a situation of dependence. The power in question derived from the king's legitimate authority to protect "liberty" in service to the "common good." Like all of the king's subjects, Indians had "liberty." Unlike the rest of the king's subjects in New Spain, the Indians' "humble, servile, and subordinated condition" entitled them to a special royal solicitude and protection. Against the unprincipled power of those who acted from private motive, they aligned themselves with the king's duty to ensure that unrestrained liberty not unhinge society altogether. "If everyone were given license to proceed according to their free will," Solórzano y Pereira noted, "liberty would perish in liberty and not only would the republic sink, but there would be no difference between our mode of government and that of the brutes."[11]

This was no mere abstraction for New Spain's indigenous people. They required no learned tomes to understand what they faced. They knew in their flesh that the alternative to dependence on the king's authority was utter abandonment. With the rope already around his neck, this may be what Fabián Martín sought to tell his Zapoteca brothers and sisters: their most realistic hope lay in seeking a genuine connection between ruled and ruler, commoner and king. We might hear in this exhortation nothing more than proof that justicia represented an illusion in service to colonial hegemony or dominance.[12] But we might also hear in it recognition that domination is not everywhere and always the same. If so, we might attend to Martín's words as a plea that the moral reciprocity between ruled and ruler not fall to the bleak instrumentalism and utter disregard for humanity that came in later centuries to be the mark of colonialism everywhere.[13] For, like the empire that gave rise to it, colonial law was not a closed and complete system. It was open and negotiable, within limits, part of a baroque sense of justice as an achievable peace, brokered by the possibility of fruitful human coexistence, more generous in some ways to the realities of difference and more alert to the unavoidability of power than later law was to become.

In effect, the decision made repeatedly by indigenous claimants to bring their grievances before the Juzgado and the audiencia amounted to a kind of politics. They would not have thought of it as such, nor would their procuradores, or Spanish officialdom more generally, for politics and law had not yet become separate spheres of human activity. But they were attempting to influence their destinies by engaging the apparatus of governance and by relying on the principles of legality—the only politics available to them in their time and place.

The condition of their political participation was their willingness, as "the feet of the republic," to pay tribute.[14] As I have argued throughout, we misunderstand this phrase if we see it as a comment fundamentally about inequality. Certainly, it amounted to a justification of the Indians' unequal status within the Spanish body politic. But it was also a leveling statement, as well as one about inclusiveness. The feet were understood to be an integral part of the body. Humble perhaps, long-suffering certainly, but no less a part of the body politic than the head. They played a different role from the head, though a critical one: without them, the republic could do little more than drag itself along the ground, a position at once undignified and unbecoming of God's plan for the human species as a whole. They could not be amputated from the body social and political—as later happened with indigenous people in Anglo-America.

By seeking amparo, by protecting posesión, by pressing for libertad, by demanding the peace of punishment against criminals, by contesting local governance, by rebelling when conditions became intolerable, and by seeking reconciliation through legal means, Indian claimants took an active part in framing their lives and the colonial world more broadly. By insisting that the laws be observed, Indian petitioners and litigants protected themselves and upheld the king's authority enshrined in those laws.[15] By his solicitude for the laws, the king sheltered his most vulnerable subjects and shored up his own power against those who so often scoffed at legality. Spanish king and indigenous vassals were thus joined in defense of law's empire in New Spain, a tacit alliance between Spain's highest power and the New World's lowliest subjects to make something of justicia's promise.[16] To the extent that justice meant more than a perquisite of privilege or a blind for domination, it was because Indian litigants took the law seriously at a crucial moment in New Spain's history. Of course, they did not do so alone; as rivers of ink and mountains of paper show, judges, procuradores, notaries, and many other Spaniards devoted endless energy and time to these cases, a story that remains to be told.[17]

There was a demotic quality to the Indians' approach to law. Indigenous voices figured integrally in the running argument over the terms of colonial rule. The breadth and variety of cases they brought before the Juzgado and the audiencia, the expansion of the amparo's ambit over the seventeenth century, their attention to the vocabulary of legal dispute, and their repeated reference to ideas transcending local circumstance all suggest that indigenous claimants knew themselves to be acting on a larger political stage. Their petitions invoked the king's name, played up their status as his vassals and tributaries, and accepted peace and the common good as a shared responsibility and haven. They might seek redress before local justices, but if they were not satisfied, they would march off to Mexico City. Nor were these solely individual voices raised to the heavens. During the seventeenth century, the común so often mentioned in petitions and lawsuits became a source of corporate identification and a platform for collective action.[18] And by making their claims, Indian litigants and petitioners, individuals and communities, came to understand that power in colonial Mexico "was widely dispersed, not concentrated in king's and notables' hands; competition rather than cooperation was the rule," for Spain's empire in the New World was partial and fragmented, torn between remote authority and local power.[19] Native claimaints did not imagine achieving anything like total control over their situation. But they did figure crucially in the competition, aware that they often fared best when they could claim the mantle of cooperation.

Indian presence in that competition complicates and enriches our sense of the early modern world in broader historical context. Where in Europe nobles and commoners increasingly resented royal absolutism, Indians in seventeenth-century New Spain had no sustained quarrel with the king's authority. Their central concern was not the absoluteness of the monarchy, but the variousness and cunning of unchecked local power.

The problem was not tribute, but the excesses of those responsible for collecting it. The issue was not royal overreaching, but that the king's long arm could not keep a tight enough rein on the locally powerful. This experience diverged sharply from what has been seen as the struggle that defined "modern" politics—the gradual revolt against monarchical rule and transcendental expectation that culminated during the eighteenth and nineteenth centuries in the emergence of a new machinery of political management called liberal democracy. Through the king's law applied locally, Mexico's Indians had found a means of confronting colonial circumstances. It was far from perfect, premised as it was on their vulnerability to exploitation. Yet it opened a channel for expressing interests, one that indigenous petitioners and litigants widened through the seventeenth century by claiming a vocabulary of legal meaning for their own use and by insisting that they be protected in their humanness, as Spanish law demanded.

This is what eroded, beginning in the eighteenth century and especially during the nineteenth century. With the dynastic shift from Hapsburgs to the Bourbons after 1700, new forces and pressures impinged on Mexico. Successive kings sought to restore royal power by increasing revenues and regaining administrative control over local power brokers. This appears to have had no immediate impact on the Indians' access to law. If anything, the number of lawsuits increased after 1750.[20] As ever, Indian claimants acted as private royal attorneys jealous of the king's laws protecting them. This litigiousness contributed to a gathering resentment against the Juzgado within Spanish officialdom. From the 1760s forward, amid a growing clamor for reform, the tribunal came under criticism from those who wanted to streamline tribute collection and put agricultural production on a more efficient footing. In the 1780s, Hipolito Villaroel, a former alcalde mayor, savaged the tribunal in recounting the "political infirmities" of New Spain: "[I]n nothing is it to be thought useful, rather it is prejudicial to the public cause and a great embarassment to the viceroys." By its power, he charged, New Spain's indigenous people had been rendered worse than useless to the crown. Not only were they lazy but they felt themselves entitled to litigate on a whim, because "the crown attorneys and audiencias want to sustain the privileges that the laws had granted in earlier times to the Indians."[21] As a result, it was no longer "credible" for alcaldes mayores to seek the Indians' "correction, subjection, and teaching." Agriculture and the royal fisc, claimed Villaroel, simply could not advance so long as the Juzgado continued to favor them. As the heat of censure rose, the Juzgado lost its potency and by the 1790s it was done, a casualty of Spain's rationalization of imperial government.[22]

Throughout the period of reforms under Bourbon kings, Hapsburg law continued to hold sway in Spanish courts.[23] The *Recopilación* of 1680 remained the chief legal text throughout the period, and widely known, or at least appealed to, as the Tule farmer's response to the tithe collector attests. There were no deep innovations in procedure; litigation continued as it had long been. Villaroel's complaints about the Juzgado indicate that the Indians still found shelter and encouragement there as late as the 1780s. The ideas behind their grievances had not been given by any legal treatise; they had been appropriated in the heat of legal conflict, their varied and unstable meanings distilled from thousands of petitions and lawsuits.

It makes no sense to think of New Spain's indigenous people as having "virtually no agenda of their own."[24] They may only infrequently have acted in a unified way, as at certain moments they did in Oaxaca in 1660–61, but amparo petitions and lawsuits suggest that they had "learned to manage the laws, the procedures and the legal memory of the conqueror."[25] They sought sanctuary in the king's amparo as loyal tributaries, understood posesión in terms of constant vigilance, found in libertad a balance between the needs of individual, community, and bien común. Through culpa they came to expect that victims would be heard and the guilty punished—Mexico City's riot of 1692 began when Indians who had gone to the archbishop and the viceroy to complain about the death of a woman at the city's granary were rebuffed.[26] By asserting their right to *voz* (voice) in village affairs and litigating over elections, they reinforced the idea of local autonomy, even while fighting over it. By rebelling, fleeing, and seeking reconciliation, they insisted on limits to what they would bear as vassals of the king, though they made clear in doing so that they were not challenging royal authority as such. And by returning again and again to the law, they refused to abandon the idea of justicia as an organizing principle of social life.

This is what we have forgotten: that the Indians of early modern Mexico had every reason to develop a politics of engagement with their rulers, in order to lead power to address their concerns. Their lives depended on it. It was neither the convulsive politics of rebellion nor a politics of pamphlets and broadsheets. It was, rather, the capillary politics of law at a time when politics and law remained intertwined.

The elements of that politics, the language and experience of their involvement with Spanish law, may indicate something about Mexico's nineteenth century. For if it is true that aspects of the liberal program were "attractive" to Indian communities from independence up through the 1860s, we must ask what allowed for the attraction and how the long history of petition and litigation influenced the way they read "the constitutional small print."[27] Did father Miguel Hidalgo succeed in mobilizing an Indian following in 1810 because his invocation of tyranny and the common good drew on deep springs of political meaning rooted in the colonial period?[28] When father Juan María Morelos spoke of libertad as freedom from unjust restraint, rather than freedom as an absolute good in its own right, and insisted that the humble still needed protection, did his hearers thrill to the familiarity of his words?[29] When later in the century Indians across Mexico heard the word *libertad* in the context of liberal politics, did they hear what liberal ideologues thought they should, or did they hear it through the filter of their own spatially defined sense of liberty-in-place, individual as well as collective, and understood in contrast to the long insistence that they were not slaves? Did the promise of egalitarianism seem an adequate compensation for the loss of royal protection? What sense did they make of private property and taxpayer status against the backdrop of a more plural experience of possession and broadly negotiable tribute payment? Did they embrace notions of individual rights, or did they worry that a regime of such rights might portend unrestrained license against their communities?

Indians' reactions to this novel political environment were complex and ambivalent, as they had been after conquest. Denied the legal advantage of their "wretchedness," they became subject to a liberalism that could not deliver the equality on which it was premised. For all its shortcomings, colonial law had recognized inequality and tried to compensate for it. Nineteenth-century liberals refused to, preferring to suppose people equal, even in the face of enormous differentials of power and capacity to play the system.[30] As they had always done, indigenous people adapted.[31] Grappling with the nineteenth century's changes, they did not reject liberal ideas out of hand but tried to recruit them to their causes and connect them to more familiar ideas. The urgency of this endeavor, and the hope that inspired it, I believe, derived from an experience of law that crystallized in the seventeenth century.

By the late nineteenth century, the direction of change was unmistakable. In 1877, fifty-six "citizens" of indigenous municipalities in Guanajuato submitted a petition to congress, asking for the "reconquest of territorial property so that it may once again be redistributed among all the citizens of the republic." Mixing liberal and colonial understandings of law and right, harkening back to the issue of the conquest's just titles, rehearsing centuries-old royal decrees, they sought to challenge royalist landholders who had opportunistically sided with the forces of independence when it became clear which way the wind was blowing. Having "reconquered their liberty" through independence, claimed the petition, Indians retained a "territorial right" preexisting the "Nation" itself.[32]

The tragedy of this petition is that the old politics of asserting the vocabulary of law and the spirit of justice no longer held sway. While such petitions found their way to the halls of congress, they gained little support among politicians and functionaries who by 1877 saw in the Indians only a backward race that blocked progress. Liberal representation in the nation's capital became the symbol of the Indians' exclusion from a political system that reproduced colonial assumptions about their incapacity while forgetting that the weak and vulnerable had always been able to seek some protection against the powerful.[33]

Taking up Indian political ideas—even in relation to what is sometimes thought of as prepolitical times—carries with it the benefit of broadening the meaning of accepted political terms and looking beyond elite discourse.[34] There is perhaps nothing more difficult than "to avoid falling under the spell of our own intellectual heritage,"[35] particularly when the object of study is remote in time, culture, and history. When we recover something of amparo, libertad, and bien común as expressed in lawsuits and amparo petitions we are able to reflect in greater depth on inequality and the relationship between ruler and ruled in our own times, on the diverse meanings of liberty, and on the idea of the common good conspicuous by its absence. When we recall that during long centuries Indian legal experience was disputacious, conflictual, and political, we may be prompted to think anew about what it means to say that in contemporary indigenous communities law emphasizes "harmony and compromise."[36] And as we ponder the role liberal ideas should play in a globalized world, we may be prompted to ask whether Mexico's Indians were not in some ways better off as subjects in the seventeenth century than as the far-less-than-equal citizens they became in the nineteenth century.[37]

We might also find ourselves questioning confident assertions regarding the rule of law.[38] Rule of law is generally seen to contrast with circumstances in which powerful individuals or groups are able to act without concern for the real or perceived arbitrariness of their decisions. In such essentially lawless situations, power is all. The conceit of the rule-of-law idea is that legality can restrain power, by impartially binding rulers and ruled alike, so that law rather than the tyranny of interest, the vagaries of personality, or the whim of the moment, *rules*. This notion has been and remains central to the culture of modern Western, and especially Anglo-American legality, and is often said to be the "first postulate of liberal political thought."[39]

The rule-of-law idea has profoundly distorted our understanding of Latin American legality. It reifies an ideal type that has never actually obtained in Latin America—or anywhere else—and at the same time belittles the long legacy of viceregal law as it actually existed.[40] I have argued that Indians in seventeenth-century Mexico took this law to heart, combatted subtle machinations and gross challenges to their interests, and ultimately claimed it as their own. This is not to say they were unaware of the extent to which practice could diverge from principle—a separation that later came to be known as *país real* and *país legal* (real country, legal country).[41] I contend, rather, that they saw the law as a means of negotiating against utter arbitrariness, not as a disembodied, impersonal force acting autonomously to check the megrims of the powerful, but as an active principle of the king's care for them, a care they needed to cultivate by their own action.[42] From their experience, they knew that the law did not announce itself, interpret itself, or enforce itself. People did so, from lowly alcaldes mayores to Spanish jurists to the king and, crucially, Indians themselves. As a result, they understood that private motive stalked all legal process, checked only by the idea of the common good defended by the king and his loyal vassals. In other words, colonial law was inherently political in the sense that it did not suppose abstract rules and regulations by themselves could finally restrain human conduct or stand apart from questions of overall rule.

From this perspective, it might be argued that Mexico's Indians entered the modern age less inclined than ordinary people in Europe and later the United States to credit the liberal story: that law had brought men under the control of an impersonal, disinterested, and nontranscendental force that could inhibit arbitrary power. New Spain's indigenous people knew better. During the seventeenth century, they had learned that law was no less manipulable than any other aspect of power, a fact that required their "rigorous attention."[43] In their experience, men were at the center of law and politics, in contrast to liberalism's confidence in depersonalized reason as the key to legal and political order.[44] The nineteenth century gave them little reason to believe the conceit that law had risen above the crass politics of interest enabled by the soft corruption of diminished hope for human community.

The charge that Mexico has lacked rule of law, therefore, may not be so much wrong as unimaginative. A more subtle critique, one that calls into question the very idea of rule of law, might go something like this: Law in postindependence Mexico never achieved what might be called a consensual hegemony around the rule-of-law idea because liberal law never succeeded as fully in masking power relations as in the United States, which faced similar problems of difference through much of its history. There, Indians and Africans—exterminated and marginalized or confined to slavery and later the prison of segregation—were placed outside the circle of "universal" law.[45] The problem of difference was set aside.[46] Law could appear fundamentally fair only by bracketing out those who had been treated most unjustly. Mexican liberals, for all that they tried, could not duplicate this feat. The Indians' entanglement with colonial justice gave them a basis for seeing past the rule of law to the myth underlying it—a foundational myth of the modern, liberal state. In the nineteenth century, they sought to understand a new situation and in doing so embraced certain liberal ideas.[47] But they remained wary, for the rhetoric of liberal legality frequently failed to match its practice, in regard to the equal rights of citizens, for example, or matched it all too well, as in the taking of communal lands to create a system of private property.[48] Perhaps this wariness, far from outright rejection, made it impossible for rule of law's myth to take full hold of indigenous imaginations. Unable fully to enlist those imaginations, state-oriented liberal elites could only strain against a situation they never quite understood, for they simply could not countenance the possibility that colonial law—or anything else from the viceregal period—might speak to the "modern" condition.

In the face of a scholarship that has tended to echo this sentiment, I hold with those who insist that we must attend to "situations that are the foundations and beginnings of our present," by writing and thinking at the seam where "mastering" Western concepts meet Latin America's historical realities, in the hope, as Augusto Salazar Bondy once put it, that "submersion in the historical substance of our communities" would allow us to discover "the values and categories that express [that substance] positively and reveal it to the world."[49]

In this regard, the crucial point is that interactions between Indians and Spaniards, and among Indians, in the seventeenth century created a new legal reality that can be characterized neither as a mere continuation of medieval notions of law nor as a failure to create rule of law. In important ways, New Spain by 1700 had rule of law, for its time and place: written law dominated legal culture, relative procedural regularity obtained, and appeals checked arbitrariness. In other ways, the rule-of-law question is beside the point. What emerged from the crucible of New Spain's seventeenth century was a legality that strove to mediate the relationship between different peoples, conquerors and conquered, living side by side, who had to be brought into an ordered relationship under a single, distant sovereign—a legality that did not (because it could not) set the problem of difference aside. No legal system had ever faced such a challenge. None has done so since. For while the Roman *res publica* came into being when patricians and plebes agreed to be ruled by a single law, which eventually included barbarians, Rome's far-flung empire did not suppose that subject peoples would live side by side with Romans in a unified social and political order. Later European empires of the nineteenth century drew on the Spanish experience in the New World, but they did not seek to create a common and shared society; those who went to these later colonies lived *among* colonial subjects, not with them. Only Spain and its indigenous subjects, through their conflicts, established an empire of law that could express and order the complexities of New World difference and permit new relationships among people who might otherwise have remained alien to one another—an experiment interrupted by the liberal advent of the nineteenth century.

Compared to the enormity and unrelenting quality of their exploitation, the litigiousness of colonial Mexico's Indians may seem little. That is, until we consider that the alternative might have been an abject silence punctuated only by the episodic violence of righteous indignation against their ill use. Suppose there had been no sixteenth-century debate over the Indians' status. Suppose the Spanish monarchy had not accepted the proposition that Indians enjoyed the same liberty as other human beings. Suppose viceroy Luis de Velasco II had not created the Juzgado. Suppose the doctrine of miserables had not been extended to the Indians and that the Indians had been discouraged from litigating because they could not pay for procuradores and court costs. Suppose Indian claimants had not been able to challenge land grabs, arbitrary imprisonment, and working conditions. Suppose they had squared off against employers, caciques, alcaldes mayores, hacendados, and mine owners without the lever of law and the space for negotiation it opened up. Suppose indigenous villages had faced dismemberment without recourse. Suppose Indians generally had despaired of the law and simply abandoned themselves to subjection—or worse. Suppose procuradores had refused to help them. Suppose native petitioners and litigants had not strained to master a powerful vocabulary of legal meaning. Suppose that the enormous monument to legality that is the records of Indian litigation at the Archivo General de la Nación and the Archivo General de Indias had never existed, because the processes that gave rise to them had never come to be.

The most remarkable thing about these records is how clearly they manifest the energy with which Indian claimants went to Mexico City to summon the law in defense of their interests and lifeways. In doing so they became part of the first early modern experiment in "cosmopolitan legality."[50] Their sphere of action was not just this or that village lost in the interior of New Spain. A given dispute might start for local reasons, but as soon as someone got it in his head to seek help in the colonial

capital, that sphere quickly expanded. Conversely, people in a village
might not think to pursue a matter against a nearby hacendado until
the king's decree banning personal service had been read out in church
one Sunday. Ideas and arguments traversed great distances and even
crossed oceans. The instruments of legality could link the local to what
we might now think of as the international, or even the global, because
the crown's authority suffused the entire structure of Spain's empire,
an authority otherwise weak against those who wielded local power so
effectively. Physically, the king was in Madrid; morally, legally, and politically, he was in every village where an Indian petitioner or litigant
invoked his name and enlisted certain principles and procedures of law
to advance a claim. Mutual awareness of these connections between indigenous villagers and the crown figured critically in defining the limits
and possibilities of colonial life.

It is true that "law gave permanence as well as form to the initial vic-
tories of force and religion" in New Spain, permitting "the organization
of empire and assur[ing] its survival."[51] It is also true that through law
Indian claimants opened up a space for conversation between colonial
rulers and colonial ruled: the empire of law—law's power to command
assent to its authority—was subject to constant negotiation.[52] In hazard-
ing their stance, native petitioners and litigants did not seek to transcend their circumstances so much as they sought to transform them in
relation to aspirations of what could be and fears of what might be. In
this way, law helped create the loosely articulated community of interests between monarch and indigenous vassals that "made the bond of
subjection more comfortable and bearable."[53]

This double effect helps account for one of the central ironies of the
Spanish conquest and colonization of Mexico: that the very problems
that may have led Indians to imagine an alternate universe in which the
Spaniards had never come, were also the ones that in day-to-day life led
them to seek vassalage as a way of protecting themselves against those
who resisted royal laws for private ends.[54] On this view, the relative
peace of colonial New Spain resulted not from the generalized application of force or from simple domination. It sprang from the very success
Indian communities had in carving out a space for themselves, a space
they ardently defended and amplified through litigation.[55]

With the coming of independence in the age of Enlightenment and
Progress, the cosmopolitan legality of the early modern period withered
as law and politics were forced into separate spheres of national experience, threatening to leave only popular religiosity as a source of identity, a site of normative commitment, and a spring for political action
in the lives of Mexico's indigenous people.[56] They did not entirely forget

their experience of colonial law; a glutinous attachment to broad legal principles and concrete practices had become common sense by 1800. But having lost the immediacy of their connection to a politics of justice and trapped within nation states led by local elites from whom there was no appeal, they struggled with only occasional success during the nineteenth and twentieth centuries to confront a situation in which they could not take as explicit a part in law's conversation as they once had. Whether the earlier practice of summoning law to their aspirations and defense could be meaningfully renewed as a form of politics remains an open question.[57]

Reference Matter

Notes

The following abbreviations are used in the notes:

AGIM   Archivo General de Indias, México, Seville, Spain
AGIP   Archivo General de Indias, Patronato, Seville, Spain
AGNC   Archivo General de la Nación, Criminal, Mexico City
AGNCR   Archivo Genreal de la Nación, Cédulas Reales
AGNGP   Archivo General de la Nación, General de Parte, Mexico City
AGNI   Archivo General de la Nación, Indios, Mexico City
AGNInq   Archivo General de la Nación, Inquisición
AGNT   Archivo General de la Nación, Tierras, Mexico City
BN   Biblioteca Nacional, Madrid, Spain
HB   Hévia Bolaños
Mss.   Manuscrito/Manuscript
RAE   Real Academia Española
Recop.   *Recopilación*
SP   Solórzano y Pereira

AGNx citations are given as volumen.expediente.foja, followed by a parenthetical two-digit year for 17th-century cases, or a 4-digit year for sixteenth-century and eighteenth-century cases, for example, 21.199.34r-37v (68) or 26.3.432v-45or (1593) or 2133.117.568r (1712). I have inserted dashes to represent missing numbers, for example 15.--.496r (74).

For frequently cited legal and juridical sources I have given volume and page citations for the edition listed in "Sources Cited" (e.g., *Recop.* 1:188r), but I have also given the more general form in parentheses as follows (I have used Arabic numerals throughout):

Burns, *Las Siete Partidas*   partida.title.law
Hévia Bolaños, *Curia philippica*   parte.parrafo.número
Nueva Recopilación de 1640 (España)   libro.título.ley
Recopilación de Indias de 1680   libro.título.ley
Solórzano y Pereira, *Política indiana*   libro.título.número
Soto, *De la justicia*   libro.cuestión.artículo

CHAPTER ONE

1. Hanke, *All Mankind*, 34–37; Todorov, *The Conquest*, 147–49; Restall, *Seven Myths*, 94–95; Seed, "The Requirement."

2. Hanke, *The Spanish*, 33–34.

3. Hanke, *All Mankind*, 37.

4. *Códice*, 132, 185–86.

5. Malagón Barceló, "Una colonización," 99.

6. The literature is vast. Some of the crucial names are Altamira (*Estudios*), Levene (*Introducción*), Ots Capdequí (*Manual*), Alfonso García Gallo, Ricardo Zorraquín Becú, and many others. Tau Anzoateguí is one of the latest members of this school (*Nuevos Horizontes*). His *Casuismo y sistema*, is an important exploration of casuistry as the baseline for trying to understand the principles that were supposed to guide judges in rendering judgments.

7. Burman and Harrell-Bond, *The Imposition*, chaps. 7–11; Benton, *Law*, chap. 4; Guha, *Dominance*.

8. Haring, *Los bucaneros*, 16.

9. See Hanke, *The Spanish*; Gibson, *Spain*, 109–11; Keen, "The Black"; Hanke, "A Modest"; Keen, "The White."

10. Hanke, "More Heat." "Irrelevant" comes from Gibson, *Spain*, 109; "alien" from Stein and Stein, *The Colonial*, 81; "separated, divorced" is from Wiarda, *The Soul*, 29. It is noteworthy that scholars hailing from such distinct historiographical camps agreed on this point.

11. Stern, *Peru's Indian*, 114–37. See also, Stern, "The Social."

12. Borah, *Justice*.

13. Borah, *Justice*, 1.

14. Stern, *Peru's Indian*, 135.

15. See, e.g., Stern, *Resistance*; Schroeder, *Native Resistance*.

16. Salvatore et al., *Crime*, 7.

17. Taylor, "Between Global," 162.

18. Kellogg, *Law*; Cutter, *The Legal*; Herzog, *La administración*, 394, 306; Haslip-Viera, *Crime*. See also, Haskett, *Indigenous*, 77–85; and Stavig, *The World*, 84–128.

19. Salvatore et al., *Crime*, 17.

20. I agree with Cutter. In defining *justice*, "[o]ne pitfall to avoid, whether as specialists or as beginning students, is to draw upon our modern Western political ideals as the litmus test. Notions such as democracy or equality before the law simply would not be found in the political ideology of colonial Spanish Americans until the eve of independence, but this is not to say justice was lacking." Cutter, "The Legal System," 58.

21. Méndez et al., *The (Un)Rule*. I have no quarrel with the idea that law in contemporary Latin America is in crisis and needs remedy. I am fairly certain, however, that contemporary problems cannot be confronted without a more adequate sense of law's past in Latin America. Such a historical project is hampered to the extent our scholarly imaginations continue to be captured by the rule-of-law idea.

22. Minow's *Latin American Law* is a recent exception to the trend.

23. Salazar Bondy, *¿Existe una filosofía?*, 38.

24. Aristotle held that "law should rule rather than any single one of the citizens" (*Politics*, iii, §XVI). Not until the late nineteenth century did the rule of law attain a clear ideological statement with Albert Venn Dicey's *An Introduction to the Law of the Constitution* (1885), in which he argued that "rule of law" rested on three basic pillars: the "supremacy" of law over arbitrary power; equality before the law; and law as a consequence of the rights of individuals as determined by courts. The *Oxford English Dictionary* gives 1883 as the first use of "rule of law" in the sense of a doctrine that subordinates power to "impartial and well-defined rules of law" (see entry 4.c under "rule"). It is worth noting that Dicey saw "the rule of law" as a "peculiarity" of English institutions, though "an Englishman naturally imagines that the rule of law . . . is a trait common to all civilised societies."

It is the easy supposition of universality that has made "the rule of law" so problematic in thinking about law and legality in Latin America. For as Dicey was careful to note, the idea itself is deeply rooted in English history, a history not shared with other nations. If anything, the acceptance of rule of law as "good for everyone" grew firmer over the twentieth century, and especially since the end of the Cold War. Tamanaha, *On the Rule*, 1. In saying this, I am concerned only that uncritical acceptance of the rule of law as the teleological unfolding of law not be projected back onto colonial Mexico's historical reality.

25. See, e.g., Gordon, "Critical," 57–125; Unger, *Law.*

26. See, e.g., Thompson, *Whigs;* Herrup, *The Common;* Erickson, *Women.*

27. Winter, *A Clearing,* 345.

28. Ibid., 105, 113–17. See also, Winter, "The 'Power' Thing," 736.

29. Although I shall not explore the matter, I intend the reference to Ortega y Gassett's insistence on the centrality of "circumstances" in human affairs.

30. This is not to say that individuals have no freedom. Rather, it is to insist that freedom not be understood in relation to the total absence of constraint. See Lakoff and Johnson, *Philosophy,* 536–38.

31. These concerns converge with those of legal anthropologists. See, e.g., Collier, *Law;* Nader, *Harmony;* Nader, *The Life;* Starr and Collier, *History.*

32. Cover, "The Supreme Court," 14, 8.

33. Ibid., 5.

34. In referring to "early modern Mexico," I have taken my cue from Dussel, who has argued that colonial expansion from the sixteenth century forward was part and parcel of the making of modernity. See Dussel, "Eurocentrism."

35. For the "consolidation" view, see Durán, *History,* xxx. For "singular complexity," see Gruzinski, *The Conquest,* 226.

36. Muro Romero, "La reforma," 47–68; Hoberman, "Hispanic," 199–218.

37. Here I am deeply indebted to Woodrow Borah, whose *Justice by Insurance* remains the bedrock for this book. His close study of the Juzgado as an institution, and his careful sampling of cases, has enabled me to build on his insights toward a fuller understanding of the Indian experience of law.

38. Haskett has noted that while "subtle shades of meaning" were sometimes lost in translation, and the presence of interpreters made "a certain amount of misrepresentation" inevitable, translations were, "for the most part . . . as accurate as the abilities of individual interpreters allowed." Haskett, *Indigenous*, 82.

39. In other words, it is a problem only if we insist on the phenomenological autonomy that grounds methodological individualism. See Lakoff and Johnson, *Philosophy*, 551–68. Put another way, I take seriously the deep implications of Ortega y Gasset's dictum regarding individual identities as being grounded in the proposition "I am I and my circumstances."

40. Cover, "The Supreme Court," 8 & n. 22.

41. There is an undeniable bias toward Mexico City in the cases. The likelihood of filing a petition or lawsuit varied inversely with distance, although cases seem more or less to track population density.

42. Winter, *A Clearing*, 351.

43. Clendinnen, *Ambivalent*, 127.

44. I agree with Benton that understanding "legal regimes" in world-historical context is crucial to making better sense of colonialism than we have, precisely because without that context law as a system of mutually constraining interactions is too easily lost to suppositions of dominance and hegemony. See Guha, *Dominance*.

45. Taylor, "Between Global," 162.

46. The problem with this formulation is that the word *politics* is an anachronism. For seventeenth-century Spaniards, *politics* still carried its Aristotelian sense of good governance in a properly constituted *polis*. It had not yet come to be understood as a generalized competition for power, nor had it taken on the "pejorative" sense it acquired in the nineteenth and twentieth centuries. Saavedra Fajardo, *Empresas;* la Real Academia Española (RAE), *Diccionario*, 3:312; Stegman, "Le mot." Here I have borrowed the title of Joseph's edited volume, *Reclaiming the Political*. See also Cañeque, *The King's*, for another effort to reclaim the political for the colonial period.

47. Maitland, *Town*, 22.

48. Tau Anzoategui, *Casuismo*, 569.

49. I was trained to that expectation, or at a minimum I learned it, though I believe that training to have been an expression of wider cultural, and especially professional, expectations regarding law.

50. This is true of all legal systems. It is the job of an overarching ideology of law—*the rule of law* for liberal systems, *justice* for colonial law—to efface this fact.

CHAPTER TWO

1. Durán, *History*, 561.

2. See Gibson, *Aztecs*, 153; Méntz, *Trabajo*, 66–67. Tlacotin were often individuals who had sold themselves into slavery pursuant to a debt they could not satisfy or because they could not pay tribute. In times of want and famine, the numbers of tlacotin generally rose substantially. For further differences be-

tween tlacotli and slaves from a European point of view, see the text accompanying footnotes 19–20 in chapter 5, below.

3. Zavala, *Las instituciones,* 191.

4. As with almost everything else, the prevalence of Indian slavery during these early years varied by region. In Oaxaca, for instance, Taylor reports there is little evidence of Indian enslavement as a form of coerced labor. Taylor, *Landlord,* 143.

5. See marginal notes accompanying the text of *Recop.* 2:194v–195r (6.2.1 & 3).

6. Simpson, *The Encomienda,* 123–44.

7. Gibson, *The Aztecs,* 224.

8. Cook and Borah, *The Aboriginal* and *Essays;* Cook and Simpson, *The Population.* Bethell, "A Note," 145–46; Gibson, *The Aztecs,* 136–40, 377–78; Gerhard, *A Guide,* 23; Baudot, *México,* 185–203; Crosby, *The Columbian,* 35–63; Cook, *Born.*

9. Martínez, *Codiciaban,* 96, 128n.73.

10. Gibson provides an extended description of the system's workings. Gibson, *The Aztecs,* 224–36.

11. Hoekstra, *Two Worlds,* 129.

12. Vitoria, *Political Writings,* 233–327.

13. *Colección de documentos inéditos relativos al descubrimiento, conquista,* 7:542–52; *Cartas de Indias,* 263–69.

14. *Colección de documentos sobre Coyoacán,* 1:39.

15. Hoekstra, *Two Worlds,* 83.

16. Prem, "Spanish Colonization," 446–47.

17. Taylor, *Landlord,* 117.

18. Gibson, *The Aztecs,* 232. Villages were often subject to the *doblas,* or double quotas, depending on the season.

19. See footnote 8, above.

20. Lockhart, *The Nahuas,* 163; Cline, *Colonial,* 157.

21. See Martin, *Rural Society,* 28–34; Taylor, *Landlord,* 195–97; Chevalier, *Land,* 172–78.

22. Gibson, *The Aztecs,* 280.

23. Melville, *A Plague,* 130. See also, *Códice,* 133.

24. Florescano, "The formation," 163; Melville, *A Plague,* 140–42.

25. Quoted in Chevalier, *Land,* 141.

26. Ordinary folk might hold land for "labor and cultivation," and pass the right to do so on to their children, but if they died without heirs, the land reverted to the community, which was generally controlled by nobles. Mass death over long periods ensured that much land did, at least technically, escheat back to the communities, in effect dispossessing commoners of property rights which, while less than full ownership, had allowed many to sustain themselves from their own labor. Gibson, *The Aztecs,* 267–68.

27. Hoekstra, *Two Worlds,* 98; Lockhart, *The Nahuas,* 163; Horn, *Postconquest* 176.

28. Ots Capdequí, *El régimen,* 72–73.

29. *Recop.* 2:92r–v (4.12.14).

30. Chevalier, *Land,* 269–70.
31. See Melville, *A Plague,* 143; Taylor, *Landlord,* 80; García Martínez, *Los pueblos,* 143, 357–60.
32. See chapters 3 and 4 below.
33. Quoted in Hoekstra, *Two Worlds,* 100.
34. This notion is traceable to Thomist ideas regarding political society.
35. See, e.g., Lockhart et al., *The Tlaxcalan,* 103–06.
36. Gerhard, "Congregaciones," 347–95.
37. This is Cline's maximum number. The minimum he gives is 8 percent. See Howard Cline, "Civil," 366. On Morelos, see Martin, *Rural,* 27–28.
38. Florescano, "The Formation," 159–60; Gibson, *The Aztecs,* 283–88. For a list of congregaciones carried out in the latter period, see Gibson 286–87.
39. Taylor, *Landlord,* 111–63; Chance, *Race,* 105; Martin, *Rural,* 27–45; Prem, "Spanish," 444–59.
40. Hoekstra, *Two Worlds,* 117; Taylor, *Landlord,* 26–27. Hoekstra refers to the lands acquired by Spaniards as the no-man's-lands between various *altepetl,* or basic pre-Hispanic political unit. Gibson agrees that while Spaniards gained land under the congregaciones, the process of congregación should not be reduced to this effect. See Gibson, *The Aztecs,* 282–83.
41. Cline, "Civil," 355–56.
42. Gibson, *The Aztecs,* 247.
43. Hoekstra, *Two Worlds,* 138.
44. Zavala y Castelo, *Fuentes,* VI:394–97, 616ff.
45. Hoekstra, *Two Worlds,* 138.
46. These were the Flowery wars, in which warriors sought to wound rather than kill, so that the captive might die on the sacrificial stone.
47. On the Chichimecas, see Jones, *Nueva Vizcaya.* On the Maya, see Farris, *Maya;* Clendinnen, *Ambivalent;* Restall, *The Maya.*
48. Lockhart et al., *The Tlaxcalan,* 77–78.
49. Just as they had to "invent" America itself. See O'Gorman, *La invención.*
50. Konetzke, *Colección,* 1:16 (the decree was dated December 20, 1503).
51. Mörner, *La corona;* Konestzke, *Colección,* 1:264–65, 464, 513; *Recop.* 2:19v–20r (6.3.21–27); 230v (6.9.11 & 13–15); 2:284r (7.4.1).
52. Cuevas, *Documentos,* 354–60. See also Llaguno, *La personalidad,* 238–70.
53. The following paragraphs draw on Heath's *Telling,* 15–36.
54. Cuevas, *Documentos,* 159.
55. AGNCR, 47.
56. See Corominas, *Breve,* 344.
57. Bernand & Gruzinski, *Histoire,* 223–35.
58. Zurita, "Breve," 97–98.
59. There is still some dispute as to the precise meaning of *calpolli.* Zurita, for instance, defines it equivocally, as "lineage or barrios" and links it explicitly to land. Zurita, "Breve," 87. See also Cline, *Colonial,* 36, 53, 87, 141, 147. The best recent account of the calpolli and its relationship to land is Horn's *Postconquest,* 111–43.

60. Zurita, "Breve," 98.
61. Soustelle, *La vie*, 20.
62. Lockhart, *The Nahuas*, 162.
63. Ibid., 45.
64. Hoekstra, *Two Worlds*, 97.
65. Bakewell, *Silver*, 35. The idea behind this migration was that settled groups, like the Tlaxcalans, would by their example persuade the Chichimecas to pacify themselves and take up a more settled, and less warlike, existence. A later group of one thousand families ended up not going, though their cabildo had originally promised they would. See Lockhart et al., *The Tlaxcalan*, 106–8.
66. Maravall, *La cultura*, 92.
67. Altman, *Emigrants*, 125, 163, 195, 201. Little is known about how many emigrants arrived on Mexican shores and precisely when. Estimates are that somewhere in the neighborhood of 200,000 Spaniards came to the New World during the sixteenth century, roughly 2,000–2,500 a year. Sánchez-Albornoz, "The Population," 1:15–17.
68. Calderón de la Barca, *Darlo todo y no dar nada*, act I. The words are pronounced by Diogenes, the Cynic philosopher, in an ironic critique of the seventeenth-century royal court. Quoted in Maravall, *La cultura*, 90, 132.
69. Suárez Figueroa, *El pasajero*, 360; Saavedra Fajardo, *Empresas*, 291 (emblema 43); Barrionuevo, *Avisos*, 1:100; Barrionuevo quoted in Maravall, *La cultura*, 341.
70. Díaz del Castillo, *Historia*, 312. See also SP, *Política*, 1:105 (1.8.25 & 28).
71. Lockhart and Otte, *Letters*, 143–46.
72. See "Soneto." I have chosen to translate "behetría" in the penultimate line as "cacophony, confusion." *Behetría* is a complicated word, with origins in medieval Spanish property law. According to *Las Siete Partidas*, behetría meant "land at the disposal of the party who lives upon it, and who has a right to select as his lord anyone that he wishes, in order to improve his condition" (Burns, *Las Siete*, 4:992 (4.25.3). Covarrubias cites this language, but indicates that in time the word became a general metaphor for "confusion," since "in behetría they have no leader to respect, everyone talks at once. And for this reason wherever there is a confusion of voices, we say behetría." Further on, the entry says that since "long experience has shown how this liberty of changing lords brought great confusion and bewilderment [desconcierto] in government, so much so as to give rise to a Castilian proverb, in which a thing without order and gone to ruin is called a thing of behetría." Covarrubias, *Tesoro*, 204.
73. "Romance a Mexico," 73v–75v. I have translated "interés" as "[self] interest." For "interes" Covarrubias gives "gain, utility, profit that one gets or expects from a thing." He offers for "interesal"—an interested person—as "one who does not do anything graciously, but always for his own interest and benefit." Covarrubias, *Tesoro*, 739.
74. See, e.g., Llaguno, *La personalidad*, 239; SP, *Política*, 1:224 (2.5.21). See also Pastor, *Crisis*, 181–82
75. Mariana, *The King*, 338–39.
76. Pastor, *Crisis*, 204.

77. Gibson, *The Aztecs,* 250–51.
78. Cline, *Colonial,* 152–59.
79. Taylor, *Landlord,* 68, 73, 75–82.
80. Horn, *Post-Conquest,* 211.
81. Hoekstra, *Two Worlds,* 142–46.
82. Gibson, *The Aztecs,* 248; Israel, *Race,* 270.
83. Burns, *Las Siete,* 2:271–72 (2.1.5); Aquinas, *The Political,* 175–76, 178–79, 182, 185.
84. Mariana, *The King,* 136 (chapter 5); Soto, *De Iustitia,* 5:886–87. See generally MacLachlan, *Spain's Empire,* 1–19.
85. Elliot, *Imperial Spain,* 249, quoting Charles Bratli, *Philippe II,* 234.
86. Aquinas, *The Political,* 120.
87. Parry, *The Spanish,* 193–94.
88. Hespanha, *Vísperas;* Burns, *Las Siete,* 3:535 (3.1.3).
89. Elliot, *Imperial Spain,* 175.
90. SP, *Política,* 3:2207 (5.15.10).
91. Cañeque, *The King's,* 76.
92. Aquinas, *The Political,* 185.
93. Ibid., 121; Maravall, "Saavedra Fajardo," 227.
94. Maravall, "Saavedra Fajardo"; Maravall, *La cultura,* 271–72.
95. Ripodas Ardanaz, "Los indios," 275–322.
96. In this paragraph I have leaned heavily on Cañeque, *The King's,* 36–37.
97. Ripodas Ardanaz, "Los indios," 311.
98. Anderson et al., *Beyond,* 177.
99. Ibid., 177–78, 168; Terranciano, *The Mixtecs,* 387.
100. Gibson, *The Aztecs,* 202.
101. Simpson, *The Encomienda,* 145–58; Gibson, *The Aztecs,* 80.
102. *Nueva colección,* 2:65.
103. Lockhart et al., *The Tlaxcalan Actas,* 97–103.
104. Ibid., 95–97.
105. Hoekstra, *Two Worlds,* 121–22.
106. *Códice,* 128–36.
107. Gilbson, *The Aztecs,* 289.
108. Horn, *Postconquest,* 32–33.
109. Hoberman, "Hispanic American Political Theory," 209.
110. Israel, *Race,* 270; Hoekstra, *Two Worlds,* 121–22.
111. MacLachlan, *Criminal,* 21; Covarrubias, *Tesoro,* 724.
112. Gibson, *The Aztecs,* 73–74, 80.
113. Offner, *Law,* 223–24; Zurita, "Breve"; Ixtlilxochitl, *Obras,* II:297–300.
114. Sahagún, *Historia,* 2:81; Zurita, "Breve," 102; Pomar-Zurita, "Relación."
115. Offner, *Law,* 47–86, 242–43.
116. Pomar-Zurita, "Relación," 29.
117. Offner, *Law,* 245–55.
118. Nor should we assume the two systems were unproblematically analogous. As Offner argues, the Texcocan legal system was chiefly "an instrument

of social control," rather than "an instrument for ensuring fair and equal treatment for all Texcocans." Offner, *Law,* 245.

119. Technically, alcaldes mayores had to account for their time in office during a posttenure *residencia.* Indians could and often did testify in such proceedings, though most may have assumed that it was not worth pursuing such small amounts, given that corregidores were only rarely punished for misconduct, and restitution was usually ordered for larger peculations—besides which raising the issue would have meant revisiting the misdemeanor that had led to the fine in the first place, matters usually best forgotten. Gibson, *The Aztecs,* 91–92.

120. Góngora, *El corregidor,* 11, 23–24.

121. Quoted in Chevalier, *La formation,* 212.

122. *Recop.*1:188r (2.15.3).

123. For the Gante quote, see Mills and Taylor, *Colonial,* 86; Zurita, "Breve," 101.

124. See Borah, *Justice,* 91–101 for details of the legislation that created the Juzgado.

125. The indispensable work on the Juzgado is Borah's social and institutional history, *Justice by Insurance.* Technical aspects of the distinction between administrative and judicial functions and the history of the Juzgado's establishment can be pursued there. Borah, *Justice,* 50–51, 91–101, 120–27.

126. Hoberman, "Hispanic," 206.

127. Ibid.

128. Maravall, "Saavedra Fajardo"; Maravall, *La cultura,* 266–304.

129. Tau Anzoategui, *Casuismo,* 40, 53,57.

130. Covarrubias, *Tesoro,* 316; Bermúdez de Pedraza, *Arte,* 135.

131. Through the sixteenth century, the crown sought to maintain unity of law between Castile and America. By the early seventeenth century, this was no longer possible, and the crown declared that only legislation passed through the Council of the Indies would be valid for the New World. Borah, *Justice,* 254; García Gallo, "La ley," 21–22:607–630.

132. Bernardo Balbuena, *La grandeza,* 13–14; Tau Anzoategui, *Casuismo,* 97; Tomás y Valiente, *Manual,* 339–40; Sy P, *Política,* 3:2092 (5.11.5).

133. Cutter, *The Legal,* 31–43.

134. Tau Anzoategui, *Casuismo,* 486.

135. See, e.g., Kellogg, *Law;* Taylor, *Landlord;* 67–110.

136. *Códice,* 132, 185–86.

137. Acosta, *De procuranda,* 516.

CHAPTER THREE

1. AGNI 12.47.190v–192v (40).

2. A league was roughly three miles. Covarrubias, *Tesoro,* 757. More colloquially, it was the distance a person could comfortably walk in an hour.

3. AGNI 9.369.184v–185r (22).

4. AGNI 11.12.9r–v (38).

5. See also Gerhard, *A Guide,* 236.

6. Throughout my discussion of cases, I will retain the spelling of place names as they appear in the documents, except that for Spanish names I will add accents. I have also added accents to personal names when they do not appear in the documents.

7. By law, procuradores had to be licensed by the king and examined by the audiencia to practice. See *Recop.* 1:272r (2.28.2 & 4 & 9).

8. Going by the AGN's Argena II electronic index and database, I found over 2,700 amparos in the Indios volumes between 1590 and 1811, of which more than 90 percent were issued in the seventeenth century.

9. My actual sample was 468, chosen by selecting every fifth case for each year listed in the results of a database search of the Indios volumes. I also examined 200–300 amparos scattered across other volumes at the AGN, especially General de Parte and Tierras. I chose the Indios amparos for sustained attention because of the long run of cases and because all were before the tribunal, which was a court of first instance for Indian litigants and petitioners.

10. Borah, *Justice,* 252.

11. Burns, *Las Siete:* 2:332–33 (2.11.1 & 3); 3:700 (3.18.18).

12. Ibid., 2:332–33 (2.10.2). For Castilian and Aragonese expressions of this principle, see Weckman, *The Medieval,* 447; Fairén Guillén, *Antecedentes.*

13. García Gallo, *Manual,* 2:956, 957.

14. Pagden, *Spanish Imperialism,* 13–36; Hanke, *The Spanish Struggle,* 23–30.

15. Vial Correa, "Teoría," 87–163.

16. Castañeda Delgado, "La condición," 9–14.

17. Velasco, *De privilegiis,* 2.3.29; Burns, *Las Siete,* 3:710 (3.18.41).

18. Exodus 23:6; Deuteronomy 24:17.

19. Castañeda Delgado, "La condición," 20–22.

20. Konetske, *Colección,* 528. See also Borah, *Justice,* 80–84.

21. HB, *Curia,* 1:50, 57.

22. Borah, *Justice,* 79.

23. Ibid., 79–119.

24. *Instrucciones,* 1:318.

25. The number dropped off in following years—thirty-nine between 1593 and 1597—after which amparos disappear from the archives until 1615. This discontinuity seems more likely to be due to accidents of archiving than to any shift in legal principle or Indian willingness to file petitions.

26. The administrative and demographic instability of these decades may explain why there were so few amparos before the creation of the Juzgado. For examples of very early cases, see Lira, *El amparo,* 17–21, and *Colección de documentos inéditos . . . sacados,* 41:142–44. My datebase search at the AGN turned up a handful of cases dating from 1582 to 1583 and no others until 1590, when the Juzgado began to take shape under Velasco. Of course, the other possibility for the lack is poor archiving practices during the sixteenth century.

27. The classic statement of the problem is contained in a polemic spanning three articles: Keen, "The Black"; Hanke, "A Modest"; and Keen, "The White."

28. Gibson, *The Aztecs,* 51–54; Prem, "Spanish," 444–60; Osborn, "Indian Land," 217–38; Lipsett-Rivera, "Indigenous," 463–83; Kellogg, *Law.*

29. HB, *Curia,* 1:57.

30. AGNI: 3.595.143r (1591); 5.314.86r (1591); 5.901.233r (1591); 6 (pt. 2).100.23r (1591); 6 (pt. 2).362.81r–v (1591); 6 (pt. 2).363.143v (1592); 6 (pt. 2).388.87r–v (1592); 4.406.121r–v (1590).

31. AGNI: 4.54.18r–v (1589); 4.141.47r (1589); 4.805.212r–v (1590); 5.314.86r (1591); 5.422.114r (1591).

32. AGNI: 5.745.199v (1591); 3.770.181r (1591); 6 (pt. 2).362.81r–v (1591); 6 (pt. 2).435.98r (1592).

33. AGNI 9.181.87r–v (19).

34. AGNI 9.277.138v (20).

35. See, e.g., AGNI: 9.244.118v (20); 10.164.63v–64r (29); 10.5.294r–v (32); 11.305.250v–251r (39); 13.37.38v–39r (40).

36. See chapter 5.

37. See, e.g., AGNI: 10.294.168v–169r (30); 10.38.209v (31); 11.136.112r–v (39); 11.274.224r (39).

38. AGNI 13.3.2r–3v (40).

39. I have extrapolated this number from my sample. The balance either could not be determined or involved both Indians and Spaniards as parties complained of. A small number of petitions were sought against mulattoes and mestizos.

40. AGNI: 18.109.84v (55); 20.73.122v–123r (56); 15.115.185v–186r (49).

41. See, e.g., Merola, *República;* SP, *Política,* 3:230 (2.6.6).

42. SP, *Política,* 2:650 (3.3.13).

43. Saavedra Fajardo, *Empresas,* 147 (empresa 22).

44. AGNI 10.143.257r (31).

45. AGNI 12.82.48v–49r (33).

46. SP, *Política,* 2:1176–77 (3.32.46). Emphasis added.

47. O'Gorman, "Bibliotecas," 877.

48. This formulation appeared in cases in Peru as well. See Stavig, *The World,* 98, 122.

49. AGNI 20.36.22v–23v (56).

50. Aquinas, *Summa,* 2:994 (I–II.90.2).

51. See Suárez, *De legibus* (19–20), 68 (1.12.3).

52. Ribadeneyra, *Tratado,* 66 (2:chap. 9); Vitoria, *Political Writings,* 40 (Q. 3, Art. 4). See generally, Pereña Vicente, *Hacia una sociologia.*

53. Covarrubias, *Tesoro,* 427; Soto, *De la justicia,* 1:10–11 (1.1.2).

54. Skinner, *The Foundations,* 1:135 passim.

55. Vitoria, *Political Writings,* 7.

56. SP, *Política,* 1:232 (2.6.6 & 8); 1:512 (3.24.3).

57. AGNI 10.140.76r–78r (29).

58. *Recop.* 2:198r (6.3.1).

59. Gerhard, *A Guide,* 66, 105.

60. Covarrubias, *Tesoro,* 482.

61. Vitoria, *Political Writings*, 239–51.
62. León Pinelo, *Tratado*, quoted in Ots Capdequí *El régimen*, 69.
63. SP, *Política*, 3:523 (2.24.45).
64. See, e.g., Soto, *De la justicia*, 1:78 (1.7.2); Mariana, *The King*, 331 (chap. 11); SP, *Política*, 2:1178 (3.32.50).
65. Soto, *De la justicia*, 1:11 (1.1.2).
66. SP, *Política*, 1:577 (2.28.9).
67. Ibid., 221 (2.5.10).
68. AGNI 5.273.73v–74r (1591).
69. See, e.g., AGNI: 4.543.153r (1590); 12.89.216r–v (40); 15.115.185v–186r (49); 19.61.31r–v (53); 17.80.102v–103r (54); 18.80.67v–68r (55); 20.166.188r (56); 27.36r–v (81); 27.154.74r–75r (81); 26.l 56.215r–v (82); 33.67r–68r (95).
70. SP, *Política*: 3:2355, 2359 (6.8.1 & 13); 1:435 (2.19.4). See also Peña Montenegro, *Itinerario*, 149.
71. Mariana, *The King*, 338.
72. SP, *Política*, 1:223 (2.5.18).
73. SP, *Política*, 2:1177 (3.32.48).
74. Letter in Israel, *Race*, 226. This letter was written in the context of a political battle over the actions of Juan de Palafox y Mendoza, archbishop of Puebla from 1640 to 1649, visitor general during the same period, charged with reviewing the performance of recent viceroys and, briefly in 1642, viceroy.
75. See Muro Romero, "La reforma," 58–59.
76. SP, *Política*, 1:521–22 (2.21.37–38).
77. AGNI 18.35.26r–29r (55). Other petitions invoking flight are AGNI: 12.127.243v–244v (40); 19.96.48v–49r (53); 17.216.211r–212r (54); 23.27.23v–24r (58); 23.161.157r–158r (58); 19.272.153r–v (60).
78. See, e.g., AGNI: 10.93.337r–v (32); 11.184.152r–v (39); 13.310.257v–258r (41); 15.115.185v–186r (49); 21.286.258v (57).
79. Covarrubias, *Tesoro*, 528 (defining "equidad"). See also, RAE *Diccionario*, 2:539.
80. SP, *Política*, 2:1254–55 (4.4.1).
81. *Recop.* 1:7r & 8r (1.2.1 & 6).
82. See, e.g., AGNI: 19.153.81r–v (53); 17.237.236r–237r (54); 18.195.145r–147v (55); 21.18.21r–26r (57); 21.180.158v–159v (57); 23.66.56v–57v (58); 23.321.285r–v (59); 19.232.128r–v (60); 19.279.156r (60); 24.167.103r–v (67); 48.44.63r–v (1723).
83. Cuevas, *Historia*, 3: 459.
84. Santa María, *Tratado*. See Tomás y Valiente, *Los validos*, 143–45. Although we must be careful, it is worth noting that Santa María's *Tratado* was available in Calderón's bookshop in Mexico City in the early 1650s. It is possible that procuradores would have read it, and its presence strongly suggests that *valimiento* was a hot-button issue of the day. O'Gorman, "Bibliotecas," 736, 847–48.
85. AGNI 18.195.145r–147v (55).
86. See, e.g., AGNI: 11.282.231r–v (39); 17.156.157v–158r (54); 18.7.5r–v (55); 18.234.170r–v (55); 19.123.63v–64r (53); 20.62.39r (56); 20.251.198r–v

(56); 21.125.117v (57); 23.179.170r–v (58); 23.313.280v (59); 29.111.100v–101r (85).

87. AGNI: 17.117.134r–v (54); 1. 54.76v–77v (54).

88. SP, *Política,* 1:224 (2.5.21).

89. AGNI 23.356.323v–325v (59).

90. Mariana, *The King,* 135; Soto, *De la justicia,* 1:11 (1.1.2); Ribadeneyra, *Tratado,* IX. See also RAE, *Diccionario,* 6:382; Covarrubias, *Tesoro,* 963.

91. Karttunen and Lockhart, *Nahuatl,* 52–89; Offner, *Law,* 247; Horcasitas, *El teatro,* 404–5.

92. Some seventeenth-century Spaniards objected to Indians' use of Spanish, thinking that it made them less humble and more prone to rascality. See Heath, *Telling,* 43.

93. Offner, *Law,* 249.

94. Maxwell and Hanson, *Of the Manners,* 26.

95. Ibid., 87–88, 133, 143–44, 166, 173–74, 186, 368–69. In rendering the titles and text of these Metaphors, I am relying chiefly on Maxwell and Hanson's "literary interpretations," and secondarily their "literal translations."

96. Molina, *Vocabulario,* pt. 1:96v, pt. 2:156r.

97. As Maxwell and Hanson note, we cannot know which came first, the gloss or the Metaphors.

98. Maxwell and Hanson, *Of the Manners,* 76–77, 136–37, 170; Molina, *Vocabulario,* pt. 1:10r, pt. 2:148v; Covarrubias, *Tesoro,* 114; RAE, *Diccionario,* 1:276.

99. Maxwell and Hanson, *Of the Manners,* 54–69, 77–79, 99–102, 124–125, 170, 177, 184; Molina, *Vocabulario,* pt. 1:19v, 28r, pt. 2:68v, 84v.

100. Beside Nahuatl, far and away the most widely spoken, there would have been Tarascan, Otomi, Huaxtecan, Mixtecan, Zapotecan, Mixe, and others even less commonly used. It is worth noting that the metaphorical relationship between amparo and shadow/shade appears also in Tarascan. See *Diccionario grande,* 1:55.

101. SP, *Política,* 1:580–81 (2.28.20 & 21).

102. AGNI 28.83.71r–72r (84). See also AGNI: 14.110.107r–v (43); 20.251.198r–v (56).

103. AGNI 14.119.114t–v (43).

104. AGNI: 14.119.114f–v (43); 29.155.130v–131r (86).

105. AGNI 17.54.76v–77v (54).

106. AGNI 13.427.372v–373r (41).

107. AGNI 24.305.200v–201v (69).

108. AGNI: 26.41.36f (1680). For a sampler of other receptor cases, see, AGNI: 12.21.176r (40); 12.181.116v (35); 15.96.68v–r (48); 15.10.76r–v (48); 17.278.270v–271r (54); 23.208.192r–193r (58); 25.267.202r–v (77); 25.369.266r (78); 29.218.174r –v (87); 32.51.57r (92).

109. See, e.g., AGNI 21.26. 231r–240v (57).

110. AGNI 21.222.192v–194r (57).

111. AGNI 11.239.195v–196r (39).

112. AGNI: 20.117.94r–95r (56); 2. 90.92r (57); 23.85.75v–76r (57); 23.85.75v–786r (58).

113. Saavedra Fajardo, *Empresas,* 147 (empresa 22).

114. AGNI: 18.245.177v–179r (55); 20.36.22v–23v (56); 30.74.64v–66r (87); 22.85.123v–124r (1714). It is unclear in the 1687 case whether the "our Lord" refers to the king or to God.

115. SP, *Política,* 1:212 (2.4.27); Peña Montenegro, *Itinerario.*

CHAPTER FOUR

1. For a later description of this process in a notary's handbook, see Juan y Colom, *Instrucción,* 158.

2. Burns, *Las Siete,* 3:850–51 (3.30.1 & 2 & 5).

3. Ibid., 3:549 (3.2.27); 3:550 (3.2.28).

4. Vitoria, *Political Writings,* 240–41. See also Pagden, *Spanish,* 18–22.

5. Peset & Menegus, "Rey," 563–99; Pagden, *Spanish,* 33–36; Solano, *Cedulario* (see, e.g., 168–69, 172–75, 177, 181–83, 193, 196–98).

6. See Zavala, *La encomienda.*

7. Zavala, *De encomienda,* 15–16.

8. *Recop.* 2:103v–104r (4.12.14), with references to decrees from 1578, 1589, and 1591. See also Solano, *Cedulario,* 15, 273–74.

9. Almandoz Garmendia, *Fray Alonso,* 119–21.

10. Ots Capdequí, *El régimen,* 50.

11. *Recop.* 2:103r (4.12.10) (quoting a royal decree of 1535).

12. *Recop.* 2:191r (6.1.30) (cédula de 1546); Burns, *Las Siete,* 3:837 (3.28.50).

13. Burns, *Las Siete,* 3:837 (3.28.50). See also, SP, *Política,* 1:115–16 (1.9.18 y 19).

14. Hoekstra, *Two Worlds,* 100–101.

15. Ibid., 100.

16. Gibson, *The Aztecs,* 274.

17. The literature on land in sixteenth-century Mexico is vast. I have relied heavily on the following: Gibson, *The Aztecs,* 257–300; Prem, *Milpa;* Ots Capdequí, *El régimen;* Hoekstra, *Two Worlds,* 89–120; Martínez, *Codiciaban;* Taylor, *Landlord,* especially chapters 3 and 4 of Zavala, *De encomienda.*

18. For the Aztecs, see Gibson, *The Aztecs,* 257; Horn, *Postconquest* 111–129; Martínez, *Codiciaban,* 81–84. For the Mixteca, see Terranciano, *The Mixtecs,* 198–220; Spores, *The Mixtecs,* 66–68. See also, Taylor, *Landlord,* 67–68; Hoekstra, *Two Worlds,* 99.

19. Gibson, *The Aztecs,* 267; Terranciano, *The Mixtecs,* 203–4; Woodrow Borah, *Justice,* 38.

20. Ots Capdequí, *El régimen,* 51–53, 69, 77. This idea had roots running back to medieval feudal arrangements. Vassals who held land were obliged to serve the king in time of war so that land ownership was not a simple matter of possession or title free and clear of obligations. See *Nueva recopilación,* 2:115 (6.8.1).

21. Iglesias, "Tierras," 217; Borah, *Justice,* 38.

22. Borah, *Justice,* 38.

23. See Solano, *Cedulario,* 45, 63, 65, 74, 78.

24. See Ots Capdequí, *El régimen*, 69.
25. García Martínez, *Los pueblos*, 238.
26. Iglesias, "Tierras," 219, 223, 229.
27. Solano, *Cedulario*, 298.
28. Kellogg, *Law*, 124.
29. For examples of fraud and other misdealings, see Gibson, *The Aztecs*, 273–74.
30. Among Indians there appears to have been a gradual acceptance of private ownership. See Phipps, *Some Aspects;* Taylor, *Landlord*, 73. See also Terranciano, *The Mixtecs*, 208–9; Hoekstra, *Two Worlds*, 120.
31. Melville, *A Plague*, 140–42; Cline, *Colonial*, 157–58.
32. Prem, *Milpa*, 228–32.
33. Burns, *Las Siete:* 3:548 (3.2.25); 5:1340; 1393; 1406 (7.7.8; 7.14.30; 7.16.1–12).
34. Solano, *Cedulario*, 41.
35. Ots Capdequí, *El régimen*, 103.
36. Iglesias, "Tierras," 223, 229.
37. Solano, *Cedulario*, 270–75.
38. Solano, *Cedulario*, 336–37.
39. Prem, "Spanish," 455.
40. Solano, *Cedulario*, 269.
41. See, e.g., AGNI: 3.356.83r (1591); 3.664.156r–v (1590); 4.54.18r–v (1589); 4.662.181r (1590); 5.717.194r–v (1591); 6 (pt. 2).388.87r–v (1592); 6 (pt. 2).435.98r (1592); 6 (pt. 2).491.108r (1592). AGNGP 4.572.159r (1591).
42. Burns, *Las Siete*, 3:844–45 (3.29.18).
43. SP, *Política*, 2:1134 (3.30.27); 1:500 (2.22.6).
44. Solórzano y Pereira later affirmed this principle. See SP, *Política*, 3:439 (2.19.24). It ultimately came to be enshrined in the *Recop.* 2:199r (6.3.9).
45. See Lira González, *El amparo*, 17.
46. Iglesias, "Tierras," 216 n.5.
47. See, e.g., AGNI: 3.506.118r (1591); 4.141.47r (1589); 4.406.121r–v (1590); 4.662.181r (1590); 6 (pt. 2).581.154r–v (1593); 6 (pt. 2).160.38r (1591).
48. Cline, "The Oztoticpac," 76–116.
49. Gibson, *The Aztecs*, 271; AGNI 4.141.47r (1589).
50. See, e.g., AGNI: 3.664.156r–v (1591); 4.543.153r (1590); 6 (pt. 1).743.199v–200r (1593).
51. Ots Capdequí, *El régimen*, 50–51, 77; Ots Capdequí, *Manual*, 2:29–37.
52. AGNI 4.543.153r (1590).
53. Taylor, *Landlord*, 78.
54. See, e.g., AGNI: 13.187.169r–v (41); 18.109.84v (55); 19.396.222r–v (61); 28.96.81v–82r (84).
55. AGNI 10.294.168v–169r (30).
56. AGNI: 12.115.77v–78r (34); 13.129.114r–v (41); 16.118.108r–109r (51). See also, e.g., AGNI: 12.89.216r–v (40); 13.79.71r–v (40); 13.187.169–v (41); 16.10.9r–v (51); 17.80.102v–103r (54); 19.61.31r–v (53); 21.209.182v (57); 25.348.353v (78); 27.154.74r–75r (81).

57. See, e.g, *Recop.* 2:149v (5.2.28), referring to a decree of Philip III from 1606. See generally, Ots Capdequí, *El régimen,* 94, 98; Ots Capdequí, *Manual,* 30.

58. See, e.g., AGNI: 19.28.13v–14r (55); 19.61.31r–v (53); 19.434.246v (61); 19.600.336r–v (63); 20.93.62v (56); 23.125.117v (58); 23.321.285r–v (59); 27.154.74r–75r (81); AGNT 2959.111.281r–v (62).

59. AGNI: 10.95.49v–50r (29); 19.61.31r–v (55); 25.348.353v (78).

60. SP, *Política,* 1:435 (2.19.4).

61. Kellogg, *Law,* 140.

62. Rojas Rabiela et al., *Vida,* 64–65, 68–69, 88–89, 180–81, 304–5.

63. AGNT 1780.3.1r–7r (60).

64. The words *su Majestad* (his Majesty) also appeared in Spanish in the original Nahuatl document.

65. Ots Capdequí, *El régimen,* 74–76. See also, *Nueva Recopilación,* 1:332v–333r (4.13.2).

66. Aquinas, *Summa,* 3:1471 (II–II.66.2). Burns, *Las Siete,* 3:533, 535 (3.2.2); 3:548 (3.2.25).

67. See Wobeser, *La formación,* apéndices, 118–217.

68. Hoekstra argues that Indian villagers tended to be less interested in riverside land than Spaniards were, in part because the soil was much softer than higher up. Hoekstra, *Two Worlds,* 100.

69. AGNT 2756.168r–187r (43); 1206.1 (cuad. 2).1r–32r. The latter case is from the eighteenth century, and the map was copied from the original, which does not appear in the record.

70. AGNI 12.101.58v–66r (29).

71. In fact, Quelatao may once have been a barrio of Capulalpa. Gerhard, *A Guide,* 159.

72. For summaries of other *cabecera* cases, see Borah, *Justice,* 203–5.

73. AGNT 1631.1 (cuad. 2).29r–98r (56).

74. Gibson, *The Aztecs,* 271. See also Taylor, *Landlord,* 108; Iglesias, "Tierras," 229; Peset & Menegus, "Rey," 580–81.

75. Gibson, *The Aztecs,* 271.

76. AGNI: 10.75.328r–v (32); 11.136.112r–v (39).

77. This procedure can be read off the cases themselves. A more systematic description of what could be involved is available in HB, *Curia,* 1:1–99.

78. AGNT 1624.5. 19r (91).

79. HB, *Curia,* 1:88 (1.17.24–25).

80. AGNT 1624.5.107r; 112r–115v; 119r–v.

81. Burns, *Las Siete,* 3:779 (3.22.5).

82. It is worth noting here that Guzmán's procurador, in seeking to impeach Tesayuca's witnesses, focused on the fact that they were reporting hearsay. He did not say that their testimony should be dismissed because they were Indians. Technically, the testimony of one Spaniard might count for the testimony of six Indians, though this doctrine appears to have been applied only exceptionally.

83. Virtually all later civil legal systems have adopted this rule, which imposes the burden of proof on the adverse claimant, who must prove superior

right in the property and prove as well that the actual possessor's title is defective. Failure on either point leaves the property in the hands of the actual possessor. See Burns, *Las Siete,* 3:550 n. 1 (3.2.38 & n. 1).

84. AGNT 1624.5.42r.

85. AGNT 127 (1ᵃ pte).2 and (2ᵃ pte.).1 (82).

86. AGNT 127 (1ᵃ pte.).2.2v.

87. Two of these testaments contain a reference of "the Virgin Mary my lawyer [abogada]." AGNT 127 (1ᵃ pte.).2.6r, 8v.

88. AGNT 127 (1ᵃ pte.).2.84v.

89. AGNT 127 (1ᵃ pte.).2.117v–119r.

90. AGNT 127 (2ᵃ pte.).1.165r–174v.

91. AGNT 127 (2ᵃ pte.).1.223r–v.

92. AGNT 226 (2ᵃ pte.).21.37.

93. AGNT 125.1.170r–194v (82).

94. AGNT 125.1.170r–287r (82).

95. This qualifies the view that indigenous attitudes oriented to production and use were holdovers from pre-Hispanic times. See Nagler, "Guatemala."

CHAPTER FIVE

1. Gerhard, *The Northern,* 184.

2. AGNI 13.327.271v–273v (41).

3. AGNI 13.326.270r (41).

4. Konestzke, *Colección,* 154–68.

5. My sample of amparos contained about 100 libertad cases, roughly one in every five.

6. *Colección de documentos inéditos . . . sacados de los archivos,* 31:211; Konetske, *Colección,* 1:6–17, 89–96; Pagden, *Spanish,* 14.

7. Hera, "El derecho," 161–64.

8. Vitoria, *Political Writings,* 233–92 (Relectio on the American Indians). The philosophical and theological complexities of these debates are discussed in Brett, *Liberty,* see especially 123–64.

9. Casas, *Apologética,* 3.136.

10. Hanke, *All Mankind.*

11. Aristotle, *Politics,* 14 (1.5.11).

12. The list of people involved in these debates is long: John Major, Matías de Paz, Bernardo Mesa, Palacios Rubios, Francisco de Vitoria, Luis de Molina, Domingo de Soto, Melchor Cano, Diego de Covarrubias, Francisco Suárez, as well as Las Casas and Sepúlveda. Arenal, "La teoría," 67–124.

13. Pagden, *Spanish,* 13–17; Vitoria, *Political,* 239–52; Soto, *De la justicia,* 2:280 (4.1).

14. Zavala, *Servidumbre;* Hanke, *All Mankind.* Sepúlveda himself argued that as Indians became better Christians, they might be granted a greater ambit of liberty commensurate to their growing capacities. In the meanwhile, they could not be reduced to actual, physical slavery.

15. Burns, *Las Siete,* 3:788 (3.22.18); 5:1478 (7.34.1). The point here is from the perspective of the individual: all individuals hate slavery and the law should help those who can make a viable claim against their individual enslavement. The law did not aim to put an end to slavery as such. As to the difference between Africans and Indians, Africans were familiar with Christianity and had a long a history of being enslaved, while Indians were neophytes to the faith and their status was tied up with theological and political justifications for conquest. Solange Alberro argues as well that "considerations of a political type" were at the root of the differential treatment of Africans and Indians before the Inquisition. See Alberro, *Inquisición,* 26.

16. Seed, *American,* 66.

17. Konetske, *Colección,* 1:89–96. For references to other cédulas, see the *Recop.* 2:194v–98 (6.2), and libro 6 more generally; *Instrucciones,* 94. See also Méntz, *Trabajo,* 70–71.

18. Thus, while theological and juridical disputes continued and, as Pagden has noted, the Thomistic natural-law view of human nature fell to a reassertion of Roman jurisprudence in the writings of León Pinelo and Solórzano y Pereira, the sixteenth-century debates left indelible marks on the legal relationship between the Spanish empire and its Indian subjects. Pagden, *Spanish,* 33–35.

19. Viqueira & Urquiola, *Los obrajes,* 78–81.

20. Méntz, *Trabajo,* 102–105. Méntz notes that while no evidence that *tlacotli* status was heritable has yet surfaced, more research is required (103). See also Clendinnen, *Aztecs,* 99–100.

21. Méntz, *Trabajo,* 72–105.

22. *Instrucciones,* 113.

23. Ibid., 129, 165–66, 213–14.

24. SP, *Política,* 1:189–91 (2.2.1–11); *Instrucciones,* 165, 214.

25. *Recop.* 2:221v–229r (6.8).

26. Florescano, "The Formation," 167.

27. Agia, *Servidumbres,* 37.

28. See AGNGP 6.499.188r–v (03).

29. Konetske, *Colección,* 1:71–85, 154–68, 335–36, 337–39; AGNGP 7.475.321r–322r (33). Which is not to say coerced labor disappeared. The "sacaindios" still worked in many areas, especially where large mining and agricultural concerns used *recogedores* to collect workers. See Méntz, *Trabajo,* 285–310.

30. Burns, *Las Siete,* 3:586, 788; 5:1478 (3.5.4; 3.22.18; 7.43.rule I).

31. See, e.g., AGNI: 11.20.14v–15r (38); 11.361.295v–297r (39); 13..129v–132r (41); 17.139.147v–148r (54); 18.224.164v–165r (55); 19.258.144v (60); 20.28.17r–v (56); 21.113.111r–112r (57); 24.165.102r–v (67).

32. SP, *Política indiana,* 1:174–77, 188–95 (2.1; 2.2); Peña Montenegro, *Itinerario,* 210, 240–41; *Recop.* 2:194v–198r (6.2).

33. Burns, *Las Siete,* 4:901 (4.5); Saavedra Fajardo, *Empresas,* 320 (emblema 47); Covarrubias, *Tesoro,* 536, 764–65, 937.

34. AGNI 13.150.129v–132r (41). Though there is no solictor's name, the petition refers to his "defender," indicating that he had help in filing.

35. Bauer, "Rural," 33.
36. Bakewell, "Mining," 139; Gerhard, *A Guide,* 236.
37. Such cases were common. Diego Martín of Queretaro filed a petition in 1660 charging that the heir of his employer had reneged on previously agreed-upon arrangements. When he had left the hacienda where he worked, the owner had kidnapped his wife and was holding her until he agreed to return. AGNI 19.326.184r (60). Matheo Sánchez and his wife, both from Jilotepec, said in 1662 that they had left the service of don Antonio de Navarrete because he refused to pay them what they had agreed on. They had fled to their own village, from which he sought to "take them by force and against their will to serve him on his estate as if they were slaves." AGNI 19.572.324r–v (62).
38. There may be additional opportunities to learn something of this when the Tribunal Superior de Justicia archive finally opens at the AGN. I have had a sneak peak and there will be much material to mine.
39. Gibson, *The Aztecs,* 220; Viqueira & Urquiola, *Los obrajes,* 80. I am indebted to John Tutino for bringing this line of thought to my attention.
40. Viqueira & Urquiola, *Los obrajes,* 193–98.
41. Konetzke, *Colección,* 1:167; AGNGP, 7.475.321r–322r (33); AGNI 18.35.26v–29v (55).
42. Boyer has explored such networks with great insight into family life. Boyer, *Lives.*
43. Cope, *The Limits,* 35; Taylor, *Drinking,* 66–67.
44. Molina, *Vocabulario,* 115r and 116r.
45. Covarrubias, *Tesoro,* 536–37, 937. "Esclavo" was defined as a "siervo," which equated to "esclavo" and in its first sense derived from the Latin "servus, qui sui iuris non est, sed alieni domino subiicitur."
46. Burns, *Las Siete,* 4:901 (4.5).
47. Maxwell and Hanson, *Of the Manners,* 173, 177, 182. It is important to note here that the title of Metaphor XXIII given as "Slave" appears in Spanish in the original. Metaphor XII, titled "Servant" by Maxwell and Hanson, appears in the original as "Servant or vassal of someone." Metaphor XXXVI, which Maxwell and Hanson title "Servant as Implement," is in fact closer to Metaphor XXIII, titled "Slave," than to Metaphor XII, titled "Servant." Indeed, the original Spanish gloss of Metaphor XXXVI is "He who is born a slave or the bastard." On *cuitlatlaça,* see Molina, *Vocabulario,* pt. 1:78r, pt. 2:27v; Karttunnen, *Analytical Dictionary,* 73.
48. SP, *Política,* 1:189, 242 (2.2.2; 2.6.45); 2:520 (2.24.32).
49. Soto, *De la justicia,* 2:300–303 (4.4.1) and 3:429–431 (5.3.1); Agia, *Servidumbres,* 100–101.
50. AGNI 19.71.55r–v (53).
51. Examples of these cases are: AGNI: 17.139.147v–148r (54); 18.167.126v (55); 19.313.175v–176r (60); 19.355.199r (61); 25.141.115v–116r (76); 26.144.206v–207r (82).
52. AGNI 17.185.181r–182r (54).
53. SP, *Política,* 1:520 (2.24.32).

54. There were exceptions in both directions, of course. Indians could be made to leave their communities pursuant to a mine repartimiento. And in "some rare cases" an Indian might be granted a license to live somewhere other than his village. *Recop.* 2:200r (6.3.18–19). This did not imply that Indians were irrevocably stuck in their villages. A woman, certainly, could marry and move to her husband's village. Beyond this, Indian men regularly left their communities for mining camps, haciendas where there was work, or the relative anonymity of the city, where they might just be taken for mestizos. But this was a liberty of movement pursued informally and in spite of law, not one that could be vindicated legally through an amparo.

55. AGNI: 17.245.242v–243r (54); 21.135.125r–v (57); 23.166.160r–161r (58); 23.236.213r–v (58). See also, AGNI: 10.311.177v–178r (30); 10.117.349v–350r (33).

56. AGNI 19.706.387r–v (64).

57. SP, *Política,* 3:520–21 (2.24.33–34).

58. The record offers no explanation of how this came to pass. It is possible that his master freed him or at least that Nicolás acted as though he had.

59. Boyer, "Honor," 152–78; Lipsett-Rivera, *"De Obra,"* 511–39; Martin, "Popular," 305–24.

60. AGNI: 17.23.35r (54); 17.95.113r–v (54); 18.21.15v (55); 19.372.209r (61); 19.443.250r–v (62); 19.672.379r (64); 20.18.17r–v (56); 21.109.108r (57); 23.76.67r–v (58); 24.165.102r–v (67).

61. Maxwell and Hanson, *Of the Manners,* 91, 145, 174.

62. Burkhart, *Holy,* 168.

63. Molina, *Vocabulario,* pt. 1:102r, 104r, 107r. Molina gives *maquixtia* as equivalent to *maquiça,* as being freed from a danger or harm, but without the sense of being removed from the hands of another given by Burkhart.

64. Molina, *Confesionario,* 108v, 113r, 116v, 117r.

65. Burkhart, *Holy,* 168; Horcasitas, *El teatro,* 274, 296, 354, 356, 358, 360.

66. Burkhart, *Holy,* 168; Burkhart, *The Slippery,* 82.

67. Molina, *Confesionario,* 70v, 116v.

68. AGNI: 23, 76.67r–v (58); 23.92.92r–v (58).

69. D'Ors, "El servicio"; RAE, *Diccionario,* 3–4:396.

70. This does not mean that under other circumstances individuals were above bending or breaking the law for personal advantage.

71. Something less than half of all amparo petitions were presented by corporate entities, usually villages. A quarter or more of petitions seeking liberty were on behalf of villages.

72. See, e.g., AGNI: 10.5.294r–v (32); 10.117.349v–350r (33); 11.218.180r–181r (39); 18.35.26v–29r (55); 20.36.22v–23r (56); 23.236.213r–v (58); 30.74.64r–66r (87).

73. AGNI 11.59.44v–45r (38).

74. AGNI 12.104.225v–226r (40).

75. Covarrubias, *Tesoro,* 765; SP, *Política,* 1:189 (2.2.2); RAE, *Diccionario,* 3–4:396.

76. Madden, *Political Theory,* 145–45. See also Parry, *The Spanish,* 175.

77. Saavedra Fajardo, *Empresas,* 320 (emblema 47).
78. Maravall, *La cultura,* 348–51.
79. Agia, *Servidumbres,* 29.
80. SP, *Política,* 2:1177 (3.32.47).
81. Redondo Redondo, *Utopía,* 154–55.
82. SP, *Política,* 1:519 (2.24.29–31).
83. *Recop.* 2:200v–201r (6.3.21–23; 6.1.10).
84. Castillo de Bobadilla, *Política,* 2:630b.
85. Examples of early cases in which liberty is mentioned in the petition are AGNI: 11.20.14v–15r (38); 12.104.225v–226r (40); 13.165.153v–154r (41); 13.257.224v (41). Cases in which the petition does not use the word *libertad* but the tribunal does are: AGNI: 10.311.177v–178r (30); 10.117.349v–350r (33); 12.242.152r–v (35); 13.172.159v (41).
86. AGNI: 11.339.319v–320–r (39); 12.76.44v–45r (33); 15.97.69v–70v (48).
87. Land cases are to be found predominantly in AGNT. Several hundred mostly seventeenth- and eighteenth-century mine and nobility cases are found in AGNGP.
88. AGNGP: 9.158.118v (43); 13.7.7r–v (70); 16.151.130r–131r (88); 14.204.179r–180r (73).
89. See, e.g., AGNGP: 5.38.8r–v (1599); 6.650.208v–290r (03); 7.283.83v–84r (32); 7.421.286v–289v (32); 8.222.151v–154r (41); AGNT 2956.117–118.229r–236r (69).
90. See, e.g., AGNGP: vol. 6.295.112v (02); AGNT: 2944.291 (00); 2961.142 (09); 2965.92 (58); 2965.105 (58).
91. See, e.g., AGNGP: 16.42.32r (87); 16.151.130r0131r (88); 18.90.86v–87v (99); 18.401.94r–v (99); 18.355.335r–336v (1702); 19.43.29r–v (1708); 23.228.168v–169r (1715).
92. See, e.g., AGNGP: 7.52.38v (32); 16.202.183r–v (88); 18.48.34r (99); 28.135.127r–128r (1731); vol. 28.156.155r (1731); AGNT: 2934.64.176r–v (47); 2941.25.37r–v (31); 2942.59.143r–145v (10); 2942.119.316r–v (32); 2951.120.253r–254v (67); 2951.152 (1682); 2951.154 (1632); 2955.7 (32); 2961.102 (10); 2963.69 (62); 2967.128 (1667); 2970.66 (06); 2972.111 (1660); 2978.55 (32); 2978.107 (32); 3365.9 (1680). Cases such as these might expand into full blown lawsuits. See Owensby, "How Juan and Leonor Won Their Freedom."
93. See, e.g., AGNI: 10.145.258r–v (31); 30.276.254r–255r (89).
94. See, e.g., AGNI: 13.165.153v–154r (41); 19.572.324r–v (62); 21.113.111r–112r (57); 23.166.160r–161r (58); 23.386.374r–v (59); 26.144.206v–207r (82).
95. *Instrucciones,* 1:663–64.
96. Griffen, *Culture,* 10–39; Gerhard, *The Northern,* 184.
97. Saavedra Fajardo, *Empresas,* 554 (emblema 72).
98. BN, MS 3195 (182r–188r).
99. Indians were commonly equated to the Israelites. In 1640, the Jesuit Colegio de San Pedro y San Pablo performed a play titled *La Comedia de San Francisco de Borja.* Its point was to pay homage to the viceroy, the Marqués de

Villena. After praising the viceroy in the *loa,* comparing him to Borja, an exemplar of humility and responsibility, the play concludes with a *tocotín,* a dance in the manner of the Indians. In it, the Indians are compared to the Israelites and the viceroy to Moses, who is exhorted to free them from the captivity of their misery at the hands of greedy Spaniards. See Luciani, "The *Comedia*," 121–41.

100. Maxwell and Hanson, *Of the Manners,* 126, 185.

CHAPTER SIX

1. "Romance en lengua."

2. Although there has been little work on these romances in the seventeenth century, eighteenth-century Spaniards and *criollos* often wrote satirical poetry voicing characters of other racial groups, complete with ungrammatical Spanish. See Hill, "Caste." The title too inclines in this direction, since it is unlikely that a half-ladino, Mexican Indian would have referred to himself as such. Finally, it is difficult to read this reaction to the theft of three roosters as a straight lament; it is simply too much ado about very little. The Indian of the poem does not lose his land, he just is not able to throw the banquet he had planned to impress his "vassals." Precisely this sort of exaggeration is what made romances such a popular form.

While we cannot know specifically what moved this author to compose the romance, the turn of the seventeenth century was a period in which New-World Spaniards faced an influx of immigrants from Spain, a growing mestizo population, and expanding horizons for Indian commoners. Under these circumstances, status anxiety appears to have been common. In this poem, the Indian comes off as a puffed-up little man who exaggerates his importance and makes grandiose what is actually trite—the classic mistake of the arriviste. In adopting a mocking tone, the Spanish author may have sought to salve the sting of watching real Indians, perhaps someone of his acquaintance, move up in a world where so many Spaniards lacked real prospects. We can imagine the laughter a Spaniard imitating an Indian's Nahuatlized pronunciation of these banalities would have provoked at a tavern among other tattered Spaniards.

Admittedly, this is a speculative reading. The alternative, that an Indian did write the poem, cannot be completely discounted. There were plenty of Indian interpreters and notaries, and since romances were meant to be performed, it is not impossible that an Indian learned the form and decided to express himself through it, though the serious tone would have been at odds with the more satirical playfulness of such romances more generally. I am indebted to Prof. Ruth Hill for her help in thinking this poem through.

3. Burns, *Las Siete,* 3:1304 (7.1.1).

4. SP, *Política,* 3:1946 (5.5.3); Burns, *Las Siete,* 5:1463 (7.31.1); Soto, *De la justicia,* 1:10–11, 38 (1.1.2; 1.1.1).

5. Burns, *Las Siete,* 684 (3.16.41).

6. For a broad view of the role of storytelling in law and legal scholarship, see Cover, "The Supreme Court"; Winter, *A Clearing,* 104–38.

7. See *Recop.* 2:169r–170v (2.10); HB, *Curia.* The *Curia*, originally published in Lima in 1600 and reissued in 1605, 1612, 1627, 1652, and 1657, was available in Mexico City libraries and bookstores during the seventeenth century. O'Gorman, "Bibliotecas," 743, 763, 771, 817.

8. HB, *Curia*, 1:43 (1.8.3).

9. Here too there was a peculiarly New World aspect to the law. While Indians could bring criminal proceedings against each other and against Spaniards before provincial alcaldes mayores, the General Indian Court in Mexico City had jurisdiction only over cases between Indians and cases in which Spaniards accused Indians. Technically, cases in which Indians accused Spaniards lay exclusively with the audiencia. The reason for this policy is obvious: Spaniards worried that the Indians would drag them to Mexico City on the slightest pretext. In practice, the Juzgado regularly dealt with cases initiated by Indians against Spaniards. Borah, *Justice*, 93.

10. SP, *Política*, 3:1889 (5.3.8); Burns, *Las Siete*, 5:1303 (part. VII, preface); 3:533 (part. III, preface).

11. Burns, *Las Siete*, 3:684 (3.16.41).

12. See Borah, *Justice*, 240–44.

13. *Recop.* 1.10.6–8.

14. Covarrubias, *Tesoro*, 386.

15. AGNC 140.4.116r–141 (26).

16. AGNC 140.4.118r.

17. AGNC 140.4, 119r–122r.

18. AGNC 140.4, 124r–v.

19. HB, *Curia*, 1:74 (1.15.1); 1:226 (3.15.7).

20. AGNC 140.4.130r–134r.

21. AGNC 140.4.134v–137r.

22. HB, *Curia*, 1:84 (1.17.2).

23. HB, *Curia*, 1:88 (1.17.21).

24. Conley and O'Barr make this point with regard to litigants, though it holds for witnesses as well. See their, *Rules*, 171.

25. HB, *Curia*, 1:227 (3.15.13); Burns, *Las Siete*, 3:677 (3.16.28).

26. Judges were responsible for rendering judgments "without any ambiguity." Burns, *Las Siete*, 3: 779 (3.22.5).

27. See Keen, *The Aztec*, 63, 80, 83, 88, 117–18; Taylor, *Drinking*, 10–45; *Instrucciones*, 1:166, 197, 214.

28. Palafox, "De la naturaleza," 253, 264–65; SP, *Política*, 1:580 (2.28.18).

29. Molina, *Confesionario*, 98r, 102v, 114v; Taylor, *Drinking*, 41.

30. Cover, "The Supreme Court," 4–68; Cover, "Violence," 1601–29; Winter, *A Clearing*, 104–38.

31. HB, *Curia*, 1:228 (3.15.20).

32. Burns, *Las Siete*, 3:777 (3.22.2).

33. Months later they filed another complaint against Juan Michaucatl for throwing the rock that killed Agustín. In January 1627 Michaucatl too was exonerated. Juan Agustín's death appears to have remained an unsolved crime.

34. Burns, *Las Siete,* 5:1303 (part. VII, prologue); 1461 (7.31.1).
35. Ceballos, *Arte,* 60.
36. Tau Anzoateguí, "Ordenes," 283–315. At least in colonial Argentina, the picota was also referred to as the "árbol de justicia." (300).
37. AGNC 590.2.25r–91 (57).
38. AGNC 590.2.39r.
39. AGNC 590.2.41r–45v.
40. AGNC 590.2.59r–60v.
41. AGNC 590.2.65r–74v.
42. AGNC 590.2.75r–77v.
43. This suggests that women's strategies discussed by Stern for late-colonial Mexico have a deeper history. See Stern, *The Secret.*
44. AGNC 590.2.78r–v.
45. The rules of torture were set out in the *Curia.* See HB, *Curia,* 1:228–32 (3.16). See also Tomás y Valiente, "Teoría," 439–85.
46. AGNC 590.2.27r–29r.
47. Burns, *Las Siete,* 5:1344, n. 1; 5:1467 (7.31.8); HB, *Curia,*1:203 (3.9.6); 1:202 (3.9.5).
48. Of course, he could have been telling the truth.
49. The Sala de Crimen in Mexico City could impose the death penalty only on a vote of three judges. *Recop.* 1: 229r (2.16.8).
50. AGNC 590.2.91v. We can only speculate as to the resonances this punishment may have had for Nahuatl speakers. Olmos's fourteenth metaphor contains an image of "the rope" by which a criminal is caught. Water also figured prominently in the Metaphors' images of punishment. In the same metaphor, the ruler "cast [the guilty party] in the river, flinging it from on high." Maxwell and Hansen, *Of the Manners,* 174. Fray Diego Durán wrote in his chronicle that under Aztec law, adulterers were to be stoned to death and then cast in rivers or left to the buzzards. Durán, *History,* 210.
51. AGNC 39.4.175–212 (41).
52. AGNC 39.4.180v–197v.
53. In referring to Rodrigo as a "son," the document uses the Nahuatl word *noconeuh.* According to Molina's bilingual dictionary, the general word for the Spanish *hijo* was *tepiltzin tetelpuch.* Women, says Molina's entry, used *noconeuh.* Molina, *Vocabulario,* 71.
54. AGNC 39.4.203r.
55. AGNC 39.4.210v.
56. AGNC 39.4.211v.
57. HB, *Curia,* 1:202 (3.9.2); 227 (3.15.11). The rule regarding minors was taken straight from *Las Siete Partidas.* Burns, *Las Siete* 5:1307 (7.1.9).
58. Burns, *Las Siete,* 3:779 (3.22.5).
59. See Burns, *Las Siete,* 3:653–684, 692–758 (3.14–18); 5:1317 (7.1.29); HB, *Curia,* 1:205–07, 225–28 (3.10; 3.15).
60. AGNC 580.5.81r–132 (78).
61. AGNC 580.5.94r.
62. AGNC 590.5.127r.

63. The underscoring is precisely what one would expect from a person charged with making a decision, as opposed to a later researcher. Almost all of the underlining seems aimed at comparing different elements of witnesses' statements against each other. Procedural details, even closing arguments and the decision itself, are not underlined.

64. AGNC 590.5.95v.

65. AGNC 590.5.91v.

66. AGNC 590.5.121r.

67. AGNC 590.5.118r–119v.

68. SP, *Política,* 1:584 (2.28.35).

69. The contrast with his own earlier conduct in handling the Tehuantepec rebellion in 1661–62 is arresting. See chapter 8 below.

70. AGNC 590.5.127r.

71. AGNC 139.24.363r–67 (96).

72. AGNC 139.24.366r.

73. AGNC 139.24, 373r–74v.

74. AGNC 139.24.376r.

75. AGNC 139.24.365r–v.

76. AGNC 139.24.372r.

77. Burns, *Las Siete,* 5:1425 (7.20.1).

78. Ibid., 5:1425–26 (7.20).

79. HB, *Curia,* 1:88 (1.17.11).

80. SP, *Política,* 1:615 (2.30.26).

81. AGNC 181.1.4r–6r.

82. AGNC 181.1.6r–10v.

83. AGNC 181.1.14v.

84. AGNC 181.1.15r–22v.

85. AGNC 181.1.25r–v.

86. AGNC 181.1.28r.

87. AGNI 11.91.74.

88. This and the following paragraph draw on Gerhard, *A Guide,* 397–98.

89. HB, *Curia,* 1:200 (3.8.11). A complainant could withdraw a complaint within thirty days of filing, as long as the defendant had not been harmed or defamed. After thirty days, defendants had to agree for a complaint to be withdrawn. There could be no withdrawal if the defendant had been subjected to judicial torture.

90. Borah, *Justice,* 307–08.

91. See, e.g., AGNC 140.4.126r.

92. AGNC 154.15.414r–470 (41).

93. AGNC 154.15.432v–433r.

94. AGNC 154.15.435r–438r.

95. HB, *Curia,* 1:229 (3.16.3–4). See also Tomás y Valiente, "Teoría"; Quevedo y Hoyos, *Libro de indicios.*

96. AGNC 154.15.451v–452r.

97. AGNC 154.15.459r–v.460r–461r.

98. See Monterroso y Alvarado, *Práctica*, 185r; Juan y Colom, *Instrucción*, 239.

99. Because Hernández had already been arrested and "defamed" by the accusation, the matter could not simply be dropped. HB, *Curia*, 1:200.

100. AGNC 154.15.469r, 469v–470r.

101. Juan y Colom, *Instrucción*, 239.

102. HB, *Curia*, 1:233 (3.17.1).

103. HB, *Curia*, 1:226–27 (3.15.11–14); 203 (3.9.6).

104. AGNC 10.15.211r–220 (74).

105. AGNC 10.15.214r–v.

106. AGNC 10.15.216v–218v.

107. Margarita was a silent party to these proceedings, most likely to preserve her reputation from further soiling. See Twinam, "Honor," 118–55. For the eighteenth century, see Twinam, "The Negotiation," 68–102.

108. Soto, *De la justicia*, 1:38.

109. Molina, *Vocabulario*, pt. 1:33r, 93v; pt. 2:137r.

110. Molina, *Confesionario*, 44, 65–72, passim. See also Burkhart, *Slippery*, 28–30.

111. *Tlatlacolli*'s general meaning in Nahuatl was "something damaged," an idea ranging from moral transgressions, to criminal wrongdoing, to moral corruption, and implied a broad harm to oneself, to society, to god, and to the cosmic order. According to Burkhart, "entropy" was the "essence of immorality," and "preservation of order" the primary moral obligation for Nahuatl speakers. Transgressors were supposed to feel not just individual guilt, but a broad unease and fear at having disturbed and disordered things, and a broad sense of sadness or sorrow regarding the act. Friars tried to liken this to Christianity's notion of pecado, and its interior sense of guilt, with only partial success. Burkhart, *Slippery*, 32–33.

112. *Recop.* 2:296r (7.8.3); Burns, *Las Siete*, 3:684 (3.16.52).

113. See AGNInq, 583.4.390r–519v for a case in which a defendant was punished for perjury.

114. The vast majority of petty criminal matters never got beyond informal proceedings conducted by Indian gobernadores and alcaldes at the village level or alcaldes mayores at a regional level. More research is needed regarding law at this level.

115. Offner, *Law*, 243.

CHAPTER SEVEN

1. Carrasco, *The Tenochca*, 207–47.

2. SP, *Política*, 3:1844 (lib. V, cap. 1, n. 2).

3. See Chapter 2. See, e.g., Vitoria, *Political*. More generally, see Pagden, *Spanish*, 13–36.

4. *Recop.* 1:126v (2.1.4); 2:149r (5.2.22).

5. SP, *Política*, 3:1844 (5.1.2).

6. According to René García Castro, caciques whose status derived from lineage traceable to pre-Hispanic dynastic rulers gradually lost authority during the sixteenth century as the colonial government realized it no longer needed an hereditary elite to rule Indian villages. García Castro, *Indios*, 172–90.

7. *Recop.* 2:199r (6.3.15); 2:198r–199r, 200r (5.3.1–4 & 10 & 15).

8. Initially, elections were supposed to be conducted in the presence of a local priest or friar to ensure proper procedures were followed. In 1622, having concluded that this gave churchmen too much influence over local government, the crown barred them, with all other Spaniards, from involving themselves in or even attending indigenous elections. See Haskett, *Indigenous*, 32.

9. Gibson, *The Aztecs*, 176.

10. Góngora, *El corregidor*, 190.

11. Martínez, *Colección*, 127–30; Lockhart et al., *The Tlaxcalan*, 111–14.

12. Gibson, *The Aztecs*, 176.

13. Castro Gutiérrez, "Conflictos," 50.

14. Karttunen and Lockhart, *Nahuatl*, 55; Molina, *Vocabulario*, pt. 2:81; Lockhart et al., *The Tlaxcalan*, 113.

15. Haskett, *Indigenous*, 33.

16. See, e.g., AGNI: 18.35.26v–29r (55); 23.50.38r–v (58); 139.27.401r–422v (41).

17. Palafox y Mendoza, "De la naturaleza," 250.

18. See Piho, *La secularización*, 119–205. Palafox's quip that the Indians would elect good governors "if left to themselves" was almost surely aimed at Franciscan friars whom he felt meddled too freely in local governance, which was one reason he sought to replace them with secular priests answerable to the bishop himself.

19. See generally, Haskett, *Indigenous*, 27–59.

20. AGNI: 13.3.2r–3v (40); 20.79.52r–v (56); 20.152.110r–v (56).

21. AGNI 24.395.273r–v (71).

22. AGNI 18.35.26v–29r (55). I have quoted some of the language from the petition, but otherwise have paraphrased it, retaining the first-person plural to signal the absence of a procurador in this case.

23. See, e.g., Horn, *Postconquest*, 44–66.

24. AGNI 14.42.46v–47v (42).

25. AGNI 14.44.48v–49r. The principales of Atoyaque made an almost identical argument in 1654. See, AGNI 17. 322.309–v.

26. AGNI:14.43.47v–48v; 14.44.48v–49r.

27. RAE, *Diccionario*, 1:643; Burns, *Las Siete*, 1:10–13 (1.2).

28. Of course, this did not hold for "bad custom," which ought to have "its leg broken." Covarrubias, *Tesoro*, 366.

29. AGNI 25.238.177v–179v (77).

30. AGNI 21.39.57r–58r (57).

31. Because the church represented a jurisdiction unto itself, the king could not order the bishop to comply. He could only "beg and charge" him with observing the law. Obedience, then, was strictly a political matter. For a general

treatment of relations between "the two majesties"—the church and the monarchy—see Cañeque's *The King's,* 79–117.

32. AGNC 139.27.401r–422v (41).

33. AGNC 139.27.403r–409v.

34. AGNC 139.27.412v.

35. AGNC 139.27.414r–422v.

36. AGNC 139.27.409r.

37. AGNC 139.27.416r.

38. See, e.g., AGNC: 139.27.401r–422v (41); 227.10.194r–244v (93); AGNI 25.238.177v–179v (77).

39. See, e.g., AGNI 19.445.251r–v (62); AGNC 227.10.194r–244v (93). This *macehualización* of politics was widespread but did not happen everywhere. See, e.g., Castro Gutiérrez, "Conflictos," 50.

40. For similar allegations of macehual involvement in elections, see: AGNI: 21.39.57r–58r (57); 25.238.177v–179v (77); AGNC 643.6.193r–236r (94). Precisely how such "force" was applied must be left to the imagination and future research.

41. For example, see the royal provision and viceregal ordinance issued in favor of the Indians of the Mines of Taxco, prohibiting justices and clergymen from being present at Indian elections. AGNT 2963.99.262r–263v (62).

42. See, e.g., AGNI: 11.499.380r–v (40); 20.79.52r (56); 21.135.125r–v (57); AGNC 580.3.53r–67v (44).

43. See, e.g., AGNC: 260.10.137v (41); 227.10.194r–244v (93); AGNI 24.49.28r (64).

44. AGNI 25.238.177v–179v (77).

45. AGNI 25.238.179v.

46. AGNC 260.10.126r–143r (41).

47. AGNI 14.61.60r–v (42).

48. AGNI: 18.287.196v–197r (55); 23.50.38r–v (58); 23.179.170r–v (58).

49. AGNI 23.356.323v–325v (59).

50. Castro Gutiérrez, "Conflictos," 60. For a list of election cases in Michoacan, see the appendix there at 62–63.

51. AGNI: 29.111.100v–101r (85); 35.87.150r (1701).

52. *Recop.* 2:147v (5.2.11); SP, *Política,* 3:1946 (5.5.2); Covarrubias, *Tesoro,* 993–94; Kartunnen and Lockhart, *Nahuatl,* 60; Lockhart et al., *The Tlaxcalan,* 113; Molina, *Vocabulario,* pt. 1:216, pt. 2:150; Maxwell and Hanson, *Of the Manners,* 87–88, 110–11, 173, 179–80, 426.

53. AGNI: 10.269.153v–154v (30); 14.123.117v–118v (43); 20.79.52r–v (56); 21.99.102r–v (57); 21.17.17–20v (57); 33.1.3r (99).

54. RAE, *Diccionario,* 5–6:335, 421; Covarrubias, *Tesoro,* 994.

55. Spaniards were intimately familiar with the notion of office as a kind of personal asset. By the seventeenth century, the sale of office had become quite common. See Parry, *The Sale; Recop.* 3:93r–98v (8.20); SP, *Política,* 3:2408–35 (6.13); León Pinelo, *Tratado,* 2a pte.:261–378.

56. AGNC: 15. 7. 88r–128v (26); 267.4.53r–73r (43); 54.4.82r–100r (44); 134. 1. 1r–27bisv (62); 227.10.194r–244v (93).

57. AGNC 29.3.32r–43v (50).

58. See Israel, *Razas*, 31, 85; *Recop.* 2:2845–285r (7.4).

59. For other cases involving broken varas, see: AGNC: 15.7.88r–128v (26); 29.3.32r–43v (50); 227.10.194r–244v (93).

60. *Recop.* 2:147v (5.2.11), from a royal order dated 1560.

61. AGNC 134.1.1r–27bisv (62).

62. *Recop.* 2:200r (6.3.12).

63. He wrote *"divino acatamiento"—divine deference.* He obviously meant *devido acatamiento* or *due deference,* a stock phrase employed when asking the court to grant a request. The slip indicates that he drew this petition up largely on his own or that it was done by an Indian notary. It also suggests that in the imaginations of many petitioners there may have been a closer connection between law and religion than petitions drawn up by procuradores generally reveal.

64. SP, *Política,* 3:2002 (5.8.3); 3:1867 (5.2.2); 1:232, 234 2.6.6 & 16); Góngora, *El corregidorz,* 221; Covarrubias, *Tesoro,* 652 (entry for "governar"). The image of the *mirror* figured prominently in Spanish political discourse, in the New World as well as the Old World. Viceroy Conde de Salvatierra was welcomed to Mexico City by an arch designed by Jesuit Alonso de Medina. Medina wrote an accompanying description of the arch entitled *Espejo de príncipes católicos.* See Cañeque, *The King's,* 27.

65. This idea that the subjects of a polity should see themselves reflected in the good ruler may have rung familiar with Nahuatl speakers. Among educated Nahua, the idea of looking to the king as a model of behavior had a long history. Olmos's Metaphors indicate that in Aztec political culture the image of the king served as an exemplary of right conduct. Line 3 in Metaphor IV lists "mirror" (*tezcatl*) as a simile for the good ruler—"he is brilliant like torchlight, like a mirror." Molina's *Vocabulario* offered "to give a good example for others" as the definition of two Nahuatl phrases in which *tezcatl/mirror* was paired with words anchored in the idea of being or giving an *example—machiotl.* One extension of this root gave *machiotlalilia,* which Molina translated as "exemplify, or put order and concert to the republic." As though to reinforce the point, Metaphor IV establishes unequivocally that a good ruler should serve as a model or standard for his people. In line four, the lord who governs is likened to a standard of length or height known as an *octacatl. Octacaana,* a variation on this root, meant "to take a model of something." Another variant, *octacatlalilia,* implied the action of citing or showing someone as a model for emulation by others. Maxwell and Hanson, *Of the Manners,* 78–79, 138–38, 170; Molina, *Vocabulario,* pt. 2:50v, 113r.

66. Covarrubias, *Tesoro,* 170; RAE, *Diccionario,* 1:490.

67. See, e.g., AGNI: 7.109.54r–55r (16); 10.73.36v–37r (29); 10.294.168v–169r (30); 11.76.58v–61r (38).

68. See, e.g., AGNI: 4.54.18r–v (1589); 9.181.87r–v (19); 10.169.377r–378v (33); 11.113.92r–v (39); 12.101.58v–66r (34); 13.205.180r–v (41); 18.35.26v–29r (55); 18.60.50r–v (55); 21.39.57r–58r (57); 21.264.231r–v (57); 23.190.181r–v (58); 23.397.387v–388r (59).

69. AGNC 43.15.350r–495v (15). Otucpa was also known as Actopan or Atocpa.

70. AGNC 43.15.381r–383r, 384v–386r.

71. AGNC 43.15.477r–v, 485r–v.

72. AGNC: 43.––.496r–530r; 43.––.531r–545v.

73. They may also have felt the tug of collective memory. Otucpa had been independent until the late fourteenth century, when it had been conquered and later incorporated as a tributary into the Tenochca empire dominated by Tenochtitlan. See Gerhard, *A Guide*, 44–46. Its status during the Aztec imperial age up to 1519 is unclear. Given what we know of the highly fragmented organization of the Triple Alliance and the tension between Tenochtitlan and many of its satellite tributaries, it would not be surprising if seventeenth-century residents resented the idea that a great-grandson of the emperor should presume to lord over them. For a detailed description of the kingdom of Tenochtitlan in the fifteenth- and sixteenth centuries, see Carrasco, *The Tenochca*, 93–132, 192.

74. See footnote 83 in chapter 2, above.

75. See, e.g., AGNC: 580.3.64v (44); 643.––.141r–142v (71); 227.10.226r (93); 643.6.2a pte.11 (1694).

76. The language quoted from cases in this and the following paragraph comes from: AGNC: 15.7.88r–128v (26); 260.10.126r–143r (41);139.––.423r–432v (41); 230.13.379r–387v (42); 580.3.53r–67v (44); 643.––.141r–145r (71); 580.7.147–180v (91); 227.10.194r–224v (93); 643.6.193r–236r (94). This language was also common in the amparo petitions.

77. Covarrubias, *Tesoro*, 69, 476, 477, 738, 897; RAE, *Diccionario*, 1:171, 543; 2:297, 307; 3:173; Molina, *Vocabulario*, pt. 1:7v, 75v, 102r, pt. 2:91r, 95r. There is no entry in Molina for "reboltoso." Instead, he uses *rebolvedor*, which Covarrubias accepted as a synonym. Covarrubias, *Tesoro*, 897. These were only the most common phrases. There are many others in these cases, including *enredos* (tangles or plots) to describe the activities of those bent on disturbing the peace; *tumultuante*, one who promotes tumults; *perturbar*, to perturb or disturb; *desorden*, disorder.

78. AGNC 227.10.226v (93).

79. Laura Nader has suggested that contemporary Zapotec communities conduct their local legal affairs in keeping with a "harmony ideology" traceable to colonial political arrangements. See Nader, *Harmony*.

80. AGNC 580.3.53r–67v (44).

81. Of course, we cannot wholly discount the possibility that these men constituted an oppressive cabal.

82. AGNC 580.7.147r–180r (91).

83. AGNC 232.27.409r–432v (33).

84. AGNC 232.27.415r.

85. AGNC 232.27.431r.

86. AGNC 138.23.392r–397r (34).

87. AGNC 41.38.523r–530r (40).

88. AGNC 48.30.499r–551v (44).

89. AGNC 48.30.544r.

90. AGNC 135.5.135r–152v (46).
91. Konestske, *Colección de documentos,* 2,1: 337–39.
92. SP, *Política,* 1:230 (2.6.1).
93. *Recop.* 2:190r–v (6.1.19).
94. AGIM/Mexico 35/Mexico 35, N. 37.9.59.1r–37r (43).
95. See Israel, *Razas,* 220–49.
96. For an in-depth account of this process as it unfolded in San Andrés Calapan, see Piho, *La secularización.*
97. AGIM/Mexico 35/Mexico, 35, N. 37.9.59.27r.

CHAPTER EIGHT

1. AGIP 230B.R 15/1.15; García, "Tumultos," 290.
2. Díaz-Polanco, *El fuego,* 9–15.
3. Díaz-Polanco, "Sociedad"; Díaz-Polanco & Sánchez, "El vigor"; Carmagnani, "Un movimiento"; Manzo, "Comercio": all in Díaz-Polanco, *El Fuego;* Barabas, "Rebeliones," 236–41; Spores, "Differential," 30–46; Rojas, *La rebelión.*
4. I am relying here on Pastor, "El repartimiento," 219–58; Menegus, "La economía," 9–64; Baskes, *Indians;* Hoekstra, *Two Worlds,* 148–57.
5. Baskes, *Indians,* 2.
6. Menegus, "La economía," 19.
7. Dahlgrem, *La grana,* 9.
8. Díaz-Polanco, *El fuego,* 103–32.
9. Sosa, *El episcopado,* 1:297.
10. See Gutiérrez-Brockington, *The Leverage;* Zeitlin, "Ranchers," 23–60.
11. AGIM 600.107r.
12. AGIM 600.128r.
13. Díaz-Polanco & Manzo, *Documentos,* 45.
14. AGIM 600.407v.
15. Manzo argues that alcaldes mayores in this area typically paid well below market values for Indian *mantas* subject to the repartimiento. Manzo, "Comercio," 111.
16. AGIM 600.407v.
17. AGIM 600.115v–116r; Díaz-Polanco y Manzo, *Documentos,* 77–78.
18. AGIP 230A. R 1.6r–9r.
19. AGIP 230.R 4/1.20v; Barabas, "Rebeliones," 239–40.
20. Part of the reason for delay was the transition from viceroy Duque de Albuquerque to Conde de Baños.
21. AGIM 600.107r–v.
22. Góngora, *El corregidor.* See also SP, *Política,* 1:521–22 (2.24.37–38).
23. *Relación cierta,* 305v. My italics.
24. AGIM 600.108r.
25. AGIM 600.107v.
26. AGIM 600.108r.
27. Burns, *Las Siete,* 4:994 (4.25.6). On the history of the word "vassallo" in sixteenth-century New Spain, see Weckman, *The Medieval,* 72–84.

28. SP, *Política*, 1:193, 387–88 (2.2.16; 2.16.63–64).
29. SP, *Política*, 1:174–187 & 413–14 (2.1.2 y ss; 2.18.10; 2.18.13).
30. AGIM 600.399v; AGIM 600.404v.
31. AGIM 600.409r.
32. *Relación cierta*, 305.
33. AGIM 600.131r. See also *Relación cierta*, 306. In a March 1660 petition addressed to the king, Indian petitioners wrote that the events in Tehuantepec had been "neither rebellion nor alzamiento."
34. AGIM 600.132r.
35. Covarrubias, *Tesoro*, 994.
36. See also, Covarrubias, *Tesoro*, entry for "alçar," 79.
37. AGIM 600.132v; *Relación cierta*, 313; AGIM 600.397v.
38. AGIM 600.405v.
39. AGIM 600.404v–405r.
40. SP, *Política*, 1:230 (2.6.1).
41. SP, *Política*, 3:2354–55 (6.8.1).
42. AGIM 600.132r.
43. AGIM 600.122r.
44. Castillo y Bobadilla, *Política*, 110; *Recop.* 2:24v (3.4.8).
45. AGIM 600.122r.
46. AGIM 600.384r; *Relación cierta*, 308.
47. AGIM 600.399v–400r.
48. *Relación cierta*, 305.
49. *Relación cierta*, 322.
50. AGIM 600.400v.
51. *Relación cierta*, 330–31.
52. *Relación cierta*, 313.
53. *Relación cierta*, p. 329–30.
54. AGIM 600.462v–463r.
55. AGIP 230A.R 4/1.6r; *Relación cierta*, 320r–v.
56. *Relación cierta*, 320v.
57. AGIM 600.401r.
58. AGIP 230A.R 1.13r–v.
59. See Díaz-Polanco, *El fuego*, 97.
60. AGIP 230A.R 4/1.9r–11r; *Relación cierta*, 323r–325v.
61. AGIP 230A.R 4/1.10r.
62. AGNI 21.39.57r–58r (57).
63. Díaz-Polanco y Manzo, *Documentos*, 147.
64. *Relación cierta*, 323.
65. Díaz-Polanco y Manzo, *Documentos*, 146.
66. The significance of this sort of imagery is discussed in Cañeque, *The King's*, 119–55.
67. *Relación cierta*, 326r–327v; AGIP 230A.R 4/1.11v–13r.
68. AGIP 230A.R 4/1.17r.
69. Díaz-Polanco, *El fuego*, anexo II, 168.
70. AGIP 230A.R 4/1.21v.

71. AGNI: 20.260.210v (56); 21.74.80v–81r (57).

72. García, "Tumultos," 279.

73. AGIP 230A.R 4/1.19v.

74. AGIP 230A.R 1.

75. AGIP 230A.R 1.6r–9r. Note that where Indian witnesses say Álvarez showed up in the middle of the night, Álvarez said he came during the day.

76. AGIP 230A.R 1.27v.

77. AGIP 230A.R 1.29v.

78. AGIP 230A.R 1.57r–62r.

79. AGIP 230A.R 1.65r–68r.

80. AGIP 230A.R 1.10r–v.

81. AGIP 230A.R 1.12r, 43r.

82. AGIP 230A.R 1.88v–97r.

83. AGIP 230B.R 15/1.7.

84. AGIP 230B.R 16/1.3r–v.

85. AGIP 230B.R 14/1.5r–v.

86. AGIM 41.44/1; 44/4; 44/8; 44/9.

87. AGIM 600.115r–117v.

88. AGIM 600.107v–108r.

89. Montemayor was a known enemy of the Duque, while he and the new viceroy Conde de Baños were allies. On the other hand, the oidores of the audiencia, with the exception of Montemayor, were on bad terms with the Conde de Baños. The details of these internecine struggles I leave to Israel's *Race,* 248–66.

90. AGNI: 19.338.191v; 19.339.191v–192r; 19.340.192r; 19.341.192r–v; 19.342.192v (all 1661).

91. AGIM 600.403r–v.

92. AGIM 600.407v. Italics added.

93. See Israel, *Race,* 262.

94. AGIP 230B.R 18/1.9r–v.

95. AGIP 230B.R 13/1.3v.

96. AGIP 230B.R 20/1.

97. AGIP 230B.R 15/1.

98. AGIP 230B.R 15/1.10v–11r. Borah cites this reversal as a voiding of the entire scheme. As I argue below, documents not available to Borah indicate that the issue dragged out much longer for other villages, until 1665, before being resolved for communities across the board. See Borah, *Justice,* 274.

99. AGIP 230B.R 18.1.

100. AGIM 600.675r–684r.

101. AGIM 600.677r–682v.

102. AGIM 230B.R 20/1.

103. AGIP 230B.R 18/1.

104. *Recop.* 2:221r–v (6.5.21); 2:216v (6.5.61).

105. AGIP 230B.R 13/1.

106. AGIM 600.680r–682v.

107. Diaz-Polanco, *El fuego,* 22.

108. AGIP 230A.R 3/1.
109. AGIP 230A.R 4/1.
110. AGIP 230B.R 17/1.3v.
111. AGIP: 230A: R 8/2; R 8/3; 230B.R 12/1.1r.
112. AGIP 230B.R 20/1.1r–v; R 20/2.1r–v.
113. AGIM 600.684v.
114. Bishop Cuevas y Dávalos briefly served as viceroy during the summer of 1664.
115. AGIM 40: 46/1.1r–v; 46/2.1r–6v; 46/3.1r–2v.
116. AGIP 230A.R 4/1.8v.
117. AGIM 600.474r–v.
118. AGIP 230A.R 4/1.8v.
119. AGIP 230B.R17/1.1; *Relación cierta,* 297.
120. *Relación cierta,* 305v–306v.
121. AGIM 600.881r.
122. Quiroga, *Libro,* 108.
123. Sariñana, *Llantos.*

CHAPTER NINE

1. Taylor, *Landlord,* 82; Pomar-Zurita, *Relaciones,* 101.
2. Gibson, *Spain,* 109; Stein and Stein, *The Colonial,* 81.
3. Others have made the same point. See, Cutter, *The Legal,* 147.
4. In other words, in seeking to understand them as "colonial subjects," we must consider the possibility that they "experienced their own image . . . in contrast to that of the colonizers" positively, not only negatively. Zavala, "Representing," 324.
5. SP, *Política,* 1:577 (2.28.9).
6. Hoberman, "Hispanic-American," 206–7.
7. Soto, *De la justicia,* 1:38; Góngora, *El corregidor,* 223.
8. Maravall, *La cultura,* 1ª pte. For a broad consideration of the world of Spanish aprovechamiento, see Seed, *American.*
9. Saavedra Fajardo, *Empresas,* 111 (empresa 17).
10. SP, *Política,* 1:223 (2.5.18).
11. SP, *Política,* 1:241 (2.6.42).
12. See Guha, *Dominance.*
13. Benton, *Law,* 253–65.
14. SP, *Política,* 1:580–81 (2.28.20 & 21).
15. This view has been attributed to Solórzano y Pereira. See Ayala, *Ideas,* 288.
16. See MacLachlan, *Spain's Empire,* 124: "In reality, justice represented a distributive compromise, not the actual realization of an abstract ideal."
17. This fact suggests a rethinking of the idea of the "scriptorial city" as a province of a small, lettered elite. Indigenous litigants may not have written most of the records that come down to us from legal encounters, but their spoken words are available for us to read, the residual efforts of Spaniards such as

Joseph de Çeli, Agustín Franco, and many other who served as procuradores for Indian ligitants and petitioners. Rama, *La ciudad,* 71–98.

18. Penry, "The Rey," has argued for the centrality of the común in eighteenth-century Alto Perú.

19. Hoberman, "Hispanic American," 209.

20. See, e.g., Taylor, *Magistrates,* 363. Though, paradoxically, the number of amparos appears to have dwindled, an issue worth further exploration.

21. Villaroel, *Enfermedades,* 94–95.

22. Lira González, "Extinción," 299–317; Borah, *Justice,* 382–13.

23. Taylor, *Magistrates,* 13. Why this should have been so is a complex question that ultimately can be addressed only by further research. Speculatively, what Villaroel saw as a bureaucratic inertia may have been part of a second-best strategy of Bourbon governance. By permitting and even encouraging indigenous claimants to bring their grievances to Mexico City, Hapsburg law had set Indian villages as a kind of check on what might otherwise have been unrestrained and unaccountable local power. A more centralized legal system simply was not an option. Even a reforming state like the Bourbons did not have the manpower to monitor goings on in the countryside directly, leaving the reforming Bourbons to rely on Hapsburg law as the only means of checking excesses at the local level. I have an anonymous reader to thank for raising this knotty question.

24. Van Young, "To See," 159.

25. Florescano, *Etnia,* 289.

26. Cope, *The Limits,* 134–36.

27. Thomson, "Popular Aspects," 275, 287.

28. Herrejón Peredo, *Hidalgo,* 15–42.

29. Taylor, *Magistrates,* 471. The phrase "freedom from unjust restraint, rather than freedom as an asbolute good in is own right" is quoted from Taylor.

30. See Guardino, *The Time,* 171–75.

31. See Guardino, *The Time;* Pastor, *Campesinos.*

32. Annino, "Ciudadanía," 87–92.

33. Borah, *Justice,* 412.

34. Lempiéière, "Reflexiones," 35–56.

35. Skinner, *Liberty,* 116.

36. See Nader, "The Crown"; Nader, *Harmony.* My point is not to deny the centrality of notions of "harmony" and "compromise" in village life. In several of the chapters above I have suggested something similar. Rather, I argue that what we now see as an emphasis on harmony in village law represents a dramatic contraction of a much wider field of legal possibility during the colonial period, when dispute and conflict appear to have been as prevalent as calls for harmony and compromise. This contraction may have taken place during the nineteenth century, as liberal legal notions replaced colonial ones and indigenous villages found themselves largely cut off from the political and legal center, where so many legal disputes played themselves. For this reason, contemporary villages remain a crucial source for understanding how and to what extent such ideas have remained alive.

37. Borah, *Justice,* 384.

38. Salvatore et al., *Crime*, 24.
39. See Thompson, *Whigs*, 258–69; Unger, *Knowledge*, 72.
40. Salvatore et al., *Crime*, 15.
41. See, e.g., Lowell, "The Real," 181–85.
42. In this they were not so different from the English of a slightly later period. See Thompson, *Whigs*, 258–69.
43. Colson, *Tradition*, 76.
44. Tau Anzoateguí, *Casuismo*, 485–86. Tau criticizes the overreliance on "state laws and regulations, without attending to revealed conditions and the existence of other modes of generating Law [Derecho]." (485).
45. "The denial of any local autonomy to Native [North] Americans on their reservations gave them less reason to update their traditions of law and order and so connect past with present." Colson, *Tradition*, 87.
46. This is Enrique Dussel's central point about Western "modernity." Though liberal ideology has characterized the modern "self" as the culmination of a historical process of individualization, the conquest of the Americas suggests that the modern self was born of the violent and still unresolved confrontation between "self" and "other." Dussel, "Eurocentrism."
47. This complex and fascinating history is still unfolding. See, e.g., Thomson, "Popular Aspects," 265–92; Guardino, *The Time*; Connaughton, "Conjuring," 459–79; Annino, "Ciudadanía"; Annino et al., "El liberalismo"; Hernández Chávez, *Anencuilco*.
48. Higgins, *Understanding*, 57–101.
49. Bolaños and Verdesio, *Colonialism*, 9. Bolaños is concerned primarily with literary texts, but the attitude he calls for makes sense for historical inquiry as well, perhaps especially with regard to legal records. Salazar Bondy, *¿Existe?*, 126.
50. Sousa Santos, *Toward*, 458–71. Sousa Santos's "cosmopolitan legality" exists in relation to contemporary global capital and liberal legality. But the sense that legality can bridge what might otherwise be seen as separate spheres of endeavor—local, regional, national, international, in Sousa Santos's case—does make sense for seventeenth-century Mexico. The idea is an important one for freeing our understanding of early modern legality from the constraints of the nation-state.
51. MacLachlan, *Criminal*, 1.
52. Here, with Benton, I depart from Guha, who leaves almost no role for agency among indigenous people in colonial settings. Law in New Spain did represent a "moment of that society's internal dynamics" by which an "alien authority" was able to impose itself upon subject peoples and through which subject peoples came to accept and adapt to their own uses and understandings a legal regime imposed from the outside. See Guha, *Dominance*, 64; Benton, *Law*, 254–60.
53. Ayala, *Ideas*, 290.
54. This is not to diminish the importance of "public" rebellions. It is simply to recognize the centrality of day-to-day means of confronting what Colson calls "superordinate power." Colson, *Tradition*, 76.

55. See Taylor, "Between Global," 153: "The relative stability of Spain's rule in America was not simply the product of extremely low levels of mobilization, poor communications, or the heavy hand of force. It had as much to do with the consent of the subjects and with their ingrained beliefs about legitimacy—like the politics of paternalism that Thompson identified as the primary basis of ruling class control in England before the nineteenth century." I agree but qualify the point in two ways. First, these "beliefs" were not only "ingrained" but learned, especially through participiation in law over the seventeenth century. Second, to the extent Taylor is talking about indigenous subjects, the "legitimacy" in which they believed was far more a matter of the context of dispute—their role as tributaries and their vulnerability to extralegal abuse—than what I see as Thompson's somewhat more passive culture of paternalism in *Whigs and Hunters*.

56. It is worth noting that Higgins, in analyzing the Chiapas rebellion begun in 1994, mentions only religion as a legacy from the colonial period on which an indigenous politics has been able to draw. And yet, the three words that so often conclude Zapatista communiqués are "Democracy! Liberty! Justice!" Although the first is a clear reference to postindependence political ideas, we might do well, given the argument presented here, to think more adventurously about the latter two. See Higgins, *Understanding*.

57. One of the three pillars of Sousa Santos's call to reenergize law's "emancipatory" potential in the context of a "cosmopolitan legality" is an unabashed "repoliticization" of law to overcome the distinction between the state and civil society. Politics, he argues, must be freed from "its confinement in the state and political society, a confinement imposed by modern political theory. Such liberation from conventional politics makes possible the repoliticization of law—which, to my mind, is the necessary condition to return to law its emancipatory energies." As an example of a contemporary effort to accomplish this, Sousa Santos points to the indigenous Zapatista movement of southern Mexico. Sousa Santos, *Toward*, 460–65. In this regard it is worth recalling that in 2001 tens of thousands of Mayan Indians marched from Chiapas to Mexico City to demand justicia from the federal government—specifically adhesion to the San Andrés accords reached in 1996—reprising and reinventing the thousands of trips made centuries earlier by those who felt they had the right to make claims before the powers that be.

Sources Cited

Acosta, José de. *De procuranda indorum salute*. Madrid: CSIC, 1984–87 [1588].

Agia, Fray Miguel. *Servidumbres personales de los indios*. Sevilla: Escuela de Estudios Hispano-Americanos de Sevilla, 1946.

Alberro, Solange. *Inquisición y sociedad en México, 1571–70*. México: Fondo de Cultura Económica, 1988.

Almandoz Garmendía, José Antonio, comp. *Fray Alonso de la Veracruz O.E.S.A. y la Encomienda Indiana en la historia eclesiástica novohispana, 1552–1556*. Madrid: Edición crítica de *De dominio infidelium et iusto bello* (1553), 1971.

Altamira, Rafael. *Estudios sobre las fuentes de conocimiento del derecho indiano*. Lisboa, 1900.

Altman, Ida. *Emigrants and Society: Extremadura and America in the Sixteenth Century*. Los Angeles: University of California Press, 1989.

Anderson, A., F. Berdan, and J. Lockhart. *Beyond the Codices: The Nahua View of Mexico*. Berkeley: University of California Press, 1976.

Aninno, Antonio. "Ciudadanía 'versus' gobernabilidad republicana en México. Los orígenes de un dilema." In H. Sabato, coord. *Ciudadanía política y formación de las naciones. Perspectivas históricas de América Latina*. México: Fondo de Cultura Económica, 1999.

Annino, Antonio, Raymond Thomas, and Joseph Buve. *El liberalismo en México*. Münster, Germany: Asociación de Historiadores Latinoamericanistas Europeos, 1993.

Aquinas, St. Thomas. *The Political Ideas of St. Thomas Aquinas*. D. Bigongari, ed. New York: Free Press, 1997.

———. *Summa Theologica*. Allen, TX, 1948, vol. 2.

Arenal, Celestio del. "La teoría de la servidumbre natural en el pensamiento español de los siglos XVI y XVII." *Historiografía y bibliografía americanistas* (1975–1976).

Aristotle. *The Politics*. Oxford University Press, 1980.

Ayala, F. Javier de. *Ideas políticas de Juan de Solórzano*. Sevilla, 1946.

Bakewell, Peter. "Mining in Colonial Spanish America." In L. Bethell. *The Cambridge History of Latin America*. Cambridge University Press, 1984. Vol. 2, 110–51.

———. *Silver Mining and Society in Colonial Mexico, Zacatecas, 1546–1700*. Cambridge University Press, 1971.

Balbuena, Bernardo. *La grandeza mexicana y compendio apologético en alabanza de la poesía*. México: Porruá, 1971.

Barabas, Alicia. "Rebeliones e insurrecciones indígenas en Oaxaca: La história de la resistencia étnica." In Alicia Barabas y Miguel Bartolomé, coords. *Etnicidad y pluralismo cultural: La dinámica étnica en Oaxaca*. México, 1986.

Barrionuevo, Jerónimo de. *Avisos, I*. Madrid: BAE, t. CCXXI.

Baskes, Jeremy. *Indians, Merchants, and Markets: A Reinterpretation of the Repartimiento and Spanish-Indian Economic Relations in Colonial Oaxaca, 1750–1821*. Stanford, CA: Stanford University Press, 2000.

Baudot, George. *México y los albores del discurso colonial*. México: Ed. Patria, 1996.

Bauer, Arnold. "Rural Workers in Spanish America: Problems of Peonage and Oppression." *Hispanic American Historical Review* 59:1 (Feb. 1979): 34–63.

Benton, Laura. *Law and Colonial Cultures: Legal Regimes in World History, 1400–1900*. Cambridge University Press, 2002.

Bermúdez de Pedraza, Francisco. *Arte legal para estudiar la jurisprudencia*. Salamanca, 1612.

Bernand, Carmen et Serge Gruzinski. *Histoire du Nouveau Monde: Les métissages (1550–1640)*. Paris: Fayard, 1993.

Bethell, Leslie. "A Note on the Native American Population on the Eve of the European Invasions." In L. Bethell, ed. *The Cambridge History of Latin America*. Cambridge University Press, 1984.

Bolaños, Félix, and Gustavo Verdesio, eds. *Colonialism Past and Present: Reading and Writing about Colonial Latin America Today*. Albany: State Universitiy of New York Press, 2002.

Borah, Woodrow. *Justice by Insurance: The General Indian Court of Colonial Mexico and the Legal Aides of the Half-Real*. Berkeley: University of California Press, 1983.

Boyer, Richard. "Honor among Plebeians: *Mala Sangre* and Social Reputation." In L. Johnson and S. Lipsett-Rivera. *The Faces of Honor: Sex, Shame, and Violence in Colonial Latin America*. Albuquerque: University of New Mexico Press, 1998.

———. *Lives of Bigamists: Marriage, Family and Community in Colonial Mexico*. Albuquerque: University of New Mexico Press, 1995.

Bratli, Charles. *Philippe II, Roi d'Espagne*. Paris, 1912.

Brett, Annabel. *Liberty, Right, and Nature: Individual Rights in Later Scholastic Thought*. Cambridge University Press, 1997.

Burkhart, Louise. *Holy Wednesday: A Drama from Early Colonial Mexico*. Philadelphia: University of Pennsylvania Press, 1996.

———. *The Slippery Earth: Nahua-Christian Moral Dialogue in Sixteenth-Century Mexico*. Tucson: University of Arizona Press, 1989.

Burman, Sandra, and Barbara Harrell-Bond. *The Imposition of Law*. New York: Academic Press, 1979.

Burns, R., ed. *Las Siete Partidas*. Philadelphia: University of Pennsylvania Press, 2001.

Cañeque, Alejandro. *The King's Living Image: The Culture and Politics of Viceregal Power in Colonial Mexico*. New York: Routledge, 2004.

Carrasco, Pedro de. *The Tenochca Empire of Ancient Mexico: The Triple Alliance of Tenochtitlan, Tetzcoco, and Tlacopan*. Norman: University of Oklahoma Press, 1999.

Cartas de Indias. Madrid, 1977.

Casas, Bartolomé de las. *Apologética historia de las indias*. M. Serrano y Sanz, ed. Madrid, 1909.

Castañeda Delgado, Paulino. "La condición miserable del indio y sus privilegios." *Anuario de Estudios Americanos* XXVIII (1971): 3e, 9–14.

Castillo de Bobadilla, Jerónimo. *Política para corregidores y señores de vasallos* . . . Amberes: Juan Bautista Verdussen, 1704.

Castro Gutiérrez, Felipe. "Conflictos y fraudes electorales en los cabildos indígenas de Michoacán colonial." *Journal of Latin American Studies* 4:2 (Dec. 1998): 41–68.

Ceballos, Gerónimo de. *Arte real para el buen gobierno de los reyes y príncipes y sus vasallos*. Toledo: D. Rodríguez, 1623.

Chance, John K. *Race and Class in Colonial Oaxaca*. Stanford, CA: Stanford University Press, 1978.

Chevalier, François. *La formation des grands domaines au Mexique. Terre et société aux XVIe–XVIIe siècles*. Paris: Institut dÉthnologie, 1952.

———. *Land and Society in Colonial Mexico: The Great Hacienda*. Berkeley: University of California Press, 1963.

Clendinnen, Inga. *Ambivalent Conquests: Maya and Spaniard in Yucatán, 1517–1570*. Cambridge University Press, 1987.

———. *Aztecs: An Interpretation*. Cambridge University Press, 1991.

Cline, Howard F. "Civil Congregations of the Indians of New Spain, 1598–1606." *Hispanic American Historical Review* 29:3 (Aug. 1949): 349–69.

———. "The Oztoticpac Lands Map of Texcoco, 1540." *Quarterly Journal of the Library of Congress* 23:2 (Apr. 1966): 76–116.

Cline, S. L. *Colonial Culhuacán, 1580–1600: A Social History of an Aztec Town*. Albuquerque: University of New Mexico Press, 1986.

Códice Mendieta. Documentos Franciscanos. Siglos XVI y XVII. Tomo I. México: Díaz de León, 1892; Guadalajara, facs. 1971.

Colección de documentos inéditos relativos al descubrimiento, conquista y organización de las antiguas posesiones españolas. Madrid: Ed. Pacheco, Cárdenas y Mendoza, 1864–89.

Colección de documentos inéditos . . . sacados de los archivos del Reino, muy principalmente del de las Indias. 1a ser. Madrid, 1864–84.

Colección de documentos sobre Coyoacán. P. Carrasco y J. Monjara-Ruiz, eds. México, 1976.

Collier, Jane Fishburne. *Law and Social Change in Zinacantan.* Stanford, CA: Stanford University Press, 1973.

Colson, Elizabeth. *Tradition and Contract: The Problem of Order.* University of Chicago Press, 1974.

Conley, John M., and William M. O'Barr. *Rules versus Relationships: The Ethnography of Legal Discourse.* University of Chicago Press, 1990.

Connaugton, Brian. "Conjuring the Body Politic from the *Corpus Mysticum*: The Post-Independent Pursuit of Public Opinion in Mexico, 1821–1854." *The Americas* 55:3 (Jan. 1999): 459–79.

Cook, Noble David. *Born to Die: Disease and New World Conquest, 1492–1650.* Cambridge University Press, 1998.

Cook, S. F., and W. Borah. *The Aboriginal Population of Central Mexico on the Eve of the Spanish Conquest.* Berkeley: University of California Press, 1963.

———. *Essays on Population History: Mexico and the Caribbean.* 2 vols. Berkeley: University of California Press, 1971–74.

Cook, S. F., and L. B. Simpson. *The Population of Central Mexico in the Sixteenth Century.* Berkeley: University of California Press, 1948.

Cope, R. Douglas. *The Limits of Racial Domination: Plebeian Society in Colonial Mexico City, 1660–1692.* Madison: University of Wisconsin Press, 1994.

Corominas, Joan. *Breve diccionario etimológico de la lengua castellana.* Madrid: Gredos, 1961.

Covarrubias, Sebastián de. *Tesoro de la lengua castellana o española.* Barcelona: S. A. Horta, 1943, fasc. de la versión de 1611.

Cover, Robert M. "The Supreme Court 1982 Term—Forewords: *Nomos* and Narrative." *Harvard Law Review* 97:4 (1983–84): 4–68.

———. "Violence and the Word." *Yale Law Journal* 95 (1985–86): 1601–29.

Crosby, Alfred. *The Columbian Exchange: Biological and Cultural Consequences of 1492.* Westport, CT: Greenwood Press, 1972.

Cuevas, Mariano, ed. *Documentos inéditos del siglo XVI para la historia de México.* México, 1975.

———. *Historia de la iglesia en México.* México, 1946.

Cutter, Charles. *The Legal Culture of Northern New Spain, 1700–1810.* Albuquerque: University of New Mexico Press, 1995.

———. "The Legal System as a Touchstone of Identity in Colonial New Mexico." In L. Roniger & T. Herzog, eds. *The Collective and the Public in Latin America: Cultural Identities and Political Order.* Portland, OR: Sussex, 2000.

Dahlgrem, Barbro. *La grana cochinilla.* México: UNAM, 1990.

Díaz del Castillo, Bernal. *Historia verdadera de la conquista de la Nueva España.* Madrid: BAE, t. XXVI.

Díaz-Polanco, Héctor, coord. *El fuego de la inobediencia: Autonomía y rebelión india en el Obispado de Oaxaca.* México, 1992.
    1. Héctor Díaz-Polanco, "Sociedad colonial y rebelión indígena en el Obispado de Oaxaca (1660)."
    2. Héctor Díaz-Polanco y Consuelo Sánchez, "El vigor de la espada restauradora. La represión de las rebeliones indias en Oaxaca (1660–61)."

3. Marcello Carmagnani, "Un movimiento político indio: La 'rebelión' de Tehuantepec, 1660–61."

4. Carlos Manzo, "Comercio y rebelión en el Obispado de Oaxaca. Tehuantepec y Nexapa, 1660–61." Díaz-Polanco, Héctor y Carlos Manzo, coords. *Documentos inéditos o muy raros para la historia de México.* México, 1982.

Diccionario grande de la lengua de Michoacán. J. Benedict Warren, ed. Morelia: FIMAX, 1991.

Dicey, Albert Venn. *An Introduction to the Study of the Law of the Constitution.* Indianapolis: Liberty/Classics, 1982.

D'Ors, Álvaro. "El servicio del derecho romano a la libertad." *Revista Chilena de Historia del Derecho* (1966): 9–21.

Durán, Diego. *History of the Indies of New Spain.* D. Heyden, trans. Norman: University of Oklahoma Press, 1994.

Dussel, Enrique. "Eurocentrism and Modernity (Introduction to the Frankfurt Lectures)," *boundary* 2 20:3 (1993): 65–76.

Elliot, John H. *Imperial Spain, 1469–1716.* New York: Penguin, 1963.

Erickson, Amy. *Women & Property in Early Modern England.* New York: Routledge, 1993.

Fairén Guillén, Victor. *Antecedentes aragoneses de los juicios de amparo.* México: UNAM, 1971.

Farriss, Nancy. *Maya Society under Colonial Rule: The Collective Enterprise of Survival.* Princeton University Press, 1984.

Florescano, Enrique. *Etnía, estado y nación: Ensayo sobre las identidades colectivas en México.* México: Nuevo Siglo Autor, 1997.

———. "The Formation and Economic Structure of the Hacienda in New Spain." In L. Bethell, ed. *The Cambridge History of Latin America.* Vol. II. Cambridge University Press, 1984, 153–88.

García, Genaro. "Tumultos y rebeliones acaecidos en México." In H. Díaz-Polanco y Carlos Manzo, coords. *Documentos inéditos o muy raros para la historia de México.* México, 1982.

García Castro, René. *Indios, territorio y poder en la provincia Matlatzinca. La negociación del espacio político de los pueblos otomianos, siglos XV–XVII.* México: CONCACULTA, 1999.

García Gallo, Alfonso. "La ley como fuente del derecho en Indias en el siglo XVI." *Anuario de historia del derecho español* 21–22 (1952–1953): 607–630.

———. *Manual del derecho español.* 1975.

García Martínez, Bernardo. *Los pueblos de la sierra: el poder y el espacio entre los indios del norte de Puebla hasta 1700.* México: El Colégio de México, 1987.

Gerhard, Peter. "Congregaciones de indios en la Nueva España antes de 1570." *Historia Mexicana* 26:3 (enero-marzo 1977): 347–95.

———. *A Guide to the Historical Geography of New Spain.* Norman: University of Oklahoma Press, 1972.

———. *The Northern Frontier of New Spain.* Princeton University Press, 1982.

Gibson, Charles. *The Aztecs under Spanish Rule: A History of the Indians of the Valley of Mexico, 1519–1810*. Stanford, CA: Stanford University Press, 1964.

———. *Spain in America*. New York: Harper & Row, 1966.

Góngora, Bartolomé de. *El corregidor sagáz: Abisos, y documentos morales; para los que lo fueren*. Madrid: 1950, originally published 1656.

Gordon, Robert. "Critical Legal Histories." *Stanford Law Review* 36:57 (Jan. 1984): 57–125.

Griffin, William. *Culture Change and Shifting Populations in Central Northern Mexico*. Tucson: University of Arizona Press, Anthropological Papers, 1969, 10–39.

Grusinzki, Serge. *The Conquest of Mexico: The Incorporation of Indian Societies into the Western World, 16th–18th Centuries*. Cambridge, MA: Polity Press, 1993.

Guha, Ranjit. *Dominance without Hegemony: History and Power in Colonial India*. Harvard University Press, 1997.

Guardino, Peter. *The Time of Liberty: Popular Political Culture in Oaxaca, 1750–1850* Durham: Duke University Press, 2005.

Gutiérrez-Brockington, Lolita. *The Leverage of Labor: Managing the Cortés Haciendas in Tehuantepec, 1588–1688*. Durham: Duke University Press, 1989.

Hanke, Lewis. *All Mankind is One: A Study of the Disputation between Bartolomé de las Casas and Juan Ginés de Sepúlveda on the Religious and Intellectual Capacity of the American Indians*. Dekalb: Northern Illinois University Press, 1974.

———. "A Modest Proposal for a Moratorium on Grand Generalizations: Some Thoughts on the Black Legend." *Hispanic America Historical Review* 51:1 (Feb. 1971): 112–27.

———. "More Heat and Some Light on the Spanish Struggle for Justice in the Conquest of America." *Hispanic American Historical Review* 44:3 (Aug. 1964): 297–304.

———. *The Spanish Struggle for Justice in the Conquest of America*. New York: Little, Brown, 1965.

Haring, Clarence. *Los bucaneros de las Indias Orientales en el siglo XVII*. Brujas, 1939.

Haskett, Robert. *Indigenous Rulers: An Ethnohistory of Town Government in Colonial Cuernavaca*. Albuquerque: University of New Mexico Press, 1991.

Haslip-Viera, Gabriel. *Crime and Punishment in Late Colonial Mexico, 1692–1810*. Albuquerque: University of Mexico Press, 1999.

Heath, Shirley Brice. *Telling Tongues: Language Policy in Mexico—Colony to Nation* (New York: Teachers College Press, 1972).

Hera, Alberto de la. "El derecho de los Indios a la libertad y la fe: La bula 'Sublimis Deus' y los problemas indianos que la motivaron." *Anuario de Historia del Derecho Español* XXVI:1 (Madrid, 1956): 89–181.

Hernández Chávez, Alicia. *Anenecuilco. Memoria y vida de un pueblo*. México, 1999.

Herrejón Paredo, Carlos. *Hidalgo. Razones de la insurgencia y biografía documental.* México: SEP, 1986.

Herrup, Cynthia. *The Common Peace: Participation and the Criminal Law in Seventeenth-Century England.* Cambridge University Press, 2000.

Herzog, Tamar. *La administración como un fenómeno social: la justicia penal de la ciudad de Quito (1650–1750).* Madrid: Centro de Estudios Constitucionales, 1995.

Hespanha, Antonio M. *Vísperas del Leviathán. Instituciones y poder político (Portugal, siglo XVII).* F. J. Bouza, trans. Madrid, 1989.

Hevia Bolaños, Juan de. *Curia philipica.* Vols. 1–2. Valladolid: Lex Nova, 1989.

Higgins, Nicholas. *Understanding the Chiapas Rebellion: Modernist Visions and the Invisible Indian.* Austin: University of Texas Press, 2004.

Hill, Ruth. "Caste Theater and Poetry in 18th-Century Spanish America." *Revista de Estudios Hispánicos* 34 (2000): 3–26.

Hoberman, Louisa. "Hispanic American Political Theory as a Distinct Tradition." *Journal of the History of Ideas* (Apr.–Jun. 1980): 199–218.

Hoekstra, Rik. *Two Worlds Merging: The Transformation of Society in the Valley of Puebla, 1570–1640.* Amsterdam: CEDLA, 1993.

Horcasitas, Fernando. *El teatro Nahuatl: épocas novohispana y moderna.* México: UNAM, 1974.

Horn, Rebecca. *Postconquest Coyoacán: Nahua-Spanish Relations in Central Mexico, 1519–1650.* Stanford, CA: Stanford University Press, 1997.

Iglesias, Miriam. "Tierras indias bajo ley española. Cuauthinchán, Puebla, México: siglo XVI." *Anuario IEHS* 13 (1998): 215–33.

Instrucciones y memorias de los virreyes novohispanos. Tomos 1–2. E. de la Torre Villar, ed. México: Porrúa, 1991.

Israel, Jonathan I. *Race, Class, and Politics in Colonial Mexico, 1610–1670.* Oxford University Press, 1975.

———. *Razas, clases sociales y vida política en el México colonial, 1610–1670.* México: Fonde de Cultura Económica, 1997.

Ixtlilxochitl, Fernando de Alva. *Obras históricas.* Vol. II. A. Chavero, ed. México: Ed. Nacional, 1952.

Jones, Oakah, Jr. *Nueva Viscaya: Heartland of the Spanish Frontier.* Albuquerque: University of New Mexico Press, 1988.

Joseph, Gilbert, ed. *Reclaiming the Political in Latin America: Essays from the North.* Durham: Duke University Press, 2001.

Juan y Colom, Joseph. *Instrucción jurídica de escribanos, abogados y jueces ordinarios de juzgados inferiores.* Madrid, 1742, 2a impresión.

Karttunen, Frances. *Analytical Dictionary of Nahuatl.* Norman: University of Oklahoma Press, 1992.

Karttunen, Frances, and James Lockhart. *Nahuatl in the Middle Years: Language Contact Phenomena in Texts of the Colonial Period.* Berkeley: University of California Press, 1976.

Keen, Benjamin. *The Aztec Image in Western Thought.* New Brunswick: Rutgers University Press, 1971.

————. "The Black Legend Revisited: Assumptions and Realities." *Hispanic American Historical Review* 49:4 (Nov. 1969): 703–19.

————. "The White Legend Revisited: A Reply to Prof. Hanke's Modest Proposal."*Hispanic American Historical Review* 51:2 (May 1971): 336–55.

Kellogg, Susan. *Law and the Transformation of Aztec Culture, 1500–1700.* Norman: University of Oklahoma Press, 1995.

Konetzke, R., ed. *Colección de documentos para la historia de la formación social de hispanoamérica, 1493–1810.* Vol. 1. Madrid: CSIC, 1953: 1493–1592.

Lackoff, George & Mark Johnson. *Philosophy in the Flesh: The Embodied Mind and Its Challenge to Western Thought.* New York: Basic Books, 1999.

Lempiéière, Annick. "Reflexiones sobre la terminología política del liberalismo." In B. Connaughton, C. Illades, y S. Pérez Toledo, coords. *Construcción de la legitimidad política en México.* México: El Colegio de Michoacán, 1999.

León Pinelo, Antonio. *Tratado de las confirmaciones reales.* [1630] Buenos Aires: Talleres s. a. Casa Jacobs Peuser, ltda., 1922.

Levene, Ricardo. *Introducción a la historia del derecho indiano.* Buenos Aires: V. Abelado, 1924.

Lipsett-Rivera, Sonia. "Indigenous Communities and Water Rights in Colonial Puebla: Patterns of Resistance." *Americas* 48:4 (1992): 463–83.

————. "*De Obra y Palabra:* Patterns of Insults in Mexico, 1750–1856." *The Americas* 54:4 (Apr. 1998): 511–39.

Lira González, Andrés. *El amparo colonial y el juicio de amparo mexicano (antecedentes novohispanos del juicio de amparo).* México: Fondo de Cultura Económica, 1971.

————. "Extinción del Juzgado de Indios." *Revista de la Facultad de Derecho de México* 26:101–02 (ene.–jun. 1976): 299–317.

————. "La voz comunidad en la Recopilación de 1680." *Poder y presión fiscal en la América española (siglos XVI, XVII y XVIII): Trabajos del VI Congreso del Instituto Internacional de Historia del Derecho Indiano en homenaje al Dr. Alfonso García-Gallo.* Buenos Aires, 1986.

Llaguno, José. *La personalidad jurídica del indio en el III Concilio Provincial de México (1585).* México: Porrúa, 1963.

Lockhart, James. *The Nahuas after the Conquest: A Social and Cultural History of the Indians of Central Mexico, Sixteenth through Eighteenth Centuries.* Stanford, CA: Stanford University Press, 1992.

Lockhart, J. F. Berdan, and A. Anderson. *The Tlaxcalan Actas: A Compendium of the Records of the Cabildo of Tlaxcala (1545–1627).* Salt Lake City: University of Utah Press, 1986.

Lockhart, James, and Enrique Otte. *Letters and People of the Spanish Indies: Sixteenth Century.* Cambridge University Press, 1976.

Lowell, W. G. "The Real Country and the Legal Country: Spanish Ideals and Mayan Realities in Colonial Guatemala." *GeoJournal* 26:2 (Feb. 1992): 181–85.

Luciani, Frederick. "The *Comedia de San Francisco Borja* (1640): The Mexican Jesuits and the 'Education of the Prince.'" *Colonial Latin American Review* 2:1/2 (1993): 121–41.

MacLachlan, Colin. *Criminal Justice in 18th-Century Mexico.* Berkeley: University of California Press, 1974.

———. *Spain's Empire in the New World: The Role of Ideas in Institutional and Social Change.* Berkeley: University of California Press, 1988.

Madden, Marie. *Political Theory and Law in Medieval Spain.* New York: Fordham University Press, 1930.

Maitland, Frederic William. *Town and Borough. Being the Ford Lectures delivered in the University of Oxford in the October term of 1897. Together with an appendix of notes relating to the history of the town of Cambridge.* London, 1898.

Malagón Barceló, Javier. "Una colonización de gente de leyes." *Estudios de historia y derecho.* México: Universidad Veracruzana, 1966.

Maravall, José Antonio. *La cultura del Barroco: análisis de una estructura histórica.* Barcelona: Ed. Ariel, 1975.

———. "Saavedra Fajardo: Moral de acomodación y carácter conflictivo de la libertad." En *Estudios de historia del pensamiento español.* Madrid: Ed. Cultura Hispanica, 1984.

Mariana, Juan de. *The King and the Education of the King (De Rege et Regis Institutione).* G. A. Moore, trans. Washington, DC: Country Dollar Press, 1948.

Martin, Cheryl English. "Popular Speech and Social Order in Northern Mexico, 1650–1830." *Comparative Studies of Society and History* 32:3 (Apr. 1990): 305–24.

———. *Rural Society in Colonial Morelos.* Albuquerque: University of New Mexico Press, 1985.

Martínez, Hildeberto. *Codiciaban la tierra: el despojo agrario en los señoríos de Tecamachaloc y Quecholac (Puebla, 1520–1650).* México: IIESA, 1994.

———. *Colección de documentos coloniales de Tepeaca.* México: INAH, 1984.

Maxwell, Judith, and Craig Hanson. *Of the Manners of Speaking that the Old Ones Had: The Metaphors of Andrés Olmos in the TULAL Manuscript.* Salt Lake City: University of Utah Press, 1992.

MacLachlan, Colin M. *Spain's Empire in the New World: The Role of Institutional Ideas and Social Change.* Berkeley: University of California Press, 1988.

Melville, Elinor G. K. *A Plague of Sheep: Environmental Consequences of the Conquest of Mexico.* Cambridge University Press, 1997.

Méndez, J., G. O'Donnell, and P. Pinheiro, eds. *The (Un)Rule of Law and the Underprivileged in Latin America.* University of Notre Dame Press, 1999.

Menegus, Margarita. "La economía indígena y su articulación al mercado en Nueva España. El repartimiento forzoso de mercancías. En Margarita Menegus, ed. *El repartimiento forzoso de mercancías en México, Perú y Filipinas.* México: UNAM 2000, 9–64.

Méntz, Brigida von. *Trabajo, sujeción y libertad en el centro de la Nueva España: Esclavos, aprendices, campesinos y operarios manufactureros, siglos XVI a XVIII.* México: Porrúa, 1999.

Merola, Jerónimo. *República orginal sacada del cuerpo humano.* Barcelona: 1587.

Mills, Kenneth, and William Taylor, eds. *Colonial Spanish America: A Documentary History.* Wilmington, DE: Scholarly Resources, 1998.

Minow, M. C. *Latin American Law: A History of Private Law and Institutions in Spanish America.* Austin: University of Texas Press, 2004.

Molina, Fray Alonso de. *Confesionario mayor en la lengua mexicana y castellana.* México: UNAM, 1984.

———. *Vocabulario en lengua castellana y mexicana y mexicana castellana.* México: Porrúa, 1970.

Monterroso y Alvarado, Gabriel. *Práctica civil y criminal y instrucción de escrivanos.* Madrid: Pedro Madrigal, 1603.

Mörner, Magnus. *La corona española y los fóraneos en los pueblos de indios de América.* Madrid: Ed. Ce Cultura Hispánica, 1999.

Muro Romero, Fernando. "La reforma del pacto colonial en Indias. Notas sobre instituciones de gobierno y sociedad en el siglo XVII." *Jahrbuch für Geschichte von Staat, Wirthschaft und Gesellschaft Lateinamerikas* 19 (1982): 47–68.

Nader, Laura. "The Crown, the Colonists, and the Course of Zapotec Village Law. In J. Starr and J. Collier, eds. *History and Power in the Study of Law: New Directions in Legal Anthropology.* Ithaca, NY: Cornell University Press, 1989.

———. *Harmony and Ideology: Justice and Control in a Zapotec Mountain Village.* Stanford, CA: Stanford University Press, 1990.

———. *The Life of the Law: Anthropological Projects.* Berkeley: University of California Press, 2002.

Nagler, Robert. "Guatemala: Indian Attitudes toward Land Tenure." *Journal of Inter-American Studies* 9:4 (1967): 619–39.

Nueva colección de documentos para la historia de México. Vol. 2. México, 1892.

Nueva recopilación de las leyes destos reynos. Madrid, 1640.

Offner, Jerome. *Law and Politics in Aztec Texcoco.* Cambridge University Press, 1983.

O'Gorman, Edmundo. "Bibliotecas y librerías coloniales, 1585–1694." *Boletín del Archivo General de la Nación.* X:4. México, 1939.

———. *La invención de América: Investigación acerca de la estructura histórica del Nuevo Mundo y del sentido de su devenir.* México: Fondo de Cultura Económica, 1958.

Osborn, Wayne. "Indian Land Retention in Colonial Meztitlan." *Hispanic American Historical Review* 53:2 (1973): 217–38.

Ots Capdequí, José María. *Manual de historia del derecho español en las Indias y del derecho propiamente indiano.* México: Ed. Losada, 1945.

———. *El régimen de la tierra en la América española durante el período colonial.* Trujillo: Universidad de Santo Domingo, 1946.

Owensby, Brian. "How Juan and Leonor Won Their Freedom: Litigation and Liberty in Seventeenth-Century Mexico." *Hispanic American Historical Review* 85:1 (Feb. 2005): 39–79.

Pagden, Anthony. *Spanish Imperialism and the Political Imagination.* New Haven, CT: Yale University Press, 1990.

Palafox y Mendoza, Juan de. "De la naturaleza del indio." In G. García, ed. *Documentos inéditos o muy raros para la historia de México.* Tomo VII. México: Carranza, 1906.

Parry, John. *The Sale of Public Office in the Spanish Indies under the Hapsburgs.* Berkeley: University of California Press, 1953.

———. *The Spanish Seaborne Empire.* New York: 1966.

Pastor, María Alba. *Crisis y recomposición social: Nueva España en el tránsito del siglo XVI al XVII.* México: Fondo de Cultura Económica, 1999.

Pastor, Roberto. "El repartimiento de mercancías y los alcaldes mayores novohispanos: Un sistema de explotación de sus orígenes a la crisis de 1810." In W. Borah, ed. *El gobierno provincial en la Nueva España, 1570–1787* México: UNAM 2002, 219–58.

Pastor, Rodolfo. *Campesinos y reformas: la Mixteca, 1700–1856.* México: El Colegio de México, 1987.

Peña Montenegro. *Itinerario para parrocos de indios: en que se tratan las materias mas particulares, tocantes a ellos, para su buena administracion.* Madrid: Ioseph Fernandez de Buendia, 1668; Madrid 1771; Guyaquil, Ecuador, 1985.

Pereña Vicente, Luciano. *Hacia una sociología del Bien Común (el Bien Común en los juristas clásicos españoles).* Madrid, 1955.

Peset, Mariano y Margarita Menegus. "Rey propietario o rey soberano." *Historia Mexicana* XLIII:4 (abr.–jun. 1994): 563–99.

Phipps, Helen. *Some Aspects of the Agrarian Question in Mexico.* Austin: University of Texas Bulletin, no. 2515, 1925.

Piho, Virve. *La secularización de las parroquias en la Nueva España y su repercusión en San Andrés Calpan.* México: INAH, 1981.

Pomar-Zurita, Juan de. "Relación de Tezcuco." *En Relaciones de Texcoco y de la Nueva España, Pomar-Zurita.* México: Salvador Chávez Hayhde, 1941.

Prem, Hans. *Milpa y hacienda. Tenencia de la tierra indígena y española en la cuenca del alto Atoyac, Puebla, México (1520–1650).* Wiesbaden, 1978.

———. "Spanish Colonization and Indian Property in Central Mexico, 1521–1620." *Annals of the Association of American Geographers* 83:2 (Sept. 1992): 444–60.

Quevedo y Hoyos, Antonio de. *Libro de indicios y tormentos: que contiene toda la práctica criminal y modo de sustanciar el proceso indicativamente.* Madrid: Francisco Martínez, 1632.

Quiroga, Pedro de. *Libro intitulado coloquios de la verdad.* Sevilla: Centro Oficial de Estudios Americanistas, 1922.

Rama, Ángel. *La ciudad letrada.* Santiago, Chile: Tajamar Editores, 2004.

Real Academia Española, La. *Diccionario de autoridades.* Madrid, 1737; Madrid: Gredos, 1969. Reprint of *Diccionario de la lengua castellana.*

Recopilación de leyes de los reynos de las Indias, 1680. Madrid: Ivlian Paredes, 1681.

Redondo Redondo, María Luísa. *Utopía Vitoriana y Realidad Indiana.* Madrid: Fundación Universitaria Española, 1992.

Relación cierta y verdadera de lo que svcedio, y a cvcedido en esta villa de Gvadalcacar Provincia de Tehuantepeque desde los 22 de março de 1660. Hasta los quatro de Iulio de 1661. BN (Madrid), Mss. 2387.

Restall, Matthew. *The Maya World: Yucatec Culture and Society, 1550–1850.* Stanford, CA: Stanford University Press, 1999.

———. *Seven Myths of the Spanish Conquest.* Oxford University Press, 2003.

Ribadeneyra, Pedro de. *Tratado de la religion y virtudes que debe tener el principe christiano, para gobernar y conservar sus estados: contra lo que Nicolás Machiavelo, y los políticos de este tiempo enseñan.* Madrid: P. Aznar, 1788.

Ripodas Ardanaz, Daisy. "Los indios y la figura jurídica del rey durante el quinientos." *Justicia, sociedad y economía en la América española (siglos XVI, XVII y XVIII): Trabajos del VI Congreso del Instituto Internacional de Historia del Derecho Indiano.* Buenos Aires, 1983.

Rojas, Basilio. *La rebelión de Tehuantepec.* México: SMGE, 1964.

Rojas Rabiela, T., E. L. Rea López, & C. Medina Lima, orgs. *Vidas y bienes olvidados: Testamentos indígenas novohispanos.* México: CIESAS, 2000.

"Romance a Mexico." BN, Mss. 19387.

"Romance en lengua de yndio mexicano medio ladino." BN (Madrid), Mss. 19387.

Saavedra Fajardo, Diego. *Empresas políticas: idea de un príncipe político cristiano representada en cien emblemas.* Murcia, 1985.

Sahagún, Bernardino de. *Historia general de las cosas de Nueva España.* A. M. Garibay, ed. México: Porrúa, 1956.

Salazar Bondy, Augusto. *¿Existe una filosofía de nuestra América?* México: Siglo XXI, 1968.

Salvatore, R., C. Aguirre, and G. Joseph, eds. *Crime and Punishment in Latin America: Law and Society since Late Colonial Times.* Durham: Duke University Press, 2001.

Sánchez-Albornoz, Nicolás. "The Population of Colonial Spanish America." In L. Bethell, ed. *The Cambridge History of Latin America.* Cambridge University Press, 1984.

Santa María, Fray Juan de. *Tratado de república y policía cristiana.* Madrid, 1615.

Sariñana, Isidro. *Llantos del Occidente en el ocaso del más claro sol de las Españas.* BN, Madrid: Vda. de Bernardo Calderón, 1666.

Schroeder, Susan, ed. *Native Resistance and the Pax Colonial in New Spain.* Lincoln: University of Nebraska Press, 1998.

Seed, Patricia. *American Pentimento: The Invention of Indians and the Pursuit of Riches.* Minneapolis: University of Minnesota Press, 2001.

———. "The Requirement: A Protocol of Conquest." In Patricia Seed, ed., *Ceremonies of Possession in Europe's Conquest of the New World, 1492–1640.* Cambridge University Press, 1995.

Las Siete Partidas del Sabio Rey don Alfonso el nono, nuevamente glosadas por el licenciado Gregorio López del Consejo Real de Indias de su Magestad. Salamanca: Andrea de Portonaris, 1555.

Simpson, Lesley. *The Encomienda in New Spain: The Beginning of Spanish Mexico*. Berkeley: University of California Press, 1966.

Skinner, Quentin. *The Foundations of Modern Political Thought*. Cambridge University Press, 1978.

———. *Liberty before Liberalism*. Cambridge University Press, 1998.

Solano, Francisco de. *Cedulario de tierras. Compilación de legislación agraria colonial (1497–1820)*. México: UNAM, 1984.

Solórzano y Pereira, Juan. *Política indiana*. Madrid: Biblioteca Castro, 1996.

"Soneto a Mexico." BN (Madrid), Mss. 19387.

Sosa, Francisco. *El episcopado mexicano*. Vol. I. México, 1962.

Soto, Domingo de. *De Iustitia et Iure*. Madrid: Instituto de Estudios Políticos, 1968.

———. *De la justicia y del derecho*. Madrid: 1967, originally published 1556.

Sousa Santos, Boaventura de. *Toward a New Legal Common Sense*. London: Butterworths, 2002.

Soustelle, Jacques. *La vie quotidiene des Aztèques à la vielle de la conquête espagnole*. Paris, 1955.

Spores, Ronald. "Differential Response to Colonial Control among the Mixtecs and Zapotecs of Oaxaca." In Susan Schroeder, ed. *Native Resistance and the Pax Colonial in New Spain*. Lincoln: University of Nebraska Press, 1998, 30–46.

———. *The Mixtecs in Ancient and Colonial Times*. Norman: University of Oklahoma Press, 1984.

Starr, J., and J. Collier, eds. *History and Power in the Study of Law: New Directions in Legal Anthroplogy*. Ithaca, NY: Cornell University Press, 1989.

Stavig, Ward. *The World of Tupac Amaru: Conflict, Community, and Identity in Colonial Peru*. Lincoln: University of Nebraska Press, 1999.

Stegman, A. " Le mot 'politique' et ses implications dans la littérature européene du début du XVIIe siècle." *Cahiers de lexicologie* II (1968): 33–47.

Stein, Stanley, and Barbara Stein. *The Colonial Heritage of Latin America. Essays on Economic Dependence in Perspective*. Oxford University Press, 1970.

Stern, Steve. *Peru's Indian Peoples and the Challenge of Spanish Conquest: Huamanga to 1640*. Madison: University of Wisconsin Press, 1982.

———, ed. *Resistance, Rebellion, and Consciousness in the Andean Peasant World, 18th to 20th Centuries*. Madison: University of Wisconsin Press, 1987.

———. *The Secret History of Gender: Women, Men, and Power in Late Colonial Mexico*. Durham: University of North Carolina Press, 1995.

———. "The Social Significance of Judicial Institutions in an Exploitative Society: Huamanga, Peru, 1570–1640." In G. Collier, R. Rosaldo, and J. Wirth, eds., *The Inca and Aztec States, 1400–1800: Anthropology and History*. New York: Academic Press, 1982, 289–320.

Suárez, Francisco. *De legibus: De Legis Obligatione—Edición crítica bilingüe*. Madrid, 1972.

Suárez de Figueroa, Christóval. *El pasajero: advertencias utilísimas a la vida humana*. Madrid: Biblioteca Renacimiento, 1913; originally published, Madrid, 1617.

Tamanaha, Brian Z. *On the Rule of Law: History, Politics, Theory*. Cambridge University Press, 2004.

Tau Anzoateguí, Victor. *Casuismo y sistema: indagación histórica sobre el espíritu del derecho indiano*. Buenos Aires: IIHD, 1992.

———. *Nuevos Horizontes en el estudio histórico del derecho indiano*. Madrid: MAPFRE, 1992.

———. "Ordenes normativos y prácticas socio-jurídicas. La justicia." *Nueva historia de la nación argentina*. Vol. 2. Buenos Aires, 1999, 283–315.

Taylor, William. "Between Global Processes and Local Knowledge: An Inquiry into Early Latin American Social History, 1500–1800." In O. Zunz and W. Taylor, eds. *Reliving the Past: The Worlds of Social History*. Chapel Hill: University of North Carolina Press, 1985.

———. *Drinking, Homicide, and Rebellion in Colonial Mexican Villages*. Stanford, CA: Stanford University Press, 1979.

———. *Landlord and Peasant in Colonial Oaxaca*. Stanford, CA: Stanford University Press, 1972.

———. *Magistrates of the Sacred: Priests and Parishioners in Eighteenth-Century Mexico*. Stanford, CA: Stanford University Press, 1996.

Terranciano, Kevin. *The Mixtecs of Colonial Oaxaca: Ñudzahui History, Sixteenth through Eighteenth Centuries*. Stanford, CA: Stanford University Press, 2001.

Thomson, Guy P. C. "Popular Aspects of Liberalism in Mexico, 1848–1888." *Bulletin of Latin American Research* 10:3 (1991): 265–92.

Thompson, E. P. *Whigs and Hunters: The Origins of the Black Act*. London: Penguin, 1975.

Todorov, Tzvetan. *The Conquest of America*. New York: Harper & Row, 1984.

Tomás y Valiente, Francisco. *Los validos en la monarquía española del siglo XVII: Estudio institucional*. Madrid: Instituto de Estudios Políticos, 1963.

———. *Manual de historia del derecho español*. Madrid: Alianza Ed., 1983.

——— "Teoría y práctica de la tortura judicial en las obras de Lorenzo Matheu y Sanz." *Anuario de historia del derecho español* 41 (1971): 439–85.

Twinam, Ann. "Honor, Sexuality, and Illegitimacy in Colonial Spanish America." In A. Lavrín, ed. *Sexuality and Marriage in Colonial Latin America*. Lincoln: University of Nebraska Press, 1989, 118–55.

———. "The Negotiation of Honor: Elites, Sexuality, and Illegitimacy in Eighteenth-Century Spanish America." In L. Johnson and S. Lipsett-Rivera. *The Faces of Honor: Sex, Shame, and Violence in Colonial Latin America*. Albuquerque: University of New Mexico Press, 1998, 68–102.

Unger, Roberto Mangabeira. *Knowledge and Politics*. New York: Free Press, 1975.

———. *Law in Modern Society: Toward a Criticism of Modern Society*. New York: Free Press, 1976.

Van Young, Eric. "To See Someone Not Seeing: Historical Studies of Peasants and Politics in Mexico." *Mexican Studies/Estudios Mexicanos* 6:1 (Winter 1990): 133–59.

Velasco, Álvarez de. *De privilegiis pauperum et miserabilium personarum*. Madrid: 1636.

Vial Correa, Gonzalo. "Teoría y práctica de la igualdad en Indias." *Historia* 3 (1964): 87–163.

Villaroel, Hipolíto. *Enfermedades políticas que padece la capital de esta Nueva España*. México: CONACULTA, 1994.

Viqueira, Carmen y José Urquiola. *Los obrajes en la Nueva España, 1530–1630*. México: CONACULTA, 1990.

Vitoria, Francisco. *Political Writings*. A. Pagden, ed. Cambridge University Press, 1991.

Weckman, Luís. *The Medieval Heritage of Mexico*. New York: Fordham University Press, 1992.

Wiarda, Howard. *The Soul of Latin America: The Cultural and Political Tradition*. New Haven, CT: Yale University Press, 2001.

Winter, Steven. *A Clearing in the Forest: Law, Life, and Mind*. University of Chicago Press, 2001.

———. "The 'Power' Thing." *Virginia Law Review* 82 (Aug. 1996): 721–835.

Wobeser, Gisela von. *La formación de la hacienda en la época colonial. El uso de la tierra y el agua*. México: UNAM, 1983.

Zavala, Iris. "Representing the Colonial Subject." In R. Jara and N. Spadaccini. *1424–1992: Re/discovering Colonial Writing*. Minneapolis: The Prisma Institute, 1989.

Zavala, Silvio. *La encomienda indiana*. Madrid, 1935.

———. *De encomienda y propiedad territorial en algunas regiones de la América española*. México: Porrúa, 1940.

———. *Las instituciones jurídicas en la conquista de América*. México: Porrúa, 1988.

———. *Servidumbre natural y libertad cristiana según los tratadistas españoles de los siglos XVI y XVII*. Buenos Aires: Peuser, 1944.

Zavala, Silvio, y María Castelo. *Fuentes para la historia del trabajo en Nueva España*. Vol. 6. México: Centro de Estudios Históricos del Movimiento Obrero Mexicano, 1980.

Zeitlin, Judith. "Ranchers and Indians in the Southern Isthmus of Tehuantepec: Economic Change and Indigenous Survival in Colonial Mexico." *Hispanic American Historical Review* 69:1 (1989): 23–60.

Zurita, Alonso de. "Breve relación de los señores de la Nueva España." En *Relaciones de Texcoco y de la Nueva España, Pomar-Zurita*. México: Ed. Salvador Chávez Hayhde, 1941.

Index

In this index an "f" after a number indicates a separate reference on the next page, and an "ff" indicates separate references on the next two pages. A continuous discussion over two or more pages is indicated by a span of page numbers, for example, "86–88." *Passim* is used for a cluster of references in close but not consecutive sequence.

Acosta, José de, Indians and Spaniards as forming a single community bound by a single law, 48

Act of Pardon, in Tehuantepec rebellion, 271

Albuquerque, Duque de, viceroy of New Spain, 252 *passim;* role of in Tehuantepec rebellion, 261f; refusing to hear Indian litigants during Tehuantepec rebellion, 282

Alcalde(s) mayor(es): as responsible for administering repartimiento, 16; as less-than-reliable enforcers of the law, 34, 43, 119; role of in securing workable outcomes, 40; synonymous with corregidor, 42; as obstructing petitioners and litigants, 50; as greedy, 71; consequences of absence of, 85; accused of acting for private ends, 197; authority of undermined by macehual, 231f; abuses of in Tehuantepec, 252 *passim;* Juan de Avellán killed in Tehuantepec, 253

Alguacil mayor/chief bailiff: engaged in private dealings, 60; importance of in local elections, 213; as holder of royal staff of justice, 230; in Tehuantepec rebellion, 255

Altepetl: defined, 23f; as seeking autonomy before conquest, 27; forces undermining after conquest, 28; caciques' power linked to persistence

of, 37; Nahuatl etymology of, 80; Spaniards often claimed land at borders of, 93; New Spain as congeries of, 211

Amparo: as available to protect Indian land during sixteenth century, 20f, 44; procedure for obtaining, 51; limited legal effect of, 51, 104; description of sample of, 52; methodological challenges of, 53; as quick, effective remedy beginning in 1590–92, 56f; as ambivalent legal form, 58; change in narratives of harm in 60 *passim;* coming of age in 1640s, 62; as pact between king and commoner, 64f; idiom of related rendered into Nahuatl, 77 *passim;* how enforced, 83ff; used early on to protect Indian lands, 98; more often filed by Indians than others, 161; compared to criminal law, 163; limitations of, 165; as form of Indian petition during Tehuantepec rebellion, 258

Apartamiento/withdrawal, from a case, 201 *passim;* from litigation over local election, 240

Appeal: in preconquest Aztec law, 41; audiencia could entertain, 43; as Nahua loan word, 77; in land cases, 114, 121, 126; in capital criminal case, 181; in case of local governance, 234, 240f; right to denied during

proper end of each individual community member vs. living for oneself, 34; as discussed by Thomist writers, 44; rooted in search for complementarities and commonalities, 44f; erosion of idea of, 45; Indians could be made to work for, 55; just law as chief ordering principle of, 64 *passim;* role in the relationship between king and subjects, 65ff; mentioned in petitions or litigation, 65f, 70, 221; as distinguished from private gain, 68, 72, 93; Spaniards often heedless of, 71; idea of dependent on distinction between public and private, 72ff; rendered into Nahuatl, 79f; as moral resource for Indians, 87, 296f; king must preserve against private interests, 93; in relation to Indians' possession of land, 93; Spaniards said to act out of private profit rather than for, 132f; Indian labor can only be appropriated pursuant to, 138; vassals obliged to, 159; and criminal law, 168; in relation to obedience, amparo, and peace, 298ff; as check on private motive in law, 305

Commoners, Indian, see Macehual(es)

Community: human beings meant to live in, 66; as basis for Indian claims to liberty, 155 *passim;* Roman municipality as basis for Indian communities, 159

Composición de tierras, history of, 20ff; in response to crisis of land in 1590s, 20, 97f, 118

Congregación: basic idea behind, 21; not just a land grab, 21f; during 1550s–1560s, 21, 26f; as undermining authority of caciques, 25, 37; subsiding of turmoil raised by, 58; of late sixteenth century, 66; in Ystapa in 1593, 199

Conquest: as historical process, 1 *passim;* enslaving of Indians and taking of land during, 13; Zurita on unmaking of Indian world by, 27; special role of Tlaxcala in, 38; Soto on, 68

Conservation: as central political problem of seventeenth century, 34; of the Indians as imperative, 69ff, 133;

141ff; of the king's state, 150; in Tehuantepec rebellion, 265

Conversion, to Christianity: related to royal protection, 2; and royal language policy, 26; as justification for occupation of New World, 55; dilemmas of for Concho Indians, 130 *passim,* 164f; and Aristotelian notions of natural slavery, 135

Convivencia, as goal of Spanish political sensibilities, 21; trumping impulse to mutual isolation of Indians and Spaniards and role of law in, 40f

Corregido(res), see *Alcalde(s) mayor(es)*

"Cosmopolitan legality," Indian litigation as early experiment in, 307; Sousa Santos on, 348n50, 349n57

Covarrubias, Sebastián de, *Tesoro:* definition of "case," 46; definition of "equity," 73; definition of "tyranny," 77n90; definition of "liberty," 142, 157; definition of "guilt," 171; definition of "custom," 219; definition of "vara," 227f; definition of "authority," 233; definition of "vassal," 260; definition of "behetría," 319n72

Criminal litigation, as a matter of public utility, 169; tangled up with village politics, 199

Cuevas y Dávalos, bishop of Oaxaca, role in Tehuantepec rebellion, 253, 263ff, 283

Custom/*costumbre:* Indians observant of, 163; in village elections, 216ff, 224f; in relation to "uso y costumbre," 217; defined, 218; as another nature, 219; keeping of ensures peace, 219

"Deed and word"/"*obra y palabra,*" see Idioms of harm

Derecho indiano, focused on jurisprudence, 3f; compared to "imposed law," 3

Derramas, laid on by friars, 36

Díaz, Bernal, on wealth as motivation for conquest, 29

Diccionario de autoridades, defining "liberty," 157; defining "custom," 218; defining "possession," 228;